OUTLINE STUDIES
IN MATTHEW

TO DALLAS THEOLOGICAL SEMINARY

Whose faculty, alumni, and students have continued
to honor the memory of the author, one of its
founders, by worthy succession to his
faithful witness, this volume is
gratefully dedicated by
his daughter.

OUTLINE STUDIES IN MATTHEW

A Devotional Commentary

by
W. H. Griffith Thomas

Foreword by
Donald K. Campbell

Editor's Preface
Winifred G. T. Gillespie

Introduction by
Warren W. Wiersbe

KREGEL PUBLICATIONS
Grand Rapids, Michigan 49501

Outline Studies in Matthew by W. H. Griffith Thomas, copyright © 1985 by Kregel Publications, a division of Kregel, Inc. All rights reserved.

Library of Congress Cataloging in Publication Data

Thomas, W. H. Griffith (William Henry Griffith), 1861-1924.
 Outline Studies in Matthew.

 Reprint. Originally published: Outline Studies in the Gospel of Matthew. Grand Rapids, Mich.: W. B. Eerdmans Publishing Co., © 1961.
  1. Bible. N.T. Matthew—Outlines, syllabi, etc.
  I. Title.
BS2576.T5 1985   226'.206   84-25109
ISBN 0-8254-3831-4

Printed in the United States of America

CONTENTS

INTRODUCTION TO THE AUTHOR

His advice to young preachers was, "Think yourself empty, read yourself full, write yourself clear, pray yourself keen—then enter the pulpit and let yourself go!"

William Henry Griffith Thomas (1861-1924) followed that counsel himself, and in so doing, he became one of the spiritual giants of his day. As a preacher and a teacher of preachers, he excelled in spiritual depth, practicality, and a simplicity of expression that made the most profound truths come alive with excitement.

His mother was widowed before he was born, and family financial demands forced him to leave school when he was fourteen. He was converted to Christ through the witness of some friends on March 23, 1878. The next year, he moved to London to work in an uncle's office.

But Griffith Thomas was determined to get an education, so from 10:30 P.M. until 2:30 A.M. each night, he gave himself to serious study. He became a lay curate in 1882, while attending lectures at King's College, London; and was ordained in 1885. Griffith Thomas belonged to that early fellowship in the Anglican Church that was unashamed to be called "Evangelical."

The day he was ordained, Griffith Thomas was admonished by the Bishop of London, William Temple, not to neglect his Greek New Testament. The young minister took that word to heart and, for the rest of his life, read one chapter a day from the Greek New Testament! This kind of devotion to God's Word shows up in his writings.

He ministered at St. Aldate's, Oxford, and St. Paul's, Portman Square (London), and in 1905 was named principal of Wycliffe Hall, Oxford, the Evangelical center for Anglicans studying for the ministry. He taught there for five years, then moved to Toronto to join the faculty of Wycliffe College, where he taught for nine years. He and has family then moved to Philadelphia and Griffith Thomas entered a wider ministry of writing and Bible conference work. He was associated with some of the leading preachers and conference speakers of his day and often spoke at the large Bible conferences.

He joined with Lewis Sperry Chafer and others to found the Dallas Theological Seminary and was to have taught there; but his death on June 2, 1924, interrupted those plans.

Back to the Bible Broadcast   WARREN W. WIERSBE
Lincoln, Nebraska

FOREWORD

Though the Gospel of Matthew is neglected in some circles as a result of the theory that the Gospel of Mark is earlier, Matthew must be seen as one of the most important books in the New Testament. It is, in fact, a bridge between the Old and New Testaments and shows, convincingly, by repeated reference to the Old Testament prophecies, that Jesus is the Messiah. The book also answers the question of Jewish believers about their future as a nation. Since the Jews had rejected their Messiah and King, was God through with them? Matthew declares that judgment would fall on that generation of Jews, but their long-promised kingdom would yet be established with His people, at the second coming of Christ.

Dr. W.H. Griffith Thomas, an Anglican scholar and teacher, believed that the Gospel of Matthew sets forth Jesus as Jehovah's King, and that the kingdom appears in this book in three forms:

1. The kingdom was preached as "at hand" by John the Baptist, Jesus, and the twelve disciples. That kingdom, Thomas insisted, was the one promised to David (2 Sam. 7:14) and referred to often by the prophets.

2. The kingdom is also described in its mystery form, in Matthew 13. Since the Jews did not receive Jesus as Messiah-King, the predicted kingdom had to be postponed. The "mysteries" describe the nature of the kingdom, in the period between the initial rejection of the kingdom and its final establishment.

3. The kingdom, foretold by the prophets, will finally be established when Christ comes a second time in power and glory (Matt. 24—25).

Declares Dr. Thomas, "Clearly, it is this thought of the Kingdom that distinguishes Matthew from the other gospels."

While insisting that Matthew is the Jewish gospel and that some of it awaits a literal interpretation in the future, there is spiritual application for believers today, in all portions.

The material in this republished volume, which was edited by Dr. Thomas's daughter, Mrs. E.H. Gillespie, takes the form of sixty studies touching all twenty-eight chapters of Matthew and is presented in expanded outline form. The studies include, in each case, introductory remarks and concluding applications. The reader will thus find in this volume a connected, devotional exposition of the biblical text.

The book is warmly commended to the Christian reading public, which will profit greatly from the sound interpretation and practical application of truth, found in these pages. In particular, those who preach and/or teach the Bible will be helped by these studies, as they observe the method of a biblical scholar, who also possessed a rare, homiletical gift.

Professor of Bible Exposition   DONALD K. CAMPBELL
Dallas Theological Seminary
Dallas, Texas

EDITOR'S PREFACE

As noted of former volumes, this one, also, contains some of the many notes on Bible passages left by my father. Like its predecessors, it was not planned as a commentary on a particular book in any sense of the term. Yet, in this case, as my work progressed, assisted by a great deal of material which had appeared during my father's lifetime in periodicals or as pamphlets, the manuscript seemed to me, in spite of its adherence to the form of the other posthumous ones, to be approaching the status of a devotional commentary — in outline — as nearly as could be attained without the guidance of the author himself. If this indeed be so, I owe it largely to a series of readings in Matthew written by my father from these very notes and published in *Daily Bible,* the magazine of an organization known as The World's Morning Watch, issues of January to June, 1917. My file of this now discontinued periodical was incomplete, and I wish to express to the New York Public Library my deep appreciation of its Photographic Service, which provided me with the necessary photostat pages from the April 1917 issue. This was located in their collection on the suggestion of Dr. James F. Rand, Librarian of Dallas Theological Seminary, to whom I am grateful also for assistance in checking certain references throughout the volume.

Once again thanks are due to the Editors of *The Sunday School Times,* of Philadelphia, for furnishing me with several sets of lesson helps on Matthew written by my father for that paper at different times in the past. They also granted me permission to use for the Introduction to the volume the contents of his pamphlet, "How to Study the Gospel of Matthew," originally published by them, and an editorial which he wrote on another occasion. I have also used by permission a booklet and several articles by him from *The Evangelical Christian,* of Toronto. Then, too, I have referred to passages in certain of my father's books in which the First Gospel is mentioned or briefly expounded. In particular, since there is bound to be some duplication if an author writes on more than one of the Gospels, those readers who undertake a comparison of this volume with *Outline Studies in The Gospel of Luke* (1984), and even with *The Apostle John* (reprinted in 1984), both issued by our present publisher, will be sure to note certain repetitions that have seemed necessary to insure as complete a coverage of Matthew's narrative as possible. Moreover, two sections of *Sermon Outlines* (1947) have been incorporated in their proper sequence.

Finally, I owe hearty thanks to Dr. Montagu Robert Lawrence,[*] of Oxford, England, for transcribing for my use his notes on Matthew taken as an undergraduate, 1905-10, at my father's weekly Greek Testament Readings for members of the University.

This volume goes forth, one hundred years after its author's birth (January 2, 1861), with the earnest prayer that its use by others may bring blessing in the study of the Word as timeless in Divine bestowal as that which its preparation has brought to its editor.

WINIFRED G. T. GILLESPIE

[*]Brother of Lawrence of Arabia.

INTRODUCTION*

I. What Is the Gospel?

The word "gospel" is never found in the New Testament with reference to a book, but always and only to "good news," and when we speak of the Gospel of Matthew we ought to understand the good news of Jesus Christ recorded by Matthew. This is seen from the first verse of Mark's Gospel, which speaks of "the beginning of the gospel of Jesus Christ, the Son of God." Thus there is in reality only one Gospel, and four presentations of it; and this is the reason why its title in the American Standard Version reads "The Gospel: —" and then heads each individual Gospel "According to" the particular Evangelist. They give four pictures of the one Christ, and their value lies in their separate though connected testimony to Him. Whatever, therefore, may be the relations between them, each should, first of all, be studied alone, in order that the impressions peculiar to it may be received and evaluated.

Yet, while we remember that "the gospel" means "good news," we shall doubtless go on referring to these records as "Gospels." This is because they give accounts in written form of that story of the life of Jesus Christ on earth which forms the foundation of the "good news" we call Christianity.

II. Why Four Gospels?

At once comes the question as to why there should be four Gospels — why one would not have been sufficient; and also why, if more than one, there are only four. There seems to be no doubt that the four are intended to express different, yet connected, aspects of the life and ministry of our Lord. As often noted, there are four Gospels and one Christ, four records with one purpose; four pictures of one Person; and four methods of recording impressions of that Person. Matthew may be said to demonstrate; Mark to depict; Luke to declare; John to describe.

---

* Adapted from the Author's pamphlet, "How to Study the Four Gospels," now out of print. Originally published by The Sunday School Times Company, the material has more recently appeared by permission as two articles in *Sunday School World*, publication of The American Sunday-School Union (issues of January and February, 1957). See also *Methods of Bible Study* (Moody Press), pp. 35-37, 73-75.

Matthew is concerned with the coming of a promised Saviour; Mark with the life of a powerful Saviour; Luke with the grace of a perfect Saviour, John with the possession of a personal Saviour. It is thus quite probable that no single Gospel could have set forth the fullness and glory of our Lord's Person and work.

When, therefore, each Gospel is read for its presentation of Christ, it will be seen that, while there is much that is identical in all of them (but especially in the first three), there is also much that is different in each. It is these differences that give rise to the conviction that the Gospels are indeed four truthful pictures of the one Lord Jesus Christ.

Further, there are some writers who speak of the "Cherubic Symbolism" of the Gospels. This may not convey much, if any, meaning to the casual reader, but in reality it suggests a great deal. As early as the second century writers saw, or fancied they saw, a likeness between the four Gospels and the symbols of the cherubic visions of Ezekiel and Revelation. The best way of stating this is to associate Matthew with the lion, Mark with the ox, or calf; Luke with the man; and John with the eagle (cf. Ezek. 1:10, Rev. 4:7). This was interpreted to mean that Matthew depicted Christ as the Jewish Messiah, the Lion of the tribe of Judah; Mark as the Servant, symbolized by the beast of burden, the ox; Luke as the Son of man, symbolized by the man; and John as the Son of God, symbolized by the eagle. There is sufficient in these suggestions to indicate the essential differences of the Gospels, and their early date shows that already the Christian Church was occupied with the relations between the four accounts of its Founder.

Another way of expressing these differences is to associate them with the passages in the Old Testament in which the Messiah is spoken of as "the Branch." Thus Matthew, the Jewish Gospel, corresponds with the prophecy, "I will raise unto David a righteous Branch" (Jer. 23:5; cf. 33:15). Mark, the Gospel of service, agrees with the description, "my servant the Branch" (Zech. 3:8). Luke, who delineates Christ as true man, illustrates the words, "the man whose name is the Branch" (Zech. 6:13). John, who is mainly concerned for the Divine Person and work of Christ, is rightly associated with the words, "the Branch of Jehovah" (Isa. 5:2). Here, again, while the thought is scarcely capable of use with any primary interpretation of the four Gospels, the spiritual application is decidedly interesting and appropriate. To the same effect are four passages from the Old Testament commencing with the word "behold." "Behold, thy king" (Zech. 9:9) represents Matthew; "Behold, my servant" (Isa. 42:1) indicates Mark; "Behold, the man" (Zech. 6:12) suggests Luke; and "Behold, your God" (Isa. 40:9) corresponds with John.

It has also been suggested that the Gospels illustrate four relationships of Christ to us. This would associate Matthew with the Prophet, Mark with the Priest, Luke with the Saviour, and John with the Son. Or, it has been said, we have in the Gospels themselves four statements of Christ's purpose in coming. Thus Matthew, true to the Jewish idea, records, "I am not come to destroy, but to fulfil" (5:17) ; Mark, illustrative of Christ's work, records, "the Son of man came not to be ministered unto, but to minister" (10:45) ; Luke, who is particularly concerned with the gospel of redemption, says that Christ is "the Son of man" who "is come to seek and to save" (19:10) ; and John appropriately associates Christ with His Father and writes that He said, "I am come in my Father's name" (5:43). Of course, this is only generally true and must not be thought to rule out other aspects and features of Christ's life in the particular Gospels. One writer, Dr. H. G. Weston, says that we may think of the Gospels as providing for our deepest spiritual needs: Matthew speaks of righteousness, Mark of sanctification, Luke of redemption, and John of life.

Or, we may consider the peoples for whom the Gospels seem originally to have been intended. Matthew is quite evidently directed to the Jews; Mark has many points of contact with the Romans; Luke is essentially suited to the Greeks; and John is applicable to all, though especially to believers among the nations. Dr. D. S. Gregory thinks that this is the best way of explaining the differences, especially because the four Gospels are thus seen to be representative of all mankind at that time, and therefore to be suitable for universal use today.

Whatever may be said of the particular character and purpose of each Gospel, they are all built on the same general plan, consisting of an introduction, an account of Christ's earthly ministry, and a conclusion. Very few dates are given, but definite turning points are indicated in the course of the story. It is customary to separate the first three from the fourth and speak of them as the "Synoptic Gospels," because they can be "viewed together" (Greek, *syn-opto*) as giving a virtually identical picture of Christ's life and work. But it is far truer to keep all four Gospels together as representing four aspects of their great subject. From time to time efforts have been made to harmonize the Gospels into one whole, but it must be confessed that none of these attempts has proved satisfactory. Indeed, it may be said, without much question, that a real harmony is impossible because each Gospel has its own characteristic features which cannot be blended with the others. It has been well pointed out that, while there are these differences between the Gospels, there is no real disagreement, because each writer was led by the Holy Spirit to present a special picture of our Lord and Saviour.

III. The General Features of Matthew

(1) The writer is quite evidently a Jew, and of course a Christian (9:9, 10; 10:3), and from the earliest days of the Church he has been regarded as Matthew (or Levi) the publican, one of the twelve Apostles. Early in the second century a writer said, "Matthew composed the oracles of God in the Hebrew tongue." Others said the same, and this became a tradition as definite as anything we possess; and yet our Gospel is in no sense a translation, but an original production in Greek. The solution of the problem is either that the word "oracles" refers to the discourses, the teaching of Christ which we now find incorporated (and so prominent) in our present Matthew, or else that Matthew wrote both in Hebrew and in Greek. There does not seem to be any real reason to doubt the possibility of the latter suggestion.

(2) The destination of this Gospel was clearly the Jews and Jewish Christians. A knowledge of the Old Testament is assumed and very many quotations from it are given. Indeed, there are about sixty of these, to say nothing of allusions, which means that there are more direct quotations from the Hebrew Scriptures than in Mark and Luke combined. It has often been pointed out that if a reader came to Matthew full of the Old Testament he would easily understand it, simply because its substance is so clearly Jewish; and we know that Christ is never called King in relation to the Church but only in reference to the Jews (cf. Matt. 10:4, 5; 15:24; Rom. 15:8), and to the world (cf. Rev. 11:15, 19:16).

(3) The purpose of the Gospel is a matter of great importance. It is, as are the others, in narrative form and is largely biographical but all through it there is a definite scheme, a sort of argument in narrative form. This, it has been suggested, displays the great wisdom and tact of the writer in not alienating Jews who might read the story. At the very outset, indeed, Jesus Christ is associated with the Jewish nation as represented by David and Abraham (1:1). Another keynote of Matthew is the word "fulfilled" (1:22), which points to the Old Testament as having predicted the coming of the Messiah. Then, too, the way in which Christ is spoken of as King, even during His infancy (2:2), is another feature that indicates the great purpose of this Gospel, which is to declare the Kingship and the Kingdom of Christ. The genealogy gives the royal succession; the message of the Baptist and of Christ Himself was: "the kingdom of heaven is at hand" (3:2, 4:17); and all the parables except three refer to "the kingdom of heaven," a phrase which is found over thirty times.

Yet another aspect of the purpose of the Gospel is the constant reference to opposition to Christ and to His rejection by the Jewish people. This note is struck very early (2:7, 13), and the hostility deepens stage by stage until, after the revelation of it in chapters 11 and 12, there is a definite change of method by Christ on this account, in chapter 13; and after this the opposition becomes deeper, stronger, and more intense until it culminates in the cross. This rejection of our Lord by the Jews naturally suggests the transference of the Kingdom to the Gentiles; and although this is essentially a Jewish Gospel, yet from the outset, as suggested by the visit of the Wise Men, there are allusions to other nations which may be said to prepare for the solemn transfer of the privileges of the Kingdom to the Gentiles. The summary of our Lord's ministry sounds this note (4:16); the announcement of the transference is made (21:43); and the Gospel ends with the commission of the Jewish disciples to proclaim the truth among all nations (28:19).

Special attention should also be given to the way in which Christ's teaching is emphasized in Matthew. There are five great sections of instruction, each ending with a similar phrase (7:28, 11:1, 13:53, 19:1, 26:1). These are all concerned with the aspects of the Kingdom: (1) its principles (chaps. 5-7);

(2) its propagation (chap. 10); (3) its progress (chap. 13); (4) its problems (chap. 18); and (5) its prospects (chaps. 24-25).

IV. The Plan of Matthew

The structure of the Gospel, when carefully studied, shows that Matthew's idea was not to set forth a chronological account of Christ's ministry, but to blend events and teachings that set forth His claims as the Messiah in fulfillment of prophecy. When this is seen, the plan of the Gospel becomes luminous with suggestion. In general, the material is divided by a phrase, found in 4:17 and 16:21, "from that time," which separates between the introduction and the ministry and the events leading up to the death of Christ. Now it is possible to proceed profitably to a detailed consideration of the contents of Matthew along these lines and in harmony with the general purpose:

A. *The King as Prophet* (1:1 to 16:20)

Part   I. *The Person of the King* (1:1 to 2:23)

1. His royal descent (1:1-17) — the genealogy.
2. His Divine origin (1:23-25) — the birth.
3. His early circumstances (2:1-23) — the infancy.

Part II. *The Preparation for the King* (3:1 to 4:16)

1. The forerunner (3:1-12) — the Baptist.
2. The consecration (3:13-17) — the baptism.
3. The testing (4:1-11) — the temptation.

Then follows an appendix (vs. 12-16) introductory to the next section, and yet summarizing the entire ministry.

N.B. Dr. G. Campbell Morgan analyzes the above material under "The Person of the King" in this suggestive way: (1) His relation to earth (1:1 to 3:12); (2) His relation to heaven (3:13-17); (3) His relation to hell (4:1-11)

Part III. *The Presentation of the King* (4:17 to 16:20)

In this section of the Gospel will be found the record of the Galilean ministry, with no reference at all to the forthcoming death.

1. Typical words and works (4:12 to 9:34).
   a. Discourses (chaps. 5 to 7).
   b. Deeds (8:1 to 9:34).
2. The mission of the Twelve (9:35 to 10:42).
3. The rise of opposition (chaps. 11 and 12).
4. The change of teaching (chap. 13).
5. Further work (chap. 14).
6. The renewal of opposition and the culmination of the ministry (15:1 to 16:20).

B. *The King as Priest* (16:21 to 28:20)

Part IV. *The Passion of the King* (16:21 to 27:66)

1. The first announcement of the cross, and its results (16:21 to 17:21).
2. The training of the Twelve (17:22 to 18:35).
3. The rise of opposition (chaps. 11 and 12).
4. The further training of the Twelve (19:23 to 20:28).
5. The last offer to the nation (20:29 to 21:17).
6. The conflict with the leaders (21:18 to 23:39).
7. The preparation of the disciples (24:1 to 25:46).
8. The accomplishment of the passion (26:1 to 27:66).

Part V. *The Power of the King* (28:1-20)

1. The resurrection (vs. 1-10).
2. The plot of the foes (vs. 11-15).
3. The commission to the disciples (vs. 16-20).

V. The Special Feature in Matthew

As remarked by most writers, the Divine purpose in this Gospel is to set forth our Lord as Jehovah's King, and it is for this reason that the material in Matthew has been selected and arranged in its present form. *The Companion Bible* points out that, compared with Mark and Luke, Matthew has no fewer than thirty-one sections peculiar to his Gospel, and that all bear more or less on the subject of the King and the Kingdom. The Kingdom appears in Matthew in three forms:

(1) At first it was preached by John the Baptist, our Lord, and the Twelve as "at hand," and there is no doubt that the Jewish hearers would know, without any need of explanation,

that the reference was to the promise to David (cf. 2 Sam. 7:14-16), and to the well-known predictions of the Kingdom all through the Prophets.

(2) Then came the Kingdom in its mysteries. The Jews would not receive the Lord Jesus as the Messiah, and so the Kingdom predicted by the prophets had to be postponed. Meanwhile, the disciples were instructed in regard to certain aspects of the Kingdom not previously made known in the Old Testament (cf. 13:17). These "mysteries" (13:11) reveal the existence of a blend of good and evil all through the interval between the rejection of the Kingdom and its official setting up according to the prophetic word.

(3) Then the Kingdom is shown once again, this time in its future glory (cf. 17:1-11); and towards the close of the Gospel Christ prophesies His coming in power and glory to set up that which the prophets had foretold (chaps. 24 and 25).

Clearly it is this thought of the Kingdom that distinguishes Matthew from the other Gospels. It is not too much to say, with Dr. A. C. Gaebelein, that only when the principle of dispensational truth is emphasized is it possible to understand this book. The references to the King, to the Jewish rejection of Him, to the transference of the Kingdom to the Gentiles, to the "mysteries" of that Kingdom, to the Church as something at that time still future (cf. 16:13-18, 18:15-17), and to the Kingdom discourses on Olivet (chaps. 24 and 25) — all these need to be kept closely in view and thoroughly mastered point by point. Otherwise, the unique, invaluable teaching of this Gospel of Matthew will neither be fully grasped nor properly appreciated by God's people.

1

THE ORIGIN OF CHRIST

Matthew 1:1-25

THE GOSPEL of Matthew opens with "the book of the generation of Jesus Christ" (1:1), thereby connecting Him with the past in Jewish history; and then it proceeds to record what was the immediate past, in telling of "the birth of Jesus Christ" (1:18).

I. The Royal Descent (1:17)

1. *The Genealogy*

   a. Beginning with Abraham, Matthew traces Christ down to "David the king" (v. 6), and then on to Joseph, husband of Mary.

   b. He abbreviates by omitting some names and giving only a selection in three sections of fourteen each; but his main thought is twofold:
      (1) Christ's royalty in Israel; and yet—
      (2) His distinction from Israel, with changed phraseology at end (cf. v. 16).

   c. This corresponds exactly with Luke's parenthetic phrase (cf. Luke 3:23); but chief points of difference between two are—
      (1) Matthew's list descends from Abraham to Jesus and is written for Jews; Luke's list ascends from Jesus to Adam and is written for all mankind.
      (2) Matthew gives genealogy of Joseph, royal line through male descent, with Christ's legal right of succession through His foster-father and guardian; Luke gives genealogy of Mary, Christ's natural line of actual physical descent and blood relationship.
      (3) Matthew shows Jesus as King of the Jews, while Luke depicts Him as Saviour of the world; and both of these aspects are true.

   d. It is significant that Jews never questioned Davidic line of Christ and, since this was absolutely essential for

Messiahship, it certainly would have been questioned had there þeen any doubt; and Joseph is clearly considered legal parent of Jesus of Nazareth (cf. 13:55, Luke 4:22, John 6:42).

e. Notwithstanding problems connected with two genealogies, early Church accepted them and circulated both Gospels.

2. *The Spiritual Message of the Genealogy*

a. It tells of Divine immanence, our Lord's nearness to and oneness with human life; He is shown to be bone of our bone and flesh of our flesh (cf. John 1:4, Eph. 5:30).

b. It contains Divine grace, because of remarkable and unusual inclusion of Gentile and of impure women in this impressively male and Jewish list (cf. vs. 3, 5, 6).

c. It teaches solemn lesson of Divine sovereignty, or transcendence, from fact that choice of God through centuries was often altogether apart from principle of primogeniture, thereby setting aside all human claims, powers, or merit; and thus He carried out His own perfect will.

II. The Divine Origin (1:18-25)

1. *Realization* (vs. 18, 19)

a. It follows that Matthew should record birth of Christ from standpoint of Joseph, while Luke emphasizes that of His mother (see Luke 1:26-56).

b. Since Jewish betrothal was equivalent to marriage, save in very exceptional cases, circumstances show Joseph's characteristic uprightness and deep concern:

(1) Bishop Handley Moule interprets Greek word translated "a just man" as one anxious to do his true duty, religious and domestic.

(2) Since there is no mention of him during Christ's public ministry, except as a supposed parent in Nazareth, there has been tacit assumption that Joseph was of mature age and judgment at time of Christ's birth, as would befit His protector, and therefore probably no longer living, at least at time of crucifixion (cf. John 19:25-27); but certainly from phrase "her firstborn son" (Matt. 1:25) it is safe to assume that children were born to him and to Mary during

years of Christ's youth or early manhood (cf. 12:46; 13:55, 56; Mark 6:3; John 7:1-10; Acts 1:14).

2. *Revelation* (vs. 20-23)

    a. But "the angel of the Lord appeared" to Joseph in dream with reassurance against fear; and announcement that imminent birth was miraculous, with its explanation, presupposes common knowledge of Holy Spirit (v. 20; cf. v. 18).

    b. Then name of Child was given, together with wonderful meaning; Jesus, N. T. counterpart of Joshua, means "Jehovah saves," or "God the Saviour," thus indicating Christ's redemptive work at very start (v. 21).

    c. Then Matthew, characteristically and with special reference to Jewish nation, gives proof O.T. Messianic passage (Isa. 7:14) that virgin birth of Christ had been foretold and was now to be fulfilled (v. 22); and it is noteworthy that he attributes these words to God as Author (cf. 2:15).

    N.B. It is true that prophecy in original setting referred to circumstances of reign of Ahaz, but O.T. passages often have secondary applications, and Matthew, under inspiration of Holy Spirit, realizing this, applies words to birth of Messiah. He also associates clearly and closely Divine source and human channel.

    d. Two names, Jesus and Immanuel, are closely connected, for He becomes our Saviour only through being "God with us" (cf. Gen. 1:1 as quite evidently complementary — "In the beginning God —" and here "God with us" and see also Heb. 1:2, Col. 1:15-17); none but present, Divine Saviour will suffice for human needs.

    N.B. Dr. Francis L. Patton once declared: "If we take the Divine Jesus out of the Synoptics, we cannot keep the human Jesus."

    e. This leads to question of whether there would have been Incarnation but for sin; however, as Dr. James Orr pointed out, this rests upon false abstraction, for God has only one plan, including at once creation of world, permission of sin, and purpose of redemption, with Incarnation integral and essential part of that one Divine plan.

3. *Recognition* (vs. 24, 25)

    a. With realization of Divine will came prompt obedience; and Joseph by marriage gave Mary at once his full protection and his tender consideration (vs. 24, 25a).

    b. When in due course holy Child was born He was named Jesus as angel had directed both Joseph and Mary (v. 25; cf. Luke 1:31); for He would indeed "save his people from their sins" (v. 21).

Conclusion

This entire chapter speaks eloquently of what has been known down the ages as the Virgin Birth of Christ. It should be noted that —

1. The story is adequately attested, since all manuscripts of both Matthew and Luke include the account of it, and it is implicit in the other N.T. books; and —

2. The story is important — nay, vital — on two grounds:

    a. It is the earthly basis of Christ's supernatural life, and the only explanation given of how a Divine Being could come into this world and take on human flesh; and thus it agrees perfectly with modern findings on the subject of heredity.

    b. It is always closely associated both with His Deity (cf. Luke 1:35), and with His atoning work (vs. 21-23).

As we ponder the heavenly origin and the human descent leading to the life and the character, the death and the resurrection of Jesus Christ, we are most surely and naturally led to His essential dissimilarity from all other beings, and we are impelled to exclaim with Thomas, "My Lord and my God!"

2

SEEKING CHRIST

Matthew 2:1, 2, 9-11

I T IS appropriate that the Gospel of the Kingdom should strike the keynote of Kingship so early as this its second chapter. Also, it is significant that the Jewish Gospel should at the outset give a preview of the extension of the Christian Church to the Gentiles as represented by the Wise Men from the East (cf. "all nations," 25:32, 28:19). The story illustrates what the Church's season of Epiphany typifies. — "the manifestation of Christ to the Gentiles" (cf. Isa. 11:10, 60:3, Jer. 16:19; etc.).

In this chapter there are four groups of people associated with the birth of Christ, and they represent varying attitudes towards the Lord and His salvation. The Wise Men are the first of these groups, and theirs was a seeking attitude. All that we actually know of them is found here, although tradition has always been fascinated by them.

I. The Position of the Wise Men

    a. Matthew does not mention either their nationality or their occupation; but tradition says they were from Persia and were philosophers and astrologers, men who studied stars as guiding human destinies in way akin to Chaldees (cf. Dan. 2:2, 4:7).

    b. Evidently they were men of rank, for they obtained courteous reception from King Herod; word "magi" is of Persian origin and denoted priestly caste or order, in later times supposed to be sorcerers, hence derivation of modern words "magic, magician."

    c. But these men certainly were representative of intellect, learning, wisdom of world, and also of wealth (cf. v. 11).

II. The Action of the Wise Men

    a. Before leaving home they received some assurance of reality of Messiah's appearance, possibly through widespread knowledge of Greek version of O.T. containing

Balaam's prophecy concerning "a Star out of Jacob" (Num. 24:17); or they may well have had their own sources of information about this famed diviner who was also Gentile from "the mountains of the east" (Num. 23:7).

b. However, nothing can be said regarding exact meaning of "his star" (v. 2), but it was almost certainly some direct revelation to these men that led them to travel so far; it may have been meteor, or perhaps some conjunction of planets, according to astronomer Johannes Kepler, 1600 years after, that had special significance for them as students of astrology.

N.B. God clearly adapts His methods of revelation, e.g., to Jews, prophecy; to shepherds, angels; and to astrologers, a star.

c. There was evidently great expectation among Gentiles at that time concerning appearance of some notable personage, as witness writers such as Tacitus, Philo, Josephus, etc.

d. Wise Men sought direction at right source (v. 1), namely, Jerusalem, metropolis of Judaism and of chosen people of God, "city of the great King" (5:35; cf. Ps. 48:2); and they recognized God as guiding them by means of star (cf. v. 10), one of great variety of Divine methods.

N.B. Here we may consider Wise Men as excellent examples of making right choice of source, e.g., of physical truth, nature; of metaphysical truth, human mind; but also of moral truth, Word of God (cf. vs. 5, 6); and, above all, choice of spiritual truth, Jesus Christ Himself (v. 11). Conversely, mistake possible here lies in seeking from Bible what is not intended of book dedicated to moral and spiritual values.

III. The Motivation of the Wise Men

a. They were quite evidently in earnest, with unsatisfied longings for truth of God; and such Divinely inspired constraint always is certain of ultimate result.

b. They sought truth with perseverance, fully conscious that journey would involve time, distance, expense, and difficulty; and this reminds us that conversion of intellectual may not be immediate.

N.B. Wise of every age must seek if they would find, and in seeking intellectual satisfaction find much. But sudden spiritual change among them rarer than among ignorant, because mental power has tendency to self-sufficiency and lack of true humility.

c. They came in attitude of reverence, to worship, and not to criticize or argue as intellectuals too often do; and thus they beautifully exemplify right spirit for "wise men after the flesh" who still, St. Paul says, "are called" (1 Cor. 1:26).

IV. The Satisfaction of the Wise Men

In the second chapter of the first Book of the Old Testament a question is asked: "Where art thou?" (Gen. 2:9). In this second chapter of the first book of the New Testament a similar question is asked: "Where is He—?" (v. 2). The first was spoken by God as to man, while the other was spoken by man as to God; and the second never would have been asked but for a necessity for the first. The wording of the second question is particularly striking: "Where is he that is born King—?"

1. *The Quest*

The Wise Men sought and found —

a. *A Person* — "Where is he—?"

(1) It was not system, though right; not theory, though true; not religion, though Divine.

(2) Man is person, so needs Person; if only intellect, system or theory would suffice, while if only conscience, religion.

(3) Christian man is person, so neither Church nor Book will satisfy; yet benefits of all these, and more, are in Person of Christ.

b. *A King* — "Where is he that is . . . King—?"

(1) That is what world needs — true, spiritual "absolute monarchy"; and individual soul needs ruling, for kingship means obedience to law and order, with consequent benefit.

(2) It was what Gabriel announced to Mary that Christ would be (cf. Luke 1:32, 33), and world will never be right till He is its King.

(3) He came both as "King of the Jews" (v. 2; cf. 27:37) and as "King of kings" (1 Tim. 6:15, Rev.

17:14) ; and although not specifically called King in connection with Church, He is its Head (cf. Eph. 1:22, 4:15, 5:23), and Lord (cf. Eph. 5:29, Col. 3:24), with same meaning spiritually.

c. *A Child* — "Where is he that is born—?"

   (1) Magi sought King and found Child; and yet what depth of meaning, for this is how Christ governs (cf. Isa. 9:6, Mark 10:15).

   (2) If Prince of Peace is to rule in men's hearts He must be received with simplicity and trustfulness of little children (cf. 18:3); so that He, and they, being brought low, are truly exalted (cf. Luke 18:14).

2. *The Response*

The Wise Men responded (v. 11) by —

a. *Experiencing Christ* — "they came . . . and saw the young child" (A.S.V.)

   (1) Christ invites everyone to come to Him (cf. 11:28), to "come and see" (John 1:39).

   (2) This means approach and look of faith (cf. John 1:29; 3:14, 15), each man personally testing Christ for himself.

b. *Acknowledging Christ* — "they fell down, and worshipped him."

   (1) Word "worship" literally means "state of worthiness," and in this case holy Child was found worthy of homage from representatives of human philosophy; "wisdom of God" (1 Cor. 1:24) was thus acknowledged by "wise men from the east" (v. 1).

   (2) Man is always at his greatest height when bowing low before God; and devotion of heart will always follow acceptance of faith.

c. *Serving Christ* — "opening their treasures they offered unto him gifts" (A.S.V.)

   (1) This was practical evidence of devotion; and valuable gifts symbolized lives surrendered to service of Christ.

   (2) Thus, sacrifice on their part was appropriate culmination of long, arduous quest of Wise Men.

Conclusion

Here is an expression of what may be termed the essence of the Christian life:

1. *Personal Contact with Christ*
   Nothing short of this will suffice; have you ever thus been brought into touch with Him?

2. *Personal Lordship of Christ*
   Nothing lower than this is of any use; does He reign over all in your life?

3. *Personal Surrender to Christ*
   Nothing less than this is possible; is yours wholehearted and sincere?   Have you impressions, aspirations, intentions in this all-important matter?   Then act, and as in feudal days of absolute lordship, say humbly to the Lord Jesus Christ:

> *Thou glorious Victor, King Divine,*
> *Shut these surrendered hands in Thine;*
> *At length my will is all Thine own,*
> *Glad vassal of a Saviour's Throne!*
> H.C.G. MOULE

3

IGNORING CHRIST

Matthew 2:4-6

IN THE DUSK of a winter afternoon it is interesting to watch firelight flickering on faces around a hearth, as with its moving fingers of light and shadow it points out the variations of thought or expectation, anxiety or serenity upon them.   So the light from the manger is cast on the characters in this chapter. We are concerned now with the chief priests and scribes who were the Jewish leaders of the day, custodians of the Hebrew religion, and teachers of the people.   It was natural that Herod, on hearing of the presence in Jerusalem of the Wise Men from the East, should inquire of these authorities where the Messiah was to be born; and their response was one of utmost significance.

I. What Was Their Attitude to Christ?

1. *They Were Men of Sufficient Learning*

   a. They knew Scriptures well, immediately quoting Micah 5:2, written nearly eight hundred years before; for evidently they recognized O.T. ever pointed forward, with prophecies unfulfilled, types with no antitypes, ceremonials unexplained, longings expressed but unsatisfied, and, above all, mystery of some great One to come unrevealed.

   b. They distinguished Bethlehem of Judea, six miles south of Jerusalem, from another place of same name to north.

2. *They Were Men of Sad Indifference*

   a. In spite of all this, they made no attempt to go there or to investigate; and they ignored testimony of Wise Men received by Herod.

   b. As today, opposition or acceptance are more easily understood than carelessness; and leaders especially should move forward, not stand still.

3. *They Were Men of Strong Prejudice*

   a. But these remained unmoved because it suited their preconceived ideas to recognize letter and ignore spirit; and doubtless they felt need to curry favor with Herod.

   b. They would even overlook parts of O.T., sacred book of which they were supposed to be custodians and interpreters, if passage would disturb existing regime and challenge their authority.

4. *They Were Men of Stolid Formalism*

   a. Mere orthodoxy truly is deadly enemy of truth; it is knowledge without life, intellect without spirit, outward respectability with inward corruption.

   b. It is found then, as now, in various shapes; e.g., ecclesiastical, with undue reliance on outward forms; evangelical, with due reliance on creed, but with no resulting spiritual experience.

II. What Is the Right Attitude to Christ?

Given knowledge of O.T., we may expect to see —

1. *Jesus the Prophet*
   a. As Scriptures were revelation of God, so One they predicted declared Him as Father, Sustainer, All in all.
   b. There should be no difficulty here, but general acceptance of His teaching as of ancient prophets.

2. *Jesus the Priest*
   a. As O.T. sacrifices and ordinances proclaimed, One they foreshadowed was uniting men to God, removing barriers of sin and guilt with their power and enmity.
   b. There should be not much more difficulty here, because human need is so great.

3. *Jesus the King*
   a. As O.T. pointed to coming Ruler, this concept of Christ goes deeper into future and is real test today, just as it was in the days of Herod and these rulers.
   b. It is brought to us by acceptance of Person of King; and there may well be difficulty in full surrender and submission, for "if He is not Lord of all, then He is not Lord at all."

Conclusion

The Christ of the Bible

1. He is —
   a. Perfect — inspiration for young and consolation for old;
   b. Present — daily, hourly, immediate help and companionship;
   c. Possessed — not only in contact of mind, but by close embrace of faith and love.

2. He may be —
   a. Opposed — helplessly, hopelessly;
   b. Accepted — joyously, wholeheartedly;
   c. Ignored — at first, but those who continue to ignore Him now must actually oppose Him later, as did these chief priests and scribes, losing all opportunity to accept Him.

Therefore, acknowledge Christ as Prophet and Teacher, admit Him as Priest and Saviour, accept Him as King and Lord, and He will teach you, save you, govern you!

4

OPPOSING CHRIST

Matthew 2:3, 4, 7, 8, 14, 16, 19

In the night of Israel's deliverance from Egypt, the blood of the Passover lamb was applied to the doorway of each house, but not to the threshold. It was a symbol of protection under which the people were to spend that night, not something to be trodden on. The Epistle to the Hebrews seems to refer to the converse of this when in 10:29 it speaks of someone who has "trodden under foot the Son of God, and hath counted the blood of the covenant . . . an unholy thing." At any rate, early in Matthew's narrative we are shown the existence of such a state of mind, a state that knows the right and yet deliberately, willfully, persistently opposes it. In its extreme form it is rare, perhaps, but it is also solemnly possible, and St. Paul speaks strongly of it as "a reprobate mind" (Rom. 1:28).

Such was the man whom we now consider as representing the third attitude to Christ in this chapter, "Herod the king" (v. 3). He was the first ruler of this name, called the Great, and was an Edomite by race, made king by the Romans. Because Herod was a cruel despot he was universally detested, even though he had rebuilt, enlarged, and enriched the Temple.

I. Fearing the Truth (vs. 3, 4, 7)

1. *Alarm* (v. 3)

   a. Statement coming from Wise Men was too serious to be disregarded, and Herod "was troubled and all Jerusalem with him"; kingship is usually associated with well-being, not with trouble.

   b. He and people should have been ready for prophetic fulfillment, not opposed to it; but, though near end of life (cf. vs. 15, 19), and world slipping away from him, Herod was not willing to lose his position to some other "King of the Jews" (v. 2).

2. *Anxiety* (v. 4)

   a. Thus it was fear that impelled his assembling of chief

priests and scribes and making his inquiry of them; he would not risk dispossession in case Messianic hopes in hearts of people might flame as fire from embers.

b. Answer (vs. 5, 6) evidently caused him acute concern regarding Child who, if Herod had only realized it, would have brought him and his people immediate blessing; he who had been terror to others now quails at thought of the Babe, because He was said to be "born King of the Jews" (v. 2).

3. *Acquiescence* (v. 7)

a. Herod virtually acknowledges Word of God in private; but he sets out to oppose it not only because of surmised opposition to himself as king, but also because his throne was founded on falsehood and murder.

b. "Conscience makes cowards of us all"; and thus guilt unmans and unnerves.

II. Fighting the Truth (vs. 8, 14, 16, 19)

1. *Deception* (v. 8)

a. Herod in request of Wise Men used word "worship," but he meant "destroy"; thus holy words were combined with wicked plans.

b. He ostensibly asked for information; but he actually plotted action leading to murder that finally resulted in wholesale slaughter.

2. *Depravity* (v. 16)

a. But God was on His throne and sent two dreams (cf. vs. 12, 13), as He had sent one to Joseph before (cf. 1:20) and would send another afterwards (cf. v. 19).

b. When Herod found himself circumvented, he was in frenzy and determined on slaughter of "Innocents," who may be regarded as first martyrs of Christian era, though at such tender age.

c. This orgy was quite in keeping with Herod's character, for he continued on throne by means of bloodshed, extending vengeance to whole families of offenders, according to history.

3. *Defeat* (vs. 14, 19)

a. Probably Herod was satisfied that he had removed threat

to throne; but God reigning supreme had protected His Son and vindicated truth of prophetic Scriptures (v. 14).

b. Soon came Herod's death (v. 19) after seventy years of bloodstained life; and end was probably hastened by events in this chapter.

c. Goaded by evil conscience, racked by disease, he awaited death; yet he still desired life and raged against God and man, for we are told by secular history that, maddened by thought of Jews' joy at his death, Herod ordered certain leaders assembled and killed.

d. This was in order that posterity might weep after all; and thus he died as he had lived, and went to his own fit place.

Conclusion

1. *Herods Are Still Working*

   a. Circumstances change, degrees of sin differ, but Herod's kind are the same.

   b. Afraid of truth and troubled by admitting its existence, they are ready to stifle conscience and act directly contrary to it.

2. *Herods Are Still Warned*

   a. Many of earth's greatest have tried to fight God — e.g., Emperor Julian the Apostate, Voltaire; but He must reign in spite of rulers taking counsel against Him and, like Herod, "against his anointed" (Ps. 2:2).

   b. They might as well try to dry up ocean or blot out sun; for the Babe of Bethlehem is now on His Father's throne as present Saviour and future Judge.

3. Therefore, there are still two ways and times in which to meet Him:

   a. Rebel now, and be ruined then; or —
   b. Surrender now, and be saved, and be honored then.

Let Him take you as His own and see what He will do — give you quietness and peace, His presence and His power. Life will be real, true, strong, blessed. You will find perfect freedom and full satisfaction as you are changed from slave to freeman, from rebel to follower, from wanderer to adherent; and pass from death to life in possession of Jesus Christ as Saviour and Lord.

5

WELCOMING CHRIST

Matthew 2:11-14, 19-23

T HOU HAST made us for Thyself, and our hearts are restless till they rest in Thee." These well-known words of St. Augustine were his expression of the realization that man is complete only in God. The Incarnation provides the means of uniting man with God and producing perfection of life. Hence, Christianity represents a right relationship between God and man, first obtained and then maintained — a mutual attitude, first adopted and then continued. Without this, man is like a timepiece with no mainspring or a steam engine with no steam.

We have seen three attitudes towards Christ at the time of His incarnation. As the Apostle Paul stated many years later, our Lord is found to be either a foundation stone or a stumbling block, according to men's relationship to Him. Now let us look at the perfect attitude, the picture of true Christian life as seen in Mary and Joseph, and with which we may test our own lives.

I. The Truth Possessed

1. *The Fact*

   a. Jesus was theirs in special sense — relation one of possession; they had not only heard of Him, as had others in this chapter, but He was theirs.

   b. This is Christianity in essence, whose first step is declared to be "He that hath the Son hath life" (1 John 5:12); for Christian who possesses Christ is divided and distinguished from man who "hath not the Son of God" and therefore "hath not life."

2. *The Message*

   a. Angel of God had brought message to both Mary and Joseph, and it was believed by each (cf. Luke 1:26-38, Matt. 1:19-25); it was brought differently — to Mary awake and to Joseph asleep — and probably their capacities for response differed, yet fact was same.

b. This is way to possess Christ — through Word of God heard and received; no matter how revelation is made or what the type of recipient, so long as fact of acceptance is certain.

II. The Truth Pre-eminent

1. *The Fact*

   a. From that time on Jesus was prominent fact in their life; they never could go back to old ways or ordinary family living.
   b. He was to be reckoned with and thenceforward put first — in Bethlehem, Egypt, Nazareth, Jerusalem.

2. *The Message*

   a. So now in spiritual things Christ is first; cf. actual wording in vs. 11, 13, 14, 20, 21 — not "Madonna and Child," as some say, but "the young child and his mother" — "that in all things he might have the preeminence" (Col. 1:18).
   b. This is secret of all true Christian life; and yet many who possess Christ are lacking here — He is not first in their lives.

III. The Truth Prized

1. *The Fact*

   a. Jesus was very dear to Mary and Joseph, spiritually as well as personally; for as Messiah He was One on whom their hopes of salvation rested (cf. Luke 1:47).
   b. As Mary's Son, moreover, He was One on whom their human affection centered; and their family hopes would be fulfilled first of all in Him.

2. *The Message*

   a. So always to His people, "How sweet the Name of Jesus sounds!" —and this also is in twofold way.
   b. Spiritually, their trust rests on Him as Saviour, and personally, their love reciprocates His love; and this is always true if Christ is both possessed and pre-eminent.

IV. The Truth Proved

1. *The Fact*

   a. Possession of Jesus caused Mary and Joseph suffering

and pain, even what amounted to persecution, outlawry, flight.

b. Up to then they had had none of these, so far as we know; but now they were plunged into trouble and difficulty.

2. *The Message*

a. Jesus brings testing; for "all that will live godly in Christ Jesus shall suffer persecution" (2 Tim. 3:12).

b. This must not come as surprise to us; for spiritual education involves pain of "drawing out" our faith and even opposition from world.

V. The Truth Preserved

1. *The Fact*

a. God was watching, keeping, guiding, blessing; His angels were near to warn and to give directions to Joseph; e.g., while perplexed (1:20); when in danger (2:13); and when danger was over (2:19).

b. God has many ways of guarding His own (cf. Ps. 115: 12); and Christianity is thus found to be both Divine and imperishable.

2. *The Message*

a. Joseph's obedience was prompt, precise, with no reluctance and no delay, and of two sorts: active (cf. v. 14), and passive (cf. v. 15), both calling for strong faith on his part; and his fear for Child's safety was used by God to guide him back to Nazareth, rather than to Bethlehem which he might well have considered to be proper home of David's heir.

b. This resulted in reassurance — "they are dead —" (v. 20); all opposition was found to be futile, and those on side of Christ, as now, had everything needed for time and for eternity.

Conclusion

1. *This is Christian Experience*

a. The truth of Christ possessed in the mind;

b. The truth of Christ pre-eminent in the life;

c. The truth of Christ prized in the heart;

d. The truth of Christ proved by testings; and —

e. The truth of Christ preserved amid opposition.

2. *This Calls for Personal Experiment*

    a. The Christian life is the only real one — perfect, power-ful, precious, permanent;

    b. But, as with a telescope whose lens must be both clear and adjusted to the point of vision, we must place our-selves humbly before God; we must allow His light to flood our souls and bring us face to face with Jesus Christ as Saviour and Friend.

Are we willing to try the experiment? If so, the experience will indeed be ours. "Blessed are all they that put their trust in him" (Ps. 2:12).

6

THE FATHER'S PLAN UNFOLDING

Matthew 2:13-23

T HE VISIT of the Wise Men must have occurred after the presentation of Christ in the temple (cf. Luke 2:22-24), for instead of the stable in which He was born it was a house in which they found Him (cf. v. 11). Also, it is implied that Mary had been too poor to offer a lamb for her purification (cf. Luke 2:24 with Lev. 12:6-8), so we may infer that the costly gifts of the Magi had not yet been presented. Their visit may even have taken place up to two years later, according to the probable length of the journey from the East after they first saw the star, and also in view of Herod's directions in verse 16.

It is possible to trace an analogy between the first two chapters of Matthew's Gospel and the first two books of the Old Testa-ment. The book of Genesis may be compared with Matthew 1:1 to 2:15, for both end with a journey into Egypt. The book of Exodus records the return of the chosen people from Egypt, and Matthew 2:16-23 tells of the return of the Child Jesus from Egypt. Parallels may be drawn, for example, between the two attempts at slaughter — of the Hebrew "men children" in Exodus and of the Innocents in Matthew — in which respectively the people and the Son were Divinely preserved; and between the forty years of Israel's wandering in the wilderness and the prob-able forty days of the holy family's sojourn in Egypt (see I, 2, b, below).

But there are three specific prophecies quoted in this passage, and all are said to have been fulfilled in the early life of our Lord:

I. The Flight and Prophecy (vs. 13-15)

1. *Divine Direction* (v. 13)

a. Immediately after Wise Men had departed, another angelic message came in a dream to Joseph; he was given both command to take flight and reason for it.

b. Again it is significant how usual order of nature is reversed as phrase found several times is "the young child and his mother" (vs. 13, 14, 20, 21) — not "the mother and child" as we say today;

N.B. Cf. also "Madonna" (my lady) with "the mother of my Lord" (Luke 1:43); and yet we ought not to ignore origin and persistence of prominence of Virgin Mary. The veneration of her, tantamount in Roman Church to worship, grew up side by side with tendency in orthodox Protestant circles to forget humanity of Christ while laying due stress on His Deity. Since heart of man needs human element as well as Divine, and yet Christ's essential humanity receded, worship of Virgin came into prominence with attractive force. Thus, best safeguard against this error is emphasis on essential, available manhood of Christ, who is demonstrated in N.T. to be humanly sympathetic as well as Divinely redemptive.

c. Destination, Egypt, beyond jurisdiction of Herod, was suitable refuge as in earlier times (cf. Gen. 12:10, 46:2-4).

2. *Human Acceptance* (vs. 14, 15a)

a. Joseph and Mary unquestioningly obeyed God's order to go and to remain in Egypt until further instructions.

b. According to some students of history, this was probably from February to April of the year A.D. 4, so that it may well have been "forty days."

c. Cause of journey would be reminder that trouble foretold by Simeon (Luke 2:34, 35) was commencing early; but it would also assure Mary that God was protecting her Child and would fulfill His word through Simeon's prayer (Luke 2:29-32).

3. *Divine Purpose* (v. 15b)

a. This was to be associated with O.T. and shown to be

in agreement with its typology, fulfillment of prophecy being both national and personal.

b. It links national life of Israel, referred to by the Lord as "my son" (Exod. 4:22, Hos. 11:1), with human life of that greater Son of God; and in both, land of Egypt played important part.

N.B. 1. Professor C. F. Keil points out that "the sojourn in Egypt, and return out of that land, had the same significance in relation to the development of the life of Jesus Christ as it had to the nation of Israel. Just as Israel grew into a nation in Egypt, where it was out of the reach of Canaanitish ways, so was the Child Jesus hidden in Egypt from the hostility of Herod."

N.B. 2. Spiritually speaking, C. G. Moore reminds us: "We are slow to take it to heart that Egypt is not merely our refuge for the time from a peril that might slay our best life, but the very place of our enrichment and enlargement. . . . 'Be thou there until, His word bids thee depart; and then thou shalt find that with a mighty hand He Himself 'will surely bring thee up again' (Gen. 46:3, 4)."

II. The Slaughter and Prophecy (vs. 16-18)

1. *Anger Resulting in Murder* (v. 16)

a. Herod soon found he had been "mocked of the wise men" and, showing his true attitude at last (cf. v. 8), vented his "exceeding" wrath upon all male children in and near Bethlehem "from two years and under" (cf. Exod. 1:16).

b. In hopes of including Jesus Christ, he took no chances as to age or locality or station — refinement of cruelty unrestrained.

N.B. Book of Common Prayer, in Collect for Innocents' Day, addresses God as having made "infants to glorify Thee by their deaths," and prays that, "by the innocency of our lives, and constancy of our faith even unto death, we may glorify Thy holy Name." By using as "Epistle" to be read a passage from Revelation (14:1-5), Reformers imply these babes to have been "redeemed from among men, being the firstfruits unto God and to the Lamb . . . without fault before the throne of God."

2. *Sorrow Refusing Consolation* (vs. 17, 18)

    a. Sadness in Bethlehem, even though perhaps children involved in so small a place were but few, was deep and real; and it is associated with well-known words of prophet Jeremiah (31:15).

    b. God's rejoinder (vs. 16,17) is noteworthy in this prophetic connection, for it includes comforting promise: "Thy work shall be rewarded . . . and they shall come again from the land of the enemy."

III. The Return and Prophecy (vs. 19-23)

1. *Enemy Dead and Return Ordered* (vs. 19-21)

    a. Before long, angel announces to Joseph in Egypt that Herod is dead who "sought the young child's life," reminding him, and us, that all opposition to Christ will be futile.

    b. Joseph is ordered to take "young child and his mother" and return to Israel, which he did; and thus, step by step, God guides, giving light enough for one duty at a time.

2. *Destination Indicated and Forecast Fulfilled* (vs. 22, 23)

    a. Joseph feared Herod's son Archelaus might follow his father's dreadful example, so hesitated to return to Judaea; but God was ready with next step, settlement in Galilee, with Nazareth, old home of Mary and Joseph, appropriate place.

    b. This decision was said to fulfill prophecy of Isaiah 11:1, blending etymology of name Nazareth (*netzer* in Hebrew, meaning rod, sprout, branch) with reputation for obscurity that town had; and it pointed to lowliness of Messiah, as shoot from prostrate tree trunk or stem of Jesse — that is, to His birth from royal family of Judah in its humble and reduced estate.

    c. This coincidence of town's name and general contempt for Galilee established association of ideas; so that Jesus being called Nazarene fulfilled this and other predictions of His humiliation.

    N.B. This should never be confused with name "Nazirite" (see Num. 6:1-21, A.S.V., where word is accurately spelled). This means "one who is separated" in sense that did not apply to our Lord.

Conclusion

In this story of some of the opening events in our Lord's earthly life we see two pictures, one from the Divine standpoint and the other from the human:

1. *Life from the Divine Side*
    a. God's Purpose — He intended every character in the drama to fulfill some vital part of it.
    b. God's Plan — He foreknew how His purpose would be carried out; by Divine interposition in explaining, warning, guiding; and by human opposition — foreseen, foretold, forewarned, and foredoomed.

2. *Life from the Human Side*
    a. Opposition — serious, but proving futile because of God's overruling providence;
    b. Obedience — expressed sometimes in activity, and sometimes in patience.

Thus, from one point of view or the other, in one way or another, God's will always is done and "all things work together for good" to those who love Him and are called by Him "according to his purpose" (Rom. 8:28).

7

THE BAPTIZER AND THE BAPTISM

Matthew 3:1-17

THE FIRST words of the chapter are indefinite as to the time of that which is here recorded, but Luke (3:1-3) gives us the exact chronology and the historical setting. Herod Antipas, the tetrarch (or petty monarch) of Galilee, was a son of Herod the Great (chap. 2) and a brother of Archelaus (2:22).

I. The Forerunner of the Messiah (vs. 1-12)

John the Baptist is one of best known personages of N.T., occupying an important position. His life is full of interest and his work calls for special attention.

1. *His General Ministry* (vs. 1-6)
    a. Message of John twofold (v. 2)

(1) Need for repentance, which means —
   (a) Change of mind and conduct;
   (b) Forsaking sin, not merely being sorry for it, which is meaning of word penitence;
   (c) Proving sincerity by baptism and confession (cf. v. 6).

(2) Imminence of Kingdom of Heaven — phrase found only in Matthew's Gospel, and one of its keys — doubtless Jewish term referring to Kingdom promised ages before by prophet Daniel (2:44), and meaning reign of God over earth:
   (a) It could soon have been established if Jews had been willing to accept Christ as King, but —
   (b) Phrase "kingdom of heaven" is not identical with "Church" or with present dispensation, which have intervened in providence of God.
   (c) Precise distinction, if any, between that and "kingdom of God" is practically, if not literally, unknown; but it is generally thought that latter term is wider and more appropriate to Gentiles, for it seems to be applied to reign of God over universe, earthly and heavenly, and over time, past, present, and future (cf. Luke 13:28-30); yet this does not explain exactly why Matthew preferred to write "kingdom of heaven."

b. Message of John shown in relation to O.T. through quotation from Isaiah 40:3 regarded by Matthew as now fulfilled:

(1) Figure is that of preparing road for coming of king (v. 3);
(2) Appearance of preacher (v. 4) was in keeping with his startling announcement, his circumstances, and his work as forerunner;
(3) Influence of testimony and effects of preaching were immediate and widespread (vs. 5, 6).

2. *His Special Ministry* (vs. 7-12)
All this naturally led to coming of religious leaders, Pharisees, and Sadducees; and then John —
a. Denounced them in plainest possible language (v. 7);

  b. Urged them to prove reality of their concern by repentant life (v. 8);

  c. Warned them not to regard themselves as specially privileged because descendants of Abraham since God was able, even of stones, to provide children for him (v. 9);

  d. Informed them that time was near when God would test life of everyone for good fruit or bad (v. 10); and —

  e. Instructed them that, while he himself was using water for baptism "with a view to repentance for the remission of sins" (v. 11, Greek), Someone was coming who would administer Holy Spirit baptism; and that, as chaff was burned near threshing-floor, there would be fire of judgment that would inevitably consume those who were found to be unreal and unfaithful in sifting and testing (vs. 11, 12).

II. The Baptism of the Messiah (vs. 13-17)

The attitude of Christ to baptism and the Baptist is most important and of great interest. It is hardly surprising that John protested and said humbly that he himself needed to be baptized of Christ. But our Lord's reply sufficed to settle matter and reveal need for —

1. *Identification*

  a. Since Christ had no sin to forsake or confess, there could be no such thing as repentance in His case; but —

  b. He showed He wished to take His place with others coming for baptism, probably believing remnant, and thus to identify Himself with His nation according to flesh in obeying God, and to "fulfill all righteousness" (v. 15).

2. *Consecration*

  a. Since Christ was looking forward to His life and work as Messiah, Anointed One, it was necessary first to be "washed with water" as was a high priest (cf. Exod. 29:4) before "anointing oil" (v. 7), symbol of Holy Spirit, was applied.

  b. There was also symbol of His reign as King — "like a dove" (v. 16), standing for peace, purity, meekness, beauty — attributes that He passes on to His subjects with His gift to them of Holy Spirit.

N.B. James Stalker once said it was "to crown the long development of His peculiar powers," and it is obvious that coronation is consequent upon royalty, never its antecedent.

c. It is evident from several other passages that our Lord in His human nature was recipient of Holy Spirit to qualify Him for His work on earth as our Redeemer (cf., e.g., Rom. 1:4, Heb. 9:14) ; and so it is natural to see in descent of Holy Spirit at His baptism actual Divine equipment of Him for work He was about to commence.

d. Immediate result of Christ's baptism, therefore, was recognition of Him by God the Father and anointing of Him by God the Holy Spirit for service that lay before Him; and this was first full manifestation of Trinity, revealing distinctions within Godhead (vs. 16, 17; cf. 28:19).
N.B. Holy Spirit here shown to be (1) Person (God Himself) ; (2) Possession (indwelling) ; and (3) Power (over sin, and for work).

Conclusion

1. *The Witness of John the Baptist*

   a. *His Character* — as expressed by the prophecy of the angel who announced his birth: "He shall be great in the sight of the Lord" (Luke 1:15) ; real greatness is goodness, tested and guaranteed by a man's relation to God.

   b. *His Message* — as recorded by the Apostle John: (1) Christ was to be the Saviour (1:29), the Bestower of the Spirit (1:33) and, therefore, the Son of God (1:34) ; (2) the people were to repent, prove their change of heart by baptism, and turn to Christ as their Saviour; or, summed up in three words, there must be repentance, surrender, trust.

2. *The Witness of Christ's Baptism*

   This act is to be regarded as of great importance in marking a crisis in the life of our Saviour (cf. Acts 1:22), coming as it did between the thirty years of obscurity and the three years of ministry thus solemnly inaugurated. There was in it a threefold supernatural manifestation:

   a. *The Opened Heavens* — appropriately indicating the Messiah's relationship to heaven as He set about His work on earth;

b. *The Descending Holy Spirit* — in the symbol of a dove alighting, to typify the purity, peace, and love that would actuate Him and characterize His ministry; and —

c. *The Divine Voice* — bearing testimony to the Father's interest in and love of the Son, with words that echo Isaiah's ages before (cf. 42:1) and are quoted in full by Matthew in another connection (12:18-21).

"Then," said Peter, relating his experience in the house of Cornelius (Acts 11:16), "remembered I the word of the Lord, how he said, John indeed baptized with water; but ye shall be baptized with the Holy Ghost."

3. *The Witness of Christian Baptism*

The difference between John's baptism of our Lord and Christian baptism is found in the latter's purpose:

a. As the Saviour, Christ identified Himself with the people of Israel and was baptized "unto repentance," even though He needed not to repent; but Christian baptism is "into the name of the Father and of the Son and of the Holy Spirit" (28:19, A.S.V.).

b. It is always associated with our relation to God and not to man, symbolizing a Divine, not a human act; and since confession of Christ covers our entire life that cannot be limited, even in its initial aspect, to one particular rite.

c. The "Name" of God always denotes His revealed character, and so Christian baptism "into the name" simply, yet blessedly, means consecration with a view to union and communion with all that we know of God — Father, Son, and Holy Spirit.

8

THE TEMPTATION OF CHRIST

Matthew 4:1-11

A NOTHER crisis in the life of our Lord was His temptation. It was a testing of Him not so much as Man, but rather as the Messiah, with special reference to His work and the establishment of His Kingdom. This is seen especially in Matthew's account, which differs from Luke's in the order of narration (cf. Luke 4:1-13). Matthew gives definite marks of time, while Luke is much more general in aim; and Matthew's order seems clearly the true order of events.

I. The Circumstances of the Testing (vs. 1, 2)

These were at once spiritual and physical, for we read of the Spirit, the wilderness, the devil, fasting, and hunger:

1. *The Fact of Temptation*
   a. Implicit here is important distinction which we may express thus: God tests, the devil tempts; and association in verse 1 of Holy Spirit and Satan reminds us God often uses temptation by Evil One, permitting it to be occasion of His testing.
   b. Devil, however, does not tempt sinful element in human nature, for that is already on his side and therefore needs no evil solicitation; rather, it is the heart pure and whole, man's "better nature," that devil assails and attempts to lead into sin.
   c. Temptation does not appeal to actual sin, but to capacity for sinning which is part of man's freedom of will; and thus it was fixed, righteous will of our Lord that Satan tried to overthrow.
   d. Further, our Lord's sympathy is definitely associated with His sinlessness (cf. Heb. 4:15); indeed, sympathy of sinfulness is weakness, not strength.
   N.B. (1) Whitham wrote: "It is the love which suffers, not the weakness which fails, that is able to help us."

(2) *The Century Bible* on Hebrews says: "The keenest agony can be known only by one who remains sinless. Others are tried till they yield, and those who yield soonest suffer least."

e. As for God's testing, word "then" (v. 1) suggests intimate connection of our Lord's temptation with His baptism and His Father's words that followed it (cf. 3:17); it was significant opportunity of determining whether these were authentic, for Christ was "led" — humanly speaking, He did not go of His own accord (cf. 6:13).

N.B. Every Christian life has two sides to its experience of God's testing: "led by the Spirit" and "tempted of the devil."

2. *The Time of Temptation*

   a. It was immediately after descent of Spirit (cf. 3:16), which was our Lord's endowment for His work; and this is very usual experience — man coming from fellowship with God to conflict with Satan, from spiritual blessing to severe testing that calls for supernatural endurance.

   b. Temptation was continuous throughout forty days (cf. Mark 1:13, Luke 4:2); but we are told only of three climactic assaults of devil upon Him.

3. *The Place of Temptation*

   a. Wilderness was fitting place for solitude and training that comes by quiet meditation.

   b. Forty days' fast in lonely spot was reminder of similar experiences of Moses (Exod. 24:18) and of Elijah (1 Kings 19:8).

4. *The Agent of Temptation*

   a. Being tempted "of the devil," original author of sin, our Lord was thereby tested in way that would prove beyond doubt His fitness for His forthcoming battle against evil.

   b. Scripture is clear that Christ believed in Satan's existence and power (cf. John 8:44); but to imply that he is omnipresent is virtually to regard him as equal with God, which is impossible.

   c. True Scriptural concept seems to be that of mighty spirit, in league with whom and under whose control are other lesser spirits of evil (cf. Eph. 2:2, 6:12); but there are few subjects that need more careful treatment than doctrine of Satan.

II. The Character of the Testing (vs. 3-10)

It was not temptation to do things evil of themselves, for object in each case was harmless; wrong was in means suggested to be used. There were three temptations, each referring to a different aspect of Christ's mission on earth:

1. *The First Temptation* (vs. 3, 4)

   a. This was concerned with Divine ideals for Kingdom, whether it was to be spiritual or material in its nature; and it involved Christ's personal relation to His Father.

   b. Since (real sense of "if" in vs. 3, 6) Christ had been declared to be Son of God (3:17), test of loyalty to Father was presented to Him; it was as though devil would imply that, assuming He was God's Son, He ought to have retained power to satisfy own hunger.

   c. But there was to be no materialism and no demagoguery; man was not to "live by bread alone" (v. 4; cf. Deut. 8:3), that is, not to consider bodily wants only.

   d. Christ rejected materialistic attitude for Himself not because it was essentially wrong to provide for natural needs, but because to use His unique relation to God would mean forsaking true human way of dependence on God; and so He answered with word "man," suggesting He was not there as Son of God, but as representative Man.

2. *The Second Temptation* (vs. 5-7)

   a. This was concerned with Divine laws for Kingdom, whether it was to be spiritual or material in its methods; and it involved Christ's official relation to His own nation, Israel.

   b. Opportunity to make striking display before Jews and thereby win them easily was natural suggestion; and Temple was mentioned because center of Jewish life.

   c. But in opposition to this came Messiah's expression of trust not only in Divine power, but in Divine program; for there was to be no charlatanism, no sensationalism, and God was not to be tempted (cf. Deut. 6:16), that is, tested presumptuously.

d. Christ thus declared that spiritual results, always excellent in themselves, can come only through observing spiritual laws; and so He answered Satan with quotation of words "thou" and "thy" which had had human application when first uttered, again identifying Himself as representative Man.

3. *The Third Temptation* (vs. 8-10)

a. This was concerned with Divine plans for Kingdom, whether it was to be spiritual or material in its approach, and it involved Christ's universal relation to world.

b. Satan offered Christ opportunity both of possessing his own enormous influence over human affairs and of avoidance of suffering — swift, painless way towards accomplishment of Christ's primary purpose; it was temptation to make short cut to throne by avoiding cross.

c. But there was to be no compromise with evil, no worldly wisdom that would seek help from Evil One who claimed to have world at his disposal (cf. 1 John 5:19, A.S.V.). *N.B.* Alexander Maclaren says: "There is much in Scripture that seems to bear out the boast that the kingdoms are at Satan's disposal, but he is the 'father of lies' as well as 'the prince of this world,' and we may be very sure that his authority loses nothing in his telling. If we think how many thrones have been built on violence and sustained by crime, how seldom in the world's history right has been uppermost, and how little the fear of God goes into the organization of society even today in so-called Christian countries, we shall be ready to feel that in this boast the devil told more truth than we like to believe."

d. Christ again declared that spiritual work must be done by spiritual means, this time on world basis as well as on more limited ones; and so He again answered Satan using quotation from O.T. that had been addressed to men in connection with their worship and service of God, thus including Himself among them as representative Man (cf. Deut. 6:13, 10:20).

Thus the three temptations were, respectively, personal, national, universal, and in three extending circles the whole era of human temptation was covered.

N.B. Dr. Jowett once characterized the three aspects of Christ's temptation thus: "In the first our Lord was tempted to be unspiritual; in the second He was tempted to be semi-spiritual; in the third He was tempted to be stupidly spiritual and to manifest a piety which was impious." Another writer has expressed it thus: the first temptation was to substitute wrong independence for good dependence; the second, to substitute wrong dependence for good independence; and the third, to accomplish right ends by wrong means.

III. The Consequences of the Testing (v. 11)

1. *To Himself*
   a. Victory was outcome of encounter, and devil left Him — yet only "for a season" (Luke 4:13), since other temptations beset Him continually during His earthly ministry.
   b. Then came God's messengers, the angels, to supply His needs (cf. 1 Kings 19:5-7, Ps. 78:25, Luke 22:43).

2. *To His Ministry*
   a. This episode, having had special reference to Christ's Messiahship, had tested His qualifications for His great office: whether He would function below principles of Kingdom and go around cross; and whether He would use wrong means to accomplish right ends.
   b. His victory showed Him fitted and ready for His work; and from innocence (purity untempted) He was led on and up to virtue (purity tempted and triumphant).
   c. It is impossible, however, to separate our Lord's redemptive work from His personal example, or His deity from His humanity:
      (1) If He could have sinned, He could not have been our Redeemer; but, also —
      (2) If He could not have been tempted, He could not have been man, and therefore one with us (cf. Heb. 2:16-18).

   We must hold both aspects of truth without being able fully to reconcile them within present limits of human knowledge.
   d. We may, therefore, hold that, from one point of view, our Lord "not able to sin," and also that, from another, He was "able not to sin."
   N.B. P. T. Forsyth suggests this passage is fully illus-

trative of *kenosis,* or Christ's self-emptying (cf. Phil. 2:7, A.S.V.), and therefore His struggle was indeed real.

3. *To His Followers*

a. *His Suffering*

   (1) No one, then, should question intense reality of Christ's temptation — "He suffered, being tempted" (Heb. 2:18); and suffering was the keener for His spotless purity.

   (2) He felt tremendous force of temptation and suffered far more than we, with our sinful nature, ever could; sinlessness obviously is much more sensitive to evil than sinfulness.

   (3) Of Adam it may be said he had liability and not tendency to sin; our Lord, on the other hand, had neither; but we, through Adam's fall, have both.

   (4) Word "perfect" used of Christ (cf. Heb. 5:8, 9), because it means not sinless (though that was true of Him), but mature, ripe, trained, and therefore fitted and ready for service.

   (5) Thus, same word can be and is used of His people (cf. 5:48; Eph. 4:12, 13), and should be their great inspiration and objective.

b. *His Sympathy*

   (1) Not only so, but through Christ's own victory over temptation He has been enabled to "suffer with" us — "touched" because "tempted" (Heb. 4:15).

   (2) This sympathy is not with wrongdoing, of course, but with weakness, and it is based not on likeness, but on unlikeness to us; for though His strength of character was severely tested it was completely victorious.

c. *His Sword*

   (1) Christ's weapon of victory was use of Scripture (cf. Eph. 6:17); for knowledge of God's Word is always secret of power.

   (2) Even though Son of God, Christ met tempter as "Son of man" by use of written Word available to man — God's wisdom, God's revelation (cf. Ps. 119:11).

N.B. In This passage we may also see a threefold aspect of true Christian life: (1) abandonment, not distrust; (2) balance, not presumption; and (3) allegiance, not betrayal.

Conclusion

There were three elements in human life to which Satan in his threefold temptation of Christ had the temerity to attempt to appeal. These were appetite, pride, and ambition. So far they are sinful they do not, of course, apply to our Lord. We know, however, that appetite is a natural element and is only wrong when abused or over-indulged. There are also right and wrong kinds of pride and ambition. All three elements make great appeal to us and are liable to lead us into sin because they are concerned with such strong desires in our human nature. With this in mind, let us consider three spiritual elements:

1. *Life's Possibilities*

We are always in danger of yielding to evil, either by abusing what is lawful, or by using what is unlawful; and the first step towards victory is the full recognition of our own sinful nature with its weakness and peril, and of the alternative if we will but accept it, which is —

2. *Life's Power*

This is the very strength of God as revealed in His Word, for whenever we take Scripture as our guide we are enabled to combat the dangers without as well as the weakness within by means of —

3. *Life's Protection*

The way of victory over evil is by acknowledging the presence of Christ by His Spirit in the heart, for when Divine grace rules within we become "more than conquerors through him that loved us" (Rom. 8:37).

9

NECESSITY

Matthew 4:3, 4

How should human life be lived? In these verses there are two theories represented, and each brings forward facts to be faced. The first was enunciated by Satan, the second by Jesus Christ:

I. The Suggestion of Satan (v. 3)

1. *The Implied Plea of Necessity*

   Given certain natural laws and human circumstances, is not duty to self clear?

   a. Necessity has compelling force on all created beings even though it is not always understood.

   b. Necessity has strong influence on man, appealing to his fears and thus darkening his judgment.

2. *The Deceitfulness of Temptation*

   a. It can pretend necessity where there is none.

   b. It can push necessity further than morally justifiable.

II. The Reply of Christ (v. 4)

1. *Necessity Not Everything*

   a. If Christ had yielded to Satan it would have been fatal admission.

   b. Law of Kingdom would have been summed up in such words as "I must live!" instead of "I must serve!"

2. *Right Is Everything*

   a. Body of man not his own in last analysis since it depends on bread made from and through God's creation; and —

   b. Likewise, spirit of man not his own since it depends upon God's power and should feed upon God's Word.

Conclusion

Since physical necessity is not everything, but right is, we sum it all up by the thought that right is the spiritual necessity on which life depends.

1. *God First*

Bread, yes — but not bread alone.

2. *God Last*

His will finally accomplished through man's trust in Him.

10

"BY THE GALILEAN LAKE"

Matthew 4:12-25

It should be borne in mind that this passage introduces the commencement not of Christ's ministry as a whole, but only of His Galilean ministry. His experiences in Judaea and Samaria (see John 1:19 to 4:42) come in before Matthew 4:12, for Christ began His work in Galilee only when the way was clear through the imprisonment of John the Baptist, which was due to what is summarized in 14:3-5. Christ could go there then without likelihood of clashing or misunderstanding. The temptation had proved His qualification to be the Messiah, and His victory over Satan had transformed His innocence into virtue.

I. General Introduction (vs. 12-17)

In verses 12-16 we have an appendix, introductory to the next section and yet summarizing Christ's entire ministry. These verses close the first general division of Matthew's Gospel (see Introduction, p. 18). Between verse 17 and 16:20, where the same phrase, "From this time," ushers in the third general division of the book, it is notable that not a single word about Christ's death is to be found. Its subject is rather His public ministry and His presentation of Himself to Israel as Messiah and King.

1. *Christ's Withdrawal from Judaea* (vs. 12, 13)

   a. This was probably only partly on account of John's imprisonment leaving Galilee without a testimony.

  b. It was also because of the increasing hostility of Pharisees (cf. John 4:1-3).

  c. It is evident, too, that change of residence from Nazareth to Capernaum was due to rejection related in Luke 4:16-31.

2. *Christ's Fulfillment of Prophecy* (vs. 14-16)

  a. He came into north according to words spoken ages before by Isaiah (9:1, 2), that the actual region might be visited by Him.

  b. They express what Christ accomplished by dispersing darkness of sin and ignorance and bringing in His light (cf. John 1:4-9).

  c. His coming was symbolic of way in which our Lord was to be "light to lighten the Gentiles" (Luke 2:32).

  d. This inclusion of Gentiles in Jewish Gospel is most important because it gives at early stage hint of "all nations" to which gospel would come (28:19).

  e. Darkness was that of sin, and light seen by people in it reveals here, as elsewhere, truths of knowledge, holiness, and joy.

  f. It is the Lord Himself who is "the light of life" (John 8:12) to those who receive Him.

  Illus.: John Ruskin says what really makes a great picture is the presence in it of what he aptly terms "heaven-light," mentioning specifically the celebrated landscape painter Turner, whose scenes are rendered more ideal, more beautiful and more sublime than reality. It is further remarked that it is this presence of "heaven-light" in human hearts and lives that makes them great, in the sight both of God and of man, transforming ordinary mortals into immortals. No wonder light is so often used by sacred oracles as the symbol of our best blessings. Paul describes gospel revelation as light (cf. Rom. 13:12, Eph. 5:8); and thus Matthew, rejoicing in "heaven-light" of Jesus, gives here this exquisite rendering of Isaiah's vision: "The people which sat in darkness saw great light; and to them which sat in the region and shadow of death light is sprung up" (v. 14).

3. *Christ's Theme for Preaching* (v. 17)

This was same as that of His forerunner — repentance in relation to Kingdom of Heaven:

a. Repentance — emphasizing necessity of turning from sin and forsaking it — expressed by two words in original:
   (1) One, most usual, means "change of mind"; and —
   (2) Other means "change of feeling" (cf. 21:29, 32; 2 Cor. 7:8), or regret, as we should say.

   When mind and feeling thus are transformed they will express themselves in entire change of conduct — simple yet searching proof of genuine repentance (cf. 2 Cor. 7:10, 11).

b. Imminence of Kingdom of Heaven — literal phrase has "of the heavens" and seems to be essentially Jewish, for found only in Matthew:
   (1) If distinguishable from wider phrase found elsewhere, "kingdom of God," as many believe, it refers to part of God's reign that involves His rule over Israel.
   (2) Jews were continually thinking of earthly kingdom, and on this account rejected our Lord's spiritual teaching of new sovereignty from heaven.

   Both aspects, repentance and kingdom, involve Lordship of Christ — "that he might be Lord" (Rom. 14:8, 9).
   N.B. Before next section, John 4:46-54 and Luke 4:16-30 may be read.

II. Preparation for the Future (vs. 18-22)

Christ's ministry was not limited to Galilee, but had reference to future:

1. *The Call of the Disciples* (vs. 18, 19, 21)
   a. It is clear this summons to Peter and Andrew presupposes commencement of discipleship recorded in John 1:35-42; they had already come *to* Christ (cf. John 1:39), and now, several months later, they were to come *after* Him (cf. Mark 1:17).
   b. Word "disciple," or learner, used first by Matthew in 5:1; and though familiar term to us, its N.T. usage is noteworthy:
      (1) Substantive found all through Gospels and Acts to describe followers of Christ (including women; cf. Acts 9:36), but not in Epistles or Revelation, perhaps because Christians addressed or described not

only had learned *about* Christ, but had also "learned Christ" (Eph. 4:20);

(2) Verb form is both active, to make disciples (cf. 28:19, Acts 14:21), and passive, to be disciples (cf. 13:52, 27:57); and —

(3) There is close interrelationship between discipleship and discipline (cf. 16:19, Heb. 5:8).

c. Peter and Andrew were now to be commissioned to special service as ministers of their Master; and it is almost certain that Luke 5:1-11 is another account of this call.

d. Summons to James and John was probably for first time, but since they were "partners with Simon" (Luke 5:7, 10), and Christ met them only "a little farther thence" (Mark 1:19), it would seem likely that they had been informed by Andrew and Peter and possibly prepared for call.

e. Reference to "hired servants" (Mark 1:20) seems to suggest men of some means and standing.

N.B. Joseph W. Kemp once pointed out that Matthew reports our Lord's use of words "Follow me" five times, calling men from lawful occupation (v. 19); parental authority (vs. 21, 22); home life (8:22); official position (9:9); and material wealth (19:21).

2. *The Response of the Disciples* (vs. 20, 22)

a. In both cases it was prompt, full, and permanent, as though it was command of king to be obeyed without hesitation, reservation, or change of heart.

b. They were to leave all fishing equipment, and in one case even their father (v. 22); and they were to be made into "fishers of men" (v. 19).

c. Thus they were to surrender everything; and another call was still to come (cf. 10:1-4) whereby they and eight others were to be made specifically apostles — not just learners and helpers, but ambassadors.

III. Personal Ministry (vs. 23-25)

Here we have a sort of summary of what is elaborated in remainder of Gospel, for this Galilean ministry is characteristic of much of Christ's work on earth:

1. *It Revealed His Three Methods* (v. 23)

   a. Teaching — instruction given; synagogue was chief place of concourse and afforded best opportunity;

   b. Preaching — gospel of Kingdom emphasized; it was to be rule of God that His Son had come to set up on earth;

   c. Healing — sickness and disease vanquished; this was because nothing was too hard for His Divine power.

2. *It Resulted in Great Blessing* (vs. 24, 25)

   a. Fame — not only in "all Galilee," to which our Lord evidently limited His own sphere at this time, but "throughout all Syria" (v. 24).

   b. Faith — not only on behalf of sick ones in general, but specifically for those afflicted by demon possession, insanity, and paralysis (v. 24).

   c. Following — "great multitudes of people" (v. 25) from all parts of country.

The new Teacher and Worker thus impressed Himself at once upon His people, and this influence deepened and extended day by day almost to the very end of His ministry.

Conclusion

Although the circumstances of the call of Christ to the disciples are never exactly duplicated today, there is a sense in which He first invites us to come to Him as our Saviour and then to follow Him as our Master — "Come" (11:28) and "Go" (28:19). The true Christian will heed both calls, the one to salvation, the other to service:

1. *The Work* — "fishers of men"

   These disciples had been catching fish, but now they were to "catch men alive" (Luke 5:10, Greek), and win them from the sea of sin to the net of God's Kingdom (cf. 13:47).

2. *The Equipment* — "to become" (Mark 1:17)

   Jesus reminds them of impossibility of doing His work without preparation, just as in their old occupation.

3. *The Secret* — "I will make you —"

   Under His guidance and imitating His example they, too, would be able to serve.

4. *The Condition* — "Come ye after me" (Mark 1:17)

The Person of Christ was the energizing and attractive influence that would enable them to learn His work and follow His example.

In proportion as we, too, follow Christ, as they did, we shall realize all that He has intended for and through us.

11

"MENDING THEIR NETS"*

Matthew 4:21

James and John were fishermen. They had been at work, and were now engaged in overhauling their nets with a view to further fishing. The wear and tear of labor had caused strain and weakness which had resulted in rents in the nets; and before they could be used again they must be repaired.

Which things are a parable, since "whatsoever things were written aforetime were written for our learning" (Rom. 15:4). "Fishers of men" is one of the titles given by Jesus Christ to His servants. Like those first ones, they are to "become" such by following Him (Mark 1:17), and their work is to be that of "catching men alive" (Luke 5:10, Greek). But their service is in danger from spiritual wear and tear and their equipment requires restoration. The strain and stress of life and work often lead to serious shortcomings, so that there is no duty of greater importance in connection with Christian service than that of "mending their nets."

Dr. F. B. Meyer observes: "It was well that the fishermen had prepared their nets, for now that they were wanted they were ready for use. Our Lord would hardly have wrought the miracle (cf. Luke 5:4-6) with nets that bore the signs of slovenly neglect. Is it any wonder that He cannot use us when we consider the pride, the worldliness, the low motives which we harbor in our hearts? He does not require of us perfection, but freedom from known sin — 'sanctified, and meet for the master's use, and prepared unto every good work' (2 Tim. 2:21)."

---

*Condensed from booklet of this title (Evangelical Publishers, Toronto), now out of print.

The word "mending" means adjustment as well as repair and is found in a number of different connections in the New Testament (cf. 1 Cor. 1:10; 2 Cor. 13:9; Gal. 6:1; Eph. 4:12; 1 Thess. 3:10; 2 Tim. 3:17; Heb. 13:20, 21; 1 Pet. 5:10). Let us see whether God will speak to us through this little phrase in His Word.

I. Their Nets — What Were They?

1. *Nets Were Means Whereby Work Was Done*

    a. Without nets fishermen would have been useless; they could not have approached nor controlled fish.

    b. Means by which Christian does his fishing for men is surely his character, source of his personal influence over others; nowadays we might refer to it as "standard equipment."

    c. Ourselves — not our gifts, but our life; not what we have, but what we are — these are our nets by which we enclose others and take them "alive" for God:

        (1) This, and nothing more, for we never really help people beyond what we ourselves are;

        (2) This, and nothing less, for it is Divine power given us whereby one life is able to help and influence another for good.

2. *Nets Were of Different Sorts*

    a. Fishermen of Galilee, according to various needs, used —

        (1) Draw-net, thrown out wide that it might by its sweep enclose great multitude of fishes (cf. 4:18, Greek);

        (2) Hauling-net, with great strength for pulling fish to land (cf. 13:47, Greek); and —

        (3) Throwing-net, ordinary one used by fishermen (cf. 4:20, Greek).

    b. It is likewise with nets of "fishers of men," for human characters differ widely:

        (1) Some are powerful, with wide sweep of influence, stirring and leading multitudes of men;

        (2) Others have great force of attraction, their influence deep rather than diffusive, strong rather than broad, personal rather than public;

        (3) Still others are quite simple in nature and limited

in power, exerting everyday influence of average or ordinary individual.

c. Yet we must never forget this third type of human character is as essential and important in its way as great and outstanding lives:

(1) We must not despise what is "ordinary," for word has both etymological and spiritual connections with "ordered" and "ordained."

(2) Our "ordinary" life is just that which God has "ordained" for us; it is "ordered" expression of His will.

(3) Apostolic band itself was composed of men of exceptional ability, like Peter and John, but there were also men of smaller caliber and ordinary influence; e.g., "There were . . . two other of his disciples" (John 21:2) — it is good that they are nameless and yet as much part of group and taking as full a share in work as others.

3. *Nets Were of Right Material and Good Quality*

a. It is probably true to say they had in particular three characteristics:

(1) Strength — because of force of water and weight of fish;

(2) Pliancy — because with all their strength they must be capable of yielding in shape to just such force and weight;

(3) Wholeness — because rents, weakness at certain points, or certain parts unavailable would cut down their usefulness in snaring and holding their contents.

b. Material and quality of "net" of character for fishing for men must be equally appropriate and excellent; it must be —

(1) Strong — if we would help others, for while weakness repels, strength attracts (cf. Eph. 6:10);

(2) Pliant — we must give and yet grasp, be pliant without being pliable, unite comprehensiveness with absence of compromise (cf. 2 Tim. 2:24-26);

(3) Whole — there must be thoroughness, reality, genuineness, sincerity if we would win and keep men (cf. Jas. 1:4).

Thou must thyself be true
If thou the truth wouldst teach.

   c. Thorough testing of character, as of net, must be made, and man is tested —
      (1) Sometimes by what he knows;
      (2) Sometimes by what he is able or willing to do; and —
      (3) Sometimes by what he possesses; but —
      (4) These are insufficient and often unreliable; only real test is what man *is* — his character which, as D. L. Moody once said, is "what a man is in the dark."

   d. Yes, "character makes the man," but for Christians Jesus Christ makes character; for as we put ourselves in His hands He first takes, then breaks, and finally makes us "meet for the master's use" (2 Tim. 2:21).

Thus, our nets are our characters — what we are. Though lacking in position, in influence, in wealth, and even in intellect, man of character will be man of power, with three essential qualities — firmness, tenderness, thoroughness — or, strength, sympathy, sincerity. Thus shall we impress and influence other lives for Christ.

II. Their Nets — Why Were They Mending Them?

  1. *It May Have Been Due to Thoughtlessness*
    a. These men may have continued work too long without thinking of examining their nets.
    b. So today — Christians are sometimes too engrossed in work to maintain its quality; outward service is disproportionate to inward communion.
    c. They do not "take time to be holy," but are influenced by modern cry, *"Laborare est orare,"* to labor is to pray, which is untrue; and they forget reverse, which is far nearer truth, "to pray is to work."
    d. We must constantly heed our Master's words, "Come ye yourselves apart . . . and rest a while" (Mark 6:31); because service for God can never take place of grace from God, and public worship, however blessed, can never displace personal communion.

2. *It May Have Been Due to Carelessness*
   a. Nets may have burst because they were not strong enough; or perhaps they were of wrong kind.
   b. So with us — our characters, and thereby our influence over others, suffer through lack of care; and we attempt work in our own strength.
   c. Carelessness of Christians often brings reproach upon their profession by means of un-Christlike spirit; and there is also failure to provide for every emergency.

3. *It May Have Been Unfaithfulness*
   a. It is possible disciples had noticed small holes but had ignored them until they became large ones.
   b. It is certain that in many Christian lives leakage comes through small weakness or failure scarcely noticeable to casual observer.
   c. But we never know what strain may be put upon us, or demand made, and if we are not careful we shall find it is—

   > *the little rift within the lute*
   > *Which by-and-by will make the music mute.*

4. *It May Have Been Disobedience*
   a. Perhaps James and John had refused to take their father's advice in fishing; for we know from parallel passage in Luke that when Christ commanded Simon to let down his "nets" (Luke 5:4), he, knowing they had been toiling all night, best time for fishing, and had taken nothing, probably felt it unnecessary to do more than cast out one "net" (v. 5).
   b. If he had thought he knew more about fishing than his Master, may not his consciousness of sin (v. 8) have been due to knowledge of this presumption and disobedience?
   c. It is certain that Christ tests His followers in such little things; and unless we obey Him fully we shall both lose blessing and hurt our influence, for no life is safe that is not obedient.
   d. Advantage of years may be lost in moment (cf. Luke 16:10), so that only by moment-by-moment loyalty can we be sure of moment-by-moment grace; if we act inde-

pendently of God in little things, we shall look for Him in
vain in the great things we attempt.

III. Their Nets — How Were They Mending Them?

1. *They Realized Their Need*

   a. This, though quite obvious, was essential; it was necessary
   to examine nets to find what work was required, like stock-
   taking in view of future business.

   b. We, too, must take time for, not self-examination so much
   as, Divine examination; we ought to spread ourselves, so
   to speak, before God, as nets are spread on shore, and ask
   Him to show us where our weakness lies and what is
   lacking in us (cf. Ps. 139:23, 24).

2. *They Worked Efficiently*

   a. Where hole had been made, there repair was effected;
   and there could be no long delay.

   b. It is exactly similar in things spiritual — rent in our
   character means something wrong in our relation to God;
   and it must be put right immediately, or loss will result.

   c. Confession is first step towards getting right with God;
   if we have passed from inner circle of His presence by
   one particular door, we must return by same door through
   confession of that sin — whether against God, against
   man, or against both.

   d. Rent of exaggeration must be mended by truthfulness; of
   impatience by restful faith; of anxiety by trustfulness; of
   procrastination by promptness; of self-confidence by humble dependence; of slothfulness by earnest energy; of
   dissimulation by absolute reality; of irritability by holy
   calm; of willfulness by willing submission; of impurity by
   holiness — whatever may be rent in our lives, we must
   mend it by its opposite.

3. *They Made Their Nets Strong for Future Use*

   a. In mending, they must have gone beyond particular rent,
   as woman in darning; for net had to be made strong again
   at that point, probably with new material.

   b. So in our process of spiritual "adjustment" or "repair"
   it is essential to go well beyond mere error, or failure,
   or sin, and ensure future progress by special provision;

and supreme secret is to be found in use of God's Word (cf. Ps. 119:11).

c. As repairing of net involved careful sewing or weaving of warp and woof, with fastenings made thoroughly strong, so we need Word of God as food and strength of soul; thus character may be set permanently by surrender and obedience.

d. As food partaken abides in body and, after we have become unconscious of its presence, builds up fabric of life, so in things spiritual; effect of great spiritual blessing does not pass away, but abides amid circumstances of life by becoming part and parcel of character.

e. The Holy Spirit of God continues to bless Word and enables us to assimilate ever increasingly its beneficent power for holy influence over others; and daily food of Word must be allowed to enter soul and then must be expressed in wholehearted consecration and consistent life to God's glory.

Conclusion

Let us take to heart these simple but solemn truths about our "nets" for "catching men alive" — our characters, our personalities, which are so often and so sadly marred and broken. Perhaps we feel we must consecrate ourselves again and again to God; yet there is really no need for all these repeated failures.

1. *Let us Present Ourselves Before God*

He will both show us our weakness and teach us the secret of His strength, for He has promised that "the Lord will be the place of repair for his people" (Joel 3:16, marg.). This is exactly what we need because, like a harbor or refuge, God will be our hope, our strength, our home.

2. *Let Us Abide in Christ*

Habit is essential to the Christian life, for it is only through good, regular procedure that character is strengthened: the habit of prayer, of Bible meditation, of daily consecration, of obedience. This will involve no slavery to form but, on the contrary, will nurture a growing freedom of spiritual life.

3. *Let Us Lead Ordered Lives*

We must keep short accounts with God, not allowing our errors or failures to go on from day to day without bringing them into His presence so that they may be dealt with at once.

Thus only shall we be kept from spiritual leakage, weakness, disaster, and be provided with all things that pertain to life and godliness. Thus we shall go from strength to strength, and be enabled to "catch men alive" to the everlasting glory of God.

> *Drop Thy still dews of quietness*
> *Till all our strivings cease;*
> *Take from our lives the strain and stress,*
> *And let our ordered lives confess*
> *The beauty of Thy peace.*
>
> JOHN GREENLEAF WHITTIER

12

THE MANIFESTO OF THE KINGDOM (1)

Matthew 5:1-48

IT IS appropriate that in this Gospel, which is occupied so largely with the Kingdom of Heaven, we should have the principles of that Kingdom set forth near the opening, in order that we may recognize the King's requirements. It was at this time, amid the profound influence of His initial words and works on earth, that our Lord felt it necessary to deliver His great manifesto and make the pronouncement that we now call the Sermon on the Mount. In view of the multitudes that were flocking around Him, He went up into a mountain, probably a comparatively small ridge, with peaks like horns, called the Horns of Hattin, which is about five miles from the Lake of Galilee, southwest of Capernaum. While our Lord spoke in the presence of the multitude, the message was intended for and directed to His disciples alone.

There is one important point, however, that should not be overlooked. St. Matthew's is the Jewish Gospel, and while there is much in this Sermon that may be applied spiritually to us today, because truth is eternal, there can be little doubt that a great deal of it still awaits a literal interpretation and application in the future. While all Scripture is written *for* us, all of it is not written *to* us or *of* us. There seems no reason to doubt that, however many spiritual applications we may make of these three chapters to Christians now, they will one day be literally fulfilled. It would seem, for instance, that the same class of Jewish believers as are often referred to in the Psalms as "the meek" (cf. 22:26, 25:9, 37:11, 69:32, A.S.V., 147:6, 149:4) will experience the actual accomplishment of verse 5 of this chapter, for they will indeed "inherit the earth" as the chosen people of God.

It is important to obtain a general view of the Sermon as a whole, and it may be outlined briefly thus: (1) The People of the Kingdom (5:1-16); (2) The Principles of the Kingdom (5:17-48); (3) The Precepts of the Kingdom (6:1 to 7:27). Accordingly, the first two of these (contained in Matthew's fifth chapter), are considered in the present study:

I. People of the Kingdom (vs. 1-16)

1. *The Character of the People* (vs. 1-12)

This passage tells Christ's followers (vs. 1, 2) not how to become citizens of the Kingdom of Heaven, but how they as citizens are to live. They are described in relation to what they *are,* which is keynote of Sermon. It has been well said that to *get* good is animal; to *do* good is human; but to *be* good is Divine. This last is emphasized in a series of statements, each commencing with word "blessed," or happy (Latin), called Beatitudes by the Church. The experience of God's people may be seen, first, in four steps, from —

a. *The Human Standpoint* (vs. 3-6)

(1) They are conscious of spiritual need — "poor in spirit" or, spiritually poor (v. 3); let us think of this as teaching blessedness of *conviction*: realization of spiritual poverty, man standing before God destitute, with no power for goodness of his own. *N.B.* Dr. Iverach of Aberdeen called poverty of spirit "the other side of greatness," declaring poor-spirited and poor-in-spirit to be directly opposed to each other, and instancing as examples of latter Isaiah 6:5, Luke 5:8, Revelation 1:17.

(2) They are ready to express spiritual need — "mourn,"

or be concerned (v. 4); this may be regarded as blessedness of *contrition*: genuine sorrow over sin.

(3) They are willing to prove spiritual need — "meek," or humble (v. 5); this will lead to blessedness of *confession,* leading to full obedience and submission. *N.B.* Lyttelton of Eton paraphrases this verse thus: "Blessed are the gentle, for to them the victory will ultimately be given"; and he speaks of mysterious strength that resides in spirit of gentleness.

(4) They are anxious to satisfy spiritual need — they "hunger and thirst after righteousness," or yearn to turn away from sin (v. 6); this may be rightly called blessedness of *conversion* — man's entire nature pursuing God's way of life.

But this spiritual need is shown to be supplied, also in four steps, from —

b. *The Divine Standpoint* (vs. 7-12)

(1) First proof of Divine supply is mercy on part of God's people — "merciful" (v. 7) — leading to blessing of *pardon* for themselves.

(2) Second proof of Divine supply is purity on their part — "pure in heart" (v. 8) — leading to blessing of *probity* for themselves through sight of God. *N.B.* "Heart" in Scripture means center of moral being and includes three elements: mind, feeling, and will; but it is not identical with "nature" and must be carefully distinguished therefrom; e.g., heart of man can be kept pure and clean by constant presence and efficacy of Holy Spirit, while his nature remains evil essentially, with presence of sin within. It is by law of counteraction that heart is kept clean. "If we say we have no sin [no evil principle within] we deceive ourselves" (1 John 1:8), yet we do not deceive anyone else, for they see, if we do not, that sin still abides with us, and will until day when we shall be forever delivered from its presence, as well as from its penalty and power.

(3) Third proof of Divine supply is peaceableness on part of God's people — "peacemakers" (v. 9) — leading to blessing of *peace* for themselves through belonging to God.

(4) Fourth proof of Divine supply is persecution of them — "persecuted for righteousness' sake" (vs. 10-12) — leading to blessing of *privilege* for themselves (cf. 2 Cor. 11:22-33) in possession of Kingdom; not only so, but beyond persecution for sake of righteousness godly people are often to be reviled for sake of their Master Himself (cf. v. 11); and they are to rejoice as well, especially in consciousness that they join in age-old struggle with evil and will share Divine reward.

Thus, man who starts as spiritually poor (v. 3) comes at length to membership in Divine family, and pauper becomes son who actually represents his heavenly Father (vs. 9, 10).

2. *The Influence of the People* (vs. 13-16)

   a. Notwithstanding so much opposition, Christians are shown to be influential in world; and their influence is mentioned under three particularly suggestive illustrations:

   (1) Salt (v. 13) — which gives savor to food (cf. 2 Kings 2:20; Job 6:6) and preserves from corruption; this means that God's people will so act as to recommend Gospel and thus to prevent moral decay occurring around them (cf. Lev. 2:14; Num. 18:19; 2 Chron. 12:5; Mark 9:49, 50; Col. 4:6).

   (2) Light of city on hill (v. 14 — which, because not hidden, is conspicuous testimony to power of godly; and, as Bishop Moule remarked, "the brighter the light in the homeland, the farther that light will penetrate into the dark places of the earth."

   (3) Lamp on stand in house (v. 15) — which, in quiet, steady shining of consistent life, not only recommends Gospel, but reveals to men true character of God.

   b. Then comes concluding application of this section, that believers are to "let" their light shine (v. 16), meaning there must be nothing in them to hinder brightness of Christ being seen; and phrase "good works" may be rendered "beautiful deeds" (cf. John 10:11), suggesting attractiveness as well as genuineness, so that men may see not us, but those characteristics which will lead them to glorify our Father in heaven.

c. Thus, our Christianity is to influence every part of our surroundings, from home in center, to city, to world at circumference; there is nothing so potent as holiness expressed in human life to reveal truth and to preserve it intact amidst error and evil.

N. B. (1) If salt becomes corrupt it is utterly useless — not like many substances that, when spoiled for one use, can be put to others. So Christians who are un-Christlike will never recommend Gospel nor preserve their surroundings from moral decay. But, mercifully, metaphor ends here, for we know power of Divine grace to restore believer to much of power and blessing.

N.B. (2) Cf. "before men" in verse 16 with "before men" in 6:1 — difference lies in motive: citizens of Kingdom were to let light shine "to glorify your Father who is in heaven," but not to "do . . . righteousness" to be seen of men, else "no reward with your Father who is in heaven."

II. The Principles of the Kingdom (vs. 17-48)

After showing character and influence of people of new Kingdom, our Lord proceeds to show that Kingdom of Heaven was object and purpose of Mosaic Law and of Prophets.

1. *The Kingdom Law in General* (vs. 17-20)

a. *Its Fulfillment* (vs. 17, 18)

    (1) In coming to establish Kingdom, Christ was not in any sense destroying old law, but fulfilling it (v. 17); word "fulfil" means to fill up and so to complete, and any law may be completed —

        (a) By obedience to it (cf. Rom. 13:8), or —

        (b) By re-issue of it in fuller form, which is primary meaning here, since contrast is "destroy," not transgress as it would have been if former meaning had been chiefly intended.

    (2) It seems clear from examples given in following verses that Christ was showing what law really meant and required, what were its ideal form and significance.

    (3) Yet He came for something more, for He said He came to "fulfil," that is, actually to accomplish "filling up" or completing of law, in His earthly life

by perfect obedience, thus realizing its ideal in His own Person.

(4) This twofold revelation about law obviously gave it deeper meaning and made it more difficult to obey; indeed, it showed quite clearly that no sinful man could ever obey it as here interpreted (cf. Rom. 3:20).

(5) Law, intended to convince of sin and of need of Christ as Redeemer and Righteousness (cf. Gal. 3:19-24), is not abrogated in Him, for every vital demand of it is as binding as ever; but when we commit ourselves to Him who has fulfilled law, we find in Him not only salvation from condemnation but also power to obey those very demands that in ourselves we were powerless to do.

(6) Thus we do not "make void the law through faith" (Rom. 3:31), but rather establish it on firmer footing than ever; we regard it not as means of justification, but rather as expression and proof of justification (cf. Rom. 8:4).

b. *Its Observance* (vs. 19, 20)

(1) Thus, difference between law and Kingdom would be one of degree, because latter was introducing righteousness (v. 20) infinitely above that characteristic of old law which only Christ Himself could fulfill (cf. Rom. 3:20); it is further contrasted with that of scribes and Pharisees, which at best held to letter only and at worst was hypocritical and unreal. *N.B.* On the contrary, God's own righteousness is "apart from the law" (Rom. 3:21) and is received "through faith in Jesus Christ" (v. 22).

(2) Christ destroys nothing but sin; all that is true, pure, and right He elevates, spiritualizes, and transforms.

(3) This, then, is His definite statement against thought of putting end to old dispensation in any violent way; rather, our Lord's emphasis is on inward and spiritual obedience to law by means of Gospel of Kingdom.

2. *The Kingdom Laws in Particular* (vs. 21-48)

Jewish character of Gospel clearly shown here because examples of Christ's laws of righteousness are contrasted with those of O.T. and deeper meaning of His teaching is indicated. Herein our Lord observed great principle of progressive revelation which is of primary importance to students of Word, for it is suited at each stage of history to moral powers of those involved. Knowledge of this principle of progress will prevent our using O.T. in any of its stages without guidance from complete revelation in Christ that is our own great heritage. God revealed Himself gradually according to particular needs, but it does not follow that what was considered necessary for one age is equally so for another. In old days God spoke partially compared with fullness of His later revelation (cf. Heb. 1:1). On the other hand, development of doctrine does not involve rejection of earlier revelation, nor does repeal mean repudiaiation, just as acceptance of noonday light does not imply denial of dawn. What God said in past was authentic revelation of His will for those ages, whether or not our fathers and we have fully understood it. In these verses, accordingly, five great contrasts are drawn, not in sense of opposition, but only of extension; and these may be considered under three headings:

a. *Christ's Laws of Life* (vs. 21-32)

These are in two departments:

(1) Individual life (vs. 21-26):

    (a) Man's primary instinct being to preserve and maintain human life, Mosaic law met this requirement in Sixth Commandment, "Thou shalt not kill" (v. 21, Exod. 20:13).

    (b) But new law of Christ went much further (v. 22) in insisting on avoidance of all quarrelsomeness and angry feelings that might so easily lead to act of murder and consequent punishment.

    (c) Thus, at outset of His teaching, our Lord emphasizes importance of thoughts, feelings, and, here, words as source of deeds; if former are right, latter will follow, so best way of avoiding wrong action is keeping "heart with all diligence" (Prov. 4:23).

    (d) True attitude of man to man follows (vs. 23-26), and frequently obedience to these simple but searching precepts — "First be reconciled to thy brother'" (v. 24) and "agree with thine adversary quickly" (v. 25) — brings blessing to our souls and those of others; in fact, spiritual revival has been known to come to individuals and to churches by means of endeavor to practice reciprocal confession of sin, reconciliation, and brotherly love, for spirit of forgiveness is spirit of Christ.

(e) But whether it is necessary to make confession to man as well as to God depends upon circumstances, i.e., if sin has wronged individual only it should be confessed to that individual; if sin was patent to all and scandal to Church, there should be some suitable public action; but confession is required only to those against whom we have sinned, and not either generally or impersonally, as to disinterested group or "confessor."

After individual comes community life, and, specifically, unit of society which is —

(2) Family life (vs. 27-32)

(a) Thus it is natural and important that, immediately after mentioning Sixth Commandment, Christ should deal with Seventh (v. 27, Exod. 20:14); for in family we have basis and guarantee of all organized society and civil life.

(b) It is literally true that every duty we owe those around us in city or countryside must first be performed in our home life, so that in God's Kingdom all that destroys or even disturbs sacredness of family is necessarily forbidden.

(c) Christ is saying (v. 28) that no sin is more terrible in its effects, both on individual and on society, than sin mentioned here; and once again He calls attention to relationship of actions with thoughts, feelings, and even, here, glances.

N.B. It has been well said Tenth Commandment places covetousness at end of list of sins as if it were climax, worse than adultery or murder; indeed, it leads to both, for it is of man's inmost heart.

(d) Further than this (vs. 29, 30), even if dearest and most useful thing in life, as represented by eye and hand, should lead us astray, we are to be prepared to sacrifice it, lest our whole being suffer loss.

(e) Then Christ proceeds to point out (vs. 31, 32) that those who transgress this commandment not only commit serious evil themselves, but are cause of others doing wrong.*

b. *Christ's Law of Lips* (vs. 33-37)

Another possibility of wrongdoing is connected with man's speech as Christ refers to Leviticus 19:11 :

(1) In some respects utterance is man's highest and most distinctive gift, his truest expression of personal character and best means of exercising influence.

(2) In connection with Kingdom of God it is particularly important not only to speak truth, but to speak this only; i.e., there is no need of overemphasis or exaggeration.

(3) However, swearing mentioned here (vs. 34-36) surely is quite separate from solemnity of legal oaths properly administered, but rather refers to practice of promiscuous swearing (cf. Jas. 5:12); it is impossible to think Christ would forbid usual method taken by magistrates to sustain authority (cf. Titus 3:1).

(4) Paul often made use of solemn affirmations equivalent to oaths (cf. Rom. 1:9, 2 Cor. 1:23, Gal. 1:20, Phil. 1:8), and same idea is found in connection with angel (cf. Rev. 10:6); our Lord allowed Himself to be put on oath as He answered question of high priest at His trial (cf. 26:63, 64); above all, God Himself is said several times to have expressed Himself with an oath (cf. Ps. 110:4, Heb. 6:13-18, 7:21).

(5) True oath consists of simple statement uttered in perfect calm and confidence under sense of God's presence; but in days of our Lord, Jews seem to

---

*For more detailed consideration of Christ's teaching about marriage and divorce, see Study No. 40, under II.

have used many oaths in common conversation, with forms of cursing and swearing almost infinite.

(6) It is against use of these that Christ warns them, bidding them to be truthful in their simple affirmations or denials; and, since warning still much needed today, among Jews and Gentiles alike, it is all the more essential that Christian speech should be strong and yet pure and true.

c. *Christ's Laws of Love* (vs. 38-48)

It is certain that we shall often be faced by those not prepared to recognize these laws of righteousness. How must we conduct ourselves towards man who refuses to be just towards us? In respect to two contrasts —

(1) We are to show love instead of vindictiveness (vs. 38-42).

(a) Superseding Mosaic injunction (cf. Exod. 21: 24, Lev. 24:20, Deut. 19:21) we have command, "resist not evil" (v. 39); we are not to resist wrongdoer by acts of violence, because our supreme desire is to do him good.

(b) But closer look at these counsels of Christ leads us to ask whether they are to be taken quite literally, since Bible is full of Oriental metaphor and symbol; and, further, Sermon in its full meaning may be applicable only to Divine Kingdom still future.

(c) Answer is almost certainly that these precepts represent profound, underlying spiritual principles to be searched out and individually applied; this is not so easy a method as literal interpretation, but it is far more genuinely spiritual and truer to genius of Christ's religion.

(d) Since Bible is not book of rules, but of principles, our interpretation of it should avoid that forced literalism that defeats its own object; for this is often impractical and even dangerous because it is apt to conflict with plain teachings found elsewhere.

(e) Had teaching of N.T. been that under no circumstances was defence of life, home, and country justifiable, license would have been given to murder, burglary, and tyranny; but teaching of love and neighborliness to all, and of brotherhood of those in Christ, saps very foundation of injustice and affords sole hope of eventual ending of cruelty of man to man.

(f) Thus while here, in Sermon meant primarily for Jewish disciples, we have command not to resist, our Lord elsewhere did resist evil and employed force (cf. John 2:15); He also assumed that circumstances might alter cases, as in mention of sword (cf. Luke 22:36-38, 49-51); and we must therefore be careful to balance varying aspects of His teaching and example.

(2) We are to show love instead of hatred (vs. 43-48)

(a) Since literal carrying out of anything like preceding verses might so easily lead to more evil instead of to good, it is probable that key to difficulty lies in these final verses of chapter; for they introduce new attitude to those who persist in enmity towards us.

(b) Yet it will be seen all this is individual and concerns man's own life alone; for nothing is said about his responsibility to defend others if those in his charge be persecuted or injured.

(c) In actual practice, man will retaliate if intruder attacks his family; and this is applicable to times of war when Christian is often compelled to "resist evil" and fight on behalf of other defenseless folk, uniting with his country on behalf of Christian principles and human liberty.

(d) This is because sin has to be taken into consideration; war in itself is wrong, always has been, always will be, but is inevitable because of human sin, and God overrules it for His own inscrutable purposes.

(e) War is opposed to Christianity, and if all men were Christians it would be abolished; since they are not, it is not always possible to be at peace with all men (cf. Rom. 12:18).

(f) Therefore we must never attempt to apply principles to cases that are manifestly outside their sphere; but in regard to ourselves spiritually we are to be under rule of love that includes all men and expresses itself by forgiveness and seeking good of others.

(g) We have here statement of principles rather than list of rules, for civil society has to do with actions and conduct; but Kingdom of God, dealing first with human heart and emphasizing character, reveals fundamental difference: one is concerned with outward life, and other with inward attitude.

(h) These final verses of chapter, then, reveal heart of Him who is love (cf. 1 John 4:16) and remind us (vs. 46, 47) of God's impartiality (v. 45).

N.B. Word "perfect" (v. 48) has in its meaning nothing whatever to suggest what is known as "sinless perfection" on part of Christ's followers, even though it also is descriptive of God. It means, rather, moral maturity (cf. 1 Cor. 2:6, A.S.V., where it is translated "full-grown"), and kindliness, as of a father, in contrast to childishness and spite often found in immature son or daughter.

As His children, we are "therefore" to imitate our heavenly Father in ways associated with context, i.e., showing love towards unthankful and evil folk, and leading lives of impartial beneficence towards all our fellow creatures (cf. Jas. 3:17, 18).

Conclusion

In this chapter God's people have been described in relation to what they are to be, and this is the keynote of the entire Sermon on the Mount. It is summed up in one word, "blessed," which is found in groups in three places in Scripture, each most interesting. First comes "blessed" in the Psalms; then follows "blessed" in the Sermon on the Mount; and lastly comes "blessed" in the Revelation. When put together they are found to constitute the full revelation of how Christ blesses His people, on earth and in heaven.

1. *Blessing on Earth—Grace*

God has blessed us with all spiritual blessings in Christ (cf. Eph. 1:3, 4), and in Him we possess all things (cf. Rom. 8:32, 2 Cor. 6:10). It is impossible to exaggerate the present blessedness of the believer (cf. Ps. 1:1-3); so far from "giving up," as is so often implied, the Christian receives abundantly, even "exceeding abundantly" (Eph. 3:20), here and now in Christ our Lord.

2. *Blessing in Heaven — Glory*

This is the crown of the Christian's present life — "most blessed for ever" (Ps. 21:6). Such heavenly blessedness is truly inconceivable, for it can be depicted only in earthly terms (cf. Rev. 22:14). It may best be summed up in the thought of the very presence of God Himself in which all true blessedness consists (cf. Rev. 21:3-7, 22:1-5).

And so, whether we think of the present or of the future, "the Lord will give grace and glory" (Ps. 84:11).

13

THE MERCIFUL (A FRAGMENT)

Matthew 5:7

W E ARE told that people full of mercy are happy people. What is mercy? According to the New Testament —

1. Mercy is a ministry to the needy (Luke 10:36, 37).

2. Mercy is an offering of self to the unpopular (Matt. 9:13).

3. Mercy is a lovingkindness to the unresponsive (Luke 6:35, 36).

4. Mercy is a part of heavenly wisdom in the face of earthly strife (Jas. 3:17).

N.B. God, who is called "the Father of mercies" (2 Cor. 1:3), and is "rich in mercy" (Eph. 3:4), will "give mercy . . . in that day" (2 Tim. 1:16, 18; cf. Matt. 25:34).

It is no wonder that Christ said, "Blessed are the merciful; for they shall obtain mercy."

14

THE MANIFESTO OF THE KINGDOM (2)

Matthew 6:1-34

W ITH THIS chapter is commenced the third section of our outline for the Sermon on the Mount. Having been introduced to the people of the Kingdom of Heaven, and to its principles, we now pass to a consideration of certain precepts of the Kingdom (6:1 to 7:27). Our Lord speaks of —

I. Some Aspects of Religious Life (vs. 1-18)

If it be true that "character makes the man," it follows that the actions expressive of character are determined by motive power. The motive of an act goes far to settle its essential moral quality. What, therefore, is to be the motive of those who are citizens of the Kingdom? Here Christ dwells on three religious acts with special reference to motive, applying the lesson just inculcated about moral purity (chap. 5). In each of these we shall see that God's glory is to be supreme (cf. vs. 1, 4, 6, 18).

1. *Giving* (vs. 1-4)

First comes an act involving our attitude to those around us:

a. In our giving we are warned of the wrong motive of being seen of men (v. 1); for craving to stand well with fellows is only too apt to enter into our religious life.

b. It is pleasant to have our benevolences praised and a satisfaction to be appreciated; but when we face real motive that all too often prompts us it is humbling to realize how much we have done simply to gain this approval of men, or at least to conform to their standards of philanthropy.

c. Only way to avoid this danger is to make and keep God real in life; for in His presence we ought to have no thought of anyone else, dominant principle of life being then "doing service, as to the Lord, and not to men" (Eph. 6:7).

d. Christ knew Pharisees and scribes had perverted great

virtues of life, such as almsgiving; instead of showing thereby superior piety and moral pre-eminence, they destroyed spiritual character of these acts and reduced them to level of sinful pride (v. 2).

e. Such hypocrites had already received their reward in approval of men; but man who puts God first is not only rewarded here with consciousness of Divine favor, but is assured of complete acknowledgment hereafter (vs. 3, 4).

2. *Praying* (vs. 5-15)

Second comes an act involving relationship to God, and the same insistence on reality should mark our prayer life:

a. *The Spirit of Prayer* (vs. 5-8)

(1) We are to pray individually and privately (vs. 5, 6) because there is no merit either in act *per se* or in flaunting of it; we are not to be like Pharisees who performed devotions in public places in order that men might be impressed by their earnestness, for antithesis between "inner chamber" (v. 6, A.S.V.) and "corners of the streets" (v. 5) is very clear.

(2) While, of course, there must also be public prayer, it is essential that all display should be avoided in any type of devotional exercise; and genuine believer should realize prayer is personal between himself and his Lord and, while no corporate worship can make up for absence of private prayer, one will be valued more highly because of other.

N.B. Human eyes may be protected from outer scene by eyelids, but ears have no such refuge; hence, both time and place for prayer should ideally be characterized by quietness. However, it is possible to turn many a circumstance of busy day into blessed opportunity for prayer:

One hearkening, even, cannot know
When I have crossed the threshold o'er;
For He alone who hears my prayer
Has heard the shutting of the door.

(3) We are to pray earnestly and definitely (v. 7), because there is no merit in length or repetition (cf. 1 Kings 18:26); we are not to be like heathen, or "Gentiles" (A.S.V.), who perverted prayer by at-

tempting to gain favor with God by superstitious practices.

N.B. Sad to say, this is still done in both pagan and sacerdotal religious exercises of today. But Christ here points out how impossible it is that God should listen because of such practices.

(4) We are to pray humbly and trustfully (v. 8), because there is no merit in ourselves — it is our heavenly Father who is omniscient and omnipotent; unlike heathen whose conception of God was of some tyrant who had to be placated by pretensions as to devotion or intention, we are to come with simplicity of little child to its parent who knows all requirements before they are asked.

b. *The Substance of Prayer* (vs. 9-13)*

This model of prayer, which we call the Lord's Prayer, though given here for use of His disciples, is brief and simple, and yet full; indeed, it demonstrates how remarkable a variety of requests may be pressed into a few earnest petitions, including virtually every desire of a prayerful heart. It is based upon spiritual relationship of children to their Father and thus teaches them that prayer should be united, confident, reverent, unselfish, regular, simple, sincere. It may be considered in three parts:

(1) The Invocation — reminding us as disciples (cf. 5:1, 6:1) of God as "our Father" (v. 9), and therefore very near even though "in heaven";

(2) The Petitions — six in number:

    (a) Three for God's glory (vs. 9, 10) — in regard to holiness of His character, coming of His Kingdom, and obedience to His will;

    (b) Three for our good (vs. 11, 12) — referring to bread for our bodies, forgiveness for our souls, and protection for our minds;

(3) The Ascription — threefold (v. 13), reminding us that our Father is "God blessed for ever" (Rom. 9:5; cf. 24:30; 1 Tim. 6:15, 16; 2 Tim. 4:18; Rev. 1:6).

---

* For fuller analysis of the Lord's Prayer, see Study No. 16, p. 92.

c. *The Sincerity of Prayer* (vs. 14, 15)

Teaching on prayer closes with a strong emphasis on petition for forgiveness, as elsewhere (cf. 18:35; Mark 11:25, 26). This is made perfectly natural by filial relationship, because, although God pardons only once as Judge (when believer trusts Christ for salvation), He pardons many times as Father during subsequent Christian experience. With this in mind, it is important to note the following:

(1) If we cannot sincerely plead our forgiveness of others, we must not expect God's attitude towards us, which includes His answers to our prayers, to be what we desire; and thus there is nothing in its way more searching than this requirement of a forgiving spirit in order to be daily forgiven and blessed.

(2) This is, of course, for those who are already disciples (cf. 5:1); indeed, it is a distinguishing mark of those who have received Divine forgiveness and salvation in Christ (cf. Eph. 4:32).

(3) Personal experience amply supports this simple yet searching principle of Christ's Kingdom; to paraphrase John 13:10, which has direct bearing on life of believer: "He who has had the bathing of perfect justification needs only the daily cleansing from defilement in the process of sanctification."

N.B. See also 1 John 1:7 — "As we are walking in the light, the blood of Jesus his Son is cleansing us, and so we have continuing fellowship with God" (with whom "we say we have fellowship," v. 6; cf. also vs. 9-11).

3. *Fasting* (vs. 16-18)

Third comes an act involving our attitude to ourselves:

a. Fasting may be called typical way of abstaining from whatever hinders growth in spiritual life; and abstinence from food is but one specific way in which spiritual action associated with idea is to be expressed.

b. It is significant that prayer and fasting are so frequently associated in N.T.; yet it is quite logical, for prayer may be said to be that by which we *attach* ourselves to God, and fasting that by which we *detach* ourselves from world.

c. Pharisees had added number of fasts to those required

by Mosaic law; and they had in this, as in other instances, proved themselves to be "hypocrites" (v. 16), disfiguring their appearance when fasting, as though to seem gaunt and undernourished.

d. Instead of this, true disciple will show by outward appearance that fasting is token of spiritual reality and no mere formal abstinence; we are not forbidden to let it be known we fast if circumstances require us to show it, but what is forbidden is doing religious act for sake of showing it, in behalf of our own advancement instead of to glory of God (cf. 1 Cor. 10:34).

As we review these three attitudes — to our fellows, to our Father, and to ourselves, we see in each case, whether in regard to almsgiving or prayer or fasting, that the emphasis is on the words "in secret" (vs. 4, 6, 18), or, on privacy as contrasted with publicity. What we are in God's sight is intended to affect with uplifting and transforming power all our outward and visible attitudes. In each case, also, we are assured of a "recompense" (vs. 4, 6, 18, A.S.V.). There is a sense in which "virtue is its own reward," but the recompense here is the inward assurance of our Father's approval. This is the supreme satisfaction of every loyal, loving heart.

From outward acts and their motives, our Lord turns to —

II. Some Aims of Religious Life (vs. 19-34)

As former part of chapter shows everything should be done as in God's sight, this section naturally follows by pointing out how often supreme devotion to Him is hindered by human needs and earthly possessions. Thus, there is great need for —

1. *Spirituality* (vs. 19-21)

a. True spirituality must be characterized by concentration and intensity of purpose in relation to Kingdom of God, so opening words of this section contrast treasure upon earth and treasure in heaven: one is corruptible and can be stolen; other is incorruptible and beyond all human depredation (vs. 19, 20).

b. Importance of this contrast is seen in statement that where treasure is there will heart be also (v. 21), since "heart" in Scripture always means center of moral being, including thought, feeling, and will; thus, to treasure heavenly things, putting God first in life and never allowing anyone or anything to take His place will be to prevent ourselves from being occupied by world.

c. While we remain in world, surrounded by earthly cares and constantly open to temptation, we are to be definitely related to heaven; as is often said, paraphrasing our Lord's words in John 17, we are to be "in the world and yet not of it."

d. In this connection we may contrast false spirituality of "hypocrites" mentioned in verses 1-18; in spite of their positions of religious leadership they were worldly-minded, trying to lay up moral and spiritual treasure on earth.

2. *Sincerity* (vs. 22, 23)

a. From heart we proceed naturally to consideration of motive in all this, as our Lord emphasizes absolute necessity of reality, using human eye to illustrate need for clearness of moral vision which transmits spiritual light (v. 22); "single" has sense of "one-fold," transparent.

b. But just as, when external eye is not normal, natural light only dazzles, making lack of sight worse, so, in regard to inner eye of soul, light of Divine revelation cannot penetrate if sin or self-will rules; in fact, it only deepens spiritual darkness (v. 23).

c. Inward eye and inward heart influence each other (cf. Eph. 1:18); and both will be transformed by inclination towards heavenly things.

3. *Service* (v. 24)

a. Still another contrast is drawn as our Lord shows impossibility of serving both God and "mammon"; and this Syriac word seems to stand for everything earthly, but especially money (cf. Luke 16:9-13), though sometimes for riches personified, or demon of cupidity.

b. If we live for God's service we cannot serve anyone or anything else; this is simply because it is impossible to exert valid feelings or desires in two opposite directions at once.

N.B. Thus we have three striking contrasts: heaven and earth, light and darkness, God and mammon; and these lead to necessity of —

4. *Security* (vs. 25-32)

a. From thought of earthly life and human needs comes possibility of anxiety and insecurity; and close connection between this and former section is seen by opening phrase, "Therefore I say unto you, Be not anxious —" (v. 25, A.S.V.), which is preferable rendering to "Take no thought" (K.J.V.).

b. Warning throughout, emphasized five times (cf. vs. 25, 27, 28, 31, 34), is against intense concern that disturbs and hinders, not legitimate consideration and care for things needed in daily life; in fact, Greek root suggests "division," or distraction of mind in different directions at once (cf. Luke 10:40, 41; 1 Cor. 7:32-35), reminding us that spiritual weakness and loss accrue from anxiety.

c. Christ tells us anxiety is at once unnecessary and futile for several reasons:

   (1) Because of nature of life (v. 25) — unworthy preoccupation with eating, drinking, or clothing to be set aside;

   (2) Because of care of Creator (v. 26) — since He takes care of birds that do not produce or store their food, we may be secure in knowledge that He as "heavenly Father" (v. 26) will not forget His children;

   (3) Because of impotence of worry (vs. 27-30) — no such concern can add to our physical height, so if we should be over-anxious about such comparative triviality as its covering, we should be rebuked by flowers of field that are more marvelously arrayed than king, with no effort on their part.

   (4) Because of heathen character of worldliness (vs. 31, 32) — anxiety over such matters really means childish distrust of God as "heavenly Father" (vs. 26, 32), even willful ignorance of His ways; it is also one of chief sources of avarice, so that by it heart indeed becomes divided or distracted (Greek) between world and God.

"Your Father knoweth," — let your heart be glad
And never grieve Him more by being sad;
   He will provide;
No good thing will His love withhold from you,

And He is with you all the journey through
    Whate'er betide.

"Your Father knoweth," — in His loving hands
How safe you are, for well He understands
    Your every need
And will supply it from His throne on high.
Trust Him, till with Him you are by-and-by
    Most blest indeed.

                              H. E. JENNINGS

d. This illustration from birds and flowers, however, does not seem to go beyond idea of futility of anxiety on part of God's children as to question of their ever being in actual want of life's necessities; and of course we must be careful not to apply to Christians in this dispensation promises of temporal blessings made to Jews.

e. Yet there is very real sense in which righteousness of life tends toward well-being in things temporal, and it is simple matter of fact that pauperism, as distinct from poverty, is not often associated with genuine Christian life; for power of Divine grace is such that Psalm 37:25 seems capable of definite application to present day.

f. There is also probability against believer and his descendants falling through sin into poverty; for he should have indwelling power through prayer to exert prevailing faith in God that will secure himself and his children from want and be a strong testimony (cf. Ps. 37:13, 14).

5. *Solicitude* (vs. 33, 34)

a. Attitude of concern may be vain or true according to its object and motive, and here, after warning against being too solicitous over temporal needs, Christ points us to a right solicitude, in behalf of God's Kingdom and righteousness.

b. His supreme requirement is that we should put Him first (v. 33a); and then we shall find He solemnly undertakes to meet every real need of ours (v. 33b).

c. Indeed, this is only way to avoid anxiety (cf. "therefore," v. 34) — to be occupied, in singleness of purpose, with living for God and His glory; for according as we put Him first, peace and rest will abide in our hearts, and Holy Spirit will so fill our souls that there will be no room for worry and care.

N.B. Someone has said: "There is a very large class and a tolerably happy one that never seeks the Kingdom at all; there is a tolerably large class and a very unhappy one that seeks it, but not first; and there is a very small and a very happy one that seeks the Kingdom and seeks it first." Someone else has put it helpfully thus: "Are not God's promises literally fulfilled to those who literally fulfill His conditions? The fulfillment is intended to depend upon wholehearted seeking of God's Kingdom and righteousness. Just so far as we are wholehearted and rely simply on the Lord, excluding from our lives all thoughts not of His Kingdom, in thought, motive and deed, does He literally fulfill His promise. An experience of this kind may not be an everyday one to most of us, but when it is, we realize something of its power, and we obtain wonderful light on the promises."

Conclusion

Once again in this Sermon emphasis is laid on character and on what we are in the sight of God. Two appeals are made:

1. *Be True* (vs. 1-24)

    a. In giving, be truly philanthropic (vs. 1-4);
    b. In praying, be truly prayerful (vs. 5-15);
    c. In fasting, be truly pious (vs. 16-18);
    d. In choosing, be truly perceptive (vs. 19-24).

2. *Be Trustful* (vs. 25-34)

    a. Anxiety is against nature, therefore senseless (vs. 25-30);
    b. Anxiety is against revelation, therefore godless (vs. 31, 32);
    c. Anxiety is against providence, therefore useless (vs. 33, 34).

Let us ask for grace to enable us to be both true and trustful in relation to our Lord.

> *Jesus, the greatest Teacher, saith*
> *To man who draws his fleeting breath:*
> *"A secret unto you I show:*
> *Behold the lilies how they grow.*

They toil not, neither do they spin,"
Their life develops from within.
They spin not, neither do they toil;
Their bulbs, deep hidden in the soil,
Without a single effort vain
Absorb the sunshine, dew and rain,
And thus without an anxious care
The lily grows, surpassing fair.
"And Solomon," the Saviour said,
"Was not more gloriously arrayed."

Christian, would you then secure
A life that daily groweth pure?
Christ unto you the way doth show:
"Consider how the lilies grow!"
Through constant and believing prayer
Cast on your God your every care
And unto Him draw ever nigh,
Accept from Him your whole supply
Of grace, of mercy, and of peace,
And thus in beauty you'll increase,
More like the blessed Master grow
Who walked unsullied here below.

To be like Christ do you aspire?
Is this your most sincere desire?
Then cast your deadly works away,
Absorb God's love from day to day;
Then you will daily grow in grace
Until you see Christ face to face.
This is the only way I know —
"Behold the lilies how they grow!"

ERNEST O'REILLY

15

PRAYER

Matthew 6:5-8

ALL THAT we know about prayer is derived from God's revelation in His Word, from which it is clear that room has been found in the constitution of the universe for prayer to be offered and answered. How, precisely, this is brought about is not revealed, but the fact of it is as unmistakable in Scripture as it is certain in the experience of all believers.

In his fine book *With Christ in the School of Prayer,* Andrew Murray points out that in the Gospels we may study prayer along two lines: Christ's teaching on the subject blended into a harmonious whole; and Christ's own life of prayer exemplified. The first of these is commenced in these verses, pointing out —

I. The Need of Prayer

- a. *"When* thou prayest" (v. 5) admits of no argument; it merely assumes Christian will pray.
- b. This is doubtless because prayer is soon found to be necessity in spiritual life, as it was in spiritual birth.
- c. It is also assumed that there will be definite times of prayer and that there is a listening Father; the great question is *how* to pray.

II. The Essentials of Prayer

1. *The Personal Approach*

   There is to be responsibility — "thou" . . . "ye" — e.g., singular second personal pronoun is used no fewer than eight times in one of these four verses (cf. v. 6).

2. *The Secret Place*

   a. There is to be privacy — "closet" (v. 6) or "chamber" (A.S.V.; cf. 24:26, Isa. 26:20, Luke 12:3), and "shut . . . door."

   b. Solitary prayer first in time and importance for Christian — quiet, free from interruption, veritable Holy of holies, for God is best met absolutely alone; nothing can take the place of what has well been called "practice of the presence of God."

   c. One needs solitude, silence, and secrecy to have senses properly adjusted — physical, intellectual, moral: head bowed and eyes closed, mind alert and undisturbed, heart and soul lifted towards heaven.

3. *The Definite Purpose*

   a. Word used for "pray" (v. 6) is used everywhere in N. T. of act of praying to God.

   b. Cognate noun, "prayer" (cf. 21:22, Luke 22:45, Acts 3:1, etc.) is literally "desire towards" God; and it includes for us both worship and request.

4. *The True Spirit*

   a. This includes sincerity and honesty (vs. 5, 6); and it excludes anything remotely dramatic or spectacular from Christian worship, public or private.

   b. As someone has said, we are to be natural in spiritual life and spiritual in natural life.

5. *The Divine Encouragement*

   a. There is to be a child's simplicity — "thy Father"

   b. There is to be a child's trustfulness — "knoweth"

   c. Thus, there is no need of "vain repetitions," that is, there should be no willful, determined hammering as at closed door.

III. The Outcome of Prayer

Fellowship with God thus established will bring —

1. *Satisfaction to the Soul*

   a. Pressures of world will be met and lifted.

   b. Reality of spiritual truth will be disclosed.

2. *Influence on the Character*

   a. Sin will be revealed and counteracted.

   b. Holiness will be encouraged and exemplified.

   c. Courage, strength, and guidance will be proved for work and witness.

   N.B. As has been well said, the Christian on his knees sees farther than the philosopher on tiptoe.

Conclusion

This lesson in the school of prayer will be learned best in a quiet place, at a quiet time, by a quiet heart. Let us *take* time, with no hurry or haste, and see what wonderful results even a few moments will bring; or let us *make* time, as we say, by arranging our habits or even, like General Gordon in the African desert or General Washington at Valley Forge, by readjusting our responsibilities. It will be well worth while.

> *At the place of prayer I'm kneeling,*
> *Life is sweetest with Him there;*
> *Deeper truths God is revealing*
> *At the place of prayer.*

A. H. ACKLEY

16

THE LORD'S PRAYER

Matthew 6:9-13

IT HAS often been asserted that the Lord's Prayer is not for present use, but for some future time connected with the Kingdom; and it does not seem to have been used as a form of prayer in assemblies for worship during the first two or three hundred years of the Christian era. Here, however, there is necessity of distinguishing between the primary interpretation and secondary application of Holy Scripture. There is surely a true and blessed sense in which we may use the Prayer now, as for centuries past, but undoubtedly its fullest meaning is still future. For example, "Thy kingdom come" addressed to "our Father" seems to look beyond the Kingdom of the Son to the time mentioned in I Corinthians 15:24, 28. In the meantime, believers of today are just as certainly the direct heirs as those to whom the Lord's Prayer was given.

In the preceding verses of this chapter Christ has told His disciples how not to pray (v. 5) and what not to pray (v. 7). He has also given positive directions on circumstances (v. 6) and content (v. 8), and now He corrects current habits of formalism in prayer by means of a model or type (cf. Luke 11:2-4). This model prayer has three striking characteristics:

brevity, simplicity, and yet completeness; everything within the limits of true prayer is, indeed, contained in it. Here in Matthew's Gospel it also has three distinct parts:

I. The Invocation (v. 9b)

1. *"Father"*
   a. This name was used by Christ some one hundred and fifty times, while word "God" was used by Him only once (see 27:46).
   b. Implied relationship for disciples is not physical by creation, nor national by Israel's adoption as people of God, but spiritual and filial in Christ Himself.

2. *"Our"*
   a. This is clearly prayer for Christians as family group — cf. "we," "our," and "us" throughout.
   b. Individual believer is not mentioned, so it is, in first instance at any rate, social form.

3. *"Which Art in Heaven"*
   a. This is literally "in the heavens" and relates to the Father's supernatural character rather than to His place.
   b. Likewise it refers to heavenly, not earthly, relationship.

II. The Petitions (vs. 9c-13a)

These fall into two parts, one having as its object God's glory, the other man's good; their order is God first, then self, then the world. Their number is usually counted as six, the first group of three being unconnected and the second group of three linked by conjunctions. The last one of the six consists of a negative as well as a positive clause, as though for emphasis.

1. *For God's Glory* (vs. 9c, 10)
   a. God's "name" — revealed character — is to be "hallowed" — known and honored (cf. Prov. 18:10).
   b. God's "kingdom" — future rule of the Father — is to be brought ever nearer (cf. 26:29, I Cor. 15:24-28).
   c. God's "will" — His universal plan — is to be done not as in Gethsemane (cf. 26:39) by individual endurance or resignation, but in all of life, by universal obedience.
   N.B. The commencement, center, and culmination of

God's purpose: (1) His Name the supreme object of honor; (2) His Kingdom the blessed sphere of realization; (3) His will the highest means of fulfillment.

2. *For Man's Good* (vs. 11-13a)

a. God's provision to be requested:

(1) Phrase in original is not "daily bread" because "this day . . . daily" is really tautological; Greek word, not found outside N.T., is, rather, "sufficient" or "needful" (cf. A.S.V. marg., also Vulgate — *supersubstantialem* — and Anglican Catechism — "needful both for our souls and bodies"; see also Prov. 30: 8, A.S.V.).

(2) Context is against anxiety (vs. 25-32), and all other petitions of Prayer are spiritual; it is likely, therefore, that food "for our souls" as well as for our bodies should be included as we pray for God's provision (cf. John 6:27).

b. God's forgiveness to be asked:

(1) Of "debts" (Vulgate), "trespasses" (vs. 14, 15), "sins" (Luke 11:4) — terms apparently interchangeable since sin is considered in Scripture both as debt owed to God and as overstepping of mark set by Him.

(2) "As we forgive" — our forgiveness of others not made ground of Divine pardon, but comparable condition ("in the same way as") under which our Father's attitude to us may also be favorable, bringing us joy and peace.*

c. God's deliverance to be implored:

(1) From "temptation," which here includes all testing, whether good or evil, for we shrink from anything beyond our own unaided strength; and adding clause expressive of desire, if testing be God's will, for His keeping power.

(2) From "evil" — either neuter word or, as in A.S.V., masculine ("the evil one"), for one comes from other.

---

*Cf. discussion of vs. 14, 15 in Study No. 14, p. 83.

N.B. Thus we have provision for present need, pardon for past guilt, and protection from future weakness.

III. The Ascription (v. 13b)

This doxology in the Syriac tongue is not found in all texts, but the similar ones used by St. Paul (cf. 1 Tim. 6:15, 16; 2 Tim. 4:18) would suggest the complete suitability of its inclusion in the Lord's Prayer, particularly with a view to the future — "the kingdom, and the power, and the glory, for ever."

Conclusion

The Lord's Prayer is at once —

1. *A Guide*

    It assures us, as we repeat it, of —
    a. The Divine purpose;
    b. The Divine blessing;
    c. The Divine simplicity; and —
    d. The Divine sufficiency.

    — and —

2. *A Test*

    It asks us, as we consider it, whether we —
    a. Put God first in filial humility;
    b. Pray always for others in family love; and —
    c. Petition for ourselves in childlike trust.

17

THE MANIFESTO OF THE KINGDOM (3)

Matthew 7:1-29

WITH THIS chapter we continue with the third part of our outline for the Sermon on the Mount, the Precepts of the Kingdom (6:1 to 7:29). The preceding chapter has dealt largely with the inner life of the Kingdom people, and this one follows with a more definite emphasis on their outer life. The connection of thought with the preceding verses is not very clear, though probably the reference is to those who may have disliked what Christ said about "hypocrites" (cf. v. 5 with 6:1-7, 16-18).

I. Some Counsels (vs. 1-12)

1. *Warning Against Judging* (vs. 1-5)

    a. Our Lord points out that true disciple will govern his life according to God's requirements; but at same time he will avoid condemning others who have not adopted his principles.

    b. This use of word "judge" (v. 1) does not refer to proper forming of opinions, but is concerned with harsh, hasty and even fanatical condemnation of neighbors; and Christ warns that anyone who indulges in fault-finding is liable to be treated similarly (v. 2).

    c. It is impossible to do this without being blind to our own faults, for concentration on others prevents proper evaluation of ourselves (vs. 3, 4); "mote" was old English word meaning anything trifling such as small splinter, or even floating dust particle or speck of dirt, while "beam" indicated large section of tree — figure of speech to remind us we are only too apt to see small faults in others while blind to great sins in our own lives.

    d. It it thus most difficult to help others without first dealing with ourselves (v. 5) and, conversely, it is easier to judge ourselves adequately while refraining from judging others.

N.B. Cf. 1 Cor. 14:29 on entirely different type of judging — exercise of Christian discernment in testimony and teaching; but even this is not to be hastily expressed (v. 30).

2. *Warning Against Lack of Judgment* (v. 6)

a. Christ is saying here that we tend, if not towards censorious preoccupation with evil, to callous trifling with what is true, pure, and holy, and these two extremes of fanaticism and profanity are to be avoided, especially because Divine omniscience, not human limitation, is essential to every just judgment.

b. But when God puts us in place where decision on questions of moral character is necessary, we must not be indifferent to fundamental distinctions; if He makes us guardians of holy things, we must avoid belittling them and allowing them to be injured and defiled.

N.B. Cf. "cast not pearls" (v. 6) with "let your light so shine" (5:16). Spiritual truths may not yet be appreciated, but good works are to be done and Christlikeness is to be manifested, in order that unspiritual men may become spiritual by means of example, if not precept.

c. Our Lord evidently wished to show real judgment that awaits false spirituality of worldly-minded people; whether it be manifested by censoriousness or by indifferentism, Christians must avoid it as essentially hypocritical, for pronouncement of harsh judgment on one hand, and disregard of true purity and holiness on other, constitute two of most subtle forms of evil.

3. *Encouragement to Confidence in God* (vs. 7-11)

a. Then follow some promises with reference to prayer, showing warnings of earlier verses should not dishearten us, since God is abundantly ready to give what we really require.

b. There is suggestive connection between two precepts, "judge not" (v. 1) and "ask" (v. 7), for we often make ourselves critics when we ought to be suppliants.

c. Yet it is only in true prayer, petition of genuine meekness, that we shall attain wisdom mentioned in earlier verses; for when we lift up our hearts to God we become far too conscious of our own shortcomings to want to interfere in affairs of others.

d. In presence of God there is no room for pride and vain self-consciousness; nothing humbles like loving-kindness of our heavenly Father.

e. Three invitations indicate gradation with climax: "ask . . . seek . . . knock" (vs. 7, 8):

   (1) Starting with request;
   (2) Leading to earnest desire; and —
   (3) Reaching to definite persistence while answer is awaited.

f. Or, we may say God deals with us as we do with our children (vs. 9, 10), who are first taught to ask; then, later on, when what they need is not so easily obtainable, we encourage them to seek; and at length we tell them they must show real earnestness until doors are opened to them.

g. True child of God will readily understand this threefold method of prayer, for with it comes assurance of His fatherly attitude and readiness to help; and His love is so great that He is only too anxious to "give good things to them that ask him"* (v. 11; cf. Luke 11:13, where "the Holy Spirit" is His answer).

4. *Encouragement to Justice for Others* (v. 12)

a. What is called the Golden Rule is based on God's willingness to give; since we have yielded ourselves to Him in prayer with perfect confidence that He will give everything that is good, we in turn are to imitate Him in our conduct towards those around us.

b. As God answers our prayer, we are to do to our neighbors what is rightly expected by Him; thus, together with confidence of faith in our approach to God, there is to be fullness of love shown to our fellows.

c. This law is definite, simple, universal, beneficent; under authority of Christ, its observance would provide solution

---

*Ed. Note: It may be of interest to readers that this was the verse quoted by the author to bring his six-year-old daughter into the full light and joy of what he always believed to have been her second birth. The father-analogy was thus found by personal experience to be compelling and precious.

of all problems, preserve all rights, enforce all duties, conciliate all differences, silence all discords, prevent all wars.

d. It is shown to be teaching of O.T. and brings Christ's Kingdom teaching full cycle back to 5:17 (cf. Rom. 13: 8-10).

II. Some Cautions (vs. 13-27)

The Sermon closes with four of these. If they are carefully observed, all spiritual dangers pointed out in these chapters will be avoided. They set forth in form of vivid contrasts:

1. *Gates and Goals* (vs. 13, 14)

a. First, we must be sure we are really entering into life, for "gate" comes first and then "way"; pilgrim has already been counseled to "knock" (v. 7) and, having entered by right gate, is to proceed along true way.

b. Way of righteousness is narrow and way of evil is wide; this is to say, former is difficult for man and requires such graces as repentance, humility, distrust of self; while latter is easy of access and associated with pride, self-righteousness, self-assertion — apparently hospitable, yet really delusive.

c. Goals of two ways are strikingly contrasted in words "life" and "destruction"; we are not to follow multitude on broad way, but to seek with few door of God's Kingdom and keep to narrow way, with difficulties for flesh that are often found to be blessings, for they require such attributes as consecration and concentration.

d. Christ's use of words "many" and "few" is probably to be interpreted historically, i.e., they describe what was then going on around Him, and were not necessarily generalization applying to all time; for careful consideration of many passages shows that through ages many more shall seek and find than miss way (cf. Isa. 11:9, Rom. 11:26, Heb. 8:11).

e. Such principles as are revealed in Romans 2 as to God's merciful dealings with men under law — in case of Jew, law of Moses, in case of Gentile, law of conscience — have application that cannot yet be estimated; we can but note that N.T. outlook on future is one much wider and fuller than many people are apt to imagine.

f. It is absolutely certain, however, that Christ will "see of the travail of his soul, and shall be satisfied" and "shall . . . justify many" (Isa. 53:11); and if there is no disappointment in store for Him there can be none for us either.

g. During His earthly life, however, there was very small proportion of believers, and there often seems to be today; yet when Kingdom of God is put first (cf. 6:33) and is entered at any cost, human life becomes real, true, precious, and satisfying — in fact, spiritual condition commences that elsewhere is described as "eternal life."

2. *Doctrine and Danger* (vs. 15-20)

a. Second caution is directed against erroneous doctrine, and danger of being misled by it in direction of mere profession is emphasized.

b. Not only, as we have seen, is it necessary to beware of crowd going astray (cf. v. 13), but we must guard against influence of false teachers (v. 15) who would lead us astray.

c. Prophet is one who represents God and declares His truth; in O.T., false prophet was prominent and God's people were urged repeatedly to test him, both by his words and by his works (cf. Deut. 13:1-5, 18:20-22).

d. Today, one of greatest dangers encountered as we walk pathway of life comes from influence of such mistaken leaders; but supreme test of them is their fruits (vs. 16, 20).

e. Character, conduct, and speech are decisive evidence of whether such men are true or false; and nature itself exemplifies this fact (vs. 17-19) in Christ's illustration of two kinds of tree, "good" and "corrupt."
N.B. Even miracles of grace cannot set aside truth; it is still sadly possible for modern-day leader to point to "a sign or a wonder" and yet to have God say, "Thou shalt not hearken unto the *words* of that prophet" (Deut. 13:1, 3; cf. 2 Thess. 2:8-12).

3. *Profession and Practice* (vs. 21-23)

a. Third caution carries warning against mere profession still further, for conversely it is not enough to avoid error and own Christ verbally as our Master; there must be

genuine obedience to His word (v. 21), for doing His
work is plainest and most convincing proof of reality of
profession.

b. Nothing is sadder or more disastrous than orthodoxy of
lip without orthodoxy of life; it is not only what we say,
but also what we are and do that constitutes true discipleship, for every truth is to be transmitted into living.

c. Even those who claim to have spoken in Christ's very
Name are to be set aside unless their work and teaching
are in accordance with will of God (vs. 22, 23); and
even testimonies in Christ's behalf will avail nothing
unless they are true to revelation given us in God's Word.

d. There is scarcely anything more solemn and heart-search-
ing than proof from Scripture that ungodly men can
actually preach with success and even do "wonderful
works" (v. 22).

N.B. We must carefully distinguish, however, between this
passage where reference is to false profession without true ˙
possession, with which our Lord will disclaim acquaintance
(v. 23), and case in Mark 9:39-41, where genuine adherent
of Jesus did not happen to be among recognized disciples;
him our Lord refused to forbid because of spirit in which
work was done — another instance of reality and power of
motive; for different men can take identical action and yet
one be right and other wrong, because of difference of
motive.

4. *Faithfulness and Foolishness* (vs. 24-27)

a. Fourth caution is presented in most striking contrast,
and with this, Sermon closes — two foundations; life
must have basis on which it is built, and the only true
one for a follower of Christ is humble acceptance of and
faithful obedience to Word of God.

b. This is how man is to be judged: one who thus hears
and practices Christ's words will be like man who builds
his house upon rock, so that, notwithstanding all opposition, it will not fall, because of its strong foundation.

c. In contrast, man who hears and does not practice Divine
truth is like one whose house has only foundation of sand;
so that, when test comes, building will fall into irreparable
ruin.

    d. Man's life is well compared to house, a connected whole reared by continuous process; and his deeds, added one by one, thus become home for his soul that ought to stand strain of testing.

    e. Thus, Sermon closes with significant and searching implication of Jesus Christ's claim to be Judge of all mankind and to separate men into two classes — those "wise" ones who heed His Word and those "foolish" ones (v. 26) who do not.

    Illus.: A Korean Christian explained to his pastor how he had learned by heart the Sermon on the Mount: "I am only an ignorant man and could not easily remember it; so I learned one verse at a time and then practiced it on my neighbors, until I had mastered the whole Sermon."

Conclusion

It is not surprising that the result of this incomparable discourse was astonishment that our Lord spoke with such authority and not in the customary way of the scribes, who merely quoted those who had preceded them (vs. 28, 29). But what is the relation of the Sermon on the Mount to Christianity today?

1. *Law and Grace*

As we have seen, it is a serious mistake to suppose that the law is repealed in the gospel (cf. 5:17). Rather, the law, transfigured and glorified, reappears in Christianity. It has been said that every utterance given in the thunderous sermons of Mount Sinai is re-echoed with heightened emphasis in the Sermon on the Mount, but it comes "silent as the night and gentle as the dew from the lips of incarnate Love." Yet it is important to understand that, while salvation is by grace and not by law, where the works of the law are wanting in the Christian life the grace of God cannot be present. Our Christian activity and service are the recognition and expression of the fact that we are saved by grace; and this is what is meant by our being "under the law to Christ" (1 Cor. 9:21).

2. *Kingdom and Church*

The Sermon, while its primary reference is to the Kingdom of Heaven, still future, has a definite and direct application to disciples today, in regard to the principles that should

actuate every life. This does not mean that the Sermon
can be literally carried out today in its entirety, because it is
concerned with principles, not rules, and it is individual, not
national. It presupposes all that has been stated in chapters
1 to 4 with reference to Christ, and it assumes the existence
of regenerate people who are following Him. Christianity
today means the cross, the resurrection, the Holy Spirit,
the Church of Christ, and the grace of God; and to the extent
that the Sermon is applied to Christians these great verities
have to be taken for granted. We may confidently state,
therefore, that since the Kingdom of Heaven may be considered in abeyance and intended to be fully realized in the
future, the Sermon can only be fulfilled now by members of
the Christian Church in so far as its principles are carried
out in the power of the indwelling Holy Spirit of God. Yet
it is only as we lift our hearts in such prayer and with such
perfect trust as are described in these chapters that
God's grace and power are received. Thus we are enabled to
be true and trustful, gracious and genuine, even as the Sermon
directs us to be.

18

CHRIST AND THE BIBLE*

Matthew 7:28, 29

IN THESE verses the Evangelist is not only reporting the
effect on the people of the Sermon on the Mount, but also
writing what became afterwards part of one of the accepted records
of Christ's authoritative "sayings" and "his doctrine" (v. 28)
which found an honored place in the Divine library. This, therefore, is a fitting place to compare our Lord and Holy Scripture
as each "the Word of God." There is a close resemblance between
the incarnate Word and the written Word, and a careful consideration of this will help in our understanding of the Bible
as the embodiment of God's revelation for human life.

Our Lord and the Scriptures are alike in the following ways:

* From an unsigned editorial by the writer in *The Sunday School
Times,* July 13, 1918, pp. 385, 386. Used by permission.

I. Their Nature

Christ and the Bible are at once human and Divine

1. *Our Lord Was Perfect in Each of His Natures, and They Were Inseparable.*

   a. Those who knew and loved Him in the flesh were impressed by His real humanity but became convinced of His equally real Divinity, and yet none of them undertakes to say exactly where Divine element ended and human began; and, in spite of all subsequent efforts to separate superhuman from human in His life and miracles, record cannot be altered without injury and even violence to its basic language.

   b. Indeed, problem of two natures of our Lord has hitherto proved insoluble; how two natures, one Divine and one human, can co-exist in unity of one personality is great psychological enigma of all ages, and yet, in spite of mystery, fact of this union can become assured and satisfying.

2. *The Bible Also Is at Once Divine and Human*

   a. Varieties of its composition reveal individualities of writers, and differences between them are manifest tokens of its essential humanity; yet it bears on its face marks of Divinity, and no other book even approaches it in this respect.

   b. Here, too, these elements are inseparable; even if scholarship does its utmost in separating and discriminating, it will be found impossible to say with accuracy and certainty where Divine element in Scripture ends and human begins.

   c. There have been discussions about inspiration all through centuries, and attempts have been made to solve problem of coexistence and combination of human and Divine elements in Holy Writ; but none of these carries us far, though fact of this union is found to be satisfying to personal experience so that we rest on assurance that "all Scripture is given by inspiration of God" (2 Tim. 3:6) and also that "holy men of God spake as they were moved by the Holy Ghost" (2 Pet. 1:21); i.e., we accept facts without discovering full explanation.

Thus the sum total of the impression, whether of Christ or

of the Bible, is a complete conviction of their real Divinity and their equally real humanity.

II. Their Infallibility

1. *Our Lord Was Infallible in His Earthly Manifestation*

   a. As Teacher sent from God, He claimed to be exponent of His Father's will and mouthpiece of Divine revelation.

   b. Believers of present day have not seen Christ in that original manifestation; nevertheless, they fully believe in His personal infallibility.

2. *We Believe the Same About the Bible*

   a. We consider that in its original manifestations, i.e., in manuscripts that came from hands of Apostles and other chosen men of apostolic times, its teaching was infallible.

   b. We do not possess these original manuscripts, for it has not pleased God to preserve them for us; but in our Bibles of today we have nearest possible approach, and this a perfectly adequate one, to original revelation.

III. Their Authority

1. *Our Lord's Authority as a Teacher Was Absolute and Final*

   a. As suggested here in Matthew's Gospel, what He said carried its own weight in authority and uniqueness (cf. Luke 4:14, 15, 22).

   b. Not only so, but elsewhere He claimed to have come to this world as revelation of God the Father (cf. 5:17; Mark 14:61, 62; John 4:25, 26; etc.); and this was taken for granted through remainder of N.T. and summed up for us by writer of Hebrews (cf. Heb. 1:1, 2).

2. *In the Same Way, We Believe the Bible To Be of Absolute and Final Authority*

   a. Because it so obviously contains revelation of God for man's spiritual life from time of Apostles to day of our Lord's second coming, this book is our supreme authority; indeed, it is our only infallible guide in all matters of moral and spiritual truth and life.

   b. Whatever truth may be more fully understood by Church as days go on, or whatever interpretations of truth may come to be accepted as correct, we are convinced they all will be discovered within limits of our present Bible.

N.B. Importance of this fact was stressed by Canon H. P. Liddon when he declared: "Authority can never trifle with the basis on which it rests without ceasing to be authority."

IV. Their Purpose

1. *Christ Was Sent Into the World To Reveal the Redeeming Love and Grace of God*

   a. This purpose of God has universal destination, since Christ was intended for whole world; He is being interpreted according to every need of every race.

   b. This purpose gives Christ an exhaustless significance; each generation, each race, finds more and more in Him of many-sided revelation of God and of His own Person and work.

2. *The Bible, in Striking Analogy, Continues To Reveal the Redeeming Grace of God*

   a. Its purpose, too, has universal application; and it is being translated into every language and dialect.

   b. It has wonderful universal significance, and new beauties are always being discovered; to use John Robinson's well-known words to Pilgrim fathers: "The Lord hath yet more light and truth to break forth from His holy Word."

V. Their Power

1. *Christ Has Personal Power*

   a. He is abundantly able to instruct, to convict, to pardon, to cleanse, to sanctify, to enlighten, and to strengthen; "where the word of a king is, there is power" (Eccl. 8:4).

   b. This personal power of Christ arises out of His revelation of God to those who will receive Him.

2. *The Bible, in Another Close Analogy, Has Literary Power*

   a. "The power of the printed page" is a well-known phrase; how much more powerful than words of men are those of God's Holy Spirit!

   b. Scriptures also have power, in Christ's stead, of instruction, conviction, conversion, pardon, cleansing, sanctification, enlightenment, strengthening; they show clearly how

God's grace may be received into minds, consciences, hearts, and wills.

> *Eye of God's Word, where'er we turn,*
> *Ever upon us! Thy keen gaze*
> *Can all the depths of sin discern,*
> *Unravel every bosom's maze.*

> *Who that has felt thy glance of dread*
> *Thrill through his heart's remotest cells,*
> *About his path, about his bed,*
> *Can doubt what Spirit in thee dwells?*

Conclusion

From all this it can be easily understood that the requirements of both the incarnate Word and the written Word are virtually identical. Each demands three conditions for both understanding and enjoyment:

1. First must come *meditation,* as we ponder our Saviour's Person and God's great Book.
2. Then will follow *trust,* as we confide both in the Lord and in His Word.
3. Out of these will proceed *obedience,* as we follow Christ's Holy Spirit and His sacred writings.

Thus we shall have in our own lives the crowning and most convincing testimony to the reality of the incarnate Word and of the written Word alike; and these are some of the aspects of the close analogy between them. The more we dwell upon them and enter into their beauty and fullness, the deeper will be our conviction that in the Lord Jesus Christ and in the Bible alike we have that which alone can save, sanctify, and satisfy the soul, because in both we have the full, perfect, and sufficient revelation of God. Occupying mind, heart, and will with Christ, and with the sacred record of His work and words, we shall live forever in the fortress of an "impregnable Rock," one upon which the storm will beat in vain, and in which there is shelter and satisfaction for time and for eternity.

19

CHRIST'S MINISTRY BY MIRACLE (1)

Matthew 8:1—9:8

T HE SERMON on the Mount is immediately followed by a number of miracles recorded in this and the succeeding chapter. Like an unbeliever who once listened to a description of a Christian's plan for his life, we might be tempted to exclaim as we finish our study of Christ's Sermon, "Beautiful! — but can it be done?" The miracles give the answer to this inquiry, showing that the ideal of the Sermon is possible by means of the power demonstrated by Christ in working them. They here form a group without regard for chronological order (the specific times being noted by Mark and Luke), in order to prove the authority of Christ. As we have seen, His ministry was described in 4:23 as consisting of both teaching and miracles, and after chapters 5 to 7 have shown the former, this section begins to deal with the latter.

Miracles in the New Testament not only are evidential, to prove Christ's Divine origin and authority, but they also serve as symbols of His spiritual purpose and as confirmations of faith for those who are already His followers. The way in which the Jews rejected Christ in spite of His miracles is striking evidence that something besides physical demonstration is needed, that is, the Divine gift of faith together with the calling of God to the individual.

In this study we shall consider a section that describes three specific miracles and includes one general account; then there is an interlude of personal dealing; and after that a second group of three miracles. After noting another and longer interlude of personal dealing (see Study No. 22), we shall consider a third group that includes four miracles (see Study No. 24).

I. Christ's Miracles in Relation to the Old Testament
   (vs. 1-17)

This first group has to do entirely with healing and is shown, in harmony with Matthew's purposes, to be a fulfillment of prophecy (cf. v. 17).

1. *The Healing of Leprosy* (vs. 1-4)

    a. Among Jews leprosy symbolized sin, and victim was regarded as unclean, not allowed to associate with God's people in worship (cf. Lev. 13).

    b. As Christ came down from mountain (v. 1), one of these met Him with words, "Lord, if thou wilt, thou canst make me clean" (v. 2); and though, as with us, use of word "if" indicates uncertainty, it was quite natural and not faithless in this case, since full truth of Christ's pitying love had not yet reached this poor man; his "if" was one of ignorance and not of unbelief.

    c. It is both ignorant and doubting "ifs" that hurt our Christian lives unless, like this leper, we take them to the Lord; he was perfectly sure of Christ's power, for he said, "thou canst—" and, resting on this knowledge and owning Christ as "Lord," he appealed to compassion that has never failed to respond.

    d. At once "if thou wilt" of his diffidence was met by sympathetic and purifying touch; and great "I will" accompanied command "be thou clean" and brought immediate and perfect deliverance (v. 3).

    e. When we bring our doubts into presence of Christ, they disappear, leaving us waiting for His word of assurance, and feeling certain it will be given; and only then are we healed of our "grievous wound."

    Jesus, Thy touch is still the same,
    For Thou unchanging art;
    This prayer I offer in Thy Name,
    Dear Saviour, touch my heart.

    Touch me, O Lord, with healing power,
    For I am sick with sin;
    Grant me, O Christ, the heavenly power
    To heal the plague within.

    Touch me, O Lord, for Thou art pure,
    Uncleanness flies from Thee;
    Thy precious blood a fountain sure
    From leprous taint shall free.

> *Touch me, O Lord; with thoughts of Thine*
> *Thy mind to me be given;*
> *My spirit fill with light Divine*
> *And guide my feet to heaven.*

    f. Relation of this miracle to O.T. is shown in Christ's reference to Moses' law of leper's cleansing (cf. Lev. 14:1-32, Deut. 24:8).

2. *The Healing of Paralysis* (vs. 5-13)

    a. This next miracle beautifully and logically follows by showing that after dealing with sin comes need of power for service, since paralysis ("palsy," v. 6) is fit symbol of helplessness of soul.

    b. Centurion was philanthropist and probably proselyte (cf. Luke 7:45); and something of his character is shown by his personal interest in his servant (v. 6), by his sense of unworthiness to receive Christ into his house in spite of gracious offer (v. 7), and, above all, by his unexpectedly implicit faith — confidence that one Divine word would be sufficient for healing (v. 8).

    c. As Roman soldier he speaks of obedience he is bound to give to superiors and of that which he requires from subordinates (v. 9); and he implies there was no need for Christ's actual presence at bedside, since even he himself was not required always personally to superintend execution of his orders.

    d. Unusual conception of Divine power is thus manifested, and with command from Christ paralysis goes (v. 13); but this miracle is accompanied also by unique expression of our Lord's admiration of such faith on part of Gentile (v. 10), and acceptance of his estimate.

    e. Relation of this miracle to O.T. is indicated by Christ's reference to patriarchs (vs. 11, 12); "children of the kingdom" referred to Jews, who were going to reject their King and would therefore find themselves outside, while those who had not had their opportunities but who had exercised "great faith" (v. 10) would be within banqueting house (cf. Song of Sol. 2:4), enjoying privileges of Kingdom.

    f. There is, of course, sense in which we may speak of Kingdom now as spiritual and invisible, within human hearts; but these verses show definitely that full and visible meaning of it has yet to be realized.

g. Then our Lord turns again to centurion and reassures him, declaring great principle that measure of faith is also measure of blessing (v. 13; cf. Ps. 81:10); and healing of servant was found later to have taken place at that very hour, incontrovertible proof of what Christ can do in response to "great faith."

3. *The Healing of Fever and Other Maladies* (vs. 14-17)

a. Third miracle occurred in house of Peter, where his wife's mother was sick with fever (v. 14); again our Lord's touch led to healing, and immediate outcome was grateful service on part of woman healed (v. 15).*

b. All these miracles evidently led to deep stirring of enthusiasm for Jesus Christ, because on evening of that day inhabitants of place brought to Him their sick, especially those possessed of demons (v. 16).

c. Relation to O.T. is shown in reference to prophet Isaiah (v. 17; cf. Isa. 53:4); and this work of healing is seen by Matthew as fulfillment of well-known text.

d. While in original Hebrew of Isaiah words have sacrificial significance, it is question whether same idea is in Matthew, for simple reason that Christ's atonement had not been made at time to which text refers; so its application seems rather to be to His ministry of healing, His sympathetic entrance into human suffering.

f. Matthew uses physical words, "infirmities" and "diseases," while Isaiah's reference was to mental "griefs" and "sorrows"; yet all are connected, as causes and effects, with sin on one hand (cf. Isa. 53:5), and with death on other (cf. vs. 8, 9), so that it is possible to think of both passages as applicable to Christ's healing miracles as well as to His atoning death.

f. For all this intense labor, therefore, Evangelist can find no more appropriate description, for sympathy and self-sacrifice must have been at least as costly to Christ as expenditure of physical force is to us; such a view seems to accord with His real humanity.

g. Christ took away disease in token of His removal of

---

*For fuller treatment of this miracle, see following Study, No. 20, p. 118.

its root, sin, at cross; and His miracles of healing may thus be said to partake of nature of atoning suffering, crowned at last by sufferings of atoning death.

N.B. R. V. Bingham wrote: "Sin is the only thing that demands expiation by blood. For if sickness needed atonement, then sickness implies a clouded conscience and broken fellowship with God. And such a cruel doctrine is denied by the most saintly men in the Church who in the direst sicknesses have had sweetest fellowship with God. We have no doubt that in the great company which Christ healed on this occasion He saw in many instances the direct results of sin, and in His healing touch He was quite generally undoing the effect of much for which He was ultimately to die. . . . In the Old Testament . . . where sickness was directly the result of sin . . . atonement was invariably introduced for the sin as God's method of dealing with the sickness . . . a real background behind Christ's ministry of healing. In this very chapter, in cleansing the leper, He specifically told him to fulfil the demands of the Mosaic law. . . . Christ was entering sympathetically into the woes, sorrow and sufferings of those to whom He came to minister; . . . it was that phase of His life referred to by a later writer when he says: 'We have not a high priest which cannot be touched with the feeling of our infirmities' (Heb. 4:15)."*

II. An Interlude of Personal Dealing (vs. 18-22)

Owing to the pressure of enthusiastic and curious crowds, Christ determined to go over to the other side of the lake (v. 18). A sudden outburst of mere human excitement might have proclaimed Him king, and this was not His purpose at that time. But before He went, certain principles of His kingly service were announced, and two interviews are recorded having to do with the subject of true citizenship in the Kingdom. The link that connects them with the preceding and following miracles is the great claim of Christ to sovereignty. Here is One who has just shown His power over sickness. Surely He is now to be put above —

---

* *The Bible and the Body,* Evangelical Publishers, Inc., 1921, p. 43.

1. *Human Comforts* (vs. 19, 20)

   a. Scribe, evidently already in general a disciple, proposed henceforward to follow Christ continuously (v. 19); but answer given him clearly showed for first time what would be cost of identification with already despised and opposed Teacher.

   b. It is as though our Lord stated that the man did not know what he said, for while animals and birds had places of protection, Son of Man could not secrete Himself from His enemies.

   c. Thus Christ emphasized essential need of sacrifice of comfort, safety and, if required, of life itself; it was solemn warning rather than definite refusal, for perhaps He saw under man's profession an element of superficiality and insincerity which demanded such caution. *N.B.* It has been pointed out that phrase "lay his head" (v. 20) is identical in Greek with phrase in John 19:30, "bowed his head"; metaphorically, then, our Lord had nowhere to lay His head till He laid it down on cross — He never rested till His work was done.

   > *He had no place whereon to lay His head,*
   >   *His life begun:*
   > *No room for Him, save in a manger-bed —*
   >   *A borrowed one.*

   > *He had no place whereon to lay His head,*
   >   *His life-work done:*
   > *A Cross His pillow, and His graveyard bed,*
   >   *A borrowed one.*

   > *Sin's suffering borne, He freely offers men*
   >   *In heaven a part:*
   > *Yet stay! He asks one resting-place again,*
   >   *'Tis but my heart!*

And surely, also, Christ is to be regarded above —

2. *Human Circumstances* (vs. 21, 22)

   a. Another disciple took opposite view, making apparently laudable, reasonable request that may have been perfectly sincere in intention, viz., for permission to recognize earthly duty first of all and delay following his Master; but wording (v. 21) does not necessarily mean his father was actually dead.

b. It was Oriental idiom to express desire to put human claims and home ties first, perhaps even to stay at home till eventual death of father freed son from filial duty (cf. Luke 9:60).

c. Reply of our Lord states His unique claim over every earthly circumstance — in effect, only spiritually dead were then to bury their physical dead; that is, purely worldly people may subordinate everything spiritual to their duty towards their own family, but Christian is to put Christ first and regard calling of his Master as highest of all obligations.

d. There may well be no end to these personal obligations if once we give Christ's cause second place, for such a plea as this disciple made is often unconscious self-deception, covering actual reluctance; but, conversely, Divine claim to our supreme affection and obedience, when recognized, ennobles and enables all earthly devotion.

III. Christ's Miracles in Relation to Human Freedom (8:23 to 9:8)

The connection between these three miracles is most interesting. They all have to do with bondage: the first to physical forces; the second to the Evil One, and the third to sin itself.

1. *Christ Sovereign Over Storm* (8:23-27)

a. On entering boat in order to cross lake, and followed by disciples, our Lord fell asleep, tired with day's work; but great storm suddenly arose, threatening to flood their craft (vs. 23, 24).

b. Disciples in their terror cried out to be saved (v. 25), at which Christ immediately awoke and rebuked first their fearfulness and lack of faith, and then winds and sea (v. 26); order of rebuke is particularly noticeable.

c. Then with revulsion of feeling men changed from extreme anxiety to limitless admiration; for they were unable to understand "what manner of man" this was (v. 27) that even natural elements of wind and water obeyed Him.

d. This incident reminds us how man, when made in image of God, was monarch of all creation; and how his fall into sin means he is no longer king but under dominion of nature which may so easily send him to destruction.

e. We also see in this story that Christ, as perfect man as well as God, was indeed "sovereign of the sea," bringing threefold calm: to His own heart as He fell asleep; to nature as He stilled elements; and to hearts of His disciples as He saved their lives.*

2. *Christ Sovereign Over Satan* (8:28-34)

a. Infinitely worse than bondage of physical nature is slavery to Evil One; and demon possession as particular form of human trouble seems to indicate that, during Christ's earthly life, special power of devil was permitted in order that our Lord's greater power might be manifested.

b. Description of these two men (vs. 28, 29) shows extent to which they were demon-possessed; and contrast between them and Christ is most impressive.

c. They recognized His power and yet realized there was nothing in common between themselves and Him; they felt His influence, they even hastened to meet Him, and yet they feared Him because their awful power was manifestly checked by His presence.

d. Identification of demons with men is also noteworthy, for they spoke, as it were, through their victims, and if cast out would be sent to place of torment; thus their evil rule over human beings would be disturbed and ended.

N.B. J. G. Simpson, in his volume entitled *Fact and Faith,* has this to say: "If Christ be indeed God, few narratives are more striking than that of the Gadarene swine. Does it not seem to lift the curtain that veils the spiritual forces that day by day are at work and deaden the meaningless disasters in the progress of history?"

e. Request to enter herd of swine (vs. 30, 31) perhaps indicates demons thought they could thus put end to Christ's work in that place, through loss to owners; if these were Jews, who were prohibited from keeping

---

*For fuller treatment, see Study No. 21, p. 121.

pigs, they would be punished by animals' destruction and be vengeful.

f. Christ thereupon permitted demons to depart in this manner (v. 32), doubtless on principle that human salvation is infinitely more important than preservation of animals (cf. 12:12); we must distinguish, however, between permission and commandment, even though, like greater mystery of permission of sin, we may not know exact reason.

g. Violence on part of herd is accounted for by tendency among gregarious creatures to follow leaders, and yet terror caused by report of miracle (v. 33) proved stronger than either anger over loss or appreciation of salvation of two men; and "whole city came out to meet Jesus" (v. 34) fearing disturbance so greatly as to beseech Him to leave their region.

h. Thus, though ruin wrought by evil spirits is terrible and far-reaching, Christ is shown able to cast out every one; and men thus delivered are seen clothed, restored to their right minds, and made fit to sit "at the feet of Jesus" (cf. Luke 8:35).

3. *Christ Sovereign Over Sin* (9:1-8)

a. Christ will not force Himself on anyone's attention and so, when besought to depart, He immediately complied (v. 1); but soon another need faced Him, and this time bondage was that of sin itself, its victim helpless, hopeless, pitiable, and yet his physical condition was only symbolic of deeper spiritual predicament.

b. Four friends of palsied man (cf. Mark 2:5) had thought solely of his physical need; but Christ evidently recognized deeper primary requirement.

c. These men saw clearly one thing to be done and did it immediately — fact that Jesus could and would heal dominated them, and they determined somehow to get their friend into His presence; and He honored their faith by speaking at once wonderful words of love (v. 2).

d. Forgiveness, or pardon, was characteristic gift of Christ — immediate, perfect, eternal, assured; no wonder He said here: "Be of good cheer."

N.B. Two other uses of phrase occur in Matthew (v. 22,

14:27) where reasons for "good cheer," or encouragement, were power and peace. See also Mark 10:49, privilege; John 16:33, protection; Acts 23:11, preservation.

e. In some respects, greatest problem of life is: Can sin be forgiven, so blotted out, in fact, that it shall no longer stand between us and God, but be removed forever as barrier to fellowship?

f. Scribes present evidently regarded it seriously, and inwardly accused Christ of being blasphemer (v. 3), charge apparently made for first time; then, not only did He trace affliction of palsied man to its secret source in sin, but He also read secret objections of scribes (v. 4) and charged them with evil thoughts, pointing out (v. 5) it would be no more difficult to say, "Thy sins are forgiven" than, "Arise and walk."

g. But, as full effect of forgiveness could not be seen by outward senses, He gave visible confirmation of it by miracle of physical healing; and so that all might know He had not spoken blasphemy Christ bestowed on man power to arise and go to his house perfectly healed (vs. 6, 7).

h. Thus Christ answered question about sin and showed He could fill this deepest human need of all by His power of forgiveness, an exclusively Divine act; no wonder multitudes "were afraid" (v. 8, A.S.V.), though this did not prevent them from glorifying God and recognizing Divine gift of authority bestowed upon Jesus Christ, for visible facts attest invisible powers.

Conclusion

Sickness, Self, Storm, Satan, Sin — powerful enemies every one, but as they pass in review we see Christ as —

1. Sensitive to human suffering, being deeply conscious of man's condition;

2. Sympathetic, since He felt not only for, but with, man in his troubles;

3. Swift to come to man's help; and —

4. Strong to overcome difficulties.

Some people have sensitivity and sympathy without swiftness and strength; others have the latter without the former. But

Christ possessed all these attributes to the very highest degree and proved Himself "a very present help in trouble," the Divine Saviour in deed and in truth.

20

THE MASTER'S TOUCH

Matthew 8:15

THERE IS a big word which describes a frequent charge against Christianity — "anthropomorphism," which has been defined as "God conceived of and expressed in language that relates to man." We are accused of "making God in our own image" in order to describe Him. But how else, or how better, may man express the One whose highest creation he is? Man is a personality no less than his Maker; therefore love, pity, justice, are necessarily ascribable to the one as well as to the other, and it is but a step to the representation of bodily form or parts, although care must be taken lest anything unworthy be ascribed to Deity. This apart, we may fearlessly use such language as, indeed, God's own Word does on almost every page. In fact, it is a vital need for, while we agree with Bishop Handley Moule that "a Saviour not quite God is a bridge broken at the other end," it is equally true that if Christ were "not quite man" the chasm of sin would be unbridged at the nearer bank. Christianity must therefore combine both aspects, unique Divinity and perfect humanity.

In this connection it is noteworthy that in several of the miracles in this chapter special emphasis is placed upon the touch of Christ, as though to show His nearness to us, His oneness with us, and His desire to enter into the fullest possible fellowship with us. As we compare several of the passages in the Gospels where we find His touch mentioned, we may discern in it a fourfold meaning.

I. Sympathy

    a. We see this on several occasions (cf. 8:3, 9:29, 20:34), although Christ could have healed, and sometimes did heal, without any such contact.

b. But that is how God saves — not from great height, but in coming down to our level; and attitude beyond mere pity is at once our encouragement and God's glory (cf. Heb. 2:14).

II. Authority

a. We want more than sympathy, however — something to give it support (cf. Luke 7:14), for it is possible for sympathy to accompany weakness.

b. Christ's words carried authority (cf. 7:29), and so did His whole life (cf. John 5:27).
Illus.: As with men such as physician, lawyer, general — authority gives assurance; in fact, it is indispensable in all leadership.

III. Power

a. But authority without power is empty and useless, and so Christ's authority is seen to have been based on power of Almighty God, His heavenly Father.

b. Here He had power over Disease, and, in later verses, over Demons and Danger; in next chapter, it is recorded, over Death and Darkness as well.

c. Cf. also Christ's power over Difficulty (cf. Luke 22:51), Doubt (cf. 17:7), Despair (Mark 9:27), Deafness and Dumbness (Mark 7:33) — in short, over all diverse and untoward circumstances of life.

IV. Blessing

a. Christ's touch not only showed sympathy, authority, and power, but brought benediction (cf. 19:13-15, Luke 24:50, Acts 11:21).

c. It is comparable with use of "right hand" in O.T., which was sign of blessing (cf. Gen. 35:18, 48:14, Ps. 16:11, 80:17, etc.).

Conclusion

1. Let us ask for His hand in acceptance (cf. 9:18, Mark 7:32).
2. Let us yield to His hand in obedience (cf. 1 Pet. 5:6).
3. Let us tell of His hand in witness (cf. Ps. 118:15-17).

Thus may we rejoice in His sympathy, obey His authority, realize His power, and praise Him for His blessing.

> *"He touched her hand, and the fever left her."*
> *He touched her hand, as He only can,*
> *With the wondrous skill of the Great Physician*
> *With the tender touch of the Son of Man.*
>
> *And the eyes where the fever-light had faded*
> *Looked up, by her grateful tears made dim,*
> *And she rose and ministered in her household,*
> *She rose and ministered unto Him.*
>
> *"He touched her hand, and the fever left her."*
> *Oh, we need His touch on our fevered hands!*
> *The cool, still touch of the Man of Sorrows,*
> *Who knows us, and loves us, and understands.*
>
> *"He touched her hand, and the fever left her."*
> *Oh, blessed touch of the Man Divine!*
> *So beautiful then to arise and serve Him,*
> *When the fever is gone from your life and mine.*
>
> *Whatever the fever His touch can heal it;*
> *Whatever the tempest His voice can still;*
> *There is only joy as we seek His pleasure;*
> *There is only rest as we choose His will.*
>
> *And some day, after life's fitful fever,*
> *I think we shall say, in the Home on high,*
> *"If the hands that He touched but did His bidding,*
> *How little it matters what else went by!"*
>
> *Ah, Lord! Thou knowest us altogether,*
> *Each heart's sore sickness, whatever it be;*
> *Touch Thou our hands! Let the fever leave us,*
> *And so shall we minister unto Thee.*
>
> E. G. CHERRY

21

"A GREAT CALM"

Matthew 8:26

Jesus Christ used three methods in His earthly ministry: miracles, teaching, training. The last had the most far-reaching importance because of the future extension of His work. Among the lessons taught the disciples, the one recorded in this passage was one of the most essential, viz., the results of unquestioning trust in their Lord.

I. A Calm Possessed

This was in the Saviour's heart as He fell asleep and was brought about by —

1. *Innocence of Life*

   a. Long day was over so He dismissed it from mind as it were, because His conscience was clear; and He was soon asleep.

   b. Good man's innocence is like downy pillow of babe; bad men must subdue his conscience first as he would thump hard cushion.

2. *Confidence in God*

   a. Christ's manhood was ideal; there was union of His will with God's, exerting implicit trust.

   b. Christ's Sonship was complete; He was willing to go step by step with His Father.

II. A Calm Created

This was in two spheres — in nature and in hearts of disciples.

1. *Storm at Sea*

   a. Tempest mentioned before fact that Christ was asleep (v. 24); so neither plash of oars, nor swell of waves, nor unsteadiness of boat were sufficient to awaken Him.

   b. Even when disciples spoke to Him, story proceeds with

complete self-possession on His part, as He immediately but unhurriedly responds.

c. There is conscious capability here; He was never at loss, so rebuked first disciples for their reckless, faithless word, "We perish!" and only then winds and sea.

> *"Commit thy way unto the Lord and trust!"*
> *There is an "also" we too oft forget,*
> *And so are plagued and worried. Oh! we must*
> *"Trust also," then our soul*
> *Shall cease to roll*
> *In restlessness, and reason, and regret.*
>
> *Commit! And then, committed, trust His word!*
> *Has He not said that He will bring thee through?*
> *Trust His strong arm, and when wild storms are heard,*
> *Believe He holds them still*
> *By His strong will;*
> *Trust Him, the Wise, the Faithful, and the True.*
>
> *Trust Him to manage all that thou dost now*
> *Commit to Him: the ship, the sails, the sea,*
> *The sailors, thy strange crew. And ask not how*
> *He will do all for thee,*
> *But trustful be;*
> *Lie down and rest, from anxious worry free.*
>
> WILLIAM LUFF

2. *Storm of Soul*

a. There had to be unworthy fear to lead them to higher one — terror before awe (cf. Mark 4:40, 41).

b. Christ, in accomplishing their deliverance, showed how close are adversity and prosperity, ill and good, danger and safety — all bridged by His mighty power.

c. Then came "great calm" into hearts and lives as well as into elements.

Conclusion

1. *The Importance of Calm*

Without it, human character is hurried and flurried, with

little chance to grow spiritually; Christian work may be harassed and embarrassed.

2. *The Sources of Calm*

Faith — never doubting Divine wisdom and power; love — receiving Christ on board our bark of life; prayer — keeping in close touch with Him "in quietness and confidence" (Isa. 30:15).

3. *The Results of Calm*

Peace in apparent loneliness — even if Christ seems to leave or forget us, we know this cannot be (cf. 28:20b); power in conflicting circumstances — even when storm is encountered in path of duty.

> *Dark was the night: the foaming deep*
> *Raged madly round; He rose from sleep,*
> *The Man, the God, the tempest's Lord.*
> *He spake! Obedient, trembling, awed,*
> *Low sank the proud waves' crested head,*
> *Far the affrighted storm-fiend fled.*

> *We sail on Life's tempestuous sea;*
> *Oh Thou, whose voice wild Galilee*
> *Heard o'er the storm-blast, speak the word*
> *Which oft since then the saints have heard!*
> *May we, when tempests baffle skill,*
> *Hear Thy commanding "Peace, be still!"*

> *Speak! And the sky of sorrow's night*
> *Is radiant with celestial light.*
> *Speak! And the wildest waves obey,*
> *And gently bear us on our way.*
> *Speak! And temptation's fiercest blast*
> *Is harmless, all its fury past.*

> *Speak! And the very winds of death*
> *Shall waft — a more than welcome breath —*
> *To fairer realms than heart conceives*
> *Or thread of happiest fancy weaves,*
> *To worlds where evil never trod,*
> *Bright as the diadem of God.*

22
INSTANCES OF CHRIST'S
PERSONAL DEALINGS
Matthew 9:9-17

As WE continue through these two chapters we see that, taken together, they may be said to exemplify Christ's authority over the three spheres — heaven, earth, and hell; over the three parts of man — spirit, mind, and body. Or, we may watch Him gaining the victory over sin, claiming human service, and introducing man to fellowship with God.

The second half of this chapter is devoted to Christ's miracles in relation to several of man's enemies, but first there is an interlude for personal contacts:

I. Dealing with Matthew* (vs. 9, 10)

1. *The Man* (v. 9)

    a. This section is especially significant since it is concerned with author of this Gospel, although his brief mention of himself in third person must be supplemented by what we are told by Mark and Luke, who call him Levi, probably his original name (cf. Mark 2:14, Luke 5:27).

    b. "Matthew" means "gift of God" and may have been name given him when he became Apostle (cf. John 1:42); in list in chapter 10 he is called "the publican" (v. 3), which means tax-gatherer, and this would indicate man of some education and business ability.

2. *The Call* (v. 9b)

    a. Form of this (cf. 4:19) seems to suggest that already there had been discipleship but now there were to be closer relationship and special service; words "Follow me" always imply two elements of trust and obedience.

    b. In any case, it was summons to Matthew while at own

---

* A fuller treatment of this passage is found in the study following (No. 23, p. 129).

business; and it implied both absolute Lordship of Christ and relative possibilities He saw in such a man.

3. *The Response* (v. 9c)

a. Claim of Christ immediately recognized, and Luke says "he forsook all" (Luke 5:29). It is surprising that Jesus should call tax-collector, but even more so that man should be ready so promptly to leave business so lucrative, with temptation to graft because taxes were not fixed as today, but "farmed" by Roman authorities.

b. His work was thus despised and he himself regarded as outcast by Jews; and so his response remarkably illustrates power of God in either conversion or consecration.

4. *The Feast* (v. 10)

a. Matthew omits fact, perhaps from modesty, that this was held in his own house; and only when we compare other Synoptic Gospels do we discover it (cf. Mark 2:15, Luke 5:29) and that Luke calls it a "great" feast.

b. It is interesting to note how Matthew's old associates (cf. v. 11) were invited to meet the new — "Jesus and his disciples" (Mark 2:15); this was at once testimony to their host's break with past and determination to lead new life, and to his conviction that Christ stood ready to receive them also.

II. Dealing with the Pharisees (vs. 11-13)

1. *The Inquiry* (v. 11)

a. Eating together has always been mark of social fellowship and at that time it even suggested moral equality; and yet Saviour and sinners, new friends and old, reclined at same table.

b. Narrow-minded Pharisees, doubtless present as spectators according to custom of time, could not understand; and instead of appealing to Christ direct, they asked disciples why their Master consorted in this way with such outcasts.

c. They may have been afraid of asking Him; or they may have hoped to raise doubts of Him in His disciples' minds.

2. *The Answer* (vs. 12, 13)

    a. Our Lord at once spoke for Himself, vindicating His position by stating fundamental truth; He reminded Pharisees that "they who are strong" (Greek) do not need doctor, "but those who are sick" (cf. 4:24), and He had come as Great Physician.

    b. Pharisees by their assumption of moral superiority really proved need of outcasts for our Lord; but at the same time they only imagined they were righteous, considering legal righteousness sufficient with God, so that they were left to realization that all men are sinners.

    c. This saying and quotation from Hosea (6:6) are found only in Matthew's account, proving that Christ had come for very purpose of bestowing mercy, and that God preferred kindness and pity to mere formal ceremonialism (cf. Deut. 10:12); and it is especially striking that Pharisees could be charged with ignorance of true meaning of very Scriptures they professed to honor and teach.

    d. If sacrifice was emphasized at expense of mercy, said our Lord, it lost its spiritual value and became act of hypocrisy (cf. 12:7), and this is equally true today of sacraments.

    e. If to show this was purpose of old dispensation as represented by prophet, much more was it object of Christ's coming to lead men to realize their sinfulness and then to repent and turn to God.

    N.B. Outcome of call of Matthew is self-evident, whether to conversion or to consecration, and whatever his work during these first days, he witnesses forever through permanent ministry of this Gospel, which Renan called "the most important book in the history of the world."

III. Dealing with the Disciples of John (vs. 14-17)

1. *The Problem* (v. 14)

    a. Apparently these men had not been ready to be guided by their master's direction to Christ as Lamb of God (cf. John 1:35), but shared views of Pharisees in regard to asceticism; they could not understand social aspects of life led by His disciples.

    b. This passage may be compared with Acts 19:1-7 to suggest improbability that John the Baptist ever "founded" a Christian Church; both his teaching and baptism were wholly preparatory and transitional — end of old dispensation rather than beginning of new.

2. *The Solution* (v. 15)

    a. Christ simply reminds these men that, just as on day of marriage, it was fitting that bridegroom, attended by his companions, should lead bride in festive procession, so fasting as expression of sorrow would be altogether inappropriate to present circumstances — His presence with His disciples.

    b. At so festive a season it was for them to show their gladness; but when He, as Bridegroom (cf. Baptist's own words in John 3:29), would be taken away from them by violent death it would then be appropriate for them to fast.

3. *The Illustrations* (vs. 16, 17)

    a. Two similes from common life follow, according to our Lord's frequent usage, showing both folly and unsuitability of uniting what is fresh with what is antiquated:

       (1) Patch made of unwrought (cf. v. 16, A.S.V.) cloth will shrink and make rent worse by placing strain on old garment;

       (2) So, also, new wine, still fermenting, will expand and burst old, worn wineskins (v. 17).

    b. Thus, antagonism between old and new is due to greater vigor of latter in its time of development and expansion, with result in both these cases that old and new perish.

    c. There is also danger that outward forms become worn or unsuitable, with strong convictions and feelings breaking through and perhaps being dissipated, such as icy exactitude of conduct or ritual versus innocence, warmth, and freshness of newer spiritual experience.

    d. First simile meets case of John's disciples, with whom old was of chief importance; they are told of impossibility of Christianity being regarded as patch to be used to fill up what is lacking in Judaism.

    e. Second simile may apply chiefly to Christ's disciples, to whom Christianity is chief concern and old Jewish forms secondary; no one would consider old container more important than fresh, thirst-quenching beverage.

f. In both cases, however, result is same: new dispensation neither continues nor mends old but rather, as new method of God with man, it must have its own way of expression and fulfillment.

N.B. Alfred Plummer suggests these illustrations teach that "the new spirit in religion requires a new form. . . . It would be fatal to mix the two systems. In the one case fasting, in the other case exemption from fasting, was the natural outcome of the conditions." We might add that Judaism is not only system that is "fatal" to "mix" with true Christianity; history has provided many illustrations of this principle, e.g., paganism, liberalism.

g. Truth of gospel is same everywhere and in all ages, but because of its wonderful adaptability to time, place, and circumstance, it is capable of constant and indefinitely varied application.

Conclusion

From this passage we may observe the threefold purpose of our Lord's personal work:

1. As with Matthew, He brought a message of redemption from sin.

2. As with the Pharisees, He brought a message of freedom from prejudice.

3. As with John's disciples, He brought a message of liberty from bondage.

All this is summed up in John 20:31, which may be paraphrased thus: These things are written that the Jews might believe that Jesus is the Christ, their Messiah; that the Gentiles might believe that He is the Son of God; and that both Jew and Gentile, by believing, might have "life in his name" (A.S.V.).

23

"MATTHEW THE PUBLICAN"

Matthew 9:9-13

I⊤ IS a well-known fact that no two people are alike in personality; but even so there are few things in the Gospels more striking than the wide variety seen in the disciples of Jesus Christ, among those twelve men who were His special assistants. This is a strong testimony to the universality of the Christian faith. It can take every form of human life and temperament and mould it so as to be of service in the cause of truth and righteousness. A noteworthy instance of this is seen in Matthew, the author of this First Gospel. All that we know of his life is to be found in the present passage and in its parallels in Mark 2:14-22 and Luke 5:27-39, and by the inclusion of his name and calling in the roll of the Twelve as he gives it in 10:3. But these sources are sufficient to enable us to note the essential features of Matthew's relation to Christ and to illustrate from them some of the vital elements of all true discipleship.

I. The Man (v. 9a)

1. *Occupation*

a. Tax-gatherer was one who elicited intense animosity on part of Jews who strongly opposed this mark of Roman domination.

b. Consequently, any Jew who took up this work was regarded as enemy of his country, a sort of profiteer and social outcast.

2. *Occasion*

a. But it was while Matthew was engaged in this despised occupation that he came into contact with Christ; no one has gone too far or sunk too low for the Lord to deal with him.

b. It is also to be noted that Christ came to Matthew at an hour when he was actually doing his daily work; this is how the Master often comes to us, taking us just as we are and dealing with us along line of our ordinary life.

II. The Master (v. 9b)

1. *Call*

a. This was a revelation of grace, for had Christ been aiming at popularity He would not have called a despised publican; rather, He would have avoided someone who was regarded as a pariah.

b. But our Lord had respect to men's needs, not to their standing in sight of others; He came to rescue sinners, so was willing to welcome all.

2. *Claim*

a. Christ's claim over Matthew is seen in words "Follow me," demanding what no human being has right to ask of another — surrender of personality — each of us being completely independent so far as personal responsibility is concerned; anything like what is called "passivity" is both wrong and dangerous.

b. This shows Christ to be more than man and that to follow Him means first to trust and then to obey Him; this is what our Lord sought from Matthew, and this is what He still seeks from each of us — that surrender of ourselves to Him as Lord and Master which will best preserve intact our personalities for purpose of living life intended for us.

III. The Disciple (vs. 9c, 10)

1. *Response* (vs. 9c, 10)

a. It was immediate; whether Matthew had known Christ before or not, his decision was made instantly and he answered call at once.

b. It was deliberate; there was no compulsion, for Christ will not have pressed followers or conscripts, and though He impels, He never compels; thus Matthew, as free agent, could have refused (cf. 19:21, 22; Heb. 11:15), but with full, free purpose of heart and will he responded.

c. It was thorough; fact that he left his work and all things connected with it is proof of his real faith in and loyalty to Christ.

2. *Testimony* (v. 10)

   a. Feast that Matthew gave in his house (cf. Mark 2:14, 15; Luke 5:29) was further proof of change from old to new, for his former companions were there and would see what it meant for him to cast in his lot with Jesus instead of with Rome.

   b. But company present was another witness to fact that Christ was ready to receive and bless outcasts; fact that they were "with him" was message of hope to those and all other lost souls.

   c. Still further, feast was fit symbol of that fellowship that was to mark Matthew's life from then on (cf. Rev. 3:20).

IV. The Encounter (vs. 11-13)

1. *Opposition* (v. 11)

   a. Christ's enemies were not slow to take advantage of situation and, exhibiting their false pride and exclusiveness, they asked why He ate with such people.

   b. Indirectness of their question, addressed to disciples rather than to Him, may have been caused by fear, or else by hope of causing trouble between them and their Master.

   c. Pharisees used every opportunity to find fault with Christ, demonstrating how far hostility to our Lord can and will go.

2. *Vindication* (vs. 12, 13)

   a. Answer of Christ to this inquiry is very striking, going far beyond particular occasion as it states some general principles of His life and work.

   b. He shows purpose of His coming — to meet needs of all those conscious of their condition; just as physician heals body, He had come to heal spiritually sick; but Pharisees were so self-satisfied they thought they needed nothing, so would get nothing.

   c. He bids them learn meaning of their own O.T. appeal to mercy rather than to sacrifice (cf. Hos. 6:6) — reminding they did not know book they professed to follow; it was sinners, not self-righteous, He had come to bless.

Conclusion

As we follow the career of Matthew we see a twofold result of this occasion:

1. *He Became an Apostle*
   a. What a privilege for despised tax-gatherer to become one of chosen Twelve!
   b. What wonderful use Christ can make of even most unpromising material!

2. *He Became an Evangelist*
   a. Doubtless this word may be applied to Matthew in both senses — preacher of *evangel* as well as writer of it; but it is as author of this first of our four Gospels, which have been precious heritage of Church throughout Christian era, that we know him today.
   b. It is Jewish Gospel, showing remarkable knowledge of O.T., with its main purpose to prove close connection of Jesus Christ with nation of Abraham, Moses, and David.
   c. It is also Gospel of Kingdom, with Christ as King; and phrase "kingdom of heaven" occurs over thirty times.
   d. It is also full of references to Israel's opposition to Christ and its rejection of Him; and Matthew's own experience of rejection by his own people was clear illustration and instance of this.

Thus, as we think of what Matthew originally was, what he became, and what he did, the outstanding message to our hearts is the sheer power of the grace of God (cf. 1 Cor. 15:10); and this is still operating today in the lives of all those who will make Matthew's wise decision, to leave all, rise up, and follow Christ.

24

CHRIST'S MINISTRY BY MIRACLE (2)

Matthew 9:18-34

Resuming the account of the miracles found in chapters 8 and 9, we may consider the final group of four as indicative of our Lord's power in relation to several of man's enemies.

I. Christ's Power Over Disease and Death (vs. 18-26)

The two stories of the girl and the woman are at once familiar, beautiful, and interrelated. The former was twelve years old (cf. Mark 5:42, Luke 8:42), and the latter had been a sufferer all that time (v. 20).

1. *Christ's Power Over Disease* (vs. 20-22)

   a. These had been twelve years of increasing weariness, of disappointment after disappointment as woman tried in vain one doctor after another (cf. Mark 5:26, Luke 8:43); but at last she found renewed hope in coming to Jesus Christ (v. 20).

   b. With profound faith she felt that, if only she could but touch His garment, she would be made whole (v. 21); as she does so, Jesus turning and seeing her, bids her to "be of good cheer" (v. 22, A.S.V.) and honors her faith by immediate healing.

   > O let me touch Thee, dearest Lord;
   >   Let others throng and press
   > With curious hearts to hear Thy word
   >   Or rend Thy seamless dress.
   >
   > Let me but touch Thee with my faith,
   >   Thy life to mine be given;
   > Virtue impart in life and death,
   >   Then raise me to Thy heaven.

   c. Mark and Luke in their fuller accounts of this miracle would remind us that blessing must not only be received, but confessed to bring full assurance (cf. Mark 5:33, Luke 8:47; see also Rom. 10:8-11); this woman had had physical healing, but spiritual blessing associated with Christ's words came only when she "told him all the truth" before them all.

2. *Christ's Power Over Death* (vs. 18, 19, 23-26)

a. Meanwhile, girl who was dead provides Christ with greatest challenge of all: since outcome of sin, with which He had often dealt, is death, can He deliver from this enemy also? (cf. 1 Cor. 15:26).

b. Hired mourners laugh Him to scorn (vs. 23, 24), representing sceptical mankind, as He asks for more room and says that girl is not dead but asleep (cf. 1 Thess. 4:13-15, 5:10).

c. But He soon shows futility of all such scorn, for entering in and taking girl by her hand He restores her to life.

d. Delay caused by interruption of woman (cf. Mark 5:22, 23; Luke 8:41, 42) must have been great test of faith for Jairus the ruler; but now his child is alive again and deeper trust was certainly experienced.

N.B. Records of three raised from dead by Christ seem to suggest progression: here little girl had just died; widow's young son at Nain (cf. Luke 7:12) was being taken out for burial; while Lazarus, mature man, had been in grave four days (John 11:17). Nothing is too great for power of Christ.

II. **Christ's Power Over Darkness and Demons** (vs. 27-34)

Two miracles are here recorded by Matthew alone, closing the series found in these two chapters:

1. *Christ's Power Over Darkness* (vs. 27-31)

a. Two blind men invoke Jesus Christ as Son of David, giving Him Messianic name as they follow after Him and appeal for His mercy (v. 27).

b. Thereupon our Lord challenged their faith (v. 28), for complete confidence is vital condition of blessing and channel of power; faith is hand that takes what God offers, link between Divine fullness and human need (v. 29).

c. Miracle was wrought with mere touch; and then, not-withstanding Christ's urgent command that they should keep healing private (v. 30), they "spread abroad his fame in all that country" (v. 31).

2. *Christ's Power Over a Dumb Demon* (vs. 32-34)

a. Here was very opposite of blind men's forthright speech — demoniac dumb through possession of evil spirit (v. 32) ; but he was brought to Christ by others and thus, again, faith was operative.

b. When miracle was wrought, dumb man spoke, and crowds were astonished at this exceptional manifestation of power, probably associating it with appearance of Messiah (v. 33).

c. But malice of Pharisees would not permit them to respond, and instead they attributed miracle to devil himself, as though our Lord were actually in league with him (v. 34) ; awful blasphemy of this charge shows to what lengths hostility to Christ on part of unregenerate men will go.

Conclusion

Thus this series of miracles is completed, and our Lord's power over nature, over circumstances, over evil spirits, and over man's body, mind, and spirit is clearly seen.

1. *Physical Power*

a. Out of thirty-three miracles worked by Christ seventeen were physical, especially intended to reveal Him as "God manifest in the flesh" (1 Tim. 3:16).

b. Ever since His days on earth Christianity has done much for human body, in hospitals and similar institutions, and in work of medical missions, thus showing Christian view of value of man's body and urgency of physical need.

2. *Spiritual Power*

a. We may go further and declare that physical healing is symbol and pledge of Christ's perfect redemption, including spirit, mind, and body.

b. He starts with salvation of spirit, proceeds to deal with mind, and guarantees that in future life there will be complete redemption for body through resurrection (cf. Rom. 8:18-25).

Thus there is no limit to our Lord's beneficent influence; and it is a constant encouragement for our faith, and a real inspiration for our love to realize that nothing is outside His interest, and nothing too great for His power.

> *Thy touch has still its ancient power,*
> *No word from Thee can fruitless fall.*

25

PROPAGATION OF THE KINGDOM (1)

Matthew 9:35-38

AFTER THE proclamation of the Divine Kingdom in the Sermon on the Mount, and the revelation of the Divine King's power in a series of miracles, it is natural to come next to the various methods adopted for the propagation of His Kingdom. This passage at once closes the preceding section of the Gospel and opens the following one. It also gives us a glimpse into the heart of Christ as Leader, and reminds us of the spirit He seeks in His followers. We notice first —

I. Our Lord's Mission (v. 35)

Narrative refers primarily to one of Christ's missionary tours, as He traveled along shore of lake, through "all the cities and villages," doing three things:

1. *Teaching* — in synagogues, where Jews met week by week — good opportunity of presenting His truth.

2. *Preaching* — concerned with gospel of Kingdom, and referring to offer to Jews of His Kingship, as already proclaimed by Baptist (cf. 3:1, 2) and by our Lord Himself (cf. 4:17).

3. *Healing* — continuing ministry of previous chapters and including "every sickness and every disease among the people."

N.B. David Livingstone once said: "God had only one and He was a medical missionary."
Then we observe —

II. Our Lord's Compassion (v. 36)

1. *His Perception* — natural that great need should be seen by Him in all its implications.

2. *His Pity* — following immediately and inevitably, for sight leads to feeling and, contemplating their condition, His great heart went out to these poor, helpless creatures who were thus like sheep without shepherd.

   (1) Words in A.S.V., "distressed and scattered," are very strong and might be rendered "harassed and prostrated," even as sheep that are lost and defenseless.

   (2) Montefiore said: "So far as we know, this pity for the sinner was a new note in religious history."

Then we note the result:

III. Our Lord's Instruction (vs. 37, 38)

1. *His Comparison* (v. 37)

   a. Number of people accessible to gospel and ready to receive it was great; and deep misery was apparent in fertile and populous districts of Galilee.

   b. Christ saw, as it were, plentiful crops overripe and wasting, and perhaps never was there a field so precious and never a harvest so intensely desired. Word "harvest" is itself significant, suggesting time for sowing had already come and gone.

   c. More than once in N.T. we find such suggestions that servants of Christ may enter at once upon work of reaping, rather than sowing and waiting for harvest (cf. John 4:35, Acts 18:10); so today we are sometimes forgetful of possibility, unready to believe fields are ripe.

   d. It is surely due to lack of spiritual insight that we fail to realize how much men are hungering for God; we are apt instead to judge hastily by cold or hostile exteriors and talk of hardness of soil and need of plowing and planting, when our Master sees crop wasting for lack of reapers.

N.B. This is first of two significant harvests mentioned by Matthew (see 13:39), one of labor, other of life. Each is mentioned once more in N.T. (cf. John 5:35, Rev. 14:14-16). They sum up whole of this dispensation, one present, other future, and are intimately connected — without present harvest no future one, and without future, present would be incomplete.

2. *His Injunction* (v. 38)

a. It was natural, in view of this great need, that Christ should urge His disciples to pray; work being now beyond His own human capacity and opportunity, there was urgent necessity to send forth more laborers under His Divine leadership.

b. As yet He was only worker, but suggestion of prayer shows that others could be obtained; prayers of disciples, moreover, would prepare them for development soon to come — their own commission and participation (see chap. 10).

c. It is impressive that Lord of harvest waits for prayers of His people; in His infinite condescension He makes Himself dependent on them.

d. Place and value of prayer in connection with missionary work is thus emphasized, and not as easiest part of it; on contrary, true prayer, such as is suggested here, is one of the most difficult tasks as well as one of supremely important methods of doing our Master's will.

Illus.: Chaplain in India felt strongly about certain matters and sought interview with Lord Kitchener. When time appointed came, he was charged by official who conducted him to be very brief, as his lordship had little time and less patience to waste on matters not connected with his office. But chaplain felt his business was of first importance and was not willing it should be disposed of as mere formality. "Well," said Lord Kitchener, "what is your business?" "My lord," was the answer, "it is not mine, it is Another's, and first of all I want to consult *Him*." "You mean," said Kitchener, "that you wish to pray? Then pray, by all means," and he let his caller have all the time he wanted.

Conclusion

Harvest time is always associated with spiritual as well as material things:

1. *The Field*

   a. It is wide (cf. "the world," 13:38).

   b. It is white (cf. John 4:35).

2. *The Lord of the Harvest*

   a. He is Possessor and Producer.

   b. His is greatest interest.

3. *The Laborers*

   a. They are few.

   b. They are sent — selected and qualified by the Lord.

   c. They are urgently needed.

4. *The Prayer*

   a. It is offered as part of service.

   b. It is answered by consideration of need.

   c. It is both offered and answered in close fellowship with Christ.

"If you cannot do anything else, you can pray!" Yes, but if you do not pray you cannot do anything else!

26

PROPAGATION OF THE KINGDOM (2)

Matthew 10:1-42

From 9:35 to 16:20 Matthew records Christ's public work with His disciples in proclaiming the Kingdom. This work was growing to such an extent that it was quite impossible for Him to do it alone, and so He commences to associate others with Himself and to add their training to His other methods of propagation, viz., teaching and miracles. This chapter is concerned with the choice and commission of the Twelve and with Christ's instructions to them. This first missionary campaign was one of great importance and real difficulty; and so, after general instructions, the Master gave His servants special counsels. By these He not only prepared the Twelve for the immediate local experience that would be encountered, but also enunciated for all those who should follow them the general principles of evangelism covering the whole time from our Lord's earthly ministry to His second coming.

I. The Call (vs. 1-4)

1. *Preparation*

    a. After prayer comes work, and it is noteworthy that disciples were sent out to answer their own petitions (cf. 9:37, 38); it is also interesting that choice of them came after our Lord Himself spent preceding night in prayer (cf. Luke 6:12, 13).

    b. They were already His disciples (cf. 4:18-22, 9:9, John 1:35-51); but now came another stage of their relationship in call to become apostles, or ones sent.

2. *Personnel*

    a. Four lists are given in N.T. of Twelve — here in Matthew, in Mark (3:13-19), in Luke (6:13-16), and in Acts (1:13); they are grouped in fours, with Peter always first.

b. There is some variation in names and order, but no contradiction among writers:

　(1) Bartholomew (v. 3) is universally identified with Nathaniel (cf. John 1:45), probably his surname ("son of Tolmai").

　(2) "Simon the Cananaean" (v. 4, A.S.V.; Greek rendering of Hebrew word) was not a "Canaanite," but a Zealot, member of strict sect, so we have in Luke 6:5, "Simon called Zelotes."

　(3) There were two men named James among Twelve — one, son of Zebedee and brother of John, and "the Less," who was son of Alphaeus and whose brother Jude, surnamed Thaddeus, was also called Lebbaeus, or "courageous" (v. 3).

c. All of disciples were from Galilee except, it is thought, Judas Iscariot, whose surname appears to indicate he came from Kerioth in Judea.

II. The Commission (vs. 5-15)

This was expressed in gift of authority (v. 1, A.S.V.), due to great need of additional workers in view of circumstances (cf. 9:36).

1. *The Men Authorized* (v. 5)

a. Word "apostle" (cf. v. 3) means one who is "sent forth" (v. 5); in addition to specific meaning that refers to Twelve, there is wider sense of Christian ambassadorship (cf. John 13:16, Rom. 16:7, 2 Cor. 5:18-20), but our Lord did entrust special work to these particular men.

b. Supreme thought was for thoroughness, rather than greatness, of work; at first, they were undeniably crude in ideas and inexperienced in methods but, trained with Divine patience and in due course equipped with Divine power, they went forth valiantly to do Christ's will.

c. It is encouraging to realize He does not despise humble instruments; these men were not drawn from influential classes of nation, but were persons of character from lower ranks.

d. It is also noteworthy that Christ uses every sort of individuality; differences of character, temperament and circumstance in these men were all utilized by Him.

e. It is also to be remembered that Christ is able to use all that is valuable in past history and varied experiences of each individual; same energies and other features that had marked these men in their various callings were laid hold of by their Master, transformed, and given new direction.

f. Christ is also ready to honor ties of kinship and friendship when they exist among His servants; the Twelve included two pairs of brothers, four partners in business, and several who were friends — all natural relations, thus made channels of higher purpose and fuller blessing.

2. *The Message Authorized* (vs. 5-7)

a. Destination of Twelve was limited — they were not to go to Gentiles, or even to Samaritans (v. 5), but only to people of Israel; time had not yet come for preaching to others.

b. Words "lost sheep" (v. 6) are impressive in their simplicity (cf. 9:36, 15:24); message was to be correspondingly simple, and yet searching, for Twelve were to tell of near approach of God's rule over human life, being concerned with "kingdom of heaven" (v. 7) still being offered to Israel.

c. While gospel would eventually be extended to Gentiles, this provisional arrangement for Israel was necessary to give God's people every opportunity to fulfill their destiny; also, it was important on principle of proceeding gradually, as in all sound movements, from center to circumference, from particular to universal; and temporary limitation to Israel would thus be condition for attainment of wider objective (cf. 8:1).

3. *The Methods Authorized* (vs. 8-15)

a. *Exercise of Faith* (vs. 8-10)

(1) Apostles' work was to support and prove their message (v. 8a); and as they themselves had received both teaching and blessing *gratis* (as Latin version has it), they were to pass these on in same way (v. 8b; cf. 2 Cor. 11:7).

(2) This led to principle on which they were to proceed — that people to whom they ministered were to

receive and help them; as messengers of Gospel they would have claim on hospitality and support.

(3) This in turn would set them free from care (vs. 9, 10); they were to trust to their work for maintenance (cf. 1 Cor. 9:14, I Tim. 5:18).

b. *Bearing of Testimony* (vs. 11-15)

(1) There followed special directions, for while Twelve were indeed sent to Israel (cf. v. 6), they were to concern themselves only with "worthy" among nation (vs. 11, 13).

(2) There was possibility of reception and also of rejection, and their message would soon reveal to them which it was to be.

(3) Any house worthy of their staying in it would find peace resting upon it; but one that did not receive them would become the poorer.

(4) When rejections became city-wide, disciples were to indicate definite refusal and even solemn contempt as they left (v. 14), because the higher the spiritual offer refused the greater would be the sin (v. 15).

III. The Counsels (vs. 16-42)

This passage is most important in connection with service for Christ, for it tells of several matters of permanent importance. Our Lord's instructions naturally follow His commission, and it will be seen that not only do they possess a remarkable unity and order, but may also cover the whole time from this point in our Lord's earthly ministry to His second coming. If the section can be arbitrarily divided between the ministry of the Twelve to Israel and the subsequent more general sphere of Christian service, we may note —

1. *Immediate Instructions* (vs. 16-23)

This section deals primarily with the period of earthly work of Christ and of lives of Apostles, referring to what was particularly necessary for those times and circumstances, in view of intense initial opposition:

a. *Wisdom and Watchfulness* (vs. 16, 17)

(1) Disciples were being sent "as sheep in the midst of wolves" (v. 16) to seek out those who would re-

ceive Kingdom, and thus early Christ forewarns them of danger and suffering.

(2) But they were to exercise caution — "beware of men" (v. 17); "sheep" were to be transformed into "serpents" in regard to wisdom (cf. Gen. 3:1) and into "doves" in regard to harmlessness, or guileless simplicity (cf. A.S.V. marg.), in sense of directness and singleness of purpose.

(3) As "serpents" they would often be able to avoid persecution without being guilty of cowardice; and as "doves" they would face inevitable persecution without compromising their position.

(4) These qualities, which seem opposed to each other in human nature, are made possible by gift of Holy Spirit.

b. *Faith and Fearlessness* (vs. 18-21)

(1) Notwithstanding extent of opposition and forms of persecution, disciples were to be full of confidence, assured of guidance in defense by presence and power of indwelling Spirit, who is here associated with God the Father (vs. 18-20).
N.B. Note emphasis in N.T. on Holy Spirit in relation to speech (cf. vs. 19, 20 with Luke 12:11, 12; John 14:26) and, later on, to remembrance of very words spoken by apostles (cf. 2 Pet. 3:2, Jude 17).

(2) All anxiety was thus to disappear because of intimate and constant relationship to their heavenly Father.

(3) Even if, as is still likely, persecution also involved severance from nearest and dearest, Christ's followers were to be faithful to Him (v. 21).

(4) Christianity, being based on new spiritual relationship, is necessarily supreme over all merely natural bonds; it need not imperil them, but does often become occasion of intense animosity on part of families.

c. *Endurance and Escape* (vs. 22, 23)

(1) Yet faithfulness to end, even in face of universal

hatred, would issue in complete salvation (v. 22; cf. 24:13, Heb. 11:27).

(2) There is also assurance of limitation to persecution in given place, for disciples were told to flee from it to another (v. 23a).

(3) Then Christ told them they would not have covered whole area of Israel before He should "be come" (v. 23b); and this coming of His has been given various applications:

(a) After sending Twelve on this specific Jewish mission in Palestine, He Himself was going in another direction (cf. 11:1), but would come to these "cities of Israel" as Son of man before close of His ministry.

(b) Or reference might be to Transfiguration, recounted by Luke in chronological sequence in same chapter as Twelve sent forth (cf. Luke 9:1-6, 27-36), for there is no doubt that Transfiguration is elsewhere described by term "coming" (16:28, 2 Pet. 1:16, 17).

(c) There is also sense in which day of Pentecost was His "coming" (cf. John 14:18, 23, 28), but through instrumentality of the Holy Spirit.

(d) Another and more probable explanation is that this mission of Twelve as continuing mission to Israel only was broken off by coming of armies of Titus in A.D. 70 and consequent dispersion of people; disciples would not have gone through whole of Judaea on their missionary work before destruction of Jerusalem and with it the "coming" of the Lord in this particular judgment upon Israel.

(e) This mission, it is said, will be taken up again under similar circumstances just before actual coming of Son of man from heaven; same exhortation, encouragement, and prophecy recurs in 24:13, 14, applicable to Jewish evangelism between our Lord's coming for and with His Church.

(f) But, whatever may be said of reference to coming, there can be no doubt that this particular mission is limited to "cities of Israel"; it has nothing whatever to do with present time, except as similar conditions of acceptance or opposition permit secondary application.

2. *Eventual Experiences* (vs. 24-42)

As noted above, remainder of chapter seems to refer to present age, from A.D. 70 until second coming of Christ. It prepared His followers for many trying experiences that would be encountered:

a. *Reassurances* (vs. 24-31)

(1) Servant is shown to be one with his Master, his mission and teaching regarded as identical with those of his Lord; if, therefore, Master has suffered, much more will household have same experience, be called by some such insulting name as Beelzebub (vs. 24, 25).

(2) But disciples were not to be afraid, for, since everything hidden will be revealed, man will be able to conceal nothing; they in turn were to declare openly and fearlessly what they had been taught by their Master in private (vs. 26, 27).

(3) Further, they were not to be afraid of those who at most could kill only body, but were to fear God whose omnipotence could deal with both soul and body in final judgment (v. 28).

(4) Not only so, but just as not a single sparrow is overlooked by God, so smallest details of their lives claim His consideration; disciples were in perfect safety since, as humblest creature has value in His sight, much more have followers of His Son (vs. 29-31).

b. *Requirements* (vs. 32-39)

(1) This would necessarily involve courage in open confession, and those who thus publicly acknowledged Christ would be rewarded with similar acknowledgment by Him above; while, on other hand, those who were afraid of testifying to their Master now would earn His solemn denial when standing before God (vs. 32, 33).

(2) Courage and cowardice are thus contrasted; Christ is to be confessed by lip and life, but He can also be denied in same twofold way.

N.B. Word "martyr" originally meant simply "witness," idea being testimony by life and by word, though leading sometimes to what we now mean by "martyrdom," witness in death.

(3) Thus, while disciples were to go forth without assurance of success, though with definite anticipation of opposition, they could be certain of God's love and care.

(4) Supreme requirement is faithfulness, and only thing to fear is unfaithfulness; worst efforts of fiercest opponents can do no real harm to Christ's faithful followers, but will be transformed into blessing, here and hereafter.

(5) This thought is developed further by His warning that they would be compelled, by very nature of their message, to set people at variance; while final object of His coming is peace (cf. Luke 2:14), and His gospel is intended to produce peace at last, yet prior to that there would have to be warfare because of natural contest between light and darkness, life and death (v. 34).

(6) Wherever gospel is received by some, it is sure to be rejected by others, even of one's own household (vs. 35, 36); and these statements are the reverse of those in verse 21, constituting one of Christ's most remarkable claims — love supreme over dearest natural affection, implying one due only to God (v. 37; cf. Luke 14:26).

In every heart He wishes to be first;
He therefore keeps the secret key Himself
To open all its chambers, and to bless
With perfect sympathy and holy peace
Each solitary soul which comes to Him.
So when we feel this loneliness, it is
The voice of Jesus saying, "Come to Me";
And every time we are "not understood"

It is a call for us to come again;
For Christ alone can satisfy the soul,
And those who walk with Him from day to day
Can never tread a solitary way.

(7) Further even than this, it would be necessary to face not only suffering, but death itself in order to follow Christ, for taking up of cross indicates readiness to endure to very end (v. 38).

(8) It is important to note that in N.T. word "cross" is always in singular, never in plural; cf. modern usage "crosses" for trials or annoyances, and even for sins or weaknesses, which have nothing to do with Christ's injunction here.*

(9) Again there is call to faithfulness, for he who shrinks from this demand and saves his physical life by unfaithfulness to Christ shall lose true life of his spirit, everything really worth having; while he who loses his life for Christ's sake will find eternal life in its deepest sense (v. 39).

N.B. "Servants for Christ's sake" (2 Cor. 4:5) — service for enlightenment of others; "fools for Christ's sake" (1 Cor. 4:10) — reproach for their edification.

c. *Rewards* (vs. 40-42)

(1) Now our Lord closes His exhortations by emphasizing honor that comes from faithfulness to Him; for he who received disciples would really receive Master, and not only so, but would actually receive God the Father (v. 40).

(2) He who receives minister of Christ because he is such will be suitably rewarded (v. 41); in fact, even least act of Christian love, such as gift of drink of cold water to child, will not go unacknowledged (v. 42).

(3) Description "little ones" indicates children as type of disciples at this time, of undeveloped mind and uncertain strength; "cup of cold water" — finest refreshment is simplest and courtesy one of commonest, yet "cold" water was scarce in Palestine, so it

---

*See following Study, No. 27, p. 150.

could be more trouble than one might think, and yet
possible to most obscure (cf. 1 Cor. 16:17).

(4) When we are ruled by personal love for our Master
we shall show affectionate hospitality to humblest of
His servants; and most trifling gift prompted by
such love is not forgotten of God.

Thus we see that in the service of Christ it is well we should
know beforehand what we are to expect. Yet, in spite of every
difficulty and danger, His "service is perfect freedom." Behind
the Master who commissions us is our Father in heaven and, as
St. Paul says, "a crown of righteousness, which the Lord,
the righteous judge, shall give" to those who "have kept the
faith" (2 Tim. 4:8).

Conclusion

Of the three methods of ministry adopted by our Lord while
on earth — preaching, miracle-working, and the training of
the Twelve — the last was the most important. This was
because their work was intended to be permanent, continuing
long after Christ Himself had returned to heaven, and being
self-perpetuating until He came again. This chapter is an
important reminder of the true place and power of the Christian worker, telling him of his potentialities and responsibilities:

1. *There Is a Work To Be Done*

   a. Christ is the Lord of the harvest.

   b. Fields of harvest are white with grain ready to be
   gathered in.

2. *There Are Men To Be Trained*

   a. Laborers are few, therefore important.

   b. They are wonderfully different, showing there is room
   for all; and yet they have real unity of purpose.

3. *There Is a Message To Be Delivered*

   a. Apostles preached coming of Kingdom of Heaven.

   b. This means for us today Christ as Lord of human life.

4. *There Were Instructions To Be Given*

   These may be summed up in two commands:

   a. "Fear not" — apostles were not to be afraid of hostility, but were to declare Divine message with courage and confidence;

b. "Care not" — in all difficulties they were to be without anxiety, being certain their Master would watch over them.

5. *There Was a Power To Be Provided*

a. This would be a gift of the Holy Spirit.

b. It was He who would enable them to do what their Master commanded.

Circumstances change, and generations of workers come and go; but these same principles of Christian service are applicable to us who are in the true "apostolic succession."

27

THE DISCIPLE AND HIS CROSS

Matthew 10:38

To the Christian of today the word "cross" is an exceedingly familiar one; indeed, it is representative of the very heart of Christianity. It comes almost as a shock, therefore, to find not only that this is the first recorded time the word was used by our Lord, but that it is the first appearance of it in all of the Scriptures. In the Gospels the word "cross" is used in two related senses, and it is noteworthy that all usages in the first sense appear before the initial usage in the second sense. Four more times we read that Christ exhorted His disciples each to take up his cross (three parallel passages: 16:24, Mark 8:34, Luke 9:23; and in Luke 14:27); and it is recorded once that He told the rich young ruler he should do the same (Mark 10:21). After these appearances of the word it is used solely, but many times over, of Christ's own cross, the instrument by which His death was brought about. The second of these connotations sheds light for us on the first, and yet, we venture to affirm, there is too often a confusion of terms. What did this word "cross" in its first sense mean to the disciples as they received their commission, with no knowledge at all as yet of the cross of Christ on Calvary and its deep significance? What was it intended to mean? When Christ spoke of taking up and bearing a cross, was it what we are apt to mean today when we speak of "cross-bearing"?

I. The Grammatical Form

1. In these passages word "cross" is always in singular, never in plural; each disciple has only one, and it is his own.
2. In modern speech, word is often in plural, e.g., "We all have crosses to bear"; and sometimes "little crosses of every day" and similar phrases are used.

II. The Original Connotation

1. Cross to Jew was solely Roman instrument of execution, so that fundamental idea connected with it is that of death, not of mere suffering or sorrow, and it was usually carried by criminal himself to place of execution (cf. John 19:17); thus our Lord's reference seems almost certainly to have been first hint to disciples of death He was about to die, though they could not yet grasp it.
2. Today, cross in this sense is apt to mean trial, burden, opposition, anything that thwarts; it is sometimes used even of "besetting sins" of so-called minor nature, such as temper, laziness, selfishness, sharpness, etc.

   Illus.: Principal James Denney tells how John Wesley once called on a gentleman who rang for a servant to put coals on the fire. The servant threw them on carelessly, so that a puff of smoke was blown out into the room. "Ah, Mr. Wesley," said his host, "these are the crosses we have to bear." "It is hardly exaggerating," adds Principal Denney, "to say that many people use the solemn designation in the same unfeeling and unintelligent fashion."

III. The Personal Use

1. The pronoun "his" is used five times in speaking of this "cross"; the sixth time it is even more emphatically described as "his own" (Luke 14:27, Greek).
2. Today, we frequently hear word used impersonally, e.g., "the crosses of this life."

IV. The Connected Actions

1. Evangelists use three different Greek verbs in this connection: "take," in sense of "receive, accept" (here); "take up," in

sense of "lift" (16:24, Mark 8:34, 10:21, Luke 9:23); and "bear," in sense of "carry" (Luke 14:27); they also employ two tenses: present, for verbs "take" and "carry," but aorist for verb "lift."

2. Modern usage is meager in comparison, for we are apt to hear only of "bearing" of cross, in sense of "enduring," even sometimes in grudging fashion.

V. The Spiritual Significance

1. We are now ready to venture paraphrase of these N.T. injunctions, so as to try to enter into deep meaning of entire concept: Our Lord was saying to each disciple, "Receive from Me your own cross which you, having lifted it, must continue to carry as you follow Me."

2. This was nothing short of full surrender — life made ready for Christ and placed unreservedly at His disposal; it was a complete agreement that His cause was something to live for or to die for, and that it might entail suffering, either by "sentence of death," as Dr. Woods Smythe put it, or by lifelong identification with Christ, the being "crucified" that is so prominent in writings of St. Paul (e.g., Gal. 2:20).

3. Indeed, as our Lord went towards Calvary, He was bearing His cross, metaphorically first and then literally, and it was appropriate He should direct those who wished to follow Him to do likewise; actually, it was impossible for them to follow Him at that time without so doing.

4. But when once our Lord was crucified He was no longer "bearing His cross" (John 19:17), and in same way it is now, strictly speaking, impossible for us to bear our cross; instead, we are "crucified with Christ" (Gal. 2:20; cf. Rom. 6:6, 11; 14:8; 1 Cor. 15:31; 2 Cor. 6:9; Gal. 5:24, 6:14).

5. But even if we allow phrase "bearing the cross" to apply to present-day experience, it must mean same to us as it meant to Christ, namely, crucifixion of self-life and death unto sin; above all, however, we can now see we must entirely avoid speaking of any personal tendency like temper or despondency in this manner, for such is not a cross, but a sin.

Conclusion

Let us of today, then, get back to the New Testament! To sum up its teaching on this subject, we can do no better than quote further from Principal Denney:

"In the lips of Jesus the word is quite unambiguous. The cross is a cross, and nothing else. There is only one for each person, and it is his own. The only use of a cross is crucifixion. It is that on which a man dies a violent and humiliating death.

"In Christ's conception the Christian is a man with something to die for; and to bear his cross daily signifies that he is ready to die for it all the time. The man who has nothing he would die for has nothing to live for: he does not know what life is.

"The ideal disciple is the martyr, and the glory of the Christian religion is the noble army of those who have died for it, from the Prince of martyrs down. Martyrdom may be life-long, or it may be consummated in an instant, but in every case it is the essence of Christianity."

28

CHRIST, THE GREAT TEACHER

Matthew 11:1-30

THE DEVELOPMENT of Matthew's narrative at this point is very significant. Christ's teaching as to the spiritual nature of the Kingdom was leading to doubt and to opposition. It has been helpfully pointed out that this chapter records four classes of those who revealed some definite attitude both towards Christ as Messiah and towards His teaching about the Kingdom. In line with Matthew's purpose in writing this Gospel, he groups certain events together, as compared with Luke's chronological account of the same period (cf. Luke 7:18-35; 10:13-15, 21, 22).

I. The Perplexed (vs. 1-15)

First class of people was represented by John the Baptist whom Herod Antipas had by this time imprisoned; and there were doubtless many other earnest folk who simply could not understand what was taking place.

1. *The Great Teacher Answers a Question* (vs. 1-6)
   a. *The Question* (vs. 1-3)
      (1) Some think loneliness and depression of prison life had led John to waver, while others think he sent message to Christ not for himself, but to establish faith of his two disciples (v. 2).
      (2) But whole story shows it was John himself who prompted inquiry, because not only is answer addressed to him, but subsequent references to multitudes (vs. 5, 6) apply only to him who was not present.
      (3) In his depression he may have expected some other manifestation of Messiahship, especially as he had proclaimed coming of a stern, severe Messiah who would judge and punish evil, and he had spoken about use of "axe" and "fire" (cf. 3:10-12).
      (4) When John heard of Jesus Christ doing nothing of this sort, but going about healing, cheering, and blessing people, he seems to have wondered whether, after all, this was the predicted Messiah or whether there might not be two Messiahs (v. 3).
      (5) Perhaps John was puzzled by absence of action that would have indicated severity and wrath like that of Elijah, instead of beneficent, genial work of Elisha; as representative of law, John may also have thought of lightning, or thunder, or fire from heaven, as at Sinai, and have been unable to understand gentleness manifested by Christ.
   b. *The Reply* (vs. 4-6)
      (1) Our Lord then sent messengers back with fresh revelation of His beneficence, reminding John the Baptist of other characteristics of Messiah and using language similar to Isaiah's in 35:5, 6 and 61: 1, 2; His works of love were true signs of Messiahship and His miracles emblems of spiritual deliverance, thereby clearly suggesting fulfillment of prophecy (vs. 4, 5).
      (2) Then Christ gave John beautiful but searching message (v. 6), telling him that man is blessed who is

not disturbed by God's infinite patience with world, His delay of judgment, and His methods of bringing blessing to mankind; to paraphrase, "Happy is he who is not caused to stumble by the way I am doing My work" — or, as C. G. Moore phrased it, "the blessedness of the unoffended" (cf. John 16:1).

(3) Hitherto, Christ had avoided publicly taking name Messiah; even now He appealed to works that John ought to recognize as Messianic without open avowal of Messiahship.

(4) Christ is still vindicated to mankind by what He does: spiritually blind, lame, leprous, deaf, and dead are continually being dealt with and blessed; and those who realize what He came to be and to do will never be "upset" if these tokens of His power are all they are at present permitted to see.

2. *The Great Teacher Asks a Question* (vs. 7-10)

It was necessary to protect John the Baptist from any wrong impression given people, either that he was lacking in faith or was being slighted; and so, immediately after departure of John's disciples, Christ vindicates His forerunner and praises him in the hearing of others by asking same question three times, "What went ye out to see?" (vs. 7, 8, 9), and by giving three different answers:

a. John was no "reed shaken by the wind" (v. 7), for he had not really wavered in his faith, nor would he.

b. John was not among those who, probably like Herod's courtiers, were living luxurious or effeminate lives typified by "soft raiment" (v. 8; cf. 3:4).

c. John was not only a prophet, but "more than a prophet" (v. 9); he was a Divine messenger (v. 10; cf. Isa. 40:3, Mal. 3:1).

3. *The Great Teacher Praises the Questioner* (vs. 11-15)

a. *John the Baptist Was Personally Great* (v. 11a)

(1) He wrote no book, founded no kingdom, led no army, "did no miracle" (John 10:41); yet Christ states that no one up to time of His coming had been greater among men because, in preparing way for

Messiah, he represented highest point of old covenant (cf. v. 13).

(2) Personally John was characterized by outstanding loyalty, unselfishness, humility, truthfulness, and fearlessness; literally, as prophesied before his birth, he is thus seen to be "great in the sight of the Lord" (Luke 1:15).

(3) John had heralded Jesus; and now Jesus was honoring John.

b. *John the Baptist Was Spiritually Significant* (vs. 11b, 12)

(1) Yet, with all his attainments, he enjoyed fewer privileges than any of Christ's immediate disciples; and there is sense in which even one occupying humble place within Kingdom of Heaven might be regarded as greater than John, with respect to faith, knowledge, and spiritual life (v. 11b).

(2) At any rate, it is clear that, not being actually inside Kingdom that Christ was then proclaiming and would one day set up, John could not possibly possess during his lifetime personal experience of our Lord's atoning death and glorious resurrection that even least in new covenant would enjoy; and thus our Lord was pointing out to His disciples what privileges were being afforded in enjoyment of greater knowledge, fuller opportunities, and higher hopes by reason of His own presence in their midst. *N.B. Contra:* It is interesting and suggestive, however, to note that Dr. Hugh McNeile in his volume *The Church and the Churches* argues against use of interpretation as to least N.T. saint being superior to John the Baptist. By calling attention to Greek phrase, literally, "he that is lesser" (cf. A.S.V. marg.) — not, as in K.J.V., "he that is least" — he maintains distinction is not between John and least N.T. saint, but between John and Jesus. Quoting John 1:26-30 and 3:30, McNeile points out that at that time in the Kingdom so understood Christ was in many respects "lesser" than John. He was being "despised and rejected" (Isa. 53:3) according to prophecy, while John was widely held as a "burning and a shining light" (John 5:35ff.); yet He who in

opening of dispensation was thus lesser than John was in reality greater than he. We must hasten to add that novelty of this interpretation naturally causes hesitation about accepting it; but certainly word "lesser," comparative of adjective, not superlative, has always been obstacle in way of usual interpretation.

(3) Next, Christ told people something of what had been happening from time John had commenced his ministry: Kingdom was being associated with violence (v. 12).

(4) It is sometimes thought that verse refers to advancement of Kingdom by violent means, such as by multitudes who thronged our Lord and would have made Him king by force (cf. John 6:15); but this does not seem true either to Greek words or to actual circumstances of Christ's life.

(5) If verb form could be rendered "useth violence," words could mean Kingdom is no quiet, secret thing, but a force publicly manifested that stirs men's minds, and that in turn those who are stirred gain it (cf. Luke 16:16); but it seems more probable it refers to those who are determined to lay violent hands on Kingdom and shape it according to own ideas.

(6) It has also been thought that, this verse being continuation of His eulogy of Baptist, our Lord is clearly characterizing John's work and testifying to its remarkable results in stirring Jewish people.

c. *John the Baptist Was Prophetically Important* (vs. 13-15)

(1) Our Lord goes on to state prophets had been prophesying all along until time of John and that, if only true significance could be grasped, he was in reality that Elijah announced ages before (vs. 13, 14; cf. Mal. 4:5, Luke 1:17).

(2) This is perhaps instance of double fulfillment of prophecy for, while John was metaphorically that Elijah of whom Malachi had spoken, it is probable that Elijah is still to appear literally before our Lord

comes again (cf. 17:10-13, Mark 9:11-12, Rev. 11:3-6).

(3) Very appropriately this testimony to multitudes about John is closed by solemn words (v. 15), proverbial expression emphasizing need of careful attention (cf. 13:9, 43; Rev. 2:7; etc.).

II. The Unreasonable (vs. 16-19)

This is second class of people revealing attitude towards Christ and His teaching at this time.

1. *The Illustration* (vs. 16, 17)

   a. Christ referred to them as "this generation" (v. 16a) — those listening to Him whom He had just characterized as "the violent" (v. 12), men at variance with His revelation of Kingdom who are determined to lay rough hands on it and shape it according to their own ideas.

   b. Illustration is of oriental game, with two groups of children, one representing first joyous and then sad scene, while other group refuses to play any game at all (vs. 16b, 17).

2. *The Application* (vs. 18, 19)

   a. Christ describes these people in relation, first to John, reminding them of way they had treated him, and then to Himself, showing they were no more satisfied with Him; and He declared they would accept neither severity and asceticism of Baptist as typified by fasting (v. 18), nor His own graciousness and sociability as typified by recent appearance at Matthew's feast (v. 19a; cf. 9:10, 11).

   b. Determined to have their own way, they would not repent with John nor rejoice with Christ — attitude with serious implications because it entirely fails to appreciate spiritual values.

   c. Yet these contradictory decisions and unreasonable criticisms actually confuted each other and thus confirmed God's wisdom in choosing His messengers and methods (v. 19b; cf. 1 Cor. 1:18-31); His truth, indeed, always justifies itself, whatever man's attitude towards it.

III. The Impenitent (vs. 20-24)

Then follows warning to third class of people, deliberate unbelievers in Christ and His teaching:

1. *Denunciation* (vs. 20-22)

   a. Attitude of unreasonable opposition led Christ to speak of other places where important work had been done (v. 20; cf. v. 1), but which remained unmoved by His presence and power.

   b. Allusion to Chorazin (v. 21), of which we know nothing more in connection with Christ, shows much of His work was done without being recorded in Gospels (cf. John 21:25); and Bethsaida is mentioned elsewhere only casually.

   c. Yet they are said by our Lord to be infinitely more guilty than Tyre and Sidon, Syrian cities to north, because they "repented not" (v. 20); this attitude may have been one of deliberate rejection, or simply one of apathy, which is often found most widely among people who have lived longest in light of gospel.

2. *Degradation* (vs. 23, 24)

   a. Spiritual eminence of Capernaum (v. 23), where, we are told, "he came and dwelt" (4:13), is implied by means of Christ's presence there on several occasions (e.g., 8:5, 17:24, John 6:59); and it is contrasted with terrible punishment that would come through neglect of such great privileges.

   b. It is solemn thought that there will be different degrees of punishment according to measure of opportunities enjoyed; and it is impressive that names and ruins of these three cities so entirely disappeared that even their location has been a matter for dispute, even as of Sodom (v. 24; cf. 10:15; Gen. 19:24, 25, 28).

   c. Thus prediction of Christ has already been literally fulfilled, to say nothing of spiritual fulfillment yet awaiting these people at day of judgment; guilt of those who despise spiritual opportunities is at once great and sad, and sometimes people and places enjoying most gracious visitations of God become most barren (cf. John 12:48, 2 Pet. 2:21). *N.B.* It has been well said: "The brighter the summer day the louder the thunderstorm; the greater grace the heavier the judgment."

IV. The Spiritually Sensitive (vs. 25-30)

Contrast between denunciation of cities of Galilee and this wonderful passage is most striking. From fearful thought of dishonor cast upon Him by them, Christ speaks in blessed consciousness of what His Father is to Him and He to His Father; and so fourth class of people mentioned in this chapter is that of spiritually receptive ones ready to respond to such a Divine revelation as this deep teaching.

1. *Their Relationship to God the Father* (vs. 25-27)

   a. Here Jesus turns from crowd and addresses His Father, thanking Him for revealing spiritual truth to "babes" — those humble enough to be willing to accept it, in opposition to "the wise and understanding" (v. 25, A.S.V.), i.e., those who thought themselves to be such, notably Pharisees whom pride prevented from receiving God's truth.

   N.B. Cf. two other times when Christ expressed thankfulness: for nourishment of physical life (John 6:11); for impending victory of life over death (John 11:41). Here it is for imparting of spiritual life to humble folk. This is also one of passages where Christ said "yes" to His Father ("yea, Father," v. 26, A.S.V.; Luke 10:21), assenting to and confirming Divine will and plan — standard for man's obedient response (cf. 9:28, 13:51, 15:27; John 11:27, 21:15; Rev. 16:7, 22:20).

   b. Then comes remarkable claim on part of Christ (v. 27); there is nothing more striking than this in any of Gospels, for it states in plainest terms absolute uniqueness of Christ in relation to the Father.

   c. Their mutual knowledge is suggested as secret of our Lord's triumph over such obstacles as doubt (cf. vs. 2-6) and disappointment (cf. vs. 20-24); and this prepares us to share it by means of His offer of perfect rest in following verses (cf. vs. 28-30).

   d. It is also stated that only through God the Son can "any man" enter into knowledge of God, the Father's revelation of Himself; and it is implied such a one must be among "babes" (v. 23) — those who are both humble and teachable.

2. *Their Relationship to God the Son* (vs. 28-30)

There very beautifully follows His appeal to them; it is because "all things have been delivered" to Christ by His Father that He is able to issue it. They are to "come" to Him, "take" His yoke, and "learn" of Him, entering thus into His promise of twofold rest:

a. *The Rest That Christ Gives* — "I will give you rest" (v. 28)*

   (1) In light of apostolic teaching (e.g., Heb. 3:7 to 4:11), this stands for salvation; and it becomes possible, of course, solely in relation to Christ.

   (2) Invitation "Come unto me" as Saviour is second of four found in Gospels: "Learn of me" (v. 29) as Teacher; "Follow me" as Master (4:19, etc.); "Abide in me" as Life (John 15:4).

b. *The Rest That Is Found* — "ye shall *find* rest unto your souls" (vs. 29, 30)

   (1) This surely represents what is known later as sanctification (e.g., 1 Cor. 1:30), and it is found solely in fellowship with Christ, through taking His "yoke" — Jewish figure for participation — and coming to "learn" of Him — accepting His instruction; thus our Lord does not promise freedom from toil but, rather, rest of soul in midst of toil.

   (2) His "burden" represents those things that He Himself places upon us, according to His perfect plan for us, in contrast to "labor" and "heavy" loads of previous experience (cf. v. 28); and this may also be contrasted with "tribulation" (John 16:33, Acts 14:22), or that which comes from men, though permitted by Him.

   (3) When this is fully realized, "yoke" of Christ does indeed prove "easy," and His "burden" assuredly is experienced as "light" (v. 30; cf. John 15:5, Phil. 4:13).

   Illus.: Mark Guy Pearse, after preaching on this

---

*For fuller treatment of this verse, see following Study, No. 29, p. 163.

text, was told by farmer's son that his father's yokes were always made heavier on one side than on the other, the light end being intended for a weaker bullock and the heavy one for a beast that was stronger. "That's why," concluded the young man firmly, "the Lord's yoke is easy and His burden light — the heavy end is upon *His* shoulder!"

> *"God doth not need*
> *Either man's work or his own gifts. Who best*
> *Bear His mild yoke, they serve Him best."*
>
> JOHN MILTON

This twofold rest satisfies the conscience with its realization of sin, the intellect in its search after truth, the heart with its tides of emotion, and the will with its consciousness of weakness. To quote the well-known words of St. Augustine: "Thou hast made us for Thyself and our hearts are restless until they rest in Thee."

Conclusion

If we might choose one attribute that this chapter suggests as a characterization for the true child of God, it might perhaps be teachableness, docility, tractability. This thought leads us back to the consideration of Christ as the Great Teacher, a description of Him very prominent in the Gospels, and leads us to note:

1. *The Features of Christ's Teaching*
   a. Graciousness (cf. Luke 4:22);
   b. Authority (cf. 7:29);
   c. Boldness (cf. John 7:26);
   d. Power (cf. Luke 4:32); and —
   e. Uniqueness (cf. John 7:46).

2. *The Message of Christ's Teaching*
   This included the Kingdom of God and the Fatherhood of God, both invariably associated with —
   a. Forgiveness of sin (cf. 9:2, 13);
   b. Power of grace (cf. Luke 19:10); and —
   c. Value of life (cf. 12:12).

3. *The Power of Christ's Teaching*

This is found to be in His Person and claim, for at every stage His teaching is a revelation of the Godhead:

a. As the Divine Prophet He revealed God to man (cf. Deut. 18:15-19; Acts 3:22, 23);

b. As the Divine Priest, He redeemed man to God (cf. Ps. 110:4; Heb. 7:17-28; 9:11-15);

c. As the Divine King, He came to rule mankind for God (cf. Ps. 2:6; 45:1-17; Heb. 1:8, 9).

Thus, it is impossible to accept Christ's teaching without accepting Himself and acknowledging His claim; that is, the gospel that He Himself *is* transcends anything He taught during His ministry on earth. A great scholar once said that the secret of learning is "to ask much, to remember much, and to teach much." Therefore, let us ask much of Christ with alertness and receptivity; let us remember much of Christ by the illumination of His Word by the Holy Spirit; and let us teach much of Christ, for knowing increases by telling and growth by impartation to others.

29

REST*

Matthew 11:28

THE SCENE of Gustave Doré's last great picture, "The Vale of Tears," is laid in a deep valley between high, steep hills. The light is dim, for the day seems drawing to a close. At the end of the valley, in the foreground of the picture, is a crowd of men and women of almost every class and station. Here is the monarch whose aspect tells how uneasy lies the head that wears a crown. There are the statesman and warrior, weary in their country's service. There are the outcast and the respectable, the sick and the whole, the aged ones bent with years, and the children of all ages, even to the sleeping babe on the breast of its

---

* Ed. Note: It may be of interest to note that this sermon in its original form was first preached in 1890, when the preacher's age was 29. It has not been materially changed.

worn, anxious mother. At the farther end of the valley can be seen, spanning the sky, a rainbow of hope, and under it the meek form of the Son of Man, bearing His cross and with beckoning hand inviting all to come to Him. The whole picture is intended to be an illustration of our text, "Come unto me, all ye that labor and are heavy laden, and I will give you rest."

Rest! Rest for the weary and heavy-laden! Rest through the Rest-Giver! That is the welcome news of the gospel. Long ages before Jesus of Nazareth came, one of His progenitors uttered some mysterious words: "The sceptre shall not depart from Judah, nor a lawgiver from between his feet, until Shiloh come; and unto him shall the gathering of the people be" (Gen. 49:10). The word "Shiloh" in this reference to the coming Messiah means "Rest-Giver." It shows how the patriarch Jacob in his old age had grasped one of the most beautiful aspects of our Lord's work. Earlier still, amid the sin and corruption of the antediluvian world, two parents had given their child the name of Noah, "Rest," evidently hoping that in him mankind might find some measure of physical stability. But that hope was vain, for the Deluge came. David in bitterness of soul cried out, "Oh, that I had wings like a dove! for then would I fly away, and be at rest" (Ps. 55:6). His aspiration, too, like that of Noah's dove (cf. Gen. 8:9), was at that time of no avail. But when, in the fullness of time, Shiloh, the Rest-Giver, appeared, the "gathering of the people" to Him as prophesied by Jacob was inspired by His own blessed invitation, "Come!"

Some modern thinkers, however, have denied that when Christ offered rest He was dealing with one of the more vital needs of humanity. What great man, they asked, who is seeking human allegiance or offering humanity service has failed to promise food, wealth, health, strength, security, glory? Was Jesus mistaken in what people needed? On the contrary, there is today less doubt than ever that Christ was referring to one of the greatest necessities of human life when He spoke of rest. Man either craves it, or, if he does not actually crave it, his life indicates an unconscious but none the less real need of it.

I. A Characterization — "all ye that labor and are heavy laden"

   1. *"Labor"*

      W. C. Dix's well-known hymn inspired by this text is

"Come Unto Me, Ye Weary," reminding us that Matthew's word for "labor" is exactly the same as one used by John — "Jesus being *wearied* with his journey" (John 4:6). What is referred to, of course, is weariness through labor; there are many forms of it, physical, mental, spiritual, such as —

a. *Weariness in Service of World*

    (1) Much work of this kind may be good as far as it goes, e.g., invention, discovery, legislation, politics, even philanthropy; yet it does not fully satisfy.

    (2) Use of physical energy or mental powers, or both, in unworthy causes can, of course, bring unrest of soul.

b. *Weariness in Service of Formal Religion*

    (1) Some men, in striving to get right with God and to work themselves into His favor, preach not His gospel but gospel of human endeavor — so much work for so much blessing, with only faint hope at last; but this does not solve problem of sin, and weariness can become veritable disease whose roots are left untouched.

    (2) Others, trained from childhood to churchgoing, even to Christian work, and surrounded by spiritual influences, know nevertheless, if they take time to think, that all is not right; and their souls are not at rest.

c. *Weariness in Service of Satan*

    (1) There are those who, by means of gross sins such as violence, drunkenness, infidelity, serve one who always pays wages in unrest, and finally rewards in coin of death.

    (2) Less offensive but equally deadly are selfishness, indifference to God, pride — of race, of face, of place — all wearying to soul of man.

d. *Weariness in Service of Self*

    (1) This is in some respects worse slavery of all, because continuous — thinking only of honor, ease, ambition, enjoyment, living for man's own ends; and these are not rest and peace.

    (2) In many cases, such service is merely putting first what should be second — tradition, livelihood, family;

but even so, it brings no satisfaction to man's soul, for "better" is indeed, too often, enemy of "best."

2. *"Heavy Laden"*

Many voices today offer to satisfy craving of man for rest, but all fail by being artificial and temporary. Man must have rest that is both real and abiding, meeting each part of his complex nature and able to survive all upheavals of life. He is "heavy laden" in fourfold way, or —

a. *Weighed Down in Mind*

(1) To be thus demands rest from anxiety, despondency, worry, despair, fear of future.

(2) To be thus is often to be besieged by doubt, difficulties, questionings, baffling problems.

b. *Weighed Down in Heart*

(1) To be thus needs rest from aimless toiling, rush of circumstances, defeats, disappointments, misunderstandings.

(2) It also needs relief from emptiness of life, bereavements, losses, failures, lack of love.

c. *Weighed Down in Conscience*

(1) To be thus needs rest from guilt, burden and bondage of sin, pressure that cannot long be resisted.

(2) To be thus is to battle with temptations, conflicts, weaknesses, fears.

d. *Weighed Down in Will*

(1) To be thus cries out for rest as it faces weakness of its efforts and weariness of its condition after struggling with forces of evil.

(2) Hard-pressed in past, it fears being mastered again with recurrence of besetting sins.

Yes, man's whole personality feels deep need of rest, surrounded as it is with unutterable sadness and with sense of solitariness even in midst of life's most crowded ways.

II. An Affirmation — "I will give you rest"

To all such weary, burdened ones comes our Lord's tender voice with —

1. *A Promise*
   a. *It Is Divine* — "I"
      (1) His is greatest possible power, will, right to respond.
      (2) His is unique, exact knowledge of need and how to supply it, filling void as ocean does coves of its shore.

   b. *It Is Faithful* — "will"
      (1) He brings sense of certainty, for He never yet broke His word.
      (2) His very presence causes great calm of spirit.

   c. *It Is Free* — "give"
      (1) He gives, not sells, not barters — His rest is *gratis,* i.e., through grace.
      (2) It is given, not merely shown or told — it is His possession to be shared.

   d. *It Is Personal* — "you"
      (1) It is appropriated by accepting and wearing Christ's yoke of shared obedience (vs. 29, 30).
      (2) It is associated with individual belief and trust (cf. Heb. 4:3).

2. *A Blessing*
   Philosophy and ethics, ideals and principles, all are important, but powerless to meet persistent, clamant demands of man's life; in Christ, however, all he desires is found in abundance, and fourfold need is met in way that satisfies every craving:

   a. *Rest of Conscience* — by mercy and righteousness of God, through pardon and assurance, freedom from penalty and power of sin (cf. Isa. 44:22, Rom. 8:1); forgiving grace of Christ flows into soul and brings "peace as a river" (Isa. 48:18).

   b. *Rest of heart* — in reception and possession of love of God — past (cf. Gal. 2:20), present (cf. Rev. 1:5, A.S.V.), and future (cf. Rom. 8:35) — and realization of Divine presence (cf. Exod. 33:14).

   c. *Rest of Mind* — through instruction and establishment by truth of God, resolving difficulties and assuring of His providences, that man may rest satisfied until all things are made clear (cf. Rom. 8:28, 1 Cor. 13:12).

d. *Rest of Will* — through control of God, to which it freely responds in obedience, and through energizing that is experienced in consecration to Christ (cf. Jer. 6:16, Heb. 4:10).

Yes, rest for man's soul is made possible by close fellowship with Christ, who would be Companion as well as Master of all mankind.

III. An Invitation — "Come unto me"

How is such a rest as this possible and available? Just by accepting an invitation:

1. *"Come"*

   a. We must heed, not shut ears, for it is Christ Himself who issues it.

   b. We must accept, not decline, for surely we are convinced that He means it.

   c. We must surrender, not merely accede, for He wants heart to yield as well as mind to assent.

   d. We must obey, not rebel, for then whole nature will follow and accept His will for it.

2. *"Unto Me"*

   a. This rest is not in circumstances, for they change.

   b. It is not in inaction, for man may be as busy as ever.

   c. It is not in heaven, though there is rest there; this rest is present, and only those who find it here and now will find it there and then, full, blessed, glorious.

   d. It is in a Person, the Person of Christ, for true rest is possible for us who are persons only in One who is Himself a Person; nothing short of personality will satisfy personality.

   N.B. As someone has written, "God's goodness to man flowed through One intensely human yet gloriously Divine, into whose arms the children crept, whose bosom from mortal clay was made, who hungered, thirsted, sorrowed, wept; and yet whose heart was the heart of God."

Therefore: Come as you are! Come all! Come now!

Conclusion

The prophet wrote long ago: "This is the rest wherewith ye may cause the weary to rest; and this is the refreshing" (Isa. 28:12); "In returning and rest shall ye be saved" (Isa. 30:15). That which has been called "the sabbath of the soul" (cf. Heb. 4:9, 10) is thus —

1. A blessed reality;
2. A genuine power;
3. A strong incentive; and —
4. A constant satisfaction.

It will enable the soul to face fearlessly all the emergencies of life because of its possession of a living Saviour and Friend, and to look forward with confidence to the crown of it all, the eternal rest of the heavenly country hereafter.

30

MOUNTING OPPOSITION

Matthew 12:1-50

It was not long before our Lord's preaching in Galilee aroused violent opposition. His ministry in both word and work compelled people to take sides either for or against Him. Again we may note that while Luke gives the chronological data that enable us to see where certain events are to be placed within this period (cf. Luke 6:1-11; 11:14-26, 29-32), Matthew, in accordance with his particular purpose, groups them together to show the development of the hostility consequent upon Christ's claim to be the King of the Jews. The present chapter gives some striking illustrations of the way in which both enemies and friends misunderstood and opposed Him.

I. Opposition from Malicious Foes (vs. 1-45)

A. Opposition Over the Sabbath (vs. 1-21)

1. *The Cause* (vs. 1-5)

a. At first sight it seems strange that Christ's teaching on Sabbath should excite such strong feeling, when He seemed not only to be correcting errors, but also relieving Jews of burdensome restrictions illegally placed on them.

b. Sabbath-keeping was marked at that time by much formality and very little spirituality; Fourth Commandment was interpreted in ways well-nigh intolerable, and it was these abuses that our Lord opposed.

c. Plucking of ears of grain (v. 1) was in itself no crime (cf. Deut. 23:25), but Pharisees wrongfully regarded it on this occasion as breach of Sabbath law, as though such action, prompted by cravings of hunger, could be fairly considered harvest work (v. 2).

d. Christ quickly reminded them of two passages they ought to have known from their own Scriptures:

   (1) I Samuel 21:1-6 (vs. 3, 4), where David *ate* on Sabbath (cf. v. 6 — "shewbread . . . taken . . . to put hot bread in the day when it was taken away" — i.e., Sabbath; cf. Lev. 24:8) ; and —

   (2) Numbers 28:9, 10 (v. 5), where priests in temple *worked* on Sabbath in course of their daily duties; thus, if all work on Sabbath was profanation, as Pharisees insisted, priests would have been continually guilty.

e. Our Lord thus showed that, while Fourth Commandment was binding, there was greater principle of human necessity making lawful certain activities on Sabbath; and, in light of that principle, there was no essential difference between disciples' ears of corn and David's shewbread.

f. We often speak of "works of necessity and mercy" (phrase derived from Westminster Confession) in our Christian observance of the Lord's Day, such as —

   (1) Sustaining life;
   (2) Serving the Lord; and —
   (3) Saving the lost.

g. Teaching about Sabbath was thus *occasion* of opposition, but we may be sure *cause* was far deeper one, or anger of Jews would not have been aroused; so next we see —

2. *The Claim* (vs. 6-8)

This was twofold:

a. Christ claimed to be "greater than the temple" (v. 6)
just mentioned (v. 5), and thus could authorize His
disciples to do what they had done; further (v. 7),
He reminded Pharisees of another statement in their
Scriptures about "mercy, and not sacrifice" (Hosea
6:6), and applied it to them.

N.B. Cf. "greater than Jonah" (v. 41); "greater than
Solomon" (v. 42); "greater than our father Abraham"
(John 8:53ff.); "greater than our father Jacob" (John
4:12ff.); "greater . . . than he that is in the world"
(1 John 4:4).

b. Christ also claimed to be "Lord even of the sabbath day"
(v. 8); and therefore He could give instructions as to
its observance:

(1) Since Sabbath was instituted for benefit of man,
and not man created in order to keep Sabbath (cf.
Mark 2:27), Son of man, as Head of humanity,
had authority over this institution; by calling Himself Lord of Sabbath, therefore, He claimed this
authority, which warranted what His disciples had
done.

(2) It is significant that this claim to Lordship of
Sabbath was made just when ceremonial and legal
part of Mosaic dispensation was coming to an end;
and this indicated Christ's Lordship did not mean
abolition, but only proper interpretation and even
transformation.

(3) He thus applied to it His own authority and, at
same time, spirit of liberty that was to be characteristic of new dispensation.

c. We thus see that in this twofold claim, to be greater
than temple and Lord of Sabbath, Christ was stating
that, as Son of man, He knew what was best for man
and, as Messiah, He represented Divine authority;
further, He was placing Himself on equality with
God and asserting that Jewish people were His people.

d. It was this beyond all else that aroused opposition of
Jewish authorities, because they recognized that in ad-

mitting this claim they would have to recognize Jesus as Messiah (cf. John 5:18, 10:30-33).

3. *The Cure* (vs. 9-14)

a. This incident was another illustration of same principle, leading to still more intense opposition on part of Pharisees; it probably took place on very next Sabbath (v. 9; cf. Luke 6:6-11), when man was in synagogue with hand shriveled and probably paralyzed (cf. 1 Kings 13:4).

b. According to some writers, healing was prohibited on Sabbath at that time, except when life was in danger; but, whether this was so or not, Jews raised question in order, if possible, to entrap Christ, evidently expecting answer enabling them to charge Him before local judges with violation of Sabbath (v. 10).

c. To this He replied with two other questions, appealing to their compassion in regard to plight of animal fallen into pit on Sabbath (v. 11), and urging that man is better than sheep (v. 12); and He added that, on this account, it is lawful to do good on Sabbath day.

d. Christ's command to man with withered hand (v. 13) is most interesting; when he was bidden to stretch forth his hand he had nothing to go by but this unexpected direction with its implied promise, for there is no reason to think that any sensation of life or power came with actual order.

e. Purely by faith in response to Christ, and instead of waiting for anything further, he simply did what Christ told him; and in honoring Christ by this act he obtained power for blessing of healing, and also, by stretching forth his hand in obedience, defied authority of Pharisees and acknowledged that of Jesus Christ.

f. All of this emphasized place and importance of Sabbath principle, now exemplified by what we call the Lord's Day;

N.B. One writer puts it usefully thus: "it (the Sabbath) was 'made for man' — for man as God made him. The Son of man, in whom God's aims for man are realized, moved in lordly liberty within the Sabbath order. To Him it was no prison, but a domain. Similarly, to His people: this commandment, like the rest, is never grievous, but full of liberty; but the unrenewed will always find its restraints irksome, for they are not sons, but captives. Nevertheless, in magnifying our liberty, let us not override the law; in shunning Pharisaic scruples in little things, let us not make greater ones of non-effect by too wide a license. If all law is summed up in love, the fulfilling of love cannot mean the breaking of law."

4. *The Consequences* (vs. 14-21)

   a. Immediate result of this Sabbath controversy was assemblage of Pharisees for purpose of plotting to put Jesus Christ to death (v. 14); His arguments had not convinced them of their error, and His miracle mercy had only intensified their hostility.

   b. When Jesus knew Jews had determined on His death He withdrew into privacy (v. 15a), not because He was afraid of them, but because His time had not yet come and there was still much work to do.

   c. Great multitudes, however, followed Him, and He bestowed upon all who needed it His blessing of healing (v. 15b), but urged them to avoid proclaiming His deeds (v. 16); for He was desirous for time being of preventing open rupture between Himself and His enemies.

   d. In harmony with Matthew's purpose, this experience of our Lord is associated with prophecy and is regarded as its fulfillment; in midst, therefore, of this sad story of growing animosity to Christ comes this beautiful passage from O.T. (Isa. 42:1-4) referring to Messiah (vs. 17-21); and every part of it is full of deepest interest to us, for it expresses what Christ always is to those who are willing to receive Him. Let us note:

     (1) *His Position* (v. 18)
God is speaker and describes Messiah as His Servant, His Chosen One, His Beloved One, One in whom He is well pleased.

     (2) *His Power* (*v. 18*)
Then follows assurance of His equipment by gift of

Holy Spirit; and this in turn is succeeded by announcement of His work among Gentiles.

His Program (v. 19)

He is beautifully pictured as One who was unobtrusive, content to be hidden in order to accomplish His work; popularity would have disturbed its progress, intensifying opposition.

N.B. It would be well for Christ's followers to learn dangers of self-advertisement and popularity-seeking; one of subtlest is longing for higher rank in Christian circles, thereby gaining opportunity for wider influence, while actual motive is very different. It is for Christ to open way and for us to abide quietly in Him, possessed of holy fear lest success come between us and Him.

Spurgeon once said reason why God does not allow many Christian workers to come home on top of harvest loads is that they might become dizzy and fall down!

(4) *His Patience* (v. 20)

Character of Messiah is then described in relation to Jewish people who, like reeds bruised and flax smoking, are regarded as bowed and smouldering under load of ecclesiastical bondage; He will bear patiently with them, enabling them to stand upright and grow strong towards God; He is sympathetic with all who are in earnest about following Him; and He will lead them gently on until complete victory for His just cause is assured.

(5) *His Promise* (v. 21)

Final outcome is to be that, nothwithstand opposition of certain Jews, there will be Gentiles who will accept Christ and Divine blessing will be bestowed; if, therefore, His disciples follow Him in this attribute of a meek and quiet spirit, their influence will resemble His and hearts everywhere will respond instinctively to gentle, Christlike lives.

The second occasion for hostility to Christ was —

B. **Opposition Over Satanic Power** (vs. 22-37)

1. *The Cure* (vs. 22, 23)

   a. Period of seclusion could not last very long, for authorities at Jerusalem had evidently influenced their party in Galilee to follow and persecute Christ (cf. Mark 3:22).

   b. There was brought to Him one who was not blind and dumb by nature but by demoniacal possession; obviously, to relieve anyone so terribly under power of enemy would be, in some respects, most difficult of all miracles and one that would make Pharisees watch Him with greater animosity than ever (v. 22).

   c. When man was healed, people in their astonishment expressed opinion that Jesus was Son of David, Messiah (v. 23).

2. *The Charge* (v. 24)

   a. Pharisees, however, evidently greatly perturbed by this declaration, did their utmost to prevent any further spread of disaffection by very different statement, actually charging that Christ cast out demons "by Beelzebub," thus professing to see in this wonderful work only an evidence of power of Satan, sovereign of evil spirits.

   b. This is very striking instance of extent to which moral depravity will go — actually trying, with implacable hostility, to account for what was patently Divine benfeicence by attributing it to malevolent forces.

   c. It also testified to popularity and power of Christ and, at same time, to credulity of unbelief and to strength of human perversity; for difficulties of unbelief usually are more serious than those of belief.

   d. To say our Lord's miracle of healing was attributable to influence of Satan was really to confess utter impossibility of accounting for Him by any merely human principles; and yet for Pharisees to admit that miracles proved Him to be Messiah would be fatal to their continued influence over people.

3. *The Challenge* (vs. 25-28)

   a. But our Lord, recognizing state of their hearts, soon

refuted this deplorable accusation with challenge that carried its own simple but striking conviction: if work had been done by Satan, then in reality he had cast himself out; for just as nation or kingdom, in order to exist, must have spirit of unity in regard to other nations, so it was absolutely impossible for Satan's kingdom of evil to be divided without falling (vs. 25, 26).

b. Then came further argument intended to appeal to Pharisees with even greater force; Christ reminded them their own people, Jewish exorcists (cf. vs. 43-45, Acts 19:13-16), were sometimes able to cast out demons, and if Satan were author of Christ's beneficent work he must also be author of what their kindred were doing (v. 27).

c. Our Lord thus admits that, at any rate up to a certain point, these Jewish people were successful in exorcism, although doubtless, like magicians of Egypt in time of Moses, they could go only to limited extent (cf. Exod. 8:18, 19); for it is evident that during our Lord's earthly life Satan was permitted to exercise special powers, in order that Christ's greater power might be the more manifest.

d. Meanwhile, solemn conclusion is forced on Pharisees that if Jesus was doing His work by Spirit of God they could be sure Kingdom of God had come upon them (v. 28); and thus, again, Christ implies He is Messiah and warns leaders of their danger in resisting Him and refusing to enter Divine Kingdom.

e. Unfortunately, as we now know, they did officially refuse Him and reject His Kingdom, which has never yet been set up; it is still future and will not be realized until the King Himself comes again.

4. *The Claim* (vs. 29-32)

a. Then Christ added, not merely another argument, but much more explicit statement of His claim that, compared with Satan, He was stronger One, Lord of God's Kingdom; casting out of devils is likened to entering into strong man's house, binding and robbing him, because stronger than he (v. 29), clearly implying spiritual victory over Satan and referring probably to earlier miracles and perhaps also to Temptation (cf. chap. 4).

b. Time was at hand when opposition in Galilee would reach its height, and so our Lord plainly states alternatives by pointing out there are only two kingdoms, Satan's and God's, with no middle realm; men are therefore compelled to be either in favor of Christ or against Him, gathering His harvest with Him or scattering it abroad (v. 30).

c. This was not at all arbitrary, because opponents of Christ already had deliberately adopted attitude of antagonism; and it is well to observe that, morally, God is to us only what we are willing to be to Him.

d. Then Christ goes on to proclaim breadth of Divine pardon for sin (v. 31a), but immediately makes an important exception, namely, that this willful state of opposition to and denial of Holy Spirit's power is beyond limit laid down; every sin, He says, even blasphemy in general, shall be forgiven, so long as men do not extend their blasphemy to deliberate opposition to Holy Spirit or disavowal of His manifest activity (v. 31b).

e. Further distinction is made between "the Son of man" and "the Holy Ghost" (v. 32), suggesting that, while men might speak against the Lord in His human manifestation, either from prejudice, ignorance, or honest doubt, and could still be forgiven, it would be altogether different when men definitely and wilfully closed their eyes to what they knew to be true and attributed goodness and power of Deity to evil source.

f. Key to this distinction is probably to be found in meaning of word translated "world" which really means "age," with parallelism suggesting "this age" (i.e., our Lord's earthly lifetime) corresponds to sin against Son of Man, and "the age to come" (i.e., Christian dispensation from Pentecost on) to sin against Holy Spirit.

g. This "sin against the Holy Ghost" is often matter of difficulty today, but there need be no real question about it; it is simply state of mind like that of Pharisees in context, unpardonable because it is continuously irreconcilable and prevents God from ever bestowing pardon He offers repentant hearts.

h. For such evil there never will be forgiveness because, when men persist in open and full rejection of plainest proofs of spiritual life and beneficent work, it is abundantly clear they are not receptive to any of God's blessings, including that of pardon for sin (cf. Rom. 1:28; Heb. 2:3, 4; 10:29; 1 John 5:16); on other hand, if this is indeed true interpretation, it is evident that wherever there is any desire to know whether "unpardonable sin" has been committed desire itself is positive proof that this sin is not involved and cannot be.

5. *The Condemnation* (vs. 33-37)

Proofs of all this are seen in two similes, for terms in which stern John the Baptist first addressed Pharisees are here taken up by lips of incarnate Love (cf. 3:7, 8, 10):

a. *Poisonous Plants* (v. 33)

(1) If tree was poisonous, i.e., Christ being regarded by Pharisees as being inspired by Satan, it was impossible for it to yield good fruit in casting out devils.

(2) This is because tree is always known by its fruit (cf. 7:16-20), by which words our Lord again shows absolute necessity of goodness in principle if there is to be goodness in practice.

b. *Poisonous Serpents* (vs. 34, 35)

(1) Like "vipers" (v. 34) with poisoned tongues, it was impossible for such people to give forth what was morally healthy because, when hearts overflow into speech, effect is like cause.

(2) They can produce only what they possess in their inmost recesses (v. 35); and since "heart" always means center of moral being and includes intellect, emotion, and will, such an attitude proves their whole personalities are wrong in sight of God, for otherwise their lives would be very different.

And so this solemn message closes with the statement that every morally useless and therefore hurtful word spoken will have to be accounted for by the enemies of Christ in that great Day (v. 36); for speech is an index of character, being among the best indications of man's true life in the sight of God; so that the Christian's way of speaking is strong evidence of his justification, God's act of grace in reckoning him as righteous (cf. Rom. 4:5), while sinners' speech will ultimately condemn him (v. 37).

Thus our Lord's relations with the Pharisees had at length reached a crucial stage, and it was essential that Christ should lay before them the weighty alternatives.

C. Opposition Over Signs (vs. 38-45)

Even these solemn warnings, however, did nothing to mitigate hostility; unabashed by defeat and rebuke, Christ's enemies persistently made a new demand, asking (v. 38), as they often did, for a material sign from Him, although they had already seen a number of miracles worked. To this appeal our Lord refused to give heed, implying that to those already having ample opportunity of accepting His claims any new physical manifestation would be useless to prove His possession of spiritual power; for a man may be physically strong and yet have spiritual weakness.

1. *The Sign of Jonah* (vs. 39-41)

    a. Only sign Jesus was ready to give was reminder of death and of life as symbolized by prophet Jonah's experience (v. 39; cf. Jonah 2:6); as he had been, as it were, buried and raised again, so Christ's death, because of sin, would lead to resurrection and to bestowal of life (v. 40).

        (1) This is one of first times when our Lord spoke of His death and added reference to His resurrection (cf. 16:21, 17:23, 20:19, 27:63, etc.).

        (2) His words "three days and three nights" are easily accepted if, as many, including present writer, believe, our Lord was crucified on fifth day of week (our Thursday), not on sixth day (our Friday). Careful study seems to indicate this probability (cf. 27:62-66; Mark 15:42; Luke 23:54; 24:1, 3, 21) — "the third day from which [Greek] these things were done." Or, working back from first day of following week (day of resurrection) would take one to fifth day, with "the day of the preparation" (27:62; cf. Mark 15:42) for Sabbath com-

mencing, according to Jewish custom, with our Thursday sunset; it was on day later, possibly at next sunset (on our Friday evening, as Sabbath itself was commencing) that Pharisees reminded Pilate of Christ's mention of "three days" (27:63), so that watch already set (27:65) might be continued one more day (27:64).

b. Christ regarded His miracles as signs (cf. John 11:41, 42), but perfect sign of His Messiahship was to be His death and resurrection, mighty manifestation of power for Pharisees and whole world; and He referred to Jonah again later (cf. 16:4).

c. Since true Messiah was exact opposite to purely earthly idea of Him that Pharisees had, our Lord's great sign to come would be altogether contrary to their carnal demand for immediate physical sign from heaven.

d. Further than this, Christ told them, men of Nineveh would condemn them because, while these repented at preaching of Jonah, presence of One greater than Jonah was arousing only opposition, and their condition of heart would go from bad to worse (v. 41).

2. *The Story of Solomon* (v. 42)

a. In same way, "the queen of the south," or "the queen of Sheba" (1 Kings 10:1-13, 2 Chron. 9:1-12), would condemn these privileged Jews on day of judgment for, while she, a Gentile, came a great distance (from southern Arabia, it is thought), and listened attentively to Solomon's wisdom, they were not willing to listen to One far greater; and this claim to be greater than both Jonah and Solomon is very impressive.

b. Jewish people, as represented by Pharisees, were showing themselves altogether incapable of making moral distinctions; they did not know light from darkness or heaven from hell.

c. In former days idolatry had been sin of their fathers, but their own evil was even worse, consisting of pride, self-righteousness, formalism — sins that were most likely of all to prevent humble, trustful, obedient acceptance of Messiah.

3. *The Simile of the Demoniac* (v. 43-45)

a. This fact is further driven home by our Lord who, reverting to subject of demon possession (vs. 22-28), uses simile with reference to state of Jewish nation and to blasphemy of Pharisees; for this man possessed of unclean spirit symbolizes nation under sway of Phariseeism, and his liberation would represent impression made by ministry of Jesus Christ.

b. Demon cast out is said to be roaming in desert, emblem of its home in another world (v. 43), from which, however, it restlessly decides to return (v. 44a) ; whereupon it finds man's soul restored and made attractive — "empty" means unoccupied, but "swept and garnished" means, not bare or stripped, but quite literally, cleaned and adorned (v. 44b).

c. Attraction for unclean spirit is that man's soul is indeed unoccupied and prepared but not inhabited by good spirit, and so demon is able to introduce sevenfold, infinitely worse evil with complete surrender to Satan; and thus former terrible state is succeeded by far more dreadful condition (v. 45a).

d. Then our Lord with great solemnity points out national issue to His hearers — "this wicked generation" (v. 45b) ; but His words also show us in our time what we need to remember continually, viz., that goodness in complete possession is only adequate protection against evil, and that only power of God can arrest man's soul from unutterable lengths to which it is by its very nature prepared to go.

II. Opposition from Injudicious Friends (vs. 46-50)

1. *The Natural Relationship* (vs. 46, 47)

a. In midst of this solemn discussion our Lord experiences remarkable interruption; certain relatives, including His mother, come to see Him, evidently expecting special consideration and immediate attention (v. 46), but they could not reach Him for crowd (cf. Luke 8:19).

b. It is probable they had heard of His attitude towards Pharisees and had come to conclusion He was going too far, or was mentally overstrained, or even unbalanced on subject of His mission (cf. Mark 3:21) ; thus they intended, obviously, to use their relationship to take

Him out of crowd and to get Him quietly to return home.

Joses the brother of Jesus plodded from day to day
With never a vision within him to glorify his clay;

. . . .

For he never walked with the prophets in God's great garden
of bliss,
And of all the mistakes of the ages the saddest, methinks, was
this:
To have such a brother as Jesus, to speak to Him day by day,
But never to catch the vision that glorified His clay.

HENRY H. KEMP

    c. But when Jesus was told who were there He knew well what their coming meant; so He apparently kept Himself aloof from them and refused to acknowledge any such claim, but without bringing any reproach upon them (v. 47).

2. *The New Relationship* (vs. 48-50)

    a. Instead, Christ takes opportunity to teach there is higher kinship, supreme over even closest earthly one; it is based on union of life with God and expressed in deeds of righteousness.

    b. Asking, "Who is my mother? and who are my brethren?" (v. 48), He gestures towards His disciples and actually states that they are His mother and brethren (v. 49) and, further, that His "brother and sister and mother" are all those who do the will of His heavenly Father (v. 50); and it is striking that He uses these words in detail, clearly originating new and holy humanity, to be known by one great characteristic, its devotion to will of God.

    N.B. Perhaps the fact that He does not introduce term "father" into list of His human family is hint of supernatural mystery associated with His virgin birth; certainly emphasis is on "my Father which is in heaven" (v. 50), with only earthly male relationship being designated as "brother" (something His followers may well ponder; cf. 23:9).

    c. Our Lord's standard is high, but also His grace is

sufficient for all those who respond; and how beautiful it is that, looking upon very weak and imperfect disciples, He could call them His very "brother and sister and mother," showing that in His view they were doing God's will and were therefore in close relationship with Himself.

d. Thus Christ maintains it is impossible to establish Kingdom of Heaven on lines of natural kinship for, as He said on another occasion, "That which is born of the flesh is flesh. . . . Ye must be born again" (John 3:6, 7); and how encouraging it is to realize ties that bind us to Him are at once beautifully natural, spiritually strong, and yet altogether supernatural.

N.B. Matthew Henry said: "All obedient believers are near akin to Jesus. . . . Nor will He ever be ashamed of His poor relations, but will confess them before men, before the angels, and before His Father."

Conclusion

The one connecting thought running through this whole chapter is that Christ was woefully misunderstood, first by foes and then by friends:

1. *The Foes Would Not Understand Him*

   a. Their minds, though able, were full of jealousy, hatred and falsehood.

   b. Our Lord met this opposition by *truth,* arguing logically from reason, and through Divine revelation declaring the will of God.

2. *The Friends Could Not understand Him*

   a. Their minds, though privileged, were full of doubt, difficulty, and concern.

   b. Our Lord met this opposition by *love,* continuing His work with great firmness but with tenderness pointing out true spiritual relationship.

Thus, the sumpreme passion of our Lord's earthly life is seen to be the doing of the will of God. Can this be said truly of us, His disciples today? Are we thus included among His family? Friends or foes we must be — there can be no middle ground.

31

MYSTERIES OF THE KINGDOM

Matthew 13:1-58

T HERE ARE few subjects more confused in ordinary thinking than that of "Kingdom truth." The New Testament teaching
associates it with both the present and the future, though very
largely with the latter. It is impossible, however, to identify the
Kingdom with any human social order, whether present or
future, and however well defined or valuable. It is something
far wider, deeper, and higher than any transformed society, now
or later. The Old Testament thought of the Kingdom was almost
exclusively Jewish, but in the New Testament the idea branches
out and widens so as to assure ultimate universality.

Care must be taken to distinguish between the growth of the
Church and the growth of the Kingdom. The Church grows by
individual additions to the Lord's people, because the Church is
not only His Body and Bride, but also the Building of which He
is the Cornerstone. The growth of the Kingdom refers to the
progress in the present age of every influence for good, including
the Church, although the power of evil is also prominent. It is
this twofold development of good and evil that is best seen in
the parables of the present chapter. The growth is shown to be
certain though hindered, and therefore gradual, with elements that,
though now mixed, will be rigidly distinguishable hereafter.

After recording Messiah's words (chaps. 5-7), His works
(chaps. 8, 9), an effort to extend His Kingdom (chap. 10), and
opposition to it (chaps. 11, 12), Matthew indicates in this
chapter that a crisis in our Lord's life was approaching. He had
been practically rejected by Israel, and it was necessary to take
steps in regard to the opposition, so an abrupt break is about to
be made in His method of teaching. It is important to observe
that for the first time the teaching takes the form of a parable,
which may be defined as "an earthly story with a heavenly meaning," or the setting forth of spiritual truths under the forms of
ordinary human life and experience. Literally, the Greek root of
our English word "parable" means "to throw beside" — either

by comparison and analogy or by contrast, pointing out similarities or dissimilarities between two ideas. There is a well-known saying that "an illustration does not walk on all fours" or, is not consistent in every detail; and this is sometimes true of the parabolic method. But it always has two effects: it reveals truth to those in earnest about seeking it, and it also conceals truth from those who are actuated simply by curiosity. Thus, men are led either to think and to question, or else to set a truth aside without giving it more than superficial attention; and their conduct is guided accordingly.

There are actually eight parables in this chapter and not merely seven as usually stated (cf. v. 52, "like unto," just as in vs. 24, 31, etc.). Probably they all were spoken in one day and in the order in which they occur here. All are expressive of various aspects of the Kingdom of Heaven and deal primarily with the results of Christ's work in the face of Jewish opposition, although the over-all progress of the Kingdom throughout the eight is particularly noteworthy. The chapter may properly be regarded as a prophecy of the history of what we now call Christendom.

I. The Change Recorded (vs. 1-3a, 10-17, 34, 35)

In these three places in chapter change of method is noted, i.e., before and after first parable, and between first four and second four parables.

1. *The Change and Its Explanation* (vs. 1-3a, 10, 11)

   a. After shift in location (vs. 1, 2) and in method (v. 3a), question arises in minds of disciples as to why Christ adopts this type of presentation (v. 10), and answer is given in striking contrast of His words — "unto you . . . to know . . . but to them . . . not" (v. 11); our Lord was followed by great crowds, and time had come for sifting and testing.

   b. Some people thought seriously of becoming disciples, but many came out of mere curiosity; to the curious, parables, in their dual role of concealment as well as revelation of truth, would have little further meaning, whereas would-be disciples might well be stimulated to go more deeply into meanings and to ask intelligent questions.

   Illus.: Husk of grain preserves kernel *from* harm and *for* use.

2. *The Application* (vs. 12-17, 34, 35)

a. Then Christ laid down great principle in form of proverbial expression (v. 12), showing that by use of our faculties we obtain more power, while avoidance of use leads to loss of what we possess, whether, e.g., of hearing, taste, brain-power, muscle, or any other function.

Illus.: Fakirs of India, with arms continuously upraised, in time experience atrophy; *contra,* surgeon's hand, sailor's eye, student's mind, all are made keener by use; momentum of falling body increases as it approaches ground.

b. Corresponding to this law in physical realm is law of spiritual capital; parables would compel people to think and if they would not exercise their minds sufficiently to discover meanings, result would be spiritual loss (v. 13).

c. All this is pointed out by words of prophet Isaiah (vs. 14, 15, quoting Isa. 6:9, 10), meaning of which is that judgment will come to those unwilling to listen and learn; for those who will not, find by-and-by that they cannot.

d. This law of moral and spiritual retribution is not arbitrary, but follows great principle of faithfulness and unfaithfulness that runs throughout whole of life; neither does it contradict offer of free salvation, for there was no intention of withholding truth from any willing to be saved.

e. Those who were in earnest would be led on by parables to deeper knowledge; and only those who were not serious-minded and sincere would find their willfulness leading to moral darkness and incapacity.

N.B. Alfred Plummer said: "Grace, like bodily food, may be rejected until the power to receive it perishes."

f. It is, of course, quite impossible that our Lord could have spoken in parables for sole purpose of not being understood; for in such case He need not have spoken at all.

g. This interpolation ends with our Lord showing His disciples (vs. 16, 17) how blessed they were in comparison with many who had lived and died ages before without knowing what was now to be revealed; and thus Twelve were prepared for new situation. (cf. also vs. 34, 35, which contains quotation from Ps. 78:2-4).

II. The Parables Recounted (vs. 3b-9, 18-33, 36-52)

These show Kingdom of Heaven from various points of view and at different times in history. They may be summarized first as follows:

1. The Four Soils — varying results (one good out of four) with good seed (vs. 3b-9, 18-22).
2. The Tares — enemy appears with bad seed (vs. 24-30, 36-43).
3. The Mustard Seed — enemy at work by means of abnormally prosperous growth (vs. 31, 32).
4. The Leaven — enemy at work through inward pollution (v. 33).
5. The Hidden Treasure — Church in world (v. 44)
6. The Pearl — Church separated from world and characterized by unity, beauty, and purity (vs. 45, 46).
7. The Drag Net — evil in world till end, then permanent separation from good (vs. 47-50).
8. The Householder — closing application to believers (vs. 51, 52).

There is thus consistency of historical interpretation. It may be noted, however, that it does not seem possible to draw strict parallels between first seven parables of this chapter and letters to seven Churches in Revelation 2 and 3; this is because in former it is difficult, if not impossible, to mark time limits, as has been attempted in latter.* It seems better, therefore, to trace all principles represented down through history together with their effect on progress of Kingdom.

One way to analyze the eight parables is as follows: No. 1, introduction, followed by three pairs: Nos. 2 and 7, beginning and end of evil; Nos. 3 and 4, evil outward and inward; and Nos. 5 and 6, good in and out of evil; and, finally, No. 8, application. For greater convenience in study, however, para-ables may rather be divided chronologically into two groups of four each:

A. The Parables Spoken to the Multitude (vs. 3b-9, 18-35)

These four were given out of doors (cf. vs. 1, 2), and refer-

---

*For fuller mention of this passage in the Book of Revelation, see the author's volume, *The Apostle John*, Kregel Publications, 1984, p. 362ff.

ences in them are to external things, such as wheat and tares, and thus to external characteristics of Kingdom without specific reference to Church.

1. *The Parable of the Four Soils* (vs. 3b-9, 18-32)

This is usually called the Parable of the Sower, as it was by our Lord (v. 18), but for convenience it may be more distinctively described as the Parable of the Four Soils, since there are three other "sowers" mentioned in subsequent parables (cf. vs. 24, 25, 31). It is one of two parables in this chapter which our Lord has explained, so that its meaning is clear.

a. *The Sower and the Seed* (vs. 3b, 18, 19)

(1) Jesus is Sower (cf. v. 27) and Word of God is seed (v. 19); since Greek masculine gender is used throughout (cf. v. 19, "This is he that was sown by the way side," A.S.V.), there seems to be blending of Person and Word.

(2) Seed is very small, but possesses life, force, and power to propagate; word is slight thing, yet may be far-reaching in effect, and much more so in case of Word of God (cf. Heb. 4:12), which demonstrates His life-giving power, His eternal wisdom, and His wonderful love.

b. *The Soils*

In sowing, seed and soil are brought together, causing some of greatest possibilities known to man; one of most important processes in creation is harvest from good soil, so that coming of sower at proper time is supreme event on which everything else may be said to hang. Given good seed, results of sowing depend on soil, and here there are four kinds and therefore four results:

(1) *The Wayside Soil* (vs. 4, 19)

(a) This was hardened by use, as footpath by feet; it represents type of life on which gospel truth has ceased to make deep impression, and birds represent emissaries of Satan who is always on watch, sometimes using innocent means to snatch away any possible influences for good.

(b) Heart has become hardened by sin and does not respond to either spoken or written Word of God; passive acceptance of impressions also hardens into indifference by means of repetition.

(c) Ground in parable was not responsible, but human heart is; outside influences trying to lead us from Christ do not compel us to do wrong, and temptation does not cause action until our assent is given (cf. Jas. 4:7, 8).

(2) *The Rocky Soil* (vs. 5, 6, 20, 21)

(a) This was not hardened — it was soft, but also shallow, a thin layer on rock into which seed could strike no deep root and, being scorched by sun, withered away; it represents those who seem to have eternal life but develop no staying power, and who receive spiritual influences just short of permanent impression — they "have no root in themselves, and so endure but for a time" (Mark 4:17).

(b) Their emotions are stirred and result seems so far to be good, but they fall away through "tribulation or persecution" (v. 21); feelings can be dangerous if not translated into action.

(c) Gospel message first enters through thought, then causes feeling, and then should inspire determination to act; cf. Rom. 10:10, where "heart" includes all three phases of human personality — intellect, emotion, will.
N.B. Greek word used in v. 21 and in parallel passage in Mark (4:17), and translated "for a while" or "for a time," is found only in two other N. T. passages: in Heb. 11:25, it is enjoyment of sin that is transitory; in 2 Cor. 4:18, it is visible, material world that is temporal, as distinguished from invisible one that is spiritual and eternal; and here and in Mark 4 it is actually Christian profession that is comparably temporary — a sad commentary on human nature.

(3) *The Thorny Soil* (vs. 7, 22)

    (a) This was pre-occupied — by thorns, which had head start over good seed; it represents those who harbor over-anxiety for things of this world and have divided hearts.

    (b) "Deceitfulness of riches" (v. 22) often blunts desire for better things; but there is also such a thing as deceitfulness or snare of poverty included in "the care of this world" and leading to worry and preoccupation of mind.

    Illus.: John Wesley once had asked financial aid in behalf of his work of a man who replied: "I have the will, but not the means." When the man had inherited money, Wesley approached him again, but was told: "I have the means, but not the will."

    (c) By lust of world (cf. 1 John 2:15-17) and in many other ways — "the lusts of other things" (Mark 4:19) — good seed becomes crushed and crowded out — choked and unfruitful (v. 22); thus, sin gets not only early start but also upper hand.

(4) *The Good Soil* (vs. 8, 32)

    (a) This soil was altogether excellent, since Greek word used is also translated "beautiful," so was both good in quality and goodly to look upon (cf. Luke 21:5); it represents those who not only listen, but also appropriate, retain, obey (cf. Ps. 119:11), and bring forth "fruit unto life eternal" (John 8:36) — "the fruit of the Spirit" (Gal. 5:22, 23) and "fruit unto holiness" (Rom. 6:22).

    (b) This "good ground" is said to have "kept giving" (v. 8, Greek) fruit; if reception accorded to gospel is thoroughly sincere, result is abundant and continuing fruit-bearing in life of believer.

    (c) But note variations even in this "beautiful

soil" — "some an hundredfold, some sixtyfold, some thirtyfold" (v. 8):

"An hundredfold" for Thee
  Of precious golden grain
Should be Thy portion in return
  For labor, grief, and pain;
My heart Thou didst prepare,
  Thy hand let fall the seed;
Thou didst Thyself reveal,
  As well as meet my need.
This fading world I'd leave behind,
  In Thee, blest Lord, my all to find!

H. H.

c. *The Summary*

(1) In many respects this parable is most searching of all, for it has to do with one of most solemn of all subjects — relation between revealed truth and issues of human life.

(2) Eternal life may easily be lost through indifference or shallowness, through mixture of good and evil, or through preoccupation with world; but if only our hearts truly receive seed of God's Word, outcome is eternal life here and hereafter.

(3) In this parable there were three failures to one success: in wayside soil it was Satan who brought to nought (v. 19); in rocky ground it was flesh (v. 21); in thorny ground it was world (v. 22) — world, flesh, devil; but in good soil there was willingness to receive Jesus Christ as Life-Giver and Conqueror over all these forces.

(4) Seed sown on wayside was sown on but not in; that on rocky ground went on and in but not down; that on thorny ground went on, in, and down, but not up; but seed on good soil went on, in, down, and up.

(5) Hardened ground may be ploughed up; shallow ground may be deepened; thorny ground may be weeded and cleansed; and good ground may be kept prepared under right influences, e.g., rainfall of Spirit and sunshine of God's presence.

(6) This leads to Christ's exhortation in v. 9 (cf. v. 43b) in which He suggests two classes of people — "with ears and with no ears" (cf. "haves and have-nots," v. 12); but all start with capacity, therefore all have responsibility for listening and need to exert effort to understand His teaching, even in face of formidable hindrances, e.g., preoccupation, procrastination, listlessness, opposition.

2. *The Parable of the Tares* (vs. 24-30, 36-43)

This is the other parable in the chapter of which we have the explanation in our Lord's own words. In spite of the theory that parables contain matter easy to understand, they often contain the deepest teaching of Christ. This one is very vivid and reads easily, yet raises some profound problems, especially three great facts of human experience that otherwise would be inscrutable mysteries. They are depicted as follows:

a. *The Sowing* (vs. 24, 25, 37-39a)

(1) *The Metaphor*

(a) As in previous parable, first Sower is Christ (v. 37); but there is striking development in symbolism of seed, which was stated in v. 19 to be Word of God (cf. Luke 8:11).

(b) When that is received into human hearts, those who receive it in turn become "good seed" (vs. 24, 38; cf. 1 Pet. 1:23), just as in nature seed grows into plant that in its turn bears seed for sowing; thus hint at such identification in Parable of Soils is here made clear (cf. v. 19ff.) — first, Word in Christian, then Christian taking Word to world.

(c) Tares were probably darnel, or ryegrass, not mere weeds, but plants so like true grain no one could distinguish them in seed or blade, but only when in ear (cf. v. 29); and if their seed was ground with corn, resulting flour is said to have been poisonous.

(d) Field is world (v. 24) and belongs to God — "his field" (v. 38; cf. Ps. 24:1); it is not

Church, so there is no reference in parable to church discipline or to schism or separation.

(e) Though it is "God's earth," world is at present largely under power of Evil One (cf. 1 John 5:19); world is against the Father (1 John 2:15), and human flesh opposes the Holy Spirit (cf. Gal. 5:19-23).

(f) Second sower is "the devil" (v. 39a), and his seed would seem to be mistaken or false professors of religion, probably worst of all hindrances to Kingdom; their presence is due to malice of Christ's "enemy" (vs. 28, 39), and to multiply them is perhaps his favorite form of opposition.

(g) Consequently, anything that obscures necessity for changed hearts, making religion merely outward and ceremonial, easy and fashionable, or even completely unnecessary, is undoubtedly not of God but of Satan.

(2) *The Methods*

(a) Good seed is sown openly as duty because of ownership, while bad seed is sown secretly in enmity and as intrusion; however, there need be no rebuke in words "while men slept" (v. 25), for they probably mean simply that tares were sown under cover of night.

(b) Devil is "squatter," one who settles on land not his own and works it for his own advantage; he has also been called "God's ape," for he counterfeits God's work, his main weapon indeed being imitation.

N.B. Cf. his third temptation of Christ, to worship him in place of God (4:9); his deception through Ananias and Sapphira (Acts 5:3), Simon Magus (Acts 8:23), Anti-Christ (2 Thess. 2:3, 4), and various imitative sects of present day.

(c) Every truth has its counterfeit, just as purest metal may oxidize, and most limpid water bear scum from foul weeds on bottom.

(3) *The Mystery*

    (a) This prompts us to ask why everything on earth is spoiled by sin, and man befouls all he touches; and we wonder why where there is good there is also evil.

    (b) It is not true, however, to say existence of good necessarily implied existence of evil, rather, good implied possibility of evil, not its actuality, because of freedom of choice granted both men and angels.

    (c) Man was placed in God's world to glorify Him, but unscrupulous enemy already fallen was present, so that witness to God might be tested and either preserved and rewarded or repudiated with resulting punishment.

    (d) It is indeed common experience of us all that where someone is trying to do good there is someone trying to hold him back; and as soon as one begins to follow Christ he has many powers of evil arrayed against him.

After the sowing comes —

b. *The Growing* (vs. 26-30a)

(1) *The Metaphor*

    (a) Keeping in mind that "chidren of the kingdom" (v. 38) are "good seed" and "children of the wicked one" are "tares" or counterfeits, it follows that their full development alone would reveal what had been "done" by "enemy" (v. 28); cf. Jude, whose readers are exhorted to withstand "certain men crept in unawares" in their own times (v. 4), but are also reminded that, at the earlier time of Exodus, it was only "afterward" that "the Lord . . . destroyed them that believed not" (v. 5).

    (b) "Servants of the householder" (v. 27), or "reapers" (v. 39), are to be "the angels" (v. 27), and surprise and perplexity at this situation are probably experienced in heaven as well as on earth; so that proposal to "go and

gather them up" immediately (v. 28) is reasonable.

(2) *The Method*

    (a) Owner's reply recognizes principle that time
alone shows reality of all things, and that be-
ginnings are insufficient for judging.

    (b) There must be opportunity for seed and for
man each to yield fruit "after his kind" (Gen.
1:11, 12); and, since premature gathering of
tares might "root up also the wheat with them,"
owner directs reapers to "let both grow together until the harvest" (vs. 29, 30).

(3) *The Mystery*

    (a) We have second enigma of life, viz., why
evil is permitted to go on unchecked; and we
learn from this parable that, while God does
not cause wrong, He does allow it not only to
exist, but also to continue.

    (b) As in case of wheat and tares, it is often im-
possible to separate good from evil in world,
e.g., influences of civilization on heathen practices, true religion and cults; so that our
Master is saying, "Let both grow together
until the harvest" (v. 30).

    (c) This principle holds good in connection with
national and world problems as recorded in
Scripture (cf. Ps. 110:1, Isa. 6:11-13, 32:13-
15, Ezek. 21:27, Dan. 7:25, Luke 21:24, Acts
3:21, Rom. 11:25, 2 Pet. 1:19, Rev. 17:17);
and it is no less true of individual believer's
perplexities (cf. Gen. 28:15; Ps. 73:16, 17;
Hos. 10:12; Mic. 7:9; Phil. 1:6; 1 Tim. 6:14;
Jas. 5:7, A.S.V.; Rev. 2:25).

    (d) What a mercy it is that we, the children of
God, are not called upon to "judge" others, for
in heaven there will doubtless be great number
of people present whom, because of insufficient
knowledge, we did not expect; and, conversely,
some of those we did expect will be absent.

But after the sowing and growing there comes inexorably—

c. *The Reaping* (vs. 30b, 39b-43)

    (1) *The Metaphor*

        (a) At harvest time division into good grain and bad is inevitable and easy; at "consummation of age" (vs. 39, 40, A.S.V. marg.), sinfulness is clearly distinguishable from righteousness.

        (b) Reapers are sent into field by owner; in this case "reapers are the angels" (v. 39), sent forth by "Son of man" (v. 41), and their work of separation and burning is seen to be absolute and eternal (vs. 41-43; cf. Rev. 14:14-16). *N.B.* This is harvest of life; see 9:37 for harvest of labor.

    (2) *The Method*

        (a) In great day of division, separation, and doom that is surely coming, no one will abide its awful scrutiny except those so joined to Christ Himself as to show in their lives reality of righteousness through repentance and faith.

        (b) This parable is full of striking contrasts, especially compared with first parable: there is contrast of two great persons, the Son of man and His enemy; another contrast we have seen in sowing and yet another in growing; but most solemn of all is contrast of two companies represented by seed — "the children of the kingdom" and "the children of the wicked one" (v. 38), differing in nature, form, growth, and destiny, but not yet entirely distinguishable.

    (3) *The Mystery*

        (a) This revelation of presence of enemy in Kingdom, working against its rightful Owner and Lord, is at once mystery and explanation.

        (b) It is mystery that there should be anyone or anything working against God, and yet we understand thereby something at least of meaning of sin; for when Christ said, "An enemy hath done this" (v. 28), He expressed to His disciples in brief form what we understand as problem of evil.

(c) God does not cause evil, but He permits and overrules it, and one day in Great Judgment evil men will be forever cast out; words "these shall go away" (25:46) will be found to be quite enough — separation from God.

(d) Every symbol has reality, and man at least takes his own fire with him to hell; life, like photographic film, will flash out its picture hereafter in light of eternity.

(e) Meanwhile, we who are "children of the kingdom" are to trust, wait, and work, looking to that great day; for it is still true that what we sow in time we reap in eternity (cf. v. 43 with Prov. 4:18).

(f) Christ's interpretation of this second parable ends with repeated warning to those who have "ears to hear" (v. 43; cf. v. 9); and thus it would seem that it, along with first parable, is given special emphasis.

Two brief parables follow which seem connected, as do two that precede and two that come after them. Since our Lord gave no recorded explanation of them, it is necessary to use caution in their interpretation. But, since they probably were spoken on the same day and form two of eight, there ought to be a consistent rendering of meaning and a harmony with the first two parables. It may be added that the most familiar interpretation is not necessarily the true one.

3. *The Parable of the Mustard Seed* (vs. 31, 32)

In this case metaphor can be indicated as follows:

a. *The Grain of Mustard Seed*

(1) Seed of mustard plant is very small, and grows into herb.
N.B. According to Walter Quincy Scott, proverbial Talmudic expression referred to it as type of anything exceedingly small. It was evidently tiniest of all seeds used in Jewish husbandry, even though not, of course, smallest known to botanical science.

(2) It does not, however, become tree, so apparently Christ meant Kingdom in this next form had become unusual, even abnormal, both in size and in character, out of all proportion to its small beginning — like garden shrub outdoing itself.

(3) We may think of Christendom under Constantine, during Middle Ages, magnified by popes or swelled by heretical sects, to illustrate false greatness; parable cannot typify true, prosperous, inward growth, for there is as yet no truly Christian nation or ethnic group, and no literally "national church" on face of earth.

b. *The Sower and the Field*

(1) "Man" who "sowed in his field" (v. 31) must, according to symbolism of first and second parables, be "the Son of man" (v. 37).

(2) Likewise, field must represent world in which Christendom finds itself.

c. *The Birds in the Branches*

(1) In first parable "the fowls" (v. 7) typify "the wicked one" (v. 19); and when similar phrase, "the birds of the air" (v. 32), is used here, descriptive of those who come and lodge in branches of this tree, we may assume it implies attempted capture of Christendom by Satan and his cohorts, or at least their patronage of it for purposes of influence.

(2) We may note they do not belong to tree but are "squatters" (cf. v. 25); when Satan and his angels can no longer destroy good seed they take shelter in its result and pollute it, using Christendom or visible Church for their own ends and often leading unsuspecting and uninstructed members astray.

(3) Thus, Christ's warning here has to do with dangers of size and of sheltering evil, and may well be applied to His own people as well as to professing church or Christendom.

N.B. Similar imagery is found in Ezek. 31:3-6 and Dan. 4:20-22.

(4) This is indeed intensification of "mystery" — not only presence of evil, but its ability to deceive and and even to give spurious size and prosperity to "kingdom of heaven" (v. 31).

4. *The Parable of the Leaven* (v. 33)

In studying this parable let us consider:

a. *The Usual Interpretation*

(1) It has been thought by many that, as parable of mustard seed stands for extensive growth of Kingdom, so parable of leaven typifies intensive growth, i.e., that leaven in this verse stands for good influences within Christendom or professing Church.

(2) According to this view, meal would be world; leaven, gospel; woman, preaching of gospel — result, permeation of world by gospel and eventual conversion of it in this dispensation.

b. *The Difficulties*

(1) Leaven appears in Scripture about thirty-five times, and in virtually every passage but this its meaning seems to be unmistakably corruption in some form; thus, there seems no valid reason why we should take symbol as found in this one verse and make it stand for something exactly contrary (cf., e.g., Exod. 12:15, Matt. 16:6, 1 Cor. 5:6-8).

(2) Meal, which in itself is good (cf. Lev. 2, A.S.V.), is permeable by either leaven or salt, which form antithesis in that same chapter between evil and good (cf. Lev. 2:11-13); but when blood of atonement was offered leaven was to be included in "new meal-offering . . . even an offering made by fire" (Lev. 23:15-21).

(3) We know that world (meal) opposes gospel, so woman hiding leaven in meal does not suggest preaching of gospel or any good work being received; instead, it would seem to be stealth of evil consistent with enemy's action in parable of tares (cf. v. 25; also possibly Rev. 2:20).

(4) When we connect "working" with leaven or yeast we mean process of fermentation leading to breakdown or decay, and result is mixture, not transfor-

mation, with sour taste (cf. 2 Thess. 2:7); and dough can be made more palatable and fermentation stopped only by "purging" (cf. 1 Cor. 5:7), or baking in heat of oven, or burning on altar, "as by fire" (1 Cor. 3:15; cf. Lev. 23:18).

(5) Conversion of whole world in present dispensation is contrary to Scripture in general and immediately contrary to preceding parables as well; furthermore, it is not true to life as we find it, because Christendom is far from being permeated with good.

c. *The Consistent View*

(1) Meal, or flour, as used in O.T. offerings was uniformly good symbol, standing for service and fellowship (cf. Gen. 18:6, Judg. 6:19, 1 Sam. 1:24, etc.); leaven represents evil, that which usually is to be left out.

(2) In combining two, woman in this parable actually was doing what law forbade (cf. Lev. 2:11); result was surely corruption, not improvement, of "the whole."

(3) Later, our Lord told His disciples to "beware of the leaven of the Pharisees and of the Sadducees" (16:6), which may be described as formalism and hypocrisy on one hand, and as materialism and rationalism on other; while that of Herodians was worldliness and self-indulgence (cf. Mark 8:15 with Matt. 14:1-11) — all undeniably evil tendencies.

(4) Later still, St. Paul wrote Corinthian Christians to purge out "old leaven" that they might "be a new lump," or loaf of bread, "as . . . unleavened" (1 Cor. 5:7); and he further instructed them to keep their feast with "unleavened bread of sincerity and truth" in place of loaf "with the leaven of malice and wickedness" (v. 8).

(5) Only consistent explanation, therefore, of this fourth parable is that Kingdom, i.e., outward, visible development of Christendom, would be permeated by form of impurity, gradually spreading

until all of it was affected; and we find record of beginning of this leaven of insincerity and sin in apostolic Church itself (cf. Acts 5:1-11), while writings of John and Paul warn of its further growth in Church of first century.

(6) Church history since then continues sad story, so that Christendom today is certainly not entirely pure, but rather is degenerating mixture of good and evil, of materialism and spirituality, of godliness and worldliness; and this destructive leaven has often made rapid advances in very center of church life, so that neither Christendom nor professing Church is pure in sight of God.

(7) Then, too, this parable was spoken to outsiders and not merely to disciples, i.e., true believers; thus, popular interpretation of it is not warranted by Scripture.

(8) We shall do well here, then, to hold fast to consistency running through God's Word as whole; and this in spite of intensified "mystery" — not only presence and prosperity of evil, but also its permeation of Kingdom until end of this age.

It was at this point that Christ did close His parables to the multitude outside (v. 34), the remainder being spoken privately to His disciples indoors (v. 36); and this action is seen (v. 35) to fulfill prophetic words of the Psalmist (Ps. 78:2). We thus pass on to:

B. The Parables Spoken to the Disciples (vs. 36-52)

When Christ had dismissed the multitude and had come with His disciples into the house, their first request was to be told the meaning of the second parable, that of the Tares (vs. 36-43). As we have seen, each point was interpreted by our Lord, with sowing, growing, and reaping especially emphasized, and was closed by a solemn application urging His audience to listen attentively to what He was saying (v. 43). Now the standpoint is to be changed from the external and visible to the internal and invisible, to characteristics not only of Christendom in general, but, as we may expect, since addressed to disciples only, of the Church in particular. From the former standpoint, results vary with reception, opposition is due to imitation, unnatural growth develops into material prosperity, and corruption is caused by evil influences. Through the remaining parables, essential principles and eternal values emerge, and the first two form another pair:

1. *The Parable of the Hidden Treasure* (v. 44)

Maintaining harmony with foregoing parables, we may interpret metaphor as follows:

a. *The Field and the Man*

   (1) Field clearly symbolizes world, as in first three parables.

   (2) There seems little doubt that, as before, man typifies our Lord, engaged this time in seeking instead of sowing.

b. *The Treasure*

   (1) This, of course, may be thought of as humanity in general but, since word "treasure" is often used of Israel, we may distinguish between this parable and next by suggesting that here specifically Jewish Church, or Hebrew Christian group, is primarily in mind (cf. Exod. 19:5, Ps. 135:4, Mal. 3:17); this, indeed, is not usual interpretation, but is here submitted because it seems more natural and consistent than one generally adopted.

   (2) Treasure was "hid" — and only Christ knew it was there to be "found"; and His estimate of it is seen throughout Gospels (cf. Luke 15, 19:1-10; John 17:6).

   (3) Treasure was hidden again; and, Kingdom having rejected and therefore postponed, we may interpret this as indicating that those in Israel believing on Him at that time, though true members of His Church, would not be revealed until later, perhaps after Pentecost, for they may well be included in three thousand forming first local church (cf. Acts 2:41-47, 4:32).

c. *The Purchase*

   (1) Meanwhile, man in parable "for joy thereof, goeth and selleth all that he hath, and buyeth that field";

and surely this joyful sacrifice and purchase form beautiful picture of our Lord's redemptive death (cf. Luke 15:6, 9, 23; Acts 20:28; 2 Cor. 8:9; Gal. 2:20; Heb. 12:2; 1 Pet. 1:18, 19).

(2) It does not seem that opposite interpretation of purchasing treasure can be upheld, i.e., Christ being found by man; for gospel being God's free gift, with man having nothing to do but accept it, makes for insuperable objection (cf. John 3:16; Rom. 6:23; 1 Cor. 15:57; Eph. 2:8, 9).

(4) Therefore, to be both consistent and true to fact, only person "man" in parable can be is Jesus Christ our Lord who "sold" all He had, His very life, for man's redemption, so that we are "bought with a price" (1 Cor. 6:20); and "mystery" in this case may well include His surprising estimate of value and hidden potentialities of lives "he hath purchased with his own blood" (Acts 20:28).

2. *The Parable of the Pearl* (vs. 45, 46)
   a. *The Man* (v. 45)
      (1) Here, again, if we are consistent, we shall see man represents Christ, this time as "a merchant man," one we would call connoisseur, who knows real gems from sham, "goodly," or first quality, from inferior.
      (2) Widely held interpretation, however, would make Christ pearl, even inspiring well-known gospel hymn, "I've Found the Pearl of Greatest Price"; but for consistency and other reasons it seems best not to do so, just as in previous parable.

   b. *The Pearl Sought* (v. 45)
      (1) It is said pearls were not precious to Hebrews, and they were not included in Aaron's breastplate with other jewels, those dug from earth (cf. Exod. 28:17-20); and it is not even clear they were mentioned at all in O.T., for word "pearls" in Job 28:18, K.J.V., is rendered "crystal" in A.S.V.
      (2) But they were very precious among Gentiles of ancient world, e.g., in Egypt and Assyria, and are mentioned several times in N.T. (e.g., 7:6, 1 Tim.

2:9) ; so this would seem to be clear reference to Church universal, composed of Jews and Gentiles, and it is beautiful and fitting symbol.

(3) Pearl is only precious gem that is product of living organism and result of injury to it; so Church of Christ is called His Body, united to Him through His sufferings, possessed by Him, and gradually built up by His Spirit (cf. 1 Cor. 12:12-27, Heb. 12:23).

(4) Pearl is also fine symbol of unity — it cannot be divided — and it also symbolizes purity and beauty; it is used for adornment, especially of royalty, so that when "the new Jerusalem" is seen "prepared as a bride adorned for her husband," her gates are found to be "twelve pearls" (Rev. 21:2, 21).

c. *The Pearl Found* (v. 46)

(1) This, then, is surely Pearl Divine Merchant Man was seeking, and, like man in parable, He "went and sold all that He had, and bought it"; and price of His Church was costly — "Himself" (Gal. 2:20, Eph. 5:25), "precious (1 Pet. 2:6), "exceeding riches of his grace" (Eph. 2:7).

(2) "Mystery" in this case is most striking of all — "the mystery of Christ . . . the church" (see Eph. 3:1-12) ; it was later made known in its fullness to St. Paul, but undoubtedly is foreshadowed here.

3. *The Parable of the Drag-Net* (vs. 47-50)

This seventh parable, last of those which give characteristic aspects of Kingdom of Heaven in its state of "mystery," complements second, that of Tares, with special reference to final separation of bad from good. Since Christ gave interpretation of final part only (vs. 49, 50), care is necessary; but this separation, judging by His emphasis on it, is undoubtedly most important part of parable.

a. *The Sea and the Fish*

(1) Sea is sphere of life and corresponds to field of other parables or world in its widest sense, where live "every kind," as seed was in field.

(2) Fish would suggest Gentile nations, as distinguished from Christian Church (Pearl and Treasure) ; and

time is "the end of the world" (v. 49, lit., "consummation of the age"), generally thought to be synonymous with Daniel's seventieth week (cf. Dan. 9:27), and so this will be after Church has gone to be with Christ (cf. 1 Thess. 4:13 to 5:11). *N.B.* Ford C. Ottman, in his book *God's Oath,* suggests that "This judicial separation is what comes before us in the net drawn to the shore. The net is cast into the sea (of the nations) immediately after the Church has been removed. Those who have refused grace in the day of grace are given up to strong delusion that they may believe a lie. Then those who have never had the truth before them — and the Church failing in her testimony shall leave many such — shall hear the 'everlasting gospel,' and shall then find their opportunity for salvation. Just and equal are the ways of God!"

b. *The Fishermen and the Net*

(1) Those who "cast" and "gather" and "draw" and separate are clearly the same — "the angels" (v. 49); so thought is not of disciples being "fishers of men" (4:19), nor is net one cast out now by gospel preaching, which is present-day method of God through men.

(2) Word here used for net indicates large one, or seine, long and semicircular, for several persons to use together by holding it at two extremes; while today's work is largely individual, one by one, through either public ministry or personal work.

(3) This process, therefore, has nothing to do with present age of grace; it is part of angels' work in future (cf. vs. 41, 42, 24:31; Rev. 14:6ff.).

(4) We may infer that God's action on world by angelic ministry, after present age is over, will be only hope for world; but union with God in Christ, our highest privilege, may and should be realized here and now.

c. *The Separation*

(1) It is certain — "so *shall* it be" (v. 49; cf. 24:40, 41); this will be only test for some.

Illus.: In Bank of England, gold sovereigns were tested by machine that discarded those under standard weight — "gathered the good into vessels, but cast the bad away" (v. 48).

(2) It is accurate — "the *angels* shall come forth and sever" (v. 49), so that there will be no mistake; and this is an encouragement to know, since at present time good is often overpowered and evil triumphant.

(3) It is definite — "the *wicked* from among the *just*" (v. 49), so that there is no middle course; people are either in Christ or not, either good or bad —" "there is no twilight in the spiritual world."

d. *The Outcome*

(1) While parable of Tares ends joyously, this parable ends on sad note; cf. "shine forth" (v. 43) with "wailing and gnashing of teeth" (v. 50).

(2) Character-forming tends towards permanence (cf. Rev. 22:11, 12, 15); and glory of Christian goodness is that it becomes habitual until it determines destiny.
Illus.: Pearl in oyster is formed layer by layer; and though light wind can bend sapling at will, full-grown tree can usually withstand storm.

(3) Judgment (cf. John 9:39, Greek) is not so much imposed on man from without as exposed from within, day by day; he is forming it by his character, good or bad, and this will be especially true at time referred to here.

(4) Thus seventh parable crowns whole of "mysteries of the kingdom of heaven" (v. 11); it speaks of end of period, just as first parable describes beginning.

When these seven parables had been uttered, our Lord asked His disciples whether they had understood them, and they replied with a good deal of assurance that they had. We know, however, that they were not completely informed as to the baffling problem of the existence of evil in the Kingdom of Heaven: e.g., failure, as in the Parable of the Soils; conflict, as in that of the Tares; and corruption, as in those of the Mustard Seed and of the Leaven; nor could they be truly enlightened until after the gift of the Holy Spirit at Pentecost (cf. Acts 1:3, 6, 2:30). But since they evidently thought they "understood all these things" (v. 51), the Master made rejoinder with —

8. *The Parable of the Householder* (vs. 51, 52)

As seven notes of scale require eighth to complete octave, so foregoing parables would have been incomplete without this last, indicating important principle and its new application.

a. *A Disciple's Responsibility*

(1) Disciples' affirmative answer to their Master's inquiry (v. 51) is countered by His "Therefore —" (v. 52); Christianity and intellect, faith and reason, are seldom contradictory, for the more we develop our reasoning powers, the more clearly will grounds for our faith shine out, so that knowledge of God will transcend purely human mental processes.
N.B. In Scripture, faith and sight are often antithetical, but faith and reason are shown to be capable of strong alliance.

(2) Fresh knowledge, Christ is saying, carries fresh responsibility; and to illustrate this He uses word "scribe"; in its original connotation word signified one who, from Ezra on, was associated with interpretation and exposition of Scripture (cf. Neh. 8:4).

(3) To us, of course, word has sinister sound, since in N.T. times so many scribes were among our Lord's most deadly foes, in league with Pharisees and chief priests against Him (e.g., chap. 23, Mark 11:18); but scribe in this parable is one who "hath been made a disciple to the kingdom of heaven" (v. 52, A.S.V.), or has been instructed with reference to it, doubtless new idea to Christ's followers of what scribe could be.

b. *A Disciple's Duty*

(1) "Treasure" of "householder" almost certainly means not his jewels, but his storeroom where he

dispenses food for family's sustenance; and, spiritually applied, this suggests threefold source of supply:

(a) First and most important is Scripture, of course, for believer needs real knowledge of its contents in order to bring from it spiritual food for himself and others; it is well, therefore, to ask ourselves what size of Biblical storehouse is ours, how much of Scripture we actually use, and whether we dispense it to others or keep it to ourselves.

(b) Second is believer's own experience, which ought to be real "treasure" to himself and others (cf. 12:35); and question here is whether our personal experience is growing and becoming more helpful.

(c) Third is experience of others, such as found in one's knowledge of life, in reading of biography, etc., and in personal contacts; and we should ask ourselves how much we draw on this valuable source of wisdom.

(2) "Things new and old" speak of old truths and new applications of them:

(a) Time is old, but seasons are new, light is old, but days are new, trees may be old, but their leaves and blossoms are new; new things are often good because they spring from old things, and if old does not bring forth new it signs its own death warrant.

(b) Principles are perpetual, but applications should be personal and therefore contemporary; in theology likewise, if new is against old it is false, but if old theology has no new and up-to-date message it is useless.

(c) There are men who, knowing old but not new are narrow, and others who, knowing new but not old, are shallow; narrow man we are apt to put on shelf, but shallow man's resources are so easily exhausted that we soon discard him also.

(d) True disciple of Christ will be so well instructed as to be able to place before his hearers
"more light and truth . . . from His holy
Word"; and there will be old truths in new
dress as well as fresh truths that are timely,
suggestive, and spiritually inspiring, because
founded on historical fact and ancient verities.

(e) Christ Himself, of course, was always bringing
forth out of O.T. "things new and old" (cf.,
e.g., 22:32, Luke 24:27); it was new book
when He opened it, and those who have fellowship with Him will handle it likewise (cf.
Ps. 92:10, 119:18).
Illus.: There was always great freshness about
teaching of Hudson Taylor, and friend asked
him reason for it. He replied: "I give out in
the afternoon and evening what God has told
me in the morning."

(f) It may be asked whether Christian can, like
tree, strike his roots down and his branches
out; answer to this may be seen in measure-
ment of new Jerusalem by angel: "The length
and the breadth and the height of it are equal"
(Rev. 21:16); our outward reach toward man
will not go farther than our inward grasp of
God's truth and our upward aspiration toward
His Divine life.

III. The Teacher Rejected (vs. 53-58)

1. *Opportunity* (vs. 53, 54)

   a. At close of parables, Jesus "departed thence . . . into
   his own country"; this was region surrounding town
   of Nazareth where He had been brought up (cf. 2:23,
   Luke 2:39-52), and had spent so much of His life,
   "about thirty years" (Luke 3:23).

   b. There He taught in synagogue, doubtless one He Himself had attended (cf. Luke 4:16-30); and His teaching
   caused great astonishment and questioning instead of
   fitting sense of high privilege.

   c. People's first question was natural one, but they gave
   it wrong answer; if only they had attributed "this wis-

dom, and these mighty works" to God, what blessings might not have been theirs!

2. *Offense* (vs. 55-57a)

a. But continued questionings indicate doubt and implied hostility; thinking they knew Him and His family so well, they were surprised that one appearing so ordinary to them should utter such extraordinary things, and therefore they took offense.

b. Familiarity might have been supposed to impress and gratify these people, but they were refusing to acknowledge anything in Jesus that went beyond their common observation; they could not understand Him because they would not accept Him as Messiah and Lord.

3. *Outcome* (vs. 57b, 58)

a. This episode shows how easily men are made willing to oppose truth if it happens to go contrary to their own preconceived ideas and inclinations; and notwithstanding all our Lord said and did in Nazareth He was unable to influence His fellow townsmen because, as He told them, "a prophet is not without honour, save in his own country, and in his own house" (v. 57).

b. It was their refusal to honor Him that turned aside stream of blessing; for we read that "he did not many mighty works there because of their unbelief" (v. 58).

c. If truth of Jesus Christ is not accepted with full submission of faith, it can lie inert in human mind like any other knowledge, unproductive of good; and, while we cannot dry up great main tide flowing on to bless other lives, we do have solemn, fatal power to keep it out of our own lives, leaving them forever unblessed in backwater of pride and unbelief.

Conclusion

It is not easy to distinguish rigidly between the Kingdom of Heaven and the Kingdom of God; the former, as we have seen, is a phrase peculiar to Matthew and may have a Jewish aspect primarily, while the latter undoubtedly refers to God's rule over the universe in the widest possible meaning of the term and expresses the highest possible conception of His relationship to mankind. This Kingdom can be summed up in three aspects:

1. *The Kingdom in the Past*

   a. This was national and exemplified in kingdoms of David and Solomon.

   b. However, since these manifestly could not realize it in its completeness, prophets continually foretold coming of Kingdom that should be perfect and everlasting (e.g., Dan. 2:44, 45).

2. *The Kingdom in the Present*

   a. This is spiritual and includes period exemplified by "mysteries" of this chapter; to see and enter it calls for new birth (cf. John 3:3, 5).

   b. We are translated by God from kingdom of darkness into "the kingdom of the Son of his love" (Col. 1:13, A.S.V.); and our life in this Kingdom is to be "righteousness, and peace, and joy in the Holy Ghost" (Rom. 14:17).

3. *The Kingdom in the Future*

   a. This will be universal; but, first of all, Christ will fulfill literally prophecies made about Him in O.T. as King of the Jews.

   b. There seems no doubt, moreover, that N.T. prophecy in Luke 1:32, 33 will be as literally fulfilled in His second coming as was verse 31 in His first.

   c. Then from Christ's Jewish Kingship will be developed His universal Kingship, and He will reign, finally delivering up the Kingdom "to God, even the Father" (cf. 1 Cor. 15:24-28); this is the last and culminating expectation of God's people, and it is for this that they pray "Thy Kingdom come!" (6:10).

DEATH OF JOHN THE BAPTIST

Matthew 14:1-12

THE TIME was one of great solemnity, for Christ was about to enter upon the closing events of His earthly life, culminating in His sacrificial death. On His rejection at Nazareth (cf. 13:54-58), He seems to have withdrawn Himself from the public gaze, apparently because John the Baptist had just been murdered by Herod Antipas (cf. v. 13a). These twelve verses describing the circumstances of John's death form a solemn sequel to chapter 11, where from prison he had communicated with Jesus and had received our Lord's high praise (vs. 1-15). The story of John's closing days is at once sad and inspiring. The three leading characters, Herod, Herodias, and John, are a striking reminder of three others in Israel's history: Ahab, Jezebel, and Elijah (see 1 Kings 19 to 21). If John came in the spirit of Elijah (cf. Luke 1:17), Herodias certainly showed the wickedness of Jezebel and Herod the weakness of Ahab; and behind these human personalities were the same unseen powers causing this notable likeness. Back of Elijah and John was the Holy Spirit inspiring them with faith and fortitude, while back of the rulers and their womankind was the Evil One inciting them to evil in word and deed.

I. Cowardice

    a. Herod is awful example of weakness; it is always tragic when men are driven to evil because afraid to resist it, and weak people inevitably become wicked because it is less trouble to consent to sin than to withstand it.

    b. Herod, although sensual and self-indulgent (vs. 3, 6), had respected John (cf. Mark 6:20), and evidently his better nature was not dead; in fact, certain good influences came into his life through preaching and example of this faithful prophet (v. 4), together with healthy fear of people's estimate of John and of probable effect on them of his death (v. 5).

c. But when call of obedience to conscience was heard, Herod's will was afraid to act; entrapped into an oath (v. 7) which it should have been virtue to break, he feared his guests (v. 9) as earlier he had feared people.

d. Rather than forfeit their good opinion, he committed sin he regretted; and thus his weakness culminated in awful crime of murder (v. 10).

e. Later, as in case of many another weak character, Herod showed superstitious fear; for, when fame of Jesus reached him, he affirmed that John the Baptist, whom he knew he had had beheaded, was risen from dead, in foolish attempt to explain mighty works being done by our Lord (vs. 1, 2).

II. Craftiness

a. This is exemplified by Herodias; it was outgrowth of her cruel, wicked nature and inflamed by John the Baptist's denunciation of highly irregular union between her and Herod (vs. 3, 4).

b. It was not her first incestuous marriage; we know from contemporary historical sources that her first husband, Herod's half-brother Philip (v.3), was her uncle and was still alive, and now she was living unlawfully with her step-uncle, Herod.

c. Because of John's straight speaking, Herodias "had a quarrel against him and would have killed him" (Mark 6:19); and for her Herod had been "reproved by him" (Luke 3:19; cf. v. 4).

d. Consumed with hatred, she was biding her time until Herod's birthday feast gave her opportunity to use her daughter's dancing to get him to commit murder (vs. 6-11); and thus there were in effect two Herods — one who "feared John" (Mark 6:20), and one who feared his friends, his so-called wife, and his people.

III. Courage

a. We may well read between lines of this portion of Scripture and imagine loneliness, silence, and mystery in such a close of so fine a career; yet John witnessed by his death as much as he had by his life and preaching.

    b. As Anglican Collect for St. John the Baptist's Day reminds us, he had not only spoken the truth and boldly rebuked vice, but had patiently suffered for the truth's sake; and all this called for courage of highest order, both physical and moral.

    c. In relation to people, his plain speaking admitted of no doubt as to his meaning (cf. Luke 3:7-14), and his thoroughness was notable, too (v. 18); and, in relation to his disciples, it took courage not to be perturbed or jealous when they not only "followed Jesus" (John 1:37), but also reported that crowds were leaving him to do the same (cf. John 3:26-30).

    d. John was thus thoroughly consistent when, with splendid fearlessness, he rebuked Herod for his sins (cf. Luke 3:19); and doubtless he was just as brave when, as Luke adds, Herod "added yet this above all, that he shut up John in prison (v. 20).

    e. As a witness, a "voice" (John 1:23) as he called himself, and a "friend of the bridegroom" (John 3:29), to whom he likened himself, John the Baptist spoke for God and spoke out plainly, bearing his remarkable testimony to Divine truth; and we can have no doubt that he faced headsman's axe with equal courage and faith.

IV. Confidence

    a. It is beautiful to read that on death of their master, John's disciples, having paid last token of respect by burying his body, turned in sorrowing love and did what was very best they could do; they "went and told Jesus" (v. 12).

    b. One of Christianity's unique characteristics is its provision for reciprocal relationship between God and man; this is called "access" in Romans (5:2) and in Ephesians (2:18, 3:12), "drawing near" in Hebrews (7:19, 10:22), and "fellowship" in First John (1:3, 6, 7,).

    c. This relationship is not monologue but dialogue, conversation; and it is summed up in Gospels by words "tell [told] Jesus."

    d. Here they are used in time of sorrow; elsewhere they appear in connection with suffering (Mark 1:30), with salvation (Mark 5:33), with service (Mark 6:30), and with seeking (John 12:22).

e. Every one of us has need of frankness and willingness to tell Christ all that is in our hearts (cf. 1 Kings 10:2); it is proof of true conversion and important difference between Christian and non-Christian.

f. How simple it is to "tell Jesus," for it is so purely a personal matter; but it is also searching, for everything has to go that we are not willing to place in His hands (cf. Ps. 66:18); and it is eminently satisfying as we pour out our souls to One who has full possession of them.

Illus.: (1) Lord Cairns defined conversion as "a personal transaction with the Lord."

(2) Manager of large hotel always has master-key by means of which he can enter every room; so Jesus Christ must have master-key of our confidence in Him in order to possess each chamber of our house of life, for "if He is not Lord of all He is not Lord at all."

Conclusion

It is surely fitting at this point in our studies in Matthew's Gospel to sum up briefly the life of the exceptional man who was Christ's forerunner, linking, as it were, the old and the new dispensations, the Jewish economy with the Christian era:

1. *The Wonderful Birth*

   a. *The Angel's Visit* — Divine message to parents was gratifying reassurance, and description of child very significant (cf. Luke 1:14-17).

   b. *The Child's Name* — This was another sign of some exceptional happening (cf. Luke 1:57-66).

   c. *The Father's Song* — Reference to part to be taken by John in plan of salvation has great bearing on his character (cf. Luke 1:67-79).

2. *The Special Training*

   a. *The Home* — Son of priest, John was to be prophet and Nazarite (cf. Luke 1:15 with Num. 6:3), so that it may easily be inferred what its influence would be.

   b. *The Desert* — Solitude, abstemiousness, and hardship — all vital factors in the making of this man (cf. 3:1-4, Luke 1:80).

c. *The Call* — When ready, Divine voice summoned him to his appointed task (cf. Luke 3:2, John 1:33).

3. *The Great Work*

a. *What It Was* — John was called to bear testimony to Jesus in three ways: as Lamb of God, One who would baptize with Holy Spirit, and as Son of God (cf. John 1:29, 33, 34) — and therefore Messiah (vs. 15, 23, 30, 31).

b. *How It Was Done* — John called for repentance and baptism with view to remission of sins, emphasizing practical reality of receiving Messiah (cf. 3:2, 8).

c. *Why This Was Necessary* — There was much hypocrisy prevalent in Israel at that time, and John's preaching emphasized sincerity proved by willingness to submit to baptism and by thorough change of life (cf. Luke 3:3-18).

4. *The Deep Perplexity*

a. *His Expectation* — Perhaps John was puzzled by being put into prison, thus stopping his work, but certainly he seems to have been perplexed concerning Messiah for whom he had proclaimed judgeship (cf. Luke 3:17).

b. *His Information* — Instead, he heard Christ was doing works of mercy and pity (see Study No. 28, on 11:1-19, p. 153); John's knowledge was limited, and his trying position probably added to his confusion.

c. *His Reassurance* — But our Lord's message in reply to John's inquiry was further revelation of mercy and blessing by miracles of healing, and with it was gentle but faithful reminder that Baptist also would be blessed if he found no cause of stumbling in Jesus Christ (cf. 11:6).

5. *The Divine Testimony*

a. *The Praise* — Our Lord, however, would not allow Pharisees or others to imagine there was any fundamental fault in John, or that message sent him was severe rebuke; so Christ proceeded to praise Baptist in no measured terms (cf. 11:7-15).

b. *The Comparisons* — Three illustrations are used to show John's true character, and then he was said to be even greater than any prophet; and yet, as John was just outside new Kingdom, in position he would not take precedence.

c. *The Result* — These words evidently made definite spiritual effect, for Christ's hearers recognized their truth (cf. Luke 7:29).

6. *The Wide Influence*

a. *During Life* — After considering sad circumstances of his death covered in our present study, are we to say that John the Baptist had failed, that angel's reference to joy at his birth was not fully justified? No, for even during life all Israel regarded him as prophet (cf. Luke 20:6); and he may be said to have laid original foundation of Christian Church, in sense that two of his disciples were first members of its nucleus (cf. John 1:37).

b. *After Death* — Herod was not only one who thought John had risen from dead (v. 2; cf. Luke 9:7), which is all the more remarkable because he himself had never done any miracles (cf. John 10:41).

c. *In Later Days*

It is very remarkable that, far away from Palestine, in Ephesus, twenty-six years later, there were disciples of John who knew only his teaching, but responded immediately to Paul's fuller revelation regarding the Holy Spirit (cf. Acts 18:24 to 19:7); and, to go outside Scripture, great Jewish historian Josephus speaks of John with awe at about A.D. 70 — so far-reaching and so deep was powerful impression of his life and ministry.

What does John the Baptist have to say to us in the present day? We read in John 10:41: "All things that John spake of this man were true." We, too, must bear our testimony to our Lord: sometimes we must be stern, as the Baptist was, in denouncing sin or warning against it; at other times we must be tender, as he was, when telling of the Lamb of God slain for sinners. We must be faithful and yet loving, for God still needs witnesses and is ready to qualify them by the gifts of His marvelous grace.

33

A FRESH SERIES OF MIRACLES

Matthew 14:13-36

IF THE three methods of influence used by our Lord during His earthly ministry — teaching, miracle-working, and the training of the apostolate — the miracles form an almost constant succession of aspects of His Divine purpose and of phases of His almighty power. After the story of the death of John the Baptist, Matthew gives three of these miracles, each with its own special message.

I. Christ Feeding Five Thousand (vs. 13-23)

This is the only miracle recorded in all four Gospels, an indication of its importance in the eyes of the Evangelists. It occurred at a crisis in our Lord's ministry and its effect was overwhelming (cf. John 6:14, 15). In Matthew's Gospel it marks the resumption of miracle-working that reveals not only the power, but also the character of Christ. In Mark and Luke it is closely connected not only with the death of John the Baptist, but also with the return of the Apostles from their tour (Mark 6:30, 31, Luke 9:10); and John records it after quoting one of our Lord's great discourses on the subject of His own Deity (John 5:19-46). This great turning-point in our Lord's life also marked the end of the year in Galilee, the preparatory stage of His ministry, and introduced His true life purpose; in fact, this miracle is seen to be a symbol of His great atoning work.

1. *A Tiring Time* (vs. 13, 14)

    a. On hearing of John's death, Christ had withdrawn into desert place on east side of lake of Galilee, to be there, perhaps, until storm had blown over, since His time for meeting Herod Antipas was not yet (cf. 23:8, Luke 9:9); but also He and His disciples were in serious need of rest (cf. Mark 6:30, 31).

    b. This, however, proved impossible through great pressure

of gathering crowd which, discovering where He had gone, followed Him on foot out of cities of region (v. 13) ; and, moved with compassion in presence of so great a multitude with sick among them, He characteristically re-commenced His work of healing (v. 14).

2. *A Pressing Need* (vs. 15-17)

   a. Place was desert, practically uninhabited, time was evening, crowd was large, need for food was urgent, and supply was scanty; disciples naturally came to ask that multitudes might be sent away to provide food for themselves, because there was no other way to satisfy their hunger (v. 15).

   b. When Christ replied there was no need for people to go away, and that disciples were to give them food, He received obvious reply pointing to scanty supply (vs. 16, 17) ; they were, of course, reckoning without their Master, who had already decided what to do (cf. John 6:6).
   N.B. To use one of Horace Bushnell's suggestive sermon titles, disciples were to learn that "Duty is not measured by ability."

3. *A Full Supply* (vs. 18-21)

   a. Then comes picturesque story of miracle (cf. Mark 6:39-44, Luke 9:14-17) : loaves and fishes which, John tells us (6:9), belonged to "a lad" who was at hand, were to be brought to Christ and seating of crowd was to be arranged in orderly way (vs. 18, 19a) ; it must have taken great faith both to carry this out, and also for people themselves to sit down.

   b. Then came our Lord's reverent testimony of blessing for bread, followed by distribution of it (v. 19b) ; and in very short time there was complete satisfaction, for after all had been filled, twelve baskets full remained for future use (vs. 20, 21 — Greek, "fragments in abundance"), or, as has often been suggested, one for each of the Twelve (cf., *contra,* 15:37).

   c. This miracle is not only marvel, but also parable; we may see in it, as in vision —

      (1) A perishing world — indicated by crowd;

      (2) A powerless Church — shown by helplessness of disciples;

(3) A perfect Saviour — exemplified by calm attitude and compassionate action of Christ.

d. Surely infinite blessing would have come to all men long since, had Church but lived out principles here embodied; for satisfaction of spiritual hunger of others is supreme purpose of both Christian Church and individual believer.

e. Furthermore, this miracle was followed on very next day by Christ's references to Himself as Bread of Life (cf. John 6:22-59); and He still says to us, as world reveals itself as hungry and perishing, "Give ye them to eat" (v. 16).*

4. *A Significant Act* (vs. 22, 23)

a. Immediately after this great day of toil and strain, our Lord sent His disciples by boat across lake, while He Himself went up into mountain for quiet time of prayer after dismissing multitude; use of word "constrained" seems to suggest they may have been unwilling to go.

b. If so, John's Gospel probably gives explanation: multitudes were so enthusiastic as result of miracle that, seeing in Christ leader who could realize all their desires, attempted there and then to "make him a king" (John 6:15); and perhaps disciples were influenced in same direction.

c. It was this tendency that Christ resisted, because He knew inner meaning of His mission and impossibility for Him to have at that time any relationship to Israel other than spiritual one; and from that day, within one year of His death, His popularity declined, for reception of His subsequent teaching at Capernaum (cf. John 6:60-66) shows how shallow and mistaken had been impressions made on people, even on "many of his disciples" (v. 66).

d. But into ear and heart of His heavenly Father He could pour out all these feelings and experiences in communion and prayer on mountain alone; and doubtless He felt very human need to refresh Himself for further work in

---

*For similar treatments of this and other outlines of this miracle, see author's volumes, *Outline Studies in Luke* (1984), *The Apostle John* (1984), Kregel Publications, and *Sermon Outlines* (1947), Wm. B. Eerdmans Publishing Co.

face of increasing opposition and before starting to
follow His disciples to opposite side of lake.

In every life there is an inmost place,
  A silent, cloistered spot, whereto the heart
  In uttermost aloneness draws apart,
  As did the ancient High Priest from his race
  To make atonement in the sacred space.
  Nor key of truest friend, nor subtle art
  Of strongest foe, that lock can break or start
Which bars admittance to this holiest place.

R. W. van Kirk

II. Christ Walking on the Water (vs. 24-33)

1. *The New Revelation* (vs. 24, 25)

    a. While Christ prayed alone in mountain, disciples were
    struggling against wind and waves to cross lake, "toiling
    in rowing" (Mark 6:48) for hours, though distance across
    was only five or six miles (v. 24).

    b. It was early morning, about three o'clock, therefore,
    when Christ went out to them, walking on water (v. 25);
    and, since He was doing what was humanly impossible,
    this was revelation of His Divine power in new and
    startling form.

    N.B. It is said that among ancient Egyptians symbol of
    impossibility was figure with two feet planted upon expanse
    of ocean.

2. *The Characteristic Response* (vs. 26-28)

    a. *Doubt and Fear* (vs. 26, 27)

        (1) Disciples were terrified, not recognizing their Master
        and thinking instinctively, as was common among
        Jews of that day, of an apparition, so that they cried
        out in their fright (v. 26); and this was certainly
        doubt of His presence.

        (2) But immediately He calmed their fears by sound of
        His voice uttering well-known phrase, "Be of good
        cheer" (v. 27; cf. 9:2, 22, Mark 10:49, John 16:33,
        Acts 23:11); and He added what they most needed to
        know, that it was indeed He Himself.

(3) We may well keep in mind that very waves that were difficulty to disciples were used as pathway for our Lord's feet; so over whatever waves of sorrow or suffering, discipline or testing. He may come to us, He will say, "Be of good cheer; it is I; be not afraid."

> *God moves in a mysterious way*
> *His wonders to perform;*
> *He plants His footsteps in the sea*
> *And rides upon the storm.*

> *Ye fearful saints, fresh courage take;*
> *The clouds ye so much dread*
> *Are big with mercy, and shall break*
> *In blessings on your head.*

> WM. COWPER

b. *Doubt and Faith* (v. 28)

  (1) Peter's rejoinder, "Lord, if it be thou —," is indeed characteristic and also very sad, for Jesus had stated fact — "It is I"; and yet His disciple, instead of accepting it, voiced mere supposition — "if—."

  (2) This was still doubt of Christ's presence, but it was strangely mingled with dawning trust — "bid me come unto thee on the water"; however, there may also have been conceit and rashness in Simon Peter, rebound from despair after physical exhaustion and danger to buoyant hope and relief on seeing his Master.

3. *The Sharp Reminder* (vs. 29-33)

  a. Now Simon is to learn his lesson; Jesus said only, "Come!" as though permitting rather than bidding, allowing His disciple to have his own way (v. 29a).

  b. All went well at first, but Peter's gaze was evidently soon diverted from his Master to effect on waves of "boisterous" wind; then fear took place of what faith he had, and he began to sink, calling out, "Lord, save me!" (vs. 29b, 30):

  (1) *Faith.* When Peter took Christ at His word the Lord bestowed upon him His own power, in which He Himself trod waters, at very moment Peter ventured on his Master's invitation; there was no

hesitation, or "trying to trust," such as many of us know, but eager bounding forth in joyous reliance, for he had only to look, to believe, and to step out.

(2) *Fear.* But when Peter allowed circumstances to come between him and Jesus, he was sure to fail; and so shall we in like case.

c. Peter's Master was near, however, for He had only to stretch out His hand to catch him, though not without rebuke for his lack of faith, since this was, in face of Christ's presence, doubt of His power; and question, "Wherefore didst thou doubt?" (v. 31) was reminder both of disciple's own weakness and of absolute necessity of his Lord's presence and power.

> *Touch me, O Lord, and let my pride*
> *Be smitten to Thy feet;*
> *O'er every foe triumphant ride,*
> *Thy victory complete.*

> *Touch me, O Lord, impart Thy peace,*
> *Thy legacy Divine;*
> *Rebuke the storm, let discord cease*
> *Within this breast of mine.*

d. As soon as Christ entered into boat, wind ceased; and then we read that all in it came and worshipped Him, acknowledging Him as Son of God (vs. 32, 33); and John adds, "and immediately the ship was at the land whither they went" (6:21).

III. Christ Healing the Sick (vs. 34-36)

1. *A Great Concourse*

a. Natural result of Christ's arrival at Gennesaret on western side of lake (v. 34) soon followed; crowds gathered, and when people "had knowledge of him" (v. 35) they sent out word through all that countryside and brought to Him their sick ones.

b. Then they besought our Lord for permission to touch but border of His garment; and, we read, "as many as touched were made perfectly whole" (v. 36).

2. *A Striking Contrast*

    a. We may compare Gennesaret with Gadara (cf. 8:34, Mark 5:17), where they actually asked Christ to depart, although He was there in same power and longing to bless; to each place according to its faith: no faith, no blessing; strong faith, overwhelming blessing.

    b. How simple and full of common sense were these people; the Lord had come and it was their great opportunity.

    c. No sick one was to be forgotten — all were to be brought to Him; and it would be enough even to touch His clothing.

May we be just as simple and faithful, that we may enjoy comparable spiritual blessing!

Conclusion

1. From the feeding of the five thousand we notice several aspects of our Master's care for human life, physical as well as spiritual:

    a. *His Motive Was Compassion.* Multitudes were suffering and He could not but concern Himself with provision for their needs.

    b. *His Manner Was Calm.* No fear, no doubt, no hesitation, but perfect quietness, restfulness, and authority characterized Him, because He knew not only "what He would do," but also that His Divine power was more than suffcient to meet the emergency.

    c. *His Method Was Co-operation.* This "utterly impossible" task was accomplished in a very simple way:

        (1) *Complete surrender.* His disciples were to begin by bringing to Christ everything of food that they possessed; and then they continued by doing what He told them and because He commanded them.

        (2) *Complete satisfaction.* This glorious outcome needed two elements:

            (a) Divine — God in Christ giving Himself as Bread of Life, to be appropriated and assimilated through simple trust in Him;

            (b) Human — individual disciples, making up His

Church, giving themselves to Christ to distribute
that Bread of Life throughout world.

Although we may well think of Christ as the calm, compassionate Saviour who has made ample provision of redemption
and power, it is to us, His people, to whom He has committed
the work of proclaiming His gospel. Like the Apostles, we
must be trustful and obedient, and then the multitudes will
be fed and all their deepest needs satisfied.

2. In connection with the miracle of Christ walking on the
water, let us contemplate our own difficulties and the way
out of them:

a. *Trial.* Anglican Catechism speaks of "the waves of this
troublesome world;" and full Christian life is well likened
to walk upon waves of trouble, of temptation, of sin, and
sin, and is impossible in our own strength.

> *Keep looking up —*
> *The waves that roar around thy feet*
> *Jehovah-Jireh will defeat,*
> *When looking up.*
>
> *Keep looking up —*
> *God only knows the way we take;*
> *But plain and clear the path He'll make*
> *If we look up.*

b. *Trust.* It is vital to remember that our Lord is not
only walking on our waters of trouble, but He often overrules them to bring great blessings into our lives, if only
we keep looking off from self and circumstances towards
Him and venturing in faith at His bidding.

> *Keep looking up —*
> *Though darkness seems to wrap thy soul;*
> *The Light of light shall fill the whole,*
> *When looking up.*
>
> *Keep looking up—*
> *Though all goes wrong and leaves thee sad,*
> *The peace of God shall make thee glad,*
> *When looking up.*

c. *Triumph.* As it was with the disciples so will it be with us, resting on His love and grace, as "they willingly received him into the ship" (John 6:21), they found Him abundantly able to bring them to "the land whither they went."

> *Keep looking up —*
> *When worn, distracted with the fight;*
> *Your Captain gives you conquering might*
> *When you look up.*
>
> *Keep looking up —*
> *When death comes, fear not thou the tomb;*
> *Your Lord smiles on you, saying "come!"*
> *Then still look up.*

A. F. MORDAUNT SMITH

Let us, then, in our Christian walk as well as in our Christian work, "trust and obey"!

> *Those who trust Him wholly*
> *Find Him wholly true.*

34

CHRIST AND JEWISH TRADITION

Matthew 15:1-20

In both Matthew and Mark the miracles recorded in the preceding chapter are closely followed by fresh opposition from the scribes and Pharisees. This time, representatives came all the way from Jerusalem (v. 1) to engage our Lord in controversy, with the accusation that His disciples transgressed "the tradition of the elders" (v. 2), and the implication that He Himself approved such alleged errors as the practice of eating with unwashed hands.

I. The Background of the Controversy

1. *The Divine Purpose*

   a. Jewish nation had been trained for their realization of God's plan in history by being shown what He meant by holiness; and root idea of this throughout their national life was separation.

   b. Various sacrifices, purifications, and other ritual institutions were outward and visible object-lessons of absolute necessity of this complete separation from evil.

   c. This principle was to enter as fully as possible into ordinary daily life and was to be demonstrated both to Jews themselves and to those around them; it was for this important reason that distinctions were made in food, dress, and custom.

2. *The Fatal Misunderstanding*

   a. Nation as a whole, however, entirely misinterpreted God's purpose for it, confusing means with end; instead of regarding themselves as spiritual people intended to bless others, Jews came to think of themselves as earthly people, superior to others.

   b. At same time, they assumed things forbidden were essentially unclean; and, acting on this view, they in-

creased list of requirements and thereby emptied law
of God of all its spiritual meaning.

II. The Error of the Pharisees (vs. 3-9)

This is the point of the present references to tradition in
Pharisees' question of Christ (v. 2), and in His countering
question of them (v. 3); and two stages of error are clearly
seen:

1. *Transgression* (vs. 3-6a)

   a. At first they transgressed God's law by their observance
      of mere tradition (v. 3).

   b. This led them, as Christ declared, actually to set aside
      true relationship of son to father and mother by allowing
      man to give to God what should have been used for main-
      tenance of his parents (vs. 4-6a)

2. *Hypocrisy* (vs. 6b-9)

   a. Outcome was that they soon made void Word of God
      by their tradition (v. 6b), and became hypocrites (v. 7)
      in heart, word, and life; and Christ once more quoted
      Isaiah to prove His point (vs. 7-9; cf. Isa. 29:13).

   b. Whenever anything is insisted on as of Divine authority
      which God has not appointed, some command of His will
      inevitably be put aside; to add to Divine commandments
      is, therefore, solemnly denounced (cf. Rev. 22:18, 19).

   c. Traditions, when once invested with anything like author-
      ity, tend to obscure commands and displace supremacy of
      Scripture; indeed, there is nothing more solemnly signif-
      icant than that in proportion as tradition, even Church
      tradition, gains sway, reverence for Scripture declines.
      N.B. It may be added, however, that no one objects to
      traditions if such have warrant in Scripture; indeed,
      we value every proper appeal to Church precedent, be-
      lieving much of it has its place and power. But this is
      very different to co-ordinating it with Scripture or, worse,
      reversing order and making Scripture subject to it.

   d. Loyalty to Word of God must take first place, or else
      vital concerns of soul, like saving faith in Christ and
      humble walking with Him, will become more and more
      widely ignored.

III. The Result of the Controversy (vs. 10-20)

1. *A Public Declaration* (vs. 10, 11)

   a. Our Lord, calling crowd nearer (v. 10), makes clean sweep of all these distinctions of tradition.

   b. He says it is not what man eats with his physical mouth, or use of food, that makes him impure; it is what goes out from his mouth morally, in form of language, that proves true character (v. 11).

2. *A Private Elaboration* (vs. 12-20)

   a. No wonder that, as disciples came to report, "the Pharisees were offended" (v. 12) by this plain statement; but Christ went on to elucidate for benefit of Twelve.

   b. He stated that mere traditions of men are plants that God has not planted; they have sprung from temporal motives and, as they have been made subject to temporal interests, they have become hindrances; for this reason, He declared, they shall at last meet with deserved fate of being "rooted up" (v. 13).

   c. Then Christ adds, with deep solemnity, that Pharisees were to be let alone; their utter blindness to everything inward and spiritual had resulted not only in awful state of their own lives, but also in their complete unfitness to guide destinies of others (v. 14).

   d. They observed with great scrupulosity many outward ordinances, and yet neglected inner and superior requirements of mercy, judgment, and love; thus they entirely perverted regulations of Levitical law which were intended to teach true nature of sin and principle of holiness.

   e. At Peter's insistence of non-comprehension (v. 15), our Lord expressed surprise, but proceeded to state once more and in fuller detail antithesis between human mouth in physical and in moral senses; He declared it distinguished between two types of defilement (vs. 16-19), one which can be overcome by nature, and other which has dreadful and solemn consequences affecting untold numbers of people.

   f. Therefore, concluded our Lord, adverting to original complaint of His opponents, "to eat with unwashen hands defileth not a man" (v. 20).

g. Vital principle was here involved by which all ordinances concerning meats were finally removed; and thenceforward every creature of God was to be regarded as good (cf. Mark 7:19, A.S.V.; 1 Tim. 4:3-7).

Conclusion

The distinction between clean and unclean was made under the Old Covenant, according to the purpose of God; but under the New Covenant all such distinctions are now done away in Christ. We should note carefully the Apostolic teaching as to this:

1. Nothing is unclean of itself (cf. Rom. 14:14).
2. To the pure all things are pure (cf. Tit. 1:16).
3. The fullness of the earth is the Lord's (cf. 1 Cor. 10:26).
4. Therefore, what God has cleansed, no one needs to call common or unclean (cf. Acts 10:14, 15).
5. All such things were but a shadow of "the things to come; but the body is Christ's" (Col. 2:16, 17, A.S.V.; cf. 1 Cor. 6:19, 20).

35

CHRIST AND GENTILE FAITH

Matthew 15:21-39

THE OPPOSITION to our Lord at this point necessitated a journey northwards outside the limits of the land of Israel (v. 21), probably for personal safety and to avoid premature violence (cf. Mark 7:24). It is striking that He should have thus been driven into the lands of heathenism by the murderous plans of His own Jewish compatriots. But the great truth of the cessation of all traditional distinctions, such as the ones implicit in the complaint of the Pharisees in the opening verses of the chapter, is soon illustrated. This is by means of the appearance, first, of a Gentile woman and, second, of a crowd largely made up of Gentiles from Decapolis (cf. Mark 7:31), on the return journey.

I. Christ and the Woman of Canaan (vs. 22-28)

Mark describes her as "a Greek, a Syrophenician by nation" (7:26), and the story of her experience is a study in our Lord's response to human faith in Him wherever found. This includes its awakening, development, testing, and reward; and there are four natural divisions, indicated by the word "answered" (vs. 23, 24, 26, 28).

A. Faith Manifested (vs. 22, 23)

1. *The Cry for Mercy* (v. 22)

   a. Outside of Israel though she might be, "one touch of nature," in this case sorrow in home, is amply demonstrated by her plea; this is on behalf of her demented daughter.

   b. This, her first cry, is primal need of every soul, "mercy," or God's favor to (positively) *un*deserving, as distinct from grace, God's favor to (negatively) *non*-deserving; mercy, because of broken law and even after outrage to love.

c. This mercy is only possible when we are willing to acknowledge Christ as Lord, as did this woman; she had doubtless but recently heard of Him, even something of His Messiahship, possibly through some neighbor.

d. She came to Him, therefore, feeling sure He could, and hoping He would, hear and help; and yet elements of her faith were mixed and it needed development and training.

2. *The Answer of Silence* (v. 23a)

a. This must have seemed strange, for Christ's response was usually so prompt and infinitely tender; but it was probably due to fact that, besides addressing Him as "Lord," she had also called Him "Son of David" (v. 22).

b. This was term properly applicable to Him only as Jewish Messiah, and therefore not for her as Gentile to use; so that she needed further enlightenment.

c. Cf. Bartimaeus (Mark 10:46-52), who used same term and found immediate response; but he was a Jew.
N.B. Four occasions are recorded on which Christ was silent:

(1) Silence of Testing — as here, when He restrained Himself in order to give more and draw out faith:

(2) Silence of Rebuke (John 8:6, 7), against sin and hypocrisy;

(3) Silence of Judgment (26:63, etc.), before His accusers, because they had lost capacity to recognize truth and righteousness; and —

(4) Silence of Yearning (27:39-44, etc.) in face of chorus of derision, because His people knew not what they did.

B. **Faith Discouraged** (vs. 23b, 24)

1. *The Interruption of Impatience* (v. 23b)

a. How narrow and selfish was request of disciples that the Lord would "send her away"; they were probably embarrased by woman's calling out in public and impatient to continue on their way.

b. Even yet they were not instructed as to their Master's

mission; and in any case it was not "after" them but "after" Christ that she was crying out in anguish over her daughter's plight.

2. *The Answer of Limitation* (v. 24)

a. Here was further test of her faith as He reminded her that He had been sent during His earthly ministry only to people of Israel; and it is noteworthy here that His life touched Gentiles hardly at all.

b. There was wisdom in this plan, for He would have lost influence over His own nation as Divinely appointed vehicle of grace had He not recognized racial situation; and it would have been premature to proclaim universality of gospel until He had first prepared way and enlisted co-workers among Jews, although day was now coming when He would begin to widen His ministry by recognition of other peoples.

c. Thus do God's plans develop — with no haste, no costly errors; and this answer of Christ's, "I am not sent but unto the lost sheep of the house of Israel," was doubtless for His narrow-minded disciples — calling their compatriots "lost sheep" — as well as for this woman, who was standing her ground nevertheless.

C. **Faith Tested** (vs. 25, 26)

1. *The Call for Help* (v. 25)

a. Genuine and pressing though her need, she first came and "worshipped him"; she could not understand, but still she adored — true posture for believer.

b. Then she uttered her second prayer; "help" was her great need, as it is ours.

c. If mercy is chiefly associated with beginning of Christian life, help is one great need all through subsequent Christian experience; we must have help against temptation, in difficulty, in sorrow, in weakness, in service — in everything and at all times.

d. This woman's prayer was short, for sorrow abbreviates by its very urgency; and no longer is He "Son of David" to her, but simply "Lord," denoting human submission.

N.B. (1) In this case prayer was "Lord, help me" — in difficulty; (2) In Peter's it was "Lord, save me" — from danger; (3) In case of thief on cross it was "Lord, remember me" — in death.

2. *The Answer of Refusal* (v. 26)

 a. Once more our Lord uttered an unpalatable truth, namely, difference between "children" and "dogs"; and this was reminder of generally accepted comparison between Jews and Gentiles.

 b. But gradually He was disciplining this woman and developing her faith; dog was animal declared unclean by law and much despised by Jews as scavenger (cf. Exod. 22:31, 1 Kings 14:11, Prov. 26:11); so that, taken at face value, this was searching test and hard saying.

D. Faith Rewarded (vs. 27, 28)

1. *The Appeal of Acquiescence* (v. 27)

 a. Her third response was "Yes, Lord" (A.S.V.) as, with magnificent faith, true humility, and mental agility, this woman of Canaan turned implied refusal into fresh appeal, seizing hold of precise term used by Christ, Greek word found only in N.T. and only in this incident (cf. Mark 7:27).

 b. He had actually said "little dogs" or, as we might say, "doggies," pets of household rather than fierce scavengers of street; and, taking up this affectionate name, she makes her claim on Him as Master of house and accepts conditions laid upon her.

 c. She disclaims desire for "children's bread" (v. 26) and asks only "crumbs which fall" (v. 27); and, with such high thoughts of Christ, "crumbs" are enough.

 d. Cf. difference now and at start of interchange: true faith is elicited, and self is first forgotten, then confronted, and finally surrendered; and thus Christ's purpose in this encounter is achieved.

2. *The Answer of Blessing* (v. 28)

 a. No wonder our Lord praised her faith and granted her request; indeed, there was double bounty bestowed —

daughter healed and mother blessed — but it had taken sorrow and supplication to bring success.

b. This woman's love for child had prompted her to come and, joined with her persistence and will power, to incite her to continue; but beneath all this she was becoming concerned with very character of Jesus Christ Himself.

c. She had nothing to go on but His Person; yet, knowing Him personally, she could doubtless read hidden encouragement and claim her blessing, even though it were only equal to portion of "little dogs."

d. Record of His responses reads to us severe and stern, but we cannot doubt that this woman's instinctive insight caught real meaning of Christ's words; it was surely because of His essential attitude that her faith persisted until it gained its desire.

e. Fellowship with the Lord Himself can indeed unlock secret of His words; and this is no less true to today.

Unanswered yet? The prayer your lips have pleaded
In agony of heart these many years?
Does faith begin to fail? Is hope departing?
And think you all in vain those falling tears?
Say not the Father hath not heard your prayer;
You shall have your desire, some time, somewhere.

Unanswered yet? Though when you first presented
This one petition at the Father's throne
It seemed you could not wait the time of asking,
So urgent was your heart to make it known.
Though years have passed since then, do not despair,
The Lord will answer you, some time, somewhere.

Unanswered yet? Nay, do not say "unanswered";
Perhaps your part is not yet wholly done;
The work began when first your prayer was uttered,
And God will finish what He has begun.
If you will keep the incense burning there,
His glory you shall see, some time, somewhere.

Unanswered yet? Faith cannot be unanswered,
Her feet are firmly planted on the Rock;

Amid the wildest storms she stands undaunted
Nor quails before the loudest thunder shock.
She knows Omnipotence has heard her prayer
And cries, "It shall be done, some time, somewhere!"

II. Christ and the Multitudes (vs. 29-39)

Our Lord had now reached the halfway mark of His earthly ministry and He was at the height of His influence. These verses continue the account of what happened during His withdrawal from the land of Israel for a time. On leaving the borders of Tyre and Sidon (cf. vs. 21, 29), He and His disciples were approaching the Sea of Galilee from the east, for Mark tells us (7:31) that they came "through the midst of the coasts of Decapolis."

A. The Blessing of Health (vs. 29-31)

1. *Convocation*

   a. People of region were evidently encouraged by miracle of healing on Canaanite woman's daughter, for they gathered in multitudes on mountain where Jesus had seated Himself, probably to rest after long journey on foot (v. 29).

   b. Many of these were doubtless outside covenant, like woman, since this episode took place in Decapolis; and this seems to be borne out by Matthew's statement that afterwards "they glorified the God of Israel" (v. 31).

   c. It is true that, so far as possible, apparently Christ confined His healing influence to chosen people; but it is notable that, when strangers came to Him in faith, He bestowed upon them also His abundant blessing.

2. *Action*

   a. These were wonderful events, and yet how simply and easily they came about; people, realizing opportunity, each thought of some suffering neighbor and gave himself to getting that person into presence of Christ.

   b. We can well imagine every upward approach thronged as though some great hospital had emptied out on to that waste place.

3. *Benefaction*

   a. All were healed, for neither variety of troubles nor their prolonged continuance made slightest difference to Great Physician (v. 30).

b. Mark tells us (7:32-37) of one specific cure, that of man who was deaf and dumb.

4. *Ascription*

a. As these people went down that mountainside they were radiant and exultant, giving glory to God (v. 31) and proclaiming, "He hath done all things well" (Mark 7:37).

b. All this is parable for today, since our Lord still sits in mount of communion and welcomes all who come near, bestowing just the blessing needed and sending away hearts and lives grateful and rejoicing.

c. If only His Church were really alive to opportunity of bringing needy ones into presence of her Master, we should see still greater things (cf. John 14:12); and our praises would be as frank and exultant as were those that day in Decapolis.

B. The Blessing of Sustenance (vs. 32-39)

This is the story of a miracle similar to that in the previous chapter. Its points of difference include the number of people fed, the number of baskets of food left over, and the time and scene. The feeding of the five thousand took place just before the Passover (cf. John 6:4), and near Bethsaida (cf. Luke 9:10); the feeding of the four thousand followed Christ's withdrawal into Gentile territory, probably about a month after Passover, and the place was the district of Decapolis (cf. Mark 7:31, 8:1). Verse 32 follows so closely upon verse 31 that it is virtually certain that this crowd of four thousand men, women, and children (v. 38), was largely made up of Gentiles. But the two miracles are linked together by Christ Himself in Matthew's next chapter (cf. 16:9, 10); and John tells us how, immediately after the first one, He spoke of Himself as the Bread of Life (John 6:26-35). Since a factual outline of this second miracle would have to be almost repetitive, let us here consider Christ Himself as satisfying the spiritual needs of men, even as He twice provided for their physical needs with "the meat that perisheth" (John 6:27).

1. *The Bread of Life Offered* (cf. vs. 32-35)

    a. Christ came to give life, to sustain it, and to satisfy it; and He always is ready to give more than we can appropriate, because His supply is infinitely beyond our absorption (cf. v. 37).

    b. The remarkable and blessed fact is that this heavenly food never cloys or palls; the more we have the more we want, and the better we enjoy it.

2. *The Bread of Life Prepared* (cf. v. 36)

    a. Bread is manufactured food, from grain adapted for human consumption; life could not be maintained directly on chemical elements of this food, and so there must be development into loaves and division into portions.

    b. Similarly, God as food of soul must be mediated to us through His Son, our Lord; and He was prepared for this function through His life, death, and resurrection (cf. John 6:51, Heb. 5:5-10).

3. *The Bread of Life Assimilated* (cf. vs. 37, 38)

    a. No substance can be food for anyone unless it is accepted and used; and Christ will never be our spiritual Bread until and unless He is appropriated by the soul.

    b. Faith is like mouth and digestion of spiritual nature; it is thus through simple trust in Christ that we assimilate and appreciate what He has done (cf. John 6:35).

4. *The Bread of Life Distributed* (cf. v. 36b)

    a. In this miracle of feeding four thousand people on seven loaves and a few fishes, Christ could have done without His disciples; but He used them as fellow laborers.

    b. So today He has committed to His people task of proclaiming His gospel, and we are called "workers together with him" (2 Cor. 6:1); and only when we are obedient and trustful, as disciples were, will multitudes be fed.

Conclusion

Let us see in this passage two pictures of Christ in relation to human life:

1. *Christ Helping and Healing*

   These related elements are particularly noteworthy:
   a. The Saviour powerful and the woman persevering;
   b. The Saviour present and the people participating.

2. *Christ Sustaining and Satisfying*

   Similar elements are necessary here also:
   a. The Saviour compassionate and the situation controlled;
   b. The disciples co-operative and the multitude content.

This is the crown of life, its perfect realization — complete acquiescence in the purpose of God; this is to delight in His will, to be like our Lord who was "content to do it," as the Book of Common Prayer has it — that is, "contained" by God's will, the complete "contents" and perfect "content" of our lives.

36

REBUKE AND WARNING

Matthew 16:1-12

In the closing verse of the preceding chapter Christ is recorded as having crossed to the opposite side of the lake, "into the coasts of Magdala" (15:39), or Magadan (A.S.V.), a somewhat obscure place; but He could not long be hidden. The Jewish leaders, Pharisees and Sadducees, were ready to confront Him, in persistent and ever deepening hostility, with another demand for a sign from heaven (v. 1). This encounter not only elicited from our Lord a rebuke to the leaders, but it also provided an object-lesson for the disciples that led to a timely warning.

I. Christ's Foes Rebuked (vs. 1-4)

1. *Two Kinds of Sign* (vs. 2, 3)

   a. Our Lord's response was first indirect, as He reminded Pharisees and Sadducees that, if they saw sky red in evening, they would think immediately of fine weather;

but, if they saw lowering sky in morning, they would expect foul weather.

b. In effect, they were told that, while they would need no further physical sign than "the face of the sky" (v. 3), they were not equally quick to read spiritual signs that were quite as plain; and He called these "signs of the times" in which they were then living.

N.B. Several related "times" are mentioned in N.T.:

(1) Time of repentance (Mark 1:15);

(2) Time of refreshing (Acts 3:19);

(3) Time of restitution (Acts 3:21);

(4) Time of results (13:30, 21:34; Mark 11:13);

(5) Time of reformation (Heb. 9:10);

(6) Time of redemption (2 Cor. 6:2).

c. Pharisees understood certain physical signs, but were utterly blind to revelation of God's spiritual dealings although, as Christ strongly implied, these were in harmony with spiritual laws and equally capable of being understood.

d. This persistence in bondage to external was characteristic of their view of earthly Messiah doing visible marvels; and so their hearts were hardened against Jesus Christ.

e. Where willing heart is there is spiritual vision, and where there is no vision there is for people neither life (cf. Prov. 29:18) nor warmth of heart; Pharisees' dullness came from their spiritual deadness, for if they had cared they would have seen (cf. 1 Chron. 12:32, 38).

2. *Their Only Sign* (vs. 1, 4)

a. Now comes (v. 4) Christ's direct reply to foes' request (v. 1); He tells them once again that only sign given them would be that of Jonah (cf. 12:39, 40).

b. This time He mentions it without any further explanation; it is as though He refers them to His former statement as sufficient and final.

c. Thus were these men shown again to be not alert men of God they thought they were, but wholly worldly at heart; and certainly they were completely incapable of understanding implications of their "sign" as foreshadowing death and resurrection of Christ, revealed further on in this chapter (cf. v. 21) to almost as uncomprehending disciples.

Matthew now records that our Lord again turned His back on His opponents and "departed" (v. 4), crossing "to the other side" (v. 5), or north-eastern end, of lake.

II. Christ's Friends Warned (vs. 5-12)

1. *The Danger Represented* (vs. 5, 6)

a. As result of opponents' request for sign, Christ is going to address words of solemn warning to His disciples; and account is introduced by mention of fact that they had forgotten to take bread with them (v. 5).

b. They were evidently preoccupied with this lack when their Master spoke to them, urging that they beware of "leaven" of Pharisees and Sadducees (v. 6), by which He clearly meant their teaching and leadership — their "doctrine" (cf. v. 12).

c. Just as request for sign came from coalition of Pharisees and Sadducees, usually utterly opposed to each other, so here "leaven" was really twofold, though essentially one in effect.

d. Pharisees represented bigotry and Sadducees rationalism, but both were expressions of essential worldliness and secularism under guise of piety; and each was error calculated to corrupt true religion, and Christ's disciples were to avoid both.

2. *The Difficulty Resolved* (vs. 7-12)

a. Disciples did not understand their Master at all and "reasoned among themselves" (v. 7) as to significance of word "leaven"; their blindness is indeed astonishing and showed how "little faith" (v. 8) they possessed after all this time.

b. Even two great miracles of feeding multitudes seem actually to have impressed these men with importance of taking loaves of bread with them rather than with need of always being in presence of an all-powerful Christ (vs. 9, 10).

c. In view of this difficulty and misunderstanding Christ explained His meaning (v. 11), implying this was no question about His power to provide bread if needed, but that He was concerned over His disciples being influenced by erroneous teaching of Pharisees and Sadducees; "then understood they" (v. 12) that He was warning them not of leaven of bread, but of that which symbolized false doctrine (cf. 13:33, 1 Cor. 5:6-8).

Conclusion

In these verses we may trace a great twofold law of the spiritual universe:

1. *As in the Case of the Jewish Leaders* —
   a. When there is keenness in executing of worldly business and dullness in grasping things spiritual, the existence of an earthbound heart is made abundantly plain.
   b. But when spiritual longings awaken, spiritual vision becomes wonderfully clear.

2. *As in the Case of the Disciples* —
   a. Such dangers as legalism and secularism, which are always particularly harmful in the Christian Church, are insidious ones.
   b. As leaven pervades the whole mass of dough, so will a single error corrupt generally held views and deprive them of spiritual value.

Let us be alert both to recognize and maintain spiritual truths, and to detect and repudiate errors in doctrine as well as in conduct.

37

CONFESSION AND REVELATION

Matthew 16:13-27

T HIS IS A point in the study of Matthew's book at which we may profitably stop and look back over what is essentially the gospel of the Kingdom. As such, it demonstrates our Lord as King: His genealogy (chap. 1); His birth (chap. 2); His inauguration (chaps. 3, 4); His laws (chap. 5 to 7); His powers (chaps. 8, 9); His progress (chap. 10). There is doubt of Him (chap. 11); opposition to Him (chap. 12). The consummation of His Kingdom is declared but postponed (chap. 13); and then there is His further work, together with heightened opposition to Him (chaps. 14 to 16:12).

Thus the story of Christ and His disciples at Caesarea-Philippi, a remote spot that lay to the north-east of the Sea of Galilee, is one of the pivots or crises of our Lord's ministry. As W. M. Clow points out in detail in his helpful volume on this chapter, *The Secret of the Lord,* it is a very important incident in His earthly life. It was then, after about two years of fellowship and instruction, that the disciples were called upon to pass a test and to bear a testimony. After every period of school life comes an examination to find out what the pupils know and feel in relation to their subject. Here it was necessary for Christ's followers, first, to report on the general impression men had of Him as they had been able to gauge it and, second, to express what they themselves really knew and felt about their Master; and then it was time for new truth to be revealed for which they would thus be prepared.

The sequence here is very striking: First came the truth about the Master, His nature and His office; then there logically followed the true conception of the nature and office of His Church, that new body to be founded because of the pending rejection by the Jews of the Kingdom that our Lord had come to preach. It was shown next that Christ must suffer, die, and rise again and then that the disciples' consecration to Him was essential to His program; and, finally, a brief mention is made of a second coming when He should at length establish His Kingdom in glory and in judgment.

It follows that from this turning point on Christ's ministry was to be private rather than public, with more frequent seasons spent apart with the Twelve, although He would continue to address the multitudes from time to time. The discussion here recorded was concerned first with —

I. The Character of Christ (vs. 13-17)

1. *The General Inquiry* (vs. 13, 14)

   a. One question that has distinguished man from man in all ages as has no other is that which our Lord here put to His disciples: "Whom do men say that I, the Son of man, am?" (v. 13)

   b. Title "Son of man" was almost certainly Messianic and often found on lips of Christ; indeed, except for Stephen (cf. Acts 7:56), and John (cf. Rev. 1:13; 14:14), no one else in N.T. uses this term (cf. Dan. 7:13).

   c. Answer disciples gave (v. 14) is very significant; they showed by it that people had varying views of Person of Jesus, but that all agreed in placing Him among nation's greatest men — Elijah, Jeremiah, John the Baptist, or some other prophet.

   d. It is interesting to observe how those who came in contact with Him felt He must be numbered among outstanding men; so far, so good, but this did not make Him different from other men except in degree.

2. *The Personal Test* (v. 15)

   a. Then Christ asked disciples what they themselves thought of Him after being in intimate relationship with Him for some time; and it would seem that former inquiry was intended to lead up to this.

   b. Hitherto He had revealed nothing personal about Himself by means of speech, leaving His character and deeds to make their own silent impression; such disclosures would have been premature, but now this inquiry was to be new stage in His disciples' preparation.

   c. His earliest words to them had been "Follow me" (4:19), implying trust and obedience; now He asks, "What do you think of me?" showing conviction is as necessary as confidence.

3. *The Definite Confession* (v. 16)

   a. This is first of two striking confessions in this story, as Simon Peter, spokesman for Twelve, bears splendid twofold testimony: to our Lord's Messiahship — "Thou art the Christ"; and to His Deity — "Thou art . . . the Son of the living God."

   b. Contrast between this reply and one in verse 14 shows great difference between impression made by Christ on men in general and on His disciples in particular.

   N.B. As an able writer has said: "This is exactly the answer which the world has never given, and never will give; it is the watershed that divides the Church from the world; it is the whole Christian creed packed into a single sentence, as in the acorn is the oak."

   c. To world Christ is only teacher or prophet; to disciple He is God and Lord; and Simon Peter's testimony is reminder of what we call our creed, i.e., substance of what is believed.

   d. There is very necessary connection between —

      (1) *Conviction,* which arises out of experience of Christ (cf. John 6:68, 69);

      (2) *Confession* (in sense of word used here), which is absolutely necessary for true spiritual life and always brings blessing (cf. 10:32, Rom. 10:8-11); and—

      (3) *Consecration,* which provides outlet both for our experience of Christ and its expression (cf. 2 Cor. 5:17 to 6:1).

   e. Another way of expressing relationship of Christian certainty with creed and conduct is to say that what we possess we profess, and what we profess we propagate; for, as in all of life, cause must produce effect.

   N.B. There was another confession which Peter made, and that time it was of love (cf. John 21:15-17); and, rather than merely asserting his devotion, he calls Christ to witness that it is genuine: "Thou knowest that I love thee."

4. *The Special Commendation* (v. 17)

   a. Our Lord at once pronounced blessing on Simon Peter, because such a declaration as he had just made would have been utterly impossible unless it came from devout heart; no human influence, no outward persuasion, no studied theology could have produced it — nothing short of personal experience of Divine revelation.

   b. Daily contact with Christ had done its work after all; it had wrought spiritual discernment which had given impetus to frank utterance of strong conviction.

   c. In commending witness, Christ obviously accepted and approved testimony; and this instance of our Lord's self-consciousness is very important, clearly indicating exactly what He thought, and knew, of Himself, for it is inconceivable that He would have allowed Peter's statement to go uncorrected had it been in error.

   d. It thus agrees with elements found on other occasions during Christ's earthly life, His recognition of His unique relation to God and His claim in regard to it; e.g., when Jews tried to stone Him, implying they did so because He made Himself equal with God (cf. John 8:59, 10:31), He never attempted to correct this assumption; and, although His enemies made it ground of their charges against our Lord before Pilate, He did not deny it, but died with this charge resting on His (cf. 26:63, 64, Luke 22:66-71).

   e. These were by no means only occasions on which He either stated, or else allowed men to believe, He was God; this can leave but one implication on His part — claim to Divine prerogatives and therefore to Deity; and herein lies force of old dilemma: "Either He is God or He is not good."

   f. When this is fully realized it is at once obvious that acceptance of Christ as Teacher, however great, is not enough; men must go much further and realize that He not only has left great precepts to be followed, but has also revealed God in His Person and has wrought Divine redemption for them.

   g. This means relationship to Him that puts Him far beyond category of even world's greatest men and constitutes Him what Paul called Him, "God over all, blessed for ever" (Rom. 9:5); thus, difference between Christ and all other men is pre-eminently one of kind, not merely of degree.

This lesson learned, the disciples were now ready for new teaching on —

II. The Church of Christ (vs. 18, 19)

A. The Divine Declaration (vs. 18)

1. *Affirmation*

   a. This is second confession in passage — Christ's of Simon; when our Lord and he first met, promise was given, "Thou shalt be called Cephas (Greek, Peter), which is by interpretation, A stone" (John 1:42), but now there is statement, "Thou art Peter."

   b. Until now, evidently, he had been only Simon, one who hears, but henceforth he was to be Peter, a stone, or rocklike; he had had elements of true manhood before but was lacking in great principle that should unite everything into one and produce essential strength and firmness.

   c. It was revelation of Person of Christ that made change, for when Peter rested his heart on Living Stone (cf. 1 Pet. 2:4), he became transformed into one of "living stones" he mentions in following verse, and was made partaker of Divine nature (cf. 2 Pet. 1:4); for when men have real personal experience of Christ weakest among them may become like rocks.

2. *Announcement*

   a. Our Lord then goes on to say, "Upon this rock I will build my church," What did He mean by "this rock"?

      (1) Some think it refers to Peter himself, and means that he should by his life and work be instrumental foundation of Christ's Church, some spiritual superiority being basis for his fitness; but, while this view is held by many modern scholars, including Roman Catholics, they have never explained why our Lord should not merely have said "upon thee" if Peter himself was meant.

      (2) Others believe "this rock" means confession of Christ's Messiahship and Deity that Peter had

just made, an interpretation which agrees with statements both of Apostle himself and of St. Paul (cf. 1 Cor. 3:11, Eph. 2:20, 1 Pet. 2:4-8); and this view is certainly more in accord with distinction there is between two words that appear in original — *Petros* (masc.) and *petra* (neut.).

(3) But perhaps, as Dr. T. M. Lindsay argues in *The Church and the Ministry in the Early Centuries,* union of these two views is more likely solution: "The rock on which the Church was to be built," writes Dr. Lindsay, "was a man confessing, not the man apart from his confession as Romanists insist, nor the confession apart from the man as Protestants urge."

(4) A more precise way of expressing comparison is to say that "this rock" probably means Jesus Christ as foundation confessed by Peter; not merely Christ in sense of one to whom vague allegiance is due, and certainly not Peter alone as delegated human being, but "Christ the Son of the living God" as acknowledged by Peter, believer responding to Divine revelation.

b. Term "church" is used here for first time; and future tense, "I will build," indicates what was begun afterwards, on day of Pentecost (cf. Acts 2:47), so that Christian Church as we know it was not as yet in existence (cf. Eph. 3:1-10).

c. Just as, in O.T., there were no Hebrews before Abraham and no Israelites before Jacob, no Christian Church was possible before there was established testimony that Jesus Christ was Messiah and Son of God (cf. Acts 20:28, 1 John 5:1); and yet, of course, there were men of God before all of these.

d. Church, with its name meaning "assembly of called-out ones," is illustrated in several ways in N. T., and among them following descriptions indicate God's purpose for its members:

(1) *Body.* With Christ as Head (cf. Eph. 1:22), it is to be to Him what our bodies are to our minds (cf. 1 Cor. 12:12, 13).

    (2) *Bride.* In relationship of love and consecration to Christ (cf. 2 Cor. 11:2, Eph. 5:25-32).

    (3) *Building.* With Christ as Chief Cornerstone (cf. Eph. 2:19-22).

    (4) *Brotherhood.* In joint manifestation of God's grace (cf., *inter alia,* Rom. 8:29, 1 Cor. 8:12, Eph. 2:5-10), to give Christ united and powerful witness (cf. Acts 1:8), and to be completed at His second coming (cf. 1 Thess. 4:13-18).

  e. Greek word translated "Hades" (A.S.V.) describes unseen world of departed spirits; "shall not prevail" seems to suggest that it shall not retain any of Christ's followers in coming struggle.

  f. Since "gates" do not fight, but open and close, our Lord here promises that not one of His people shall be kept from Him by power of unseen world, but shall be with Him forever (cf. Rev. 1:18); it is His striking way of assuring disciples that death will have no permanent power against new organism, significant statement in view of disclosure in v. 21.

B. The Definite Commission (v. 19)

1. *The Duty of Discipleship* (v. 19a)

  a. With words "I will give unto thee the keys of the kingdom of heaven," Christ assigns duties on earth to Peter symbolic of His own heavenly authority (cf. Isa. 22:22, Rev. 3:7); but since He does not say "keys of the Church," it must be kept in mind that He has now reverted to subject of "the kingdom of heaven."

  b. These words refer to way in which Peter was chosen as instrument to open door of Kingdom: for he was to urge Jews to accept Christ as King and Messiah on day of Pentecost (cf. Acts 2:29-36); and he was also to offer Him later on as Lord, Judge, and Saviour to Gentiles, in persons of Cornelius and his household (cf. Acts 10:34-43).

2. *The Duty of Discipline* (v. 19b)

  a. To be distinguished from duty of admitting above, words "bind" and "loose" are well-known Jewish formula for "prohibiting" and "permitting"; and, taken with word "whatsoever" (not whomsoever), referring to things (not persons), they imply power of discipline over conduct (cf. Acts 5:1-11, 8:18-24).

b. This authority, as well as that above, predicated Peter's position of leadership in early Church, and yet it was afterwards given to all disciples (cf. 18:18, John 20: 23); it included preaching of gospel of forgiveness and its alternatives and did not refer to any special qualifications bestowed on Christian ministry only.

c. Passage thus refers to necessity of Church having its own prohibitory and permissory laws and regulations; and this was clearly one of its most important functions.

d. Thus, while Peter was leader at first, difference between him and others was one of degree, not of kind; his authority cannot be continuous, or transmissible, as Roman Church alleges, for there is no such direction given in N. T. and no proof, or even hint, of its ever being done.

e. Nor was any supreme authority exercised by Peter over rest of Twelve (cf., *contra*, Acts 8:14, 11:2, 15: 13-21); so that our Lord's commission was purely personal recognition of personal confession, promising special stewardship in days to come.

N.B. (1) Kingdom of Heaven is to be distinguished from Church as larger and wider conception, for Kingdom is heavenly reign of God over all things earthly predicted in O.T. (cf. Dan. 2:44, 7:27), and of course Church is part of it. Kingdom of Heaven is phrase peculiar to Matthew, mentioned by him thirty-two times, and seems to have distinctly Jewish aspect. Yet it is also earthly sphere of Kingdom of God, phrase mentioned only five times in First Gospel, but also in other N.T. books; this is individual now (cf. Rom. 14:17) because of mankind's revolt, but is to be universal hereafter (cf. Luke 13:28, 29). Some things are common to both Kingdoms, but some are different, such as spiritual life (cf. John 3:3) and mere profession (cf. Matt. 13). Rejection of Kingdom of Heaven led to establishment of Church through necessity for Christ to suffer rather than to take up His reign immediately, and to this there must be witness; and Church is not mentioned in O.T., but is something newly revealed (cf. Eph. 3:1-12), with Christ its Head (cf. Eph. 1:22, 23). James, however, does use O.T. quotation (cf. Amos 9: 11, 12) to deduce foreshadowing of organization made up of Jews and Gentiles (cf. Acts 15:13-18). Thus, three spheres, Kingdom of God, Kingdom of Heaven, and Church are not synonymous, not identical, but their borders may be said to touch, and partially to coincide. This may be illustrated by thinking of two interlocking circles within a third and larger one.

(2) James Orr writes helpfully on this subject as follows: " 'Church' and 'Kingdom' are not precisely the same, for the 'Kingdom' . . . is a name for God's rule in all departments. . .; but the Church is still the one society which visibly represents God's Kingdom in the world, and it exists for the ends of this Kingdom. It is the association of the members of the Kingdom in their directly religious capacity, for the purposes of fellowship, of worship, of testimony, of edification, of the furtherance of the Gospel at home, and of the evangelization of the world abroad."

The character or Person of Christ and the Church or Body of Christ are now shown to be linked by —

III. The Cross of Christ (vs. 20-23)

Examination of disciples is now passed and it is time for new teaching; and after approval comes discipline.

1. *The Divine Revelation* (vs. 20, 21)

   a. First came restriction (v. 20) as to continuing to proclaim Jesus as the Christ or Jewish Messiah; up to this moment, indeed, He and His disciples had preached only Kingdom of Heaven, but now emphasis is to be radically changed.

   b. Christ tells them for the first time of necessity of redemption by way of cross (v. 21); until this time nothing definite had been said about it, all earlier allusions having been vague (cf. 1:21; Mark 2:20; John 2:19-21; 3:14, 15; 6:51).

   c. Now there is fivefold revelation of cross:

   (1) Its place ("he must go unto Jerusalem");

(2) Its experience ("he must . . . suffer many things");

(3) Its source ("the elders and chief priests and scribes");

(4) Its extent ("he must . . . be killed"; and —

(5) Its result ("he must . . . be raised again the third day").

N.B. Also, Christ had hitherto alluded only in vague terms to His resurrection (cf. 12:38-40, John 2:19-21); but now, whenever He mentions His death, He adds reference to His rising again (cf. 17:22, 23; 20:18, 19).

d. Obviously circumstances were calling for this further revelation; storms were threatening and end was approaching.

e. Hostility of Jews was coming to head and prevented their being warned of what was so soon to happen; disciples had, therefore, to face future and, instead of looking immediately for Messiah's Kingdom, they needed to be reminded of great facts of sin and redemption.

2. *The Disciple's Response* (v. 22)

a. No wonder that, in the face of so astonishing and unwelcome a statement, Peter, doubtless elated by what Christ had just said to him personally (vs. 17-19), "took him" apart (perhaps by grasping His arm or hand) and actually rebuked Him.

b. But literally Peter's words seem to have been, "Have pity on Thyself, Lord, spare Thyself; this must not be permitted"; it was doubtless well meant though impulsively and mistakenly said.

c. It was appeal to put pain and sorrow out of Christ's life, very idea of which was intolerable to Peter; for it must have seemed to him that such a close to his Master's ministry would be end of all love, fellowship, and hope among Twelve, as well as suffering for our Lord.

d. Peter did not realize way in which God would bring about His Kingdom of righteousness, and that, instead of defeat, there would be final victory; cf. "pity thyself" with "deny himself" (v. 24).

3. *The Master's Rebuke* (v. 23)

   a. It was now Christ's turn, and His retort is most impressive, with terrible epithet "Satan" striking contrast to assurance of Divine approbation and blessing just given; and Greek word translated "mindest" (A.S.V.) is strong one, indicating attitude that caused Peter to "speak like a man and not like God," as this phrase has been translated (cf. 1 Cor. 2:12).

   b. It shows entire bent of Peter's moral and intellectual being was in wrong direction; for he had actually given voice to devil's own suggestion of "short cut" to throne by avoiding cross (cf. 4:8, 9).

   c. Perhaps, however, we may infer from Peter's subsequent silence that this answering rebuke of our Lord was well taken; at any rate, later on he showed clearly he had learned this particular lesson (cf. 1 Pet. 2:19-25).

IV. The Confession of Christ (vs. 24-26)

Out of newly revealed circumstances further teaching was given; and, so far from lessening in severity, it was frank statement of terms of discipleship and its alternatives.

1. *A Solemn Reminder* (v. 24)

   a. Christ went on to tell His disciples that not only was He to die, but that they also must be willing to die; and that true discipleship was thus not only confession of Him by creed, but also and chiefly by conduct and consecration.

   b. Its characteristics were seen to be —

      (1) Loyalty — "if any man will" — firm resolve;

      (2) Life — "come" — outward action; and —

      (3) Lowliness — "after me" — humble position.

   c. Its conditions were shown —

      (1) In relation to self — "deny himself" — not denying certain things to self, but abjuring and ignoring it; literally, doing to it what Peter later mistakenly did to Christ (cf. 26:69-75), renouncing it, knowing it not;

      (2) In relation to world — "take up his cross" — nothing to do with what are sometimes described as "crosses,"

but simply attitude of readiness to do or to suffer, or full consecration (cf. 10:38, q.v.);

(3) In relation to Christ — "follow me" — trust without question, obedience without hesitation, and emulation without reservation.

2. *A Paradoxical Result* (vs. 25, 26)

As stated by our Lord in these two verses, it is twofold:

a. Life can be saved only by losing it; and losing it for Christ's sake is only way of finding or possessing it (v. 25);

b. World can be gained only by forfeiting this new-found life; and yet nothing in whole wide world is fair exchange for value of human soul.

Illus.: It has been said there are at least three instances in Scripture of bad bargains: Esau sold his birthright for what is known as a mere "mess of pottage" — literally, "this red stuff" of which he did not even know the name. Judas sold his Lord for thirty pieces of silver. And, as Christ tells us here, he makes a bad bargain who, to gain the whole world, loses his own soul.

V. The Coming of Christ (v. 27)

On this first occasion when our Lord revealed to His perplexed followers solemn fact of His approaching death and deep meaning of their discipleship, He bids them also look further forward to another time when they would be associated with Him:

1. *His Coming in Glory* (v. 27a)

a. Our Lord, during later part of His earthly ministry, laid special stress not only on His death, but also on His second coming.

b. As His death was to be "for the life of the world" (John 6:51) and "a ransom for many" (20:28), so His coming was to be crown of His revelation and completion of His Messiahship (cf. Heb. 9:28).

2. *His Coming with Rewards* (v. 29b)

a. Second Advent of Christ is to be constant hope of His followers; and so this verse includes Christ and Christians.

b. As their salvation is present, free gift, so their rewards are to be future attainments; and thus passage links two great events for Christians, Christ's death and His coming again.

Conclusion

Each of these great revelations may be summed up in two words as follows:

1. *The Character of Christ*
   a. Its Experience.
   b. Its Expression.

2. *The Church of Christ*
   a. Its Strength.
   b. Its Safety.

3. *The Cross of Christ*
   a. Its Obligation.
   b. Its Offense.

4. *The Confession of Christ*
   a. Its Appeal.
   b. Its Alternative.

5. *The Coming of Christ*
   a. Its Glory.
   b. Its Gain.

The experience of Christ by Christians confirms the truth of a fundamental issue — who and what He is. Like St. Peter and St. Paul of old, they know whom they have believed, and are persuaded that He has effected a revolution in their lives which no one merely human could possibly bring about. They may not always be able to give a clear, full statement of the theology of Christ's Person, work, and coming any more than could the Apostle when he made his memorable confession at Caesarea-Philippi; but they know positively that their personal experience of their Lord is a practical, yea, a pragmatic proposition that can be put to the test by all who are willing to try it in the simple way of repentance and trust.

> *What the hand is to the lute,*
> *What the breath is to the flute,*

What is fragrance to the smell,
What the spring is to the well,
What the flower is to the bee,
That is Jesus Christ to me!

What the mother to the child,
What the guide in pathless wild,
What is oil to troubled wave,
What is ransom to the slave,
What is water to the sea,
That is Jesus Christ to me!

38

THE TRANSFIGURATION AND ITS SEQUEL

Matthew 16:28—17:21

I T IS important to link together the last verse of chapter 16 and the following account, because there can be no doubt that at least the primary application of the former is to the Transfiguration (cf. Mark 9:1, 2, Luke 9:27, 28). Immediately after these words of Christ comes the record of that event, with a specific point of time mentioned in all three Synoptic Gospels (cf. also 2 Pet. 1:16-18). The words are quoted as the conclusion of what Christ said when for the first time He mentioned His sufferings, and when in each case there was also a mention of the glory to follow. Six days after the words were spoken, three who had been standing in our Lord's presence did for a brief moment see "the Son of man coming in his kingdom."

I. The Divine Glory (16:28 to 17:13)

1. *The Example* (16:28)

   a. Some of those present who had been perplexed by teaching about cross (16:21) would be permitted to see example of Christ's glory and foretaste of His perfected Kingdom.

   b. This manifestation was important pivot, occurring about midway in His ministry; and its great significance to Peter is clearly shown in what he wrote later, calling it "the power and coming of our Lord Jesus Christ . . . his majesty . . . honour and glory" (1 Pet. 1:16-18).

2. *The Experience* (17:1-3)

   a. Three disciples, Peter and James and John (v. 1) were men representative not only of Twelve, but probably, as Dr. Scofield suggests, of Israel in future kingdom; and the same three are selected elsewhere as eye-witnesses (cf. Mark 5:37, 14:33, etc.).

   b. Christ's being "transfigured before them" (v. 2) about eight days after His initial teaching concerning cross indicates correct order: first, suffering, then, glory; and manifestation of such glory would reassure disciples' puzzled hearts as to suffering.

   c. Christ's glory is rarely mentioned in Gospels; yet it is often theme of Daniel and of Revelation, and is frequently emphasized in Paul's Epistles.

   d. Here it is particularly significant that two heavenly visitants, Moses and Elijah (v. 3), were actually engaged in conversation about very subject, cross of Christ (cf. Luke 9:31), which had been such a stumbling-block to disciples; and it is evident cross now loomed very large before our Lord.

   e. This may be noted from marked position occupied in Gospels by His death; cf. number of pages in ordinary English Bible devoted to last week of our Lord's life as compared with number given to preceding period of His three-year ministry.

   f. It is to be noted here that only now was Moses' prayer to enter Canaan granted (cf. Exod. 33:12-17; Deut. 34:1-4); and his request, "I beseech thee, show me thy glory" (Exod. 33:18) was fully answered (cf. "his face," v. 2, with "Thou canst not see my face," Exod. 33:20; cf. also 2 Cor. 4:6).

3. *The Error* (vs. 4-8)

   a. Peter must have felt great surprise to hear as subject of conversation in mount very theme that had so shocked him, his Master's death; yet, with his usual impulsiveness, he could only express satisfaction at being there to do something, i.e., to provide shelters for Christ, Moses and Elijah (v. 4; cf. Mark 9:6, Luke 9:33), and thus to prolong experience.

b. But he was soon told by voice from above that Jesus Christ was God's Son and that time had come to hear Him; and implication is that other two were but servants, and disciples were to give heed to Him alone (v. 5).

c. It is, therefore, not without point that, after He had aroused them with a touch from their attitude of awe and fear (vs. 6, 7), they "saw no man, save Jesus only" (v. 8); this was lesson they had to learn, and so do we, for uniqueness of Christ is as vital today as ever.

d. In this picture of Divine glory we, like these three disciples, are enabled to see cross was not end, but only means towards end; for that was to be glorious consummation of everything that our Lord had come to perform.

e. We know Peter learned this lesson well, i.e., that suffering must precede glory, both for our Lord and for His followers (cf. 1 Pet. 4:13); and while Kingdom was still one theme of His teaching it was understood now to be always future (cf. 18:1, 28; 19:12, 14, etc.).

4. *The Explanation* (vs. 9-13)

a. On way down from mountain Christ charged three disciples not to tell anyone what they had seen until after His resurrection (v. 9); this was because time had not yet arrived for full revelation of Messiah's glory as seen on Mount of Transfiguration (cf. 2 Pet. 1:16-18).

b. This injunction immediately prompted inquiry from disciples about Elijah, apparently to ask why he had departed instead of accompanying them: if he was to come before Messiah (v. 10; cf. Mal. 3:1, 4:5, 6), how was it his visit was at once so secret and so brief?

c. Christ's reply confirmed teaching that Elijah was indeed to come "and restore all things" (v. 11); this was based on these O.T. prophecies of Jewish restoration to Divine favor and national glory (cf. Acts 3:21).

d. He added, however, that Elijah had already come, i.e., that prophecy had been fulfilled in appearance of John the Baptist (v. 12; cf. 11:14); but, just as Jewish people had not known him in his character as forerunner of Messiah, and had allowed him to die, so Son of man would also suffer at their hands.

e. There seems no doubt that prophecy in Malachi, like many

other O.T. passages, has twofold interpretation; secondary and symbolic meaning referred to John at Christ's first coming; and then primary fulfillment would be in Elijah's appearing literally before Christ's second coming.

f. Nor is there any real discrepancy between Baptist's own words (John 1:21) and these; he rightly denied being literal Elijah, while our Lord here teaches he was symbolical Elijah of prophecy.

g. This entire section, suggesting Scripture to be fulfilled in wider sense than appears on surface, shows how often God's Word is found to be much deeper and fuller in meaning than its mere words seem to imply; and it is therefore wise to follow disciples' example and ask Divine guidance in its interpretation.

II. The Human Contrast (vs. 14-21)

Contrast between mountain and valley experiences is here, as so often, very solemn and striking. On Mount of Transfiguration Christ was manifested in all His glory, while below in valley His disciples were baffled, defeated, and disappointed — shown up in all their pitiful inadequacy.

1. *The Great Failure* (vs. 14-17)

a. In absence of Christ, nine remaining disciples, surrounded by crowd (v. 4), probably mocking them, had been confronted by man with epileptic son (v. 15, A.S.V.), who badly needed relief from characteristic symptom of disease — periodic falling down in fit, which exposed him to such dangers as fire and water; and they had failed to heal him (v. 16).

b. Our Lord promptly rebuked disciples, calling them not only "faithless," but "perverse generation" (v. 17); this was probably because they had gone back to ways of this world and, instead of acting in dependence on Divine Spirit, had revealed state of spiritual weakness.

c. This called for great forbearance on Christ's part, for He asked, "How long shall I bear with you?" (A.S.V.); and then He commanded, "Bring him hither to me!" (cf. 14:18).

2. *The Great Lesson* (vs. 18-21)

a. Christ then "rebuked the devil" (v. 18), and put forth

His mighty power whereby this demon was cast out and boy healed immediately of his malady.

b. When disciples drew their Master apart, confessing their defeat and appealing for its explanation, they were told it was indeed due to their lack of faith (vs. 19, 20); and this is all the more striking because their failure was unwarranted, since some time before Christ had given them power to do this very thing (cf. 10:1), and they had done it (cf. Mark 6:13).

c. When this father had brought his son to them, therefore, there was no reason at all why demon should not have been at once sent forth; but evidently there had been spiritual depletion through lack of faith, and their power became paralyzed.

d. Assuming we may read disputed verse 21 with K.J.V. (and words do appear in Mark 9:29), they were told this kind of faith could be procured only by means of prayer and fasting; power evidently was not absolute but conditional, and they had not fulfilled conditions so as to maintain its constant supply.

e. These represent two different, yet connected, attitudes of soul to Christ:

(1) Prayer is that by which we *attach* ourselves to God and things of spiritual world;

(2) Fasting is that by which we *detach* ourselves from things of time and sense, whether it be from food, or pleasure, or lawful ambition and ordinary occupation.

f. When these two attitudes are characteristic of us there is Divine contact with our souls, bringing spiritual power, constant blessing, and abiding fellowship; and this would seem to be usual order — fasting, or disregard of creature comforts or secular preoccupation, because absorbed in prayer — including worship, thanksgiving, and intercession.

g. It is not too much to say that today, face to face with huge needs and complexities of modern life, there are many demons Christian Church has failed to cast out; and this failure, too, is unwarranted when provision for success has been made, is so simple, and has been utilized so often in past years by God's faithful, obedient servants.

Conclusion

There are two interesting things about the Greek verb translated "transfigured": the first is that our English verb "metamorphosed," with its more familiar noun form "metamorphosis," transformation, is an exact transliteration; and the second is that in the two other passages where the Greek verb is used it is actually translated by the Engish word "transformed." There is, therefore, —

1. *Transformation by Renewal of Mind* (cf. Rom. 12:2)
   This is in relation to will of God the Father.

2. *Transformation by Sight of Divine Glory* (cf. 2 Cor. 3:18)
   This is in relation to the Spirit of God.

Then, as we read in Luke's version of the Transfiguration, there is —

3. *Transformation by Act of Prayer* (cf. Luke 9:28, 29)
   a. This, of course, is in relation to the Son of God, for in this parallel passage we are told that it was "as he prayed" that our Lord's "countenance was altered," or made different.
   b. Correlating this with what He said about prayer at end of passage in both Matthew and Mark, we see great importance of prayer to Christian witness:
      (1) Seven Greek words are used for it in N.T., denoting need, desire, supplication, consecration, fellowship inquiry, agreement.
      (2) Seven requirements for it are given in N.T.: confidence, fasting, watching, obedience, forgiveness, thanksgiving, joy.

These are but a few of the indications of God's will concerning His people's transformation by means of prayer. When the full force of His Word on this subject is allowed to impress itself on our souls, the immediate and ever-increasing result will be a life of prayer; and through that will come a life of power, peace, purity, progress, and praise.

My inmost soul, O Lord, to Thee leans like a growing flower
Unto the light; I do not know the day nor blessed hour
When that deep-rooted, daring growth we call the heart's desire
Shall burst and blossom to a prayer within the sacred fire

Of Thy great patience, grow so·pure, so still, so sweet a thing
As perfect prayer must surely be; and yet my heart will sing.
Because Thou seem'st sometimes so near, close-present God, to me
It seems I could not have a wish that was not shared by Thee;
It seems I cannot be afraid to speak my longings out,
So tenderly Thy gathering love enfolds me round about;
It seems as if my heart would break if, living in the light,
It should not lift to Thee at last a bud of flawless white,
And yet, my helpless heart, how sweet to grow, and bud, and say
The flower, however marred or wan, shall not be cast away!

39

FURTHER TRAINING OF THE TWELVE (1)

Matthew 17:22—18:35

As we have seen, Christ now was chiefly devoting His
time and attention to His disciples, revealing, as they became
spiritually ready, deep truths about Himself, His Church, and the
future. From this point onwards, although the multitudes were
met and taught from time to time, our Lord's main consideration
was the training of the Twelve. Fresh revelations had been
followed by the Transfiguration, which had revealed as never before His glory, to be understood in conjunction with what He had
said about His cross. Then followed the miracle at the foot of
the mountain (17:14-21), and another period of special preparation of the Apostles, the lessons taught being chiefly concerned
with a true spirit of humility as an important requirement of true
discipleship, one certainly becoming to those who were soon to
face the cross and then to represent to the world the One who
had hung thereon, He who was meek and lowly in heart.

I. An Example of Humility (17:22-27)

1. *A Solemn Reminder* (vs. 22, 23)

    a. First Christ again announces His death, and as we look
       back to previous chapter and forward to next mention
       of subject we note striking progression in detail:

       (1) The stark fact — "he must . . . suffer . . . and be
           killed" (16:21);

(2) The initial means —"shall be betrayed" (v. 22);

(3) The final agents — "the chief priests and scribes . . . shall condemn him . . . and shall deliver him to the Gentiles . . . to crucify" (20:18, 19).

b. This, then, is first, solemn intimation that our Lord's own followers would have some part in His death; and immediate result was distress (v. 23), incomprehension and fear (cf. Mark 9:32, Luke 9:45).

2. *A Submissive Action* (17:24-27)

a. *The Levy* (vs. 24, 25a)

(1) Incident followed that was truly expressive of this very humiliation of Christ in contrast with His glory at Transfiguration: application was made to Peter for "tribute" (v. 24), or temple tax (cf. Exod. 30:11-16), payment of half-shekel (A.S.V.) made by Jews in support of sanctuary, thereby acknowledging God's claim on them.

(2) Perhaps request was made in strict observance of duty and with proper courtesy; or collectors may have wanted to see whether Jesus made same plea for tax exemption as Jewish teachers did.

(3) Peter at once replied, in zeal for his Master's honor, that of course He paid (v. 25a); and this assertion was probably actuated by surmise that Christ would not wish to be behind others in any legal obligation.

b. *The Lesson* (vs. 25b, 26)

(1) Then Christ, in His omniscience, anticipated (A.S.V.) Peter's mention of this exchange with tax-collectors and took initiative in order to teach him lesson; this was not argument against paying tax (cf. v. 27), but reminder of right motive.

(2) Point of our Lord's question is that kings do not demand taxes from their own children, but from their subjects; no boy-prince, for instance, would be expected to pay tax to his father the king.

(3) It should be noted there is no reference at all here to Jews as sons and Gentiles as strangers, since this was solely Jewish tax; and Peter clearly grasped what his Master meant, answering that those outside king's

family circle paid tax; whereupon our Lord rejoined that this implied his sons were exempt (v. 26).

(4) We should mark well this pronouncement as significant claim made by Jesus to be occupying unique relation to God as compared with other Jews; He is God's Son, but they are only God's subjects.

c. *The Law* (v. 27)

(1) In order, however, to fulfill law and to prevent anyone's being disturbed or offended, our Lord associates Himself with His disciples and tells Peter to go catch a fish and find in its mouth coin that will meet required payment for both of them; with perfect knowledge He saw where fish was and what was in its mouth, for all nature was at His command.

(2) Thus there was association between Christ and His followers, and yet clear distinction; He fulfilled every requirement of earthly law, even though He was equal with His heavenly Father (cf. Phil. 2:6-8).

(3) Although His claim to Divine Sonship was now clear (cf. 16:16, 17:5), He would not put stumbling-block before "them," i.e., those who were merely God's servants; and we know it was not only His humility, but His love that prevented Him from giving offense (cf. Rom. 13:10).

N.B. This was only miracle worked in any sense for His own benefit (cf. 4:4), and even this was primarily for sake of others.

II. An Exposition of Humility (18:1-14)

1. *The Significant Question* (vs. 1, 2)

a. Questions asked from time to time of Christ by His disciples are of much interest as revealing their mental grasp of great moral truths; and here is characteristic inquiry as they contemplated Messianic Kingdom and their own place in it, for their one thought is of relative prominence (v. 1).

b. This shows them still unable to understand Christ's teaching about Cross as principle of life, or even object-lesson of tribute money He had just ("in that hour," A.S.V.) tried to teach them; He therefore used little child from crowd (v. 2) as another object-lesson, of reality of goodness rather than of degrees of greatness.

2. *The True Spirit* (vs. 3-6)

Not only so, but Christ raises prior question as to whether disciples were even in Kingdom, to say nothing of occupying particular positions therein; thus, subject involved two important considerations:

a. *How To Enter the Kingdom of Heaven* (v. 3)

(1) Our Lord here points out that unless disciples did "turn and become as little children" (A.S.V.) they should not even enter Kingdom; and turning means renunciation which is very essence of repentance, with Greek verb here in active voice, implying definite action, and also change in relation to God evoked by new perception of His requirements.

(2) We are to "turn" to God and from sin, pride, selfishness and, indeed, from everything included in self-assertion; and this is infinitely more than penitence or mere sorrow for sin.

N.B. Well-known words of Anglican Catechism as simple definition of repentance cannot well be improved upon: "Repentance whereby we forsake sin"; nor can this verse from old hymn for children:

> *Repentance is to leave*
> *The sins we loved before,*
> *And show that we in earnest grieve*
> *By doing them no more.*
>
> A. J. TAYLOR

(3) We are also to "become as little children," and reference, of course, is not to intellectual or physical childhood, childishness, but only to moral elements associated with child-life, childlikeness; child possesses undeveloped mind but genuine and often well-developed conscience.

(4) Several characteristics of childhood may well be included in our Lord's thought:

      (a) Teachableness — child is usually eager to learn and be correctly informed;

      (b) Trustfulness — child's simple faith is very beautiful and appealing;

      (c) Tenderness — child's compassion is deep and easily moved.

b. *How To Be Great in the Kingdom* (vs. 4-6)

  (1) Now our Lord goes on to answer question raised by disciples (v. 1), indicating that, having once entered Kingdom, one must meet certain requirements to become "greatest" in it; and these are summed up in His words about one who will "humble himself as this little child" (v. 4).

  (2) Childlike Christian humility will surely manifest itself in such attributes as —

      (a) Simplicity — absence of anything doubtful or lacking in genuineness;

      (b) Sincerity — with motives always clear and pure;

      (c) Sensitivity — conscience always tender and nature sympathetic.

  (3) Our Lord went on to teach, in connection with child, that this humility of character will express itself in lowly service:

      (a) Reception of such a child in Christ's name was regarded as equivalent to reception of Himself (v. 5); and —

      (b) Peril of failure was shown in solemn possibility of making Christian child "to stumble" (v. 6, A.S.V.), and penalty is grave; so that whether as parents, teachers, or Christian workers, we should make childhood special concern.

        N.B. Three other commands on subject are also to be noted and observed: (1) "Despise not" (v. 10); (2) "forbid not" (19:14); and (3) "provoke not" (Eph. 6:4, Col. 3:21).

  (4) All this is expressive of humility in action, true greatness being found in stooping and serving "least of these" (25:40); and it was not in lordship or

authority, as our Lord told disciples on two other
similar occasions (cf. 20:25-27, Luke 22:24-27) —
"even as the Son of man came not to be ministered
unto, but to minister" (20:28; cf. Phil. 2:7).

Thus we have two directions in connection with Kingdom:
first, for entering it, and then for becoming truly great in it;
and spirit of child is seen to be way for both.

Illus.: A little girl asked her mother whether one could
feel the soul, or hear it, or see it. Her mother replied: "No,
the soul cannot be felt nor heard, but sometimes it seems as
though we can see it in the eyes." "Let me see yours,"
said the child; and when in her mother's eyes she saw her
own image reflected she exclaimed, "Oh Mother, your soul
is a little child!"

3. *The Vital Principle* (vs. 7-9)

Keeping child before Him, Christ continued His teaching:

a. *The Danger of Offending* (v. 7)

(1) In most solemn terms our Lord showed awful peril
of becoming occasion of stumbling to others; for,
while mankind in general will have trouble because
of its sin, it is far more serious when such offenses
are caused by false or faulty disciples of Christ.

(2) Such a man will not only cause "woe unto the
world," but there will be "woe to that man" himself;
and instances like those of Judas (cf. 26:24) and
Caiaphas (cf. John 11:49-52, 18:14) show what
our Lord meant.

b. *The Necessity of Self-Discipline* (vs. 8, 9)

(1) This danger of causing another to stumble is so
serious that there must be no failure in dealing faithfully with sin in one's own life, even though it involve most precious elements.

(2) As solemn illustration, Christ declares that even if
some valuable member of body leads to offense, it
had better be put aside; for it would be infinitely
preferable to be lacking in any one of these things
than that, through us, other people are caused to
stumble or our own life wholly lost.

(3) This shows sin is thing to be dreaded most, whether

in ourselves or in relation to others, and it should therefore he hated most; for terrible indeed will be fate of those who cause others to go wrong and to be hindered in spiritual things.

4. *The Consequent Warning* (vs. 10-14)

a. Having spoken thus solemnly, our Lord urges avoidance of despising, or minimizing importance of, little ones like child before them; and He goes on to link with this warning statement that would seem to indicate special providential interest in them (v. 10).

b. Words "their angels" are avowedly difficult, with two main explanations:

(1) We know nothing about angels beyond what Scripture teaches or suggests, and we must not indulge in vain speculation; while it is clear God uses angels to do His bidding on behalf of His people (cf. Heb. 1:14), there does not seem to be sufficient evidence of individual "guardian angels" or even of contemporary Jewish belief in them.

(2) On other hand, reference to angels in general does not explain personal pronoun "their" (v. 10) or corresponding "his" in speaking of Peter (cf. Acts 12: 15); so that there is something to be said for view that phrase may refer to glorified spirits of departed little ones occupying place of special privilege in heaven because of innocence of evil.

c. Whichever interpretation we adopt, nothing could more effectually enhance respect with which such "little ones" (children or young believers) should be treated than such an assurance of special privilege; and this is context of oft-quoted statement of our Saviour coming "to save that which was lost" (v. 11).

d. He Himself showed this spirit by being willing to seek and save even one, as conscientious shepherd would concern himself over single lost sheep out of flock of hundred (vs. 12, 13; cf. Luke 15:3-7); "even so," declared our Lord, it was not God's will that one little child should be lost (v. 14).

> *I wonder what to Thee*
> *Must I, blest Lord, be worth,*
> *Since Thou wouldst leave Thy heavenly home*
> *Through such a lowly birth,*
> *And take that journey drear,*
> *In distance far from God,*
> *To seek one object of Thy love,*
> *E'en me, my loving Lord.*
> *"The ninety and nine" were left behind*
> *This one poor, wandering sheep to find!*

    e. This whole passage also teaches that Christ's redemption includes children and that therefore children as such are saved — precious knowledge when so many of race still die in childhood; yet, of course, when old enough to be morally responsible, they, too, must choose (cf. 1 Tim. 4:6, 2 Tim. 1:5).

All through this solemn message, then, our Lord is emphasizing spirit of humility which will mean absence of hurtfulness and presence of helpfulness towards others. With this spirit actuating them disciples would be saving, serving, and blessing instruments to those for whom Christ was about to die.

III. An Expression of Humility (vs. 15-35)

This is threefold:

1. *Reconciliation* (vs. 15-18)

    a. Christian life is never one-sided, especially in its corporate aspect; not only is one believer not to offend another, but provision is made in case he is trespassed against.

    b. There may well be deep consciousness of wrongdoing against him which he desires to have put right; but motive emphasized is that of gaining, or winning goodwill of, brother who has done injury (v. 15).

    c. First line of approach is individual and private (cf. 5:24), and this will call for personal tact and humility; if this method fails next step, social approach, is to be used, its aim being that, through united appeal, same object may be realized (v. 16).

    d. Then, if this step should fail, third step is to be taken, and Church, congregation of God's people, is to take collective action (v. 17; cf. 1 Cor. 5, 2 Cor. 2:6); and if erring brother "will not hear the Church" he is to be solemnly treated as an outsider, i.e., separated from its fellowship.

N.B. Words "hear the Church" thus clearly refer to discipline, not to doctrine, to testimony rather than to instruction.

e. Of course these directions involve difficulty, and our Lord recognized this; He uttered some remarkable words setting forth authority of Church and showing it would be justified in taking such action (v. 18).

f. This power was thus left to Church, not finally to ministry alone (cf. 16:19), for similar words in plural are recorded in John 20:23 as spoken to company including at least two who had not been numbered among Twelve (cf. Luke 24:33-36); and these words, with preceding verses 21 and 22, would seem to form John's account of Great Commission found in other three Gospels under various forms of expression, and they are surely applicable to whole Church equally with Synoptic statements.

g. All leading commentators believe words cannot be limited to ministry, but refer to our Lord's commission to whole Church (as represented in upper room) to declare gospel and its alternatives.

2. *United Prayer* (vs. 19, 20)

a. Now comes significant reference to prayer (v. 19); and by its place here Christ implies continuing hope of overcoming difficulties in Church and of winning fellow Christian.

b. Word translated "agree" is musical term (cf. Luke 15:25) from which we get our word "symphony": "if two of you shall symphonize —" or "harmonize" — two voices blending in beautiful and self-effacing agreement.

c. Prayer, therefore, is more than request of one individual; and it is kept from being solitary and even selfish or proud by being exercised in conjunction with others of like mind.

d. Union in prayer is one of most potent influences of Christianity; and this "symphony" of God's people is sure harbinger of spiritual blessing, such as, in present case, reconciliation, or conversion, or sanctification.

N.B. There is awful contrast in Acts 5:9 where same word is used, Ananias and Sapphira being said to have "symphonized" to "tempt the Spirit of the Lord" by uniting their voices in lying instead of in praying.

e. Thus, Church as whole was to exercise still another form of authority; and our Lord sets His seal upon individual influence culminating in united prayer by stating categorically (not promising) that wherever "two or three are gathered together" in His Name there He is "in the midst" (v. 20).

N.B. Here are three other blessed uses of word "together":
(1) "Quickened together" (Eph. 2:5) in regeneration;
(2) "Laborers together" (1 Cor. 3:9) for service;
(3) "Gathering together" (2 Thess. 2:1) at second coming of Christ.

f. This is opportunity for emphasizing statement of fact in this verse rather than making of promise, called by F. B. Meyer one of "the present tenses of the blessed life"; as always, promises are to be expected, but facts are to be accepted, e.g., "The Lord *is* my Shepherd"; "— my light and my salvation" — and equally He *is* here "in the midst" and we do not have to ask Him to come.

g. All we know about prayer is derived from God's revelation in His Word, from which it is clear room has been found in constitution of His universe for prayer to be offered and answered; but how precisely this is brought about is not revealed, though fact is as obvious in Scripture as it is certain in experience of all true believers.

3. *Forgiveness* (vs. 21-35)

During our Lord's ministry problems of many kinds came before Him, sometimes raised by His disciples, at other times by outer circle of hearers, and yet again by His enemies. Here is one on great subject of forgiveness, suggested by one who was frequently asking meaning of things, Simon Peter:

a. *The Problem Stated* (v. 21)

(1) This inquiry probably was prompted by our Lord's

counsel regarding treatment of sinning brother; it would be natural to ask guidance in its practical application.

(2) Or, question may have been caused by resentment at, first, tax-gatherer's question seeming to reflect on Master's integrity (cf. 17:24) and, second, dispute about greatness (cf. vs. 1-4) reflecting on disciples' own lack of humility.

(3) Jewish rabbis are said to have taught people to bear injury three times and then to regard duty as done; if this is so, Peter's suggestion of "seven times" was liberal extension and could be regarded as magnanimous.

(4) He was at once childlike and childish in the form of his question: childlike, in mildness which was prepared to forgive seven times; childish, in belief that fixed rule, or repetition of so many times and no more, would be large-hearted.

(5) But since further question at once arises as to what would be done if brother asked forgiveness eighth time, it is evident that rule to limit to seven times could not possibly apply to every case.

b. *The Solution Given* (v. 22)

(1) Our Lord's reply shows He meant to urge unlimited forgiveness; this is God's method, and has been well called "celestial arithmetic" of forgiveness.

(2) This is how problem was to be solved: life was to be lived not by law, but by love; and it was not to be governed by rule, but by application of principle in widest possible way:

(a) Rule is law for given circumstance, mainly acting from without, and limited;

(b) Principle is law for all circumstances, applied from within, and limitless.

(3) For children and childlike people rules are necessary; and civilized nations are often compelled to deal in this way with uncivilized races.

(4) Jews in O.T. times were morally and spiritually children, and so needed rules and regulations of

Mosaic Law; but later on, with Christianity, came change from rule to principle, and N.T. is therefore concerned with principles rather than with rules, of which this matter of forgiveness is one striking instance.

(5) Instead of specific direction on all matters of conduct, we have been given one great principle covering everything: "Do all to the glory of God" (1 Cor. 10:31); it is for us to apply this to thought, word, and deed.

(6) It is often more difficult to live by principle than by rule, but the Holy Spirit illuminating God's Word has been given us for this purpose.

N.B. Other applications of rule versus principle according to N.T. standards are: neighborliness, prayer, Bible-reading, worship, conduct, guidance, giving, Sabbath-keeping. All of these, and many more, are governed not by outward restraint, but by inward constraint, for Christianity is impelling, not compelling.

(7) How surprised Peter must have been by difference between his seven and his Master's seventy times seven! — if seven stands for perfection, what multiplied perfection is Divine forgiveness! Cf. "for He will abundantly pardon" (lit., "multiply to pardon," Isa. 55:7; cf. Eph. 4:32, Col. 3:13).

c. *The Answer Illustrated* (vs. 23-24)

Then comes one of those wonderful parables by means of which our Lord taught some of His deepest truths:

(1) *The Forgiving King* (vs. 23-27)

   (a) A heavy debt (vs. 23-25). King, in general accounting, reckoned one of his servants owed him ten thousand talents; and, as man had nothing with which to pay, he was ordered to be sold with his family and all he had, that debt might be canceled.

   (b) An earnest prayer (v. 26). Servant thereupon appealed abjectly to his master to have patience with him; and he promised to pay debt in full if given time.

   (c) A generous act (v. 27). King, moved with

compassion at his servant's plight, released him, and actually forgave him debt; but, we may note, servant was not forgiven until he came to his lord in humility.

(2) *The Unforgiving Servant* (vs. 28-30)

  (a) Unreasoning violence (v. 28). But this man, forgiven so very much, proved heartlessly cruel in face of almost identical and immediate circumstance; and this in spite of contrast between two debts that could hardly be more striking — ratio of ten million dollars to sixteen dollars, illustrating most graphically difference between "seven" and "seventy times seven" (v. 22).

  (b) Merciless retaliation (vs. 29, 30). In the face also of almost identical plea (v. 29; cf. v. 26), servant failed to follow his master's good example; and so fellow servant went to prison "till he should pay the debt" (v. 30).

(3) *The Terrible Result* (vs. 31-34)

  (a) Discovery (v. 31). In this case, as so often, man's fellows were observant of his conduct, especially because he had been so privileged.

  (b) Rebuke (vs. 32, 33). Privilege led also to unanswerable logic of his master's words, "I forgave thee . . . shouldest not thou also have had compassion . . . ?"

  (c) Punishment (v. 34). Some interpret word translated "tormentors" as simply "jailers," while others take it literally to signify torture rather than slavery, original sentence (cf. v. 25); if latter, that servant's last state was far worse than his first, in accordance with his own savage cruelty (cf. v. 28).

No doubt our Lord used figures of talents and pence to show in most marked contrast that our obligation to God towers far above paltry debts our fellows owe us. Indeed, every human being is by his very nature indebted to his God so enormously that he himself can never pay what was due originally and what is daily accruing. How much more is this true of those of us who have been "bought with a price" (1 Cor. 7:23; cf. 1 Peter 1:18, 19)! And so the chapter closes with —

d. *The Principle Applied* (v. 35)

Implicit in Christ's concluding words are —
   (1) The reason for forgiveness — because to disciple other disciple is "his brother";
   (2) The nature of forgiveness — thorough and sincere — "from your hearts";
   (3) The standard of forgiveness — that of God Himself — "my heavenly Father"; and —
   (4) The alternative of forgiveness — certain, universal retribution — "so likewise shall . . . do also unto you, if ye . . . forgive not every one . . . their trespasses."

Conclusion

From this chapter we learn three great lessons:

1. *The Blessedness of Being Humble*
   a. Teaching of N.T. emphasizes importance of considering others, especially those weaker in the faith; in particular, St. Paul distinguishes between strong and weak brethren, calling upon former to help, not hinder, latter (cf. Rom. 14:1 to 15:3).
   b. He also teaches, as our Lord does here, that those overtaken by sin are to be dealt with kindly, tenderly, sympathetically; and there is to be a spirit of humility tempered by definite purpose of spiritual restoration (cf. Gal. 6:1-3).
   c. Thus, in everything and in various ways, humility is shown to be one of prime requirements of true discipleship; and it has close relation to —

2. *The Blessedness of Being Forgiving*
   a. Unforgiving spirit is shown in parable to lead to hatred, one of saddest features of human life; for hatred and peace never go together, whether individually or nationally.
   b. No character can be regarded as in any sense Christian

which does not possess element of pity, mercy, and forgiving love.

c. Forgiveness of others will be immediate, free, full, and permanent; for these are characteristics of —

3. *The Blessedness of Being Forgiven*

a. As God's forgiveness springs from love, not law, so consciousness of how He has loved and forgiven us will do more than anything else to make us tenderhearted towards our brethren; and there will be, not extenuation of sin, but compassion on sinner.

b. Forgiveness in Scripture is not only remission of penalty, but removal of sin itself; like God, we are to forgive and forget (cf. Jer. 31:35, Heb. 8:12).

c. Thus, Divine love expresses itself both in God's forgiveness of us through Christ and in our forgiveness of others; we experience God's love, and then we exercise it, and in so doing find we experience it again (cf. 1 John 4:19, A.S.V.; Eph. 4:32).

d. Thus, validity of petition in the Lord's Prayer is fully supported: "Forgive us . . . as we forgive" (6:12); and never must we forget emphasis placed by Christ on "forgivingness" as guarantee and proof of "forgiveness" (cf. Mark 11:25, 26), which is eloquently echoed by St. Paul (Eph. 4:32).

Yes, if we are humble we shall be forgiving, and whenever we forgive we show most clearly that we have been forgiven.

40

HUMAN PROBLEMS IN CHRIST'S MINISTRY

Matthew 19:1-26

W ITH THE closing words of the previous chapter our Lord ceased His training of the disciples for a time and left Galilee for Judaea, beyond the river Jordan (v. 1). Several different phases of His ministry may be noted from this chapter:

I. A Physical Problem (v. 2)

a. This was perennial need of people for healing; it is no wonder that, having heard such words and seen such deeds, great multitudes followed Christ from place to place.

b. Amid training of disciples and parrying hostility of Jewish leaders, crowds were not forgotten; they again received His blessings of healing, and Mark tells us that He also "taught them again" (Mark 10:1).

II. A Moral Problem (vs. 3-12)

1. *The Public Exchange* (vs. 3-9)

a. Our Lord's enemies would not leave Him alone for long, however; and now Pharisees did their best to involve Him in serious conflict by question about marriage and divorce (v. 3).

b. This inquiry elicited striking statement from Christ, reminding them of primal purpose of God for male and female; and His picture of earliest human life, man and woman united to each other and to God, is beautiful evidence of similar Divine purpose for mankind today (vs. 4, 5).

c. Indeed, this holy relationship as original plan of God demands special attention at present time; and force of argument consists in original essential unity of male and female in Adam (v. 6).

d. It is impossible, moreover, to exaggerate importance of Christ's principle concerning marriage; it completes creation as perfect communion of life and as figure of spiritual union between Christ Himself and His Church (cf. Eph. 5:22, 23).

N.B. It is also important to observe our Lord's testimony to record in Genesis; as before pointed out, He refers to account there as historical fact and bases His argument on literal expressions found therein (cf. Gen. 1:27; 2: 24).

e. But enemies of Christ could not allow matter to rest there; in quick rejoinder (v. 7) they asked Christ how, in view of this original purpose for marriage, there could be any divorce granted, as it was by law of Moses (cf. Deut. 24:1).

f. They evidently wished to entangle our Lord by making Him commit Himself on one side or other of disputes then raging on marriage, adultery, and divorce; but He countered by telling them arrangement for divorce was necessitated solely by sin of man, his failure to carry out God's original purpose (v. 8).

g. Moses did not intend to facilitate divorce, but only to regulate it and to diminish its incidence by means of legal provision to be observed; for all such laws, dealing with sinful men as they did, could never maintain perfect standard of original requirement.

h. Thus there was to be no premium on evil, since marriage was intended to be indissoluble; and not even separation could be tolerated except for one heinous sin against marriage (v. 9).

N.B. Otherwise further and deeper evil would ensue; "her which is put away" (v. 9) would seem to refer to wife of man who has in some arbitrary manner and for insufficient cause separated himself from her. She remains his lawful wife in sight of God though nominally she has been divorced; and thus man continues to be her husband, and both are equally unable to marry another.*

---

*Ed. Note: It may be appropriate and helpful here to quote a question on remarriage once asked of the writer and his answer:

"Can a divorced Christian, who has obtained divorce because of the only justifiable Christian reason, but who has himself or herself been free from

2. *The Private Explanation* (vs. 10-12)

   a. Our Lord's disciples, evidently astonished by this severe standard, suggested that, in view of what had been said, it could not be good to marry (v. 10); and His reply did not mitigate this severity.

   b. He first stated that this pronouncement of His was not for everyone (v. 11); and then He said frankly that there were cases in which celibate life was not only expedient for individual, or unavoidable by him, but could and would be made to further interests of God's Kingdom (v. 12).

   c. We are surely to infer that marriage was not shown by this further consideration of it to be low in Christ's esteem; rather, He was warning disciples circumstances might arise in which single life would better serve cause of God (cf. 1 Cor. 7:7, 29-35; 1 Tim. 4:1-5).

   d. It is serious error to exalt either celibacy above marriage or marriage above celibacy; instead, question is one to be carefully considered by each individual Christian and settled in sight of God as best may work out for His glory and extension of His Kingdom.

III. A Social Problem (vs. 13-15)

1. *The Bringing of the Children* (v. 13a)

   a. It is striking that, immediately following searching moral teaching connected with disturbed home relationships, innocent children, so often victims of these, were brought to Christ for laying on of hands and prayer; and this suggests sharp contrast of ideal Christian home.

   b. It is also interesting to note possible rendering in Luke's wording in parallel passage is "they kept on bringing even their infants" (Luke 18:15); for this suggests parents' approval of our Lord's ministry.

   c. In all three Synoptics, moreover, pronouns "they" and "them" in Greek are masculine, implying there were fathers, as well as "mothers of Salem," present; doubtless

that guilt, marry again without thereby committing sin?" "I am of opinion that he or she can. I know that many honored Christian men think otherwise, but I always distinguish between the innocent and guilty parties, believing that the former can, and the latter cannot, marry again."

they united in thus bringing their little ones to Christ in solemn act of dedication.

2. *The Blundering of the Disciples* (v. 13b)

   a. Again disciples erred, evidently considering children beneath notice of such a Person as our Lord; so that they rebuked parents.

   b. Or perhaps they were merely provoked by intrusion, forgetting so soon lessons taught by means of child set "in the midst of them" (18:2) and exhortation to "despise not one of these little ones" (18:10).

3. *The Blessing of the Lord* (vs. 14, 15)

   a. Christ's action in response was another proof of His infinite grace; for He showed deep displeasure (Mark 10:14) as He rebuked disciples who would have driven these children away (v. 14), and with matchless words of welcome laid His hands on little ones (v. 15) and blessed them (cf. Mark 10:16).

   b. In view of His phrase "of such is the kingdom of heaven," it is impossible to doubt children are capable of union with Christ; furthermore, there are intimations all through N.T. that great atoning sacrifice at Calvary included unselfconscious childhood, as well as comprehending manhood and womanhood, in its wondrous efficacy and blessing.

   c. Parents of these children brought to Christ were performing high duty of offering their little ones to God in their infancy; for it is never enough to care only for family's health, education, and deportment.

   d. It is, indeed, an inadequate parent who is concerned merely for children's physical welfare or worldly success; his supreme duty is to consider their souls, for if only parents and teachers were as anxious about spiritual realities as they are for education and position, homes and schools would be not merely very different, but also bear constant witness to childhood's essential relationship to God.

   e. As noted in connection with previous chapter (18:11), children need regeneration and, when of age of accountability, must choose for themselves; but little ones, especially as "children of the covenant" included in Christ's redemptive work, are His until and unless they reject Him.

IV. A Spiritual Problem (vs. 16-26)*

As our Lord passed on His way (cf. v. 15, Mark 10:17), one came to Him who, we know, was rich (v. 22, Mark 10:22, Luke 18:23), young (vs. 20, 22), and a ruler (Luke 18:18).

1. *The Problem* (vs. 16-20)

  a. *The Inquiry*

    (1) This rich young ruler came to Christ in quest of "eternal life" (v. 16); with all his advantages he was evidently conscious of something lacking that our Lord might supply.

    (2) There seems to have been true earnestness and genuine self-dissatisfaction; he longed for some unattained bliss and was ready to take pains to procure it.

    (3) There is nothing more striking than testimony to Christ afforded in his thus coming; but perhaps his estimate of what was "good thing" (v. 16) to be done was too superficial.

    (4) He clearly had notion that eternal life was to be won by good deeds; thus his question was blend of good and evil, his purpose being right but his plan of attaining it wrong.

  b. *The Response* (vs. 17-19)

    (1) Point of our Lord's counterquestion lies in first word, "Why" and was evidently intended to deepen young man's conception of "good" and so awaken consciousness of imperfection; He does not deny goodness to Himself, but causes man to consider reason why he should have used adjective that strictly and literally applies only to God (v. 17a).

    (2) Then Christ meets young ruler on his own ground of law, testing him by reminder that way unto life was still way of law; and, though he evidently expected to be ordered to do something new or brilliant,

---

*For another and fuller treatment of this passage, see following Study, No. 41, p. 285.

he was referred to old and familiar duties (vs. 17b-19).

c. *The Rejoinder* (v. 20)

(1) Young man, with evident disappointment and some impatience, claimed to have fulfilled all this; and he wanted to know what yet was lacking.

(2) It is striking that Christ had referred only to those commandments that define man's relation to his neighbors and had said nothing about deeper and more fundamental duty in relation to God; and yet young ruler did not seem to notice this omission as he made his claim, for his soul was evidently lacking in something essential (cf. Luke 10:25-28).

2. *The Pronouncement* (vs. 21, 22)

a. *The Offer* (v. 21)

(1) Then came application of test, made by our Lord with look of affection (cf. Mark 10:21), but revealing to young man simple yet searching fact that requirements were not yet complete; he must not only give up his wealth to help poor, but do so also in order to cast in his lot with lowly Man of Nazareth and become His disciple, one of those whom world was spurning.

(2) This would involve revolution of his entire life, because at that time Jesus was becoming practically an outcast by nation's leaders; but there would be in future compensating "treasure in heaven" for eye of faith.

N.B. It is striking to observe in this passage two stages of godly life: (1) "If thou wilt enter into life —" (v. 17); and (2) "If thou wilt be perfect —" (v. 21); that is, be mature and ripe in experience (cf. 5:48) as contrasted with mere elementary step and immature condition.

b. *The Refusal* (v. 22)

(1) It was all this that made young man, unwilling to accept Christ's offer of earthly discipleship and heavenly treasure, go away both "sorrowful" and indignant (as one meaning of word indicates); he had come "running" (Mark 10:17) and full of hope,

but went away dejected (cf. Mark 10:22) and un-
settled, back to his old life.

(2) It is clear that his wealth was only occasion, not cause,
of his trouble: real cause was unwillingness to surrender to Christ and put Him first, or, to express
deeper meaning implied, failure to keep "first and
great commandment" (cf. 22:37, 38); so this rich
young ruler lost probably finest opportunity that
would ever come to him.

3. *The Peril* (vs. 23-26)

a. *The Application* (vs. 23, 24)

(1) From these words of Christ, with their reiterated
emphasis, we seem to sense his deep pity for this
mistaken young man as he departs unwilling to surrender his life to God.

(2) Metaphor of camel and needle's eye, whether literal
or figurative, points out to disciples with all possible clarity great difficulty of entrance into Kingdom
for such as he.

b. *The Assurance* (vs. 25, 26)

(1) Disciples were astonished at this, showing how entirely opposed they still were to true, spiritual conception of Kingdom (v. 25); but though possession
of wealth was occasion for this man's stumbling at
Christ's authority, same spirit of unwillingness to
surrender may be shown by poorest of men, occasion
alone being different.

(2) Christ did not minimize difficulty, but reassured His
puzzled disciples by stating that, while such surrender
was impossible with man, it was wholly within power
of God and could be accomplished through His grace
(cf. 17:20).

Conclusion

We may trace an impressive connection between the four sections
of this passage; it is discipleship, a very important subject for
the Twelve at that time. The first two headings may be grouped
together:

1. *Frailty in Discipleship* (vs. 1-12)

    a. Health. There are those who need healing touch of Christ on body and soul before they can follow Him fully.

    b. Home. There are those who need help of Christ to settle domestic difficulties before they and their families can be true disciples of Him.

2. *Features of Discipleship* (vs. 13-15)

    True following of Christ is shown in four characteristics of childhood:

    a. Dependence;

    b. Humility;

    c. Love; and —

    d. Obedience.

3. *Failure in Discipleship* (vs. 16-26)

    Qualifications, fulfilled in case of children, were not possessed by rich young ruler. Instead, he showed —

    a. Independence, desiring to go his own way;

    b. Self-sufficiency, setting his own standards;

    c. Selfishness, giving no thought to others; and —

    d. Disobedience, owning no master but himself.

In particular, the striking contrasts brought together in this passage should enable us all to see clearly the dangers of failing to put Christ first in life.

41

"HE WENT AWAY SORROWFUL"*

Matthew 19:22

O NE OF the finest testimonies that our Lord Jesus Christ ever received during His earthly ministry was given Him unintentionally by the Pharisees, when they exclaimed: "This man receiveth sinners!" (Luke 15:2). It was one of the glories of His life on earth that He welcomed the sinful, the outcast, the rejected of men. No heart coming in contact with Him failed to feel and know His sympathy, His deep and lively interest. Similarly, it is the peculiar glory of Christianity that it receives sinners, too; that it deals with sin.

But there are many people who would not be affected in the least by that message, "This man receiveth sinners." They have never been brought into personal contact with crime or vice and their consequent degradation. It is of no use speaking to these people about the outcast or the moral leper, for all their life long they have been surrounded by good and moral influences, some even by spiritual influences, and they have no imagination for putting themselves in the position of those who have not been so fortunate. Their education has been of the best, their refinement of the highest. What are we to do with such people? Ah, Christianity has another message for such as they: This Man receives "good" people, persons of inwardly moral as well as outwardly ethical life, of good social position, who pay their debts, who are upright, respectable, exemplary citizens. Jesus Christ receives such people, those whose natures have in their backgrounds by centuries of good influences that which is ideally noble and fine.

---

*Ed. Note: For this Study I have been assisted by a stenographic report of one of my father's best-known sermons. He would preach it on a Sunday morning, and in the evening its companion sermon, using the text, "He went on his way rejoicing" (Acts 8:39). For an outline of this latter sermon see *Outline Studies in the Acts of the Apostles*, (Wm. B. Eerdmans Publishing Company, 1956) pp. 158-162. These two titles appear also in a suggestive list of five addresses on "Turning-points in Life," the other three being: "He went away in a rage" (2 Kings 5:12); "He went out . . . a leper" (2 Kings 5:27); and "He went out, not knowing whither" (Heb. 11:8).

Jesus Christ does have a message for the prodigal, thank God, but He also has a message for the elder brother. Not only does He speak to the young man who, as we say, has sown his wild oats, but He also has a message for the young man who has no wild oats to sow.

In this story of the rich young ruler coming to Christ, we may see that, while there is indeed a point at which these good, outwardly moral, upright people and He may meet, there is also a point at which they often separate, perhaps forever. We may notice —

I. A Splendid Promise

1. *This Man Was Young, Rich, and Powerful*

    a. Prospect and potential of youth is one of greatest advantages in every department of life.

    b. Wealth is great advantage, too, for it is not wrong to have it, only to let it have you; it is not wrong to have it as stone under feet, only to have it as rock above to crush you.

    c. This rich young man was also man of power and influence in his community; whatever is meant by term "ruler" (Luke 18:18; cf. John 3:1), there is no doubt he occupied some responsible position in Jewish temple or state.

2. *This Man Was Intelligent, Earnest, and Moral*

    a. He was evidently man of intelligence who had been giving thought to realities, not trivialities; he had considered such great issues as eternal life.

    b. His mind occupied with these great subjects, he was earnest and enthusiastic; for he came "running, and kneeled to" Jesus (Mark 10:12) before asking Him important question.

    c. Above all, he was a moral young man; this we also know from story, that he kept law and that his life was above reproach.

Young, rich, influential, intellectual, earnest, moral — here was man to be admired and envied, man of splendid promise, fine example of what culture, education, and social standing can do. And yet he had —

II. A Serious Problem

1. *This Man Was Not Satisfied*

   a. All these advantages were his, but he came to Jesus with question: "Good Master, what good thing shall I do to inherit eternal life?" (v. 16).

   b. He was in search of chief good, eternal life; and yet we do not suppose he knew fully what it meant, as we do (cf. John 17:3).

   c. But there was something above and beyond his experience that he could only call "eternal life"; and he was prepared to do almost anything in order to obtain it.

2. *This Man Was Bearing Testimony to Jesus Christ*

   a. He acknowledged that our Lord could tell him what he, with all his advantages, did not know, viz., how to obtain eternal life; and when man has that idea of Christ there is no doubt in his mind as to Christ's ability to answer.

   b. Problems can be solved and difficulties met if there is spirit of trust, earnestness, and humility; and we may imagine this young man's eyes lighting up with hope of great discovery as he knelt at Jesus' feet.

III. A Significant Inquiry

Our Lord's dealing with this young man was twofold:

1. *A Counter Question*

   a. Christ looks down upon kneeling figure and asks, "Why callest thou me good? There is none good but one, that is, God" (v. 17a).

   b. Modern emphasis almost invariably is placed on word "me," e.g., by Unitarians and agnostics; but this would mean Jesus Christ denied He was good, and is one of those arguments that, by proving too much, proves nothing at all.

   c. In Greek, emphasis is on word "Why," or, "What is your reason for associating term with me, when it refers, strictly speaking, only to God?"

   d. Christ was already answering young man's question by trying to probe his motives; and to do this He tested his use of language and thought behind it.

2. *A Challenge*

   a. Then our Lord went on to meet this man on his own ground; by telling him, "If thou wilt enter into life, keep the commandments" (v. 17b), He was holding up to him mirror of law in order that he might see himself and answer his own question (cf. Jas. 1:22-25).

   b. By reciting specific commandments (vs. 18, 19), Christ continued His testing, using standard of Divine law to gauge young man's real condition before God.

IV. A Shallow Rejoinder

1. *A Self-Attested Record*

   a. Young man's reply, "Master, all these have I kept since my youth up" (v. 20), if truthful, represents fine achievement; but it is notable he now drops adjective "good."

   b. No wonder our Lord questioned spirit of man who used it, for one who could thus boast of keeping all commandments must have thought, first of all and chiefly, of himself as "good"; and so form of address had probably been mere form, as was customary when speaking to rabbis and teachers of that day.

2. *A Sincere Regret*

   a. Young man, having stated his case, rephrases his question: "What lack I yet?" (v. 20); and in this puzzled request for information there was real disappointment.

   b. He had doubtless expected to be told something new and remarkable to do in order to "inherit eternal life" (v. 22); but here he is sent back to commandments that seem so obvious and familiar as to be trite (cf. Naaman's attitude in 2 Kings 5:11, 12).

   c. Natural, perhaps, but how shallow and lacking in perception was his reaction; for no mention had been made of first four commandments, regarding duty to God, only of remainder, about duty to neighbors.

   d. In spite of shallowness, however, there was also sincerity; and our Lord can deal with people as they are, even if vain or superficial, so long as they are in earnest to depth they have.

V. A Supreme Test

1. *The Divine Attitude*

a. We are told by Mark (10:21) that "Jesus beholding him loved him"; and we may picture those tender eyes of our Lord resting upon this attractive, earnest young man kneeling there.

b. As always, Christ saw into heart of man and knew possibilities of his life; and, like kind physician who knows he must hurt to heal, our Lord showed tender regard before He stated severe conditions of acceptance of eternal life.

2. *The Direct Answer*

a. To continue with Mark's version, we read that Christ replied in young man's own words: "One thing thou lackest"; and here was fine opportunity for him to respond at precise point of his life's greatest need.

b. But in all three accounts this "one thing" was manifold — fivefold, in Matthew's wording: "Go, sell that thou hast, and give to the poor, . . . and come and follow me" (v. 21).

c. Therefore we must not stop with first three, "Go, sell, give," but remember our Lord said also, "Come, follow"; for this was how He would remind young man what eternal life really meant.

d. It was not something to be "done" or "inherited"; it was not achievement, but attitude; not possession, but condition.

e. Specifically, eternal life was attitude of heart towards One who was speaking to this young inquirer, and it was condition of soul in His holy sight; inherent in it, surely, was surrender to Him as more than man.

VI. The Sad Result

1. *The Refusal*

a. Let us wait for a moment in silence, looking down at that lovable, earnest, attractive fellow as he kneels there; he has heard these five words, Go, Sell, Give, Come, Follow, and we wonder on which side the scales will drop, but now our hearts sink within us.

b. "When he heard that saying, he went away sorrowful"

(v. 22); and word used in Mark's Gospel (10:22) indicates his countenance fell, lowered with annoyance.

c. There was no argument, no appeal, no expostulation; and thus he departed both angered and sad.
   N.B. Latter word is strong one, used by Matthew of our Lord in Gethsemane (cf. 26:38).

2. *The Reason*

a. It is essential now to ask why this young man "went away sorrowful"; and it is easy question to answer at once — because he was rich, and those riches prevented him from obeying Jesus.

b. But quick, easy answer is not always right one, and if we look more closely we shall see wealth possessed was not reason of his going away; it was only occasion of it, and this is important distinction.

c. This young man's great test came to him by means of those riches, but they were not underlying cause of his failure to pass it; for Christ's call meant not merely giving up his money in connection with eternal life or even in order to benefit poor.

d. It meant complete revolution in his life: it meant giving up old position of leadership and following despised Jesus of Nazareth; it meant casting in his lot with those twelve disciples, most of them of humble origin, and going from place to place as recognized follower of One out of favor in high places.

e. It meant entire surrender of his life to Jesus Christ, and that he was not prepared to make; so, to repeat, his possession of riches was only occasion by which unwillingness to surrender expressed itself.

f. That is why so many poor people, and people who are neither rich nor poor, fail to realize application of this incident to them; for Christ comes to every man, rich, or poor, or comfortably off, and asks his wholehearted surrender.

g. It so happened this man was tested in region of his pocketbook, as we should say, but other men are tested in other regions and departments of their lives and may be equally unwilling to make surrender; underlying

cause is same in every case, though occasion may differ —
e.g., pleasure, ambition, bad habits.

VII. A Solemn Lesson

1. *The Departure*

a. This young man, then, unwilling to make that surrender,
"went away sorrowful"; and last thing we hear of him
as he turns corner and disappears out of sight is when
disciples look around, saying one to another, "How
difficult it must be for man like that to enter Kingdom
of Heaven!" (cf. v. 25)

b. Before all these disciples, who might have been his faithful companions, he went away; and he doubtless returned
to his own surroundings, where he was acknowledged as
ruler and perhaps fawned upon by those who respected
wealth and power.

2. *The Darkness*

a. No doubt, too, he lived his own life; and finally, dying
his own death and given funeral of rich man, went, like
Judas, to his own place, place of darkness forever.

b. That is, if this rich young ruler never came back again
to Jesus — and Gospels are, of course, silent on this
point; we can scarcely doubt, then, that life of his was
wasted, spiritually speaking, for one lack only — unwillingness to surrender to Christ as Lord and, living in
light as He is in light, to have fellowship with people of
God.

Illus.: See that magnificent locomotive, each part of its
mechanism perfect, its crew ready; but it does not move,
because it has as yet no steam, no power. Or look at that
watch, splendidly made, every part of its movement
ready, escapement and balance-wheel and jewels, but
lacking one thing: it has no mainspring as yet, and therefore cannot be wound, given power to go. And look at
that young man, splendid athlete, best student in his
college, fine specimen of manhood, wanting nothing —
but just one thing — Christ as motive power of his life!

Conclusion

This, then, is the point at which Jesus Christ meets "good"

people — and often has to leave them. The separation comes because they are unwilling to make wholehearted surrender to Him, the secret of eternal life, here and hereafter. This is the point, too, where they are proved to be not truly good, for their hearts are unregenerate.

But there are many Christians who have the same difficulty. They know very well that their lives, though professedly "good" and upright, are not what they ought to be. There is weakness, there is instability of character, there are variations of experience, sometimes joyous and sometimes the opposite; and the reason for all that changeableness is that Christians are unwilling to surrender fully to their Saviour, to put Him first in their lives. "For this cause," St. Paul wrote, "Jesus Christ both died and rose and revived, that he might be Lord" (Rom. 14:9).

Is He the Lord of our life? Or are we unwilling to make that surrender? If so, our life will always be weak and poor and worthless, whether we are Christians or whether we are not. Jesus Christ must be first, with no mental reservations, no moral reservations, no spiritual reservations — Jesus Christ first; and then everything else will fall into its proper place.

Man of business, is that true of you? Is Jesus Christ first in your life? What about those transactions that are just a little shady, perhaps, not quite right, not very, very wrong, but still doubtful? Do you put Jesus Christ first when these proposals are made to you? Do you allow Him to be the first in every part of your life — in your home, in your office, in your workshop, or wherever you are? Brothers and sisters, men and women, how is it with you? Christ is standing now near the throne-room of your will, and He claims full possession of it. Are you willing to decide for Jesus Christ? Good intentions are splendid in their place, but by themselves they are of no service whatever. Aspirations may be fine, but aspirations by themselves will never lead us to the feet of Christ. Resolutions and convictions are necessary, but by themselves they will never lead us to eternal life. There must be decision on the part of the believer. He must consciously and definitely take Christ as his Lord; and it must also be so with those who have never found Christ — He must be Lord as well as Saviour. Let all of us, then, give hearts and lives in complete surrender to Jesus Christ not only as Saviour, but also as Lord.

42

FURTHER TRAINING OF THE TWELVE (2)

Matthew 19:27—20:28

To continue the training of the disciples became, at this point in Christ's ministry, His well-nigh entire concern. He had spoken to them of doctrine (16:5-12); of devotion (16:21-27); and of discipline, with emphasis on humility and forgiveness (chap. 18). Then came an interval of dealing with others (19:1-26). Now comes the present passage, in which our Lord sets forth three more aspects of His teaching with reference to the Kingdom:

I. Rewards in the Kingdom (19:27-30)

1. *Self-sacrifice Recognized* (vs. 27-29)

   a. Rich young ruler, mentioned in preceding passage, had just turned away from Christ when Peter interposed, stating he and his fellow disciples had done very thing this young man had refused to do; and, since they had "forsaken all, and followed" their Master, he naturally, but in rather calculating fashion, wanted to know what they should have in return (v. 27).

   b. It is true they had not much to leave, e.g., their fishing, tax-collecting, etc.; and yet it was "all" to them, just as it would have been to rich man (cf. Luke 18:22), for they had broken with their past in following Christ, and that is seldom easy.

   c. In any case, our Lord honored it because, though small, it was indeed all they had; and He at once tells them this surrender of theirs would be rewarded:

      (1) There would be heavenly blessings (v. 28); they should sit on thrones in His future Kingdom, "judging" their fellow countrymen.
      N.B. (1) Word "regeneration," occurring twice in N.T., here clearly means new physical state or circumstances; while in Titus 3:5 it refers to second

birth of believer, or introduction of living being into new spiritual state. (2) Mention of "twelve thrones" has puzzled some in relation to our Lord's knowledge of Judas' intention of betraying Him (cf. John 6:70, 71); but promise is to those "which have followed" Him, and this was obviously going to be untrue of Judas. It also goes without saying that Christ's foreknowledge included substitution of Matthias for Judas (cf. Acts 1:15-26) to make up "twelve." (3) C. I. Scofield suggests this verse discloses how promise of Isa. 1:26 will be fulfilled.

(2) There would even be earthly increase (v. 29); and in all ages it has been found blessedly true that Christian received "an hundredfold" of that which gives these things their great value and deep satisfaction — described by Psalmist as "great reward" (Ps. 19:11) and by Luke as "manifold more" (Luke 18:30).
N.B. (1) In eyes of world today, for instance, Peter has certainly received his "hundredfold" in fame and influence. (2) But, to take illustration nearer our own level, surrendered believer has much wider horizon, closer touch with hearts of men, higher spiritual education, broader influence, more and finer friendships, etc., as his Christian life develops and deepens.

> *"An hundredfold" from Thee,*
> *Bestowed in heavenly grace*
> *On them who chose their lives to lose*
> *With Thee to have a place;*
> *Possessions here below,*
> *Greater by far above,*
> *Thy presence here, Thy glory there,*
> *Their portion endless love.*
> *Then may our hearts leave all behind,*
> *Unhindered joy in Thee to find!*
> H.H.

(3) Above all, there would be that which young ruler sought but refused — "everlasting life" (v. 29); and

since Matthew, unlike Mark and Luke, does not specify time of this, we may perhaps infer he understood it to start here and now (cf. John 5:24) for those who surrender fully to Christ.

2. *Self-assertion Rebuked* (v. 30)

a. With this encouragement, however, came Christ's solemn warning that order of recognition and size of reward would not be always as disciples apparently expected.

b. Thus rewards in Kingdom are not determined by fact or amount of service, but rather by its true quality as determined by motive and spirit.

c. Mark tells us Christ included "persecutions" (10:30) in His promised "hundredfold"; and this would show these were not to be regarded as drawbacks, but as part of gain.

II. Recognition in the Kingdom (20:1-16)

Our Lord then gave Peter and his fellow disciples illustration of His warning about last being first and first last, and this parable carries principle further into whole subject of service for Him.

1. *The Righteousness of the Master*

a. Parable depicts justice on part of householder, for laborers in each category agree to work and are content to receive either specific wage (cf. vs. 2, 13) or "whatsoever is right" (vs. 4, 7).

b. Circumstances may vary, and some workers may have fewer opportunities; but, so long as our Master is just to all, He may surely be generous to some if He sees fit (cf. vs. 14, 15).

c. There must, therefore, be no envy of other people's blessings; nor can there be any spirit of bargaining on part of Christian worker (cf. vs. 10-12).

d. However, there are also those "first" who will not be "last," and those "last" who will not be "first"; we may be sure "the judge of all the earth" will "do right" (Gen. 18:25).

2. *The Realization of the Rewards*

a. Kingdom of Christ has its compensations in present; for

everything attains its highest possible value in union with Him (cf. 1 Cor. 3:21-23).

b. Then in future will come crown and culmination of life, for God's purposes are not fulfilled here; they stretch over to world to come (cf. Mark 10:30, Luke 18:30, 1 Cor. 3:13, 14).

3. *The Risks of the Kingdom*

a. These must not be overlooked, for there may be wrong spirit in worker and unfaithfulness in work.

b. Or, there may be spasmodic zeal and intermittent work on part of some.

c. Results will be absence of reward and loss of blessing, though worker himself will be saved, "yet so as by fire" (1 Cor. 3:15).

N.B. It is useful to compare Christ's three parables dealing with rewards: (1) According to quantity of work when ability is equal (25:14-20); (2) according to ability when it varies (Luke 19:12-27); and (3) according to motive and thoroughness of worker (as here).

III. Rank in the Kingdom (20:17-28)

1. *The Revelation* (vs. 17-19)

a. Again Christ predicts His approaching death, taking His disciples apart privately for purpose (v. 17); this is third such announcement.

b. First referred only to fact (cf. 16:21); second added means — betrayal (cf. 17:22); and now comes further information regarding condemnation by rulers, and maltreatment and crucifixion by Gentiles (vs. 18, 19a).

c. Also, light of resurrection again breaks through darkness (v. 19b); such statements are numerous and form integral part of Christ's teaching concerning Himself (cf. 12:40, 16:21, 17:23, 27:63, John 2:19-22).

d. It is impressive to note this announcement can be nothing but prediction based on our Lord's supernatural foreknowledge; and to us it seems surprising that disciples did not grasp such very definite statements (cf. Luke 18:34).

2. *The Request* (vs. 20, 21)

a. Indeed, it was at this juncture that solemn subject was

broken in upon, and that by mere question of precedence amongst disciples; and situation is infinitely pathetic because cross itself was only short time ahead.

b. Our Lord's thoughts were full of His betrayal, trial, mocking, scourging, crucifixion, and then His empty tomb; but although He has told disciples of these things before there is no word of sympathy from them, no expression of sorrow or dismay this time (cf. 17:23).

c. Instead, there was family conspiracy between two of them and their mother to steal march on others by requesting priority in Kingdom; and yet these two were later to be among truest and best men of their day, trusted apostles of Christ, His nearest and dearest, leading witnesses and future martyrs (cf. Acts 12:2, Rev. 1:9).

d. Mother of Zebedee's sons, James and John, is thought to have been Salome (cf. 27:56 with Mark 15:40, 16:1); and it has been thought she was sister of our Lord's mother (cf. 27:56 with John 19:25).

N.B. This would obviate problem of two sisters with same name, making John 19:25 list four women instead of three, as Broadus suggests.

e. Perhaps James and John prompted their mother to approach Christ with them (cf. Mark 10:35); or it may be that if her human relationship to Him did exist it made her bold enough to make her request and encourage her sons to join her.

f. Her outward act of reverence (v. 20) evidently meant recognition of Jesus Christ as Messiah and future King, implying ordinary Jewish view that Kingdom would be earthly one; or else she had been told of His promise of "twelve thrones" (19:28) recently made; at any rate, she desired best positions in Kingdom for her sons (v. 21).

N.B. This prayer was ignorant prayer, and reminds us of futile prayer (Deut. 3:26); while among other types of prayer are mentioned, e.g.: sorrowful (1 Sam. 1:10); agonizing (Luke 22:44); joyful (Phil. 1:4); private (Matt. 6:16); public (Acts 2:42); parting (Acts 20:36); instant, or stedfast (Rom. 12:12); unceasing (1 Thess. 5:17).

3. *The Refusal* (vs. 22, 23)

   a. Instead of being angry at this interruption, our Lord uttered patient reminder of real character of His Kingdom by speaking again of that which lay before Him; and use of plural includes sons as well as mother (v. 22a).

   b. He spoke of His own "cup" of sorrow and asked whether they were able to drink of it, and of His own "baptism" of suffering; and they so little understood profound meaning of His inquiry that they declared themselves able to participate (v. 22b).

   c. Christ then promised they should follow Him in sorrow and suffering; but He went on to say He could not grant request about position and rank in Kingdom because it was simply not in His gift (v. 23), doubtless part of His self-emptying (cf. Phil. 2:7, A.S.V.).

   d. His authority was limited at that time by obedience to His Father's will; but, He declared, God's own purpose would be carried out in future.

4. *The Rebuke* (vs. 24-27)

   a. It is not surprising that this request for two resulted in natural indignation on part of ten; for it would seem effort had been intended to obtain special positions for James and John without regard to rights of others and, indeed, without their knowledge (v. 24).

   b. But their attitude was really just as sinful as ambition of James and John; and so Christ gently rebukes them all by declaring again that His Kingdom would be altogether different from those of earth (vs. 25, 26a).

   c. Real greatness would come only from service, and Christ significantly refers to two grades: work of ordinary servant (v. 26), and that of bondslave (v. 27); so that one who would be "great" must render service, while he who would be "chief" must be willing to enter actual bondage (cf. Rom. 1:1, Tit. 1:1, Jas. 1:1).

   Illus.: It has been said of these two verses that they contain "the greatest bit of business truth ever put into a single sentence." If this be true from worldly standpoint, much more is it so from moral and spiritual points of view. Service is one of the secrets of success.

5. *The Reminder* (v. 28)

    a. Then Christ closed this colloquy by speaking of His own life as supreme example of such high and holy service; in fact, He *"came* to minister."

    b. In addition, He told disciples, He "came . . . to give his life a ranson for many"; and certainly, if we read Gospels just as they stand, vicarious death of Jesus was clearly in view from outset of His earthly appearance (cf. 1:21 Luke 1:47, 2:11, 30, 35).

    c. Word "ransom" means payment made in order to redeem another life (cf. Gal. 3:13, Rev. 5:9), and Greek preposition here translated "for" not only means "instead of," but also appears elsewhere as part of actual word used for "ransom" (1 Tim. 2:6); so that Christ's sacrificial substitution, while but one aspect of N.T. teaching on atonement, is all-important one.

    d. Thus, honors of Kingdom are not to be allotted in accordance with man's thoughts and desires, but to be distributed by God in harmony with truth and justice; for they will be bestowed on great principle of cross, in which disciples are identified with their Master in both suffering and service.

    e. Christ's humblest servant shall thus share honor with Him who, though He was God, yet became man, taking upon Him form of servant and humbling Himself even to death of cross (cf. Phil. 2:7, 8).

Conclusion

Running through the entire passage is the question of self; in case of Peter, James, and John there was selfishness manifested, while in the character of our Lord the very opposite, selflessness, is clearly seen.

1. *The Danger of Self*

    a. Self takes various forms, and against them all we need to be on our guard: self-esteem, self-assertion, self-consciousness, self-confidence, self-satisfaction, self-pleasing, self-indulgence, self-centeredness, and self-will.

    b. There is also ambition, one of the strongest influences on human life; when properly exercised, it is an incentive to the achievement of higher things.

c. Yet ambition has great peril if fixed on unworthy objects or engaged in the setting aside of other people; there is, indeed, a Greek word rendered by the English word "envy," which is sinful because it involves success at the expense of the rights of others.

d. Another Greek word is translated "zeal," used by St. Paul to tell us of the three ambitions in his life: he was ambitious to be right with Christ here and hereafter (cf. 2 Cor. 5:9); he was ambitious to preach the gospel where Christ had not been named (cf. Rom. 15:20); and he was ambitious to be quiet and simple in his daily life (cf. 1 Thess. 4:11), this last passage having been well rendered — "Be ambitious, but have no ambition."

2. *The Safeguard from Self*

a. The only way of meeting this serious peril is by substituting Christ for self, and saying with St. Paul: "Not I, but Christ" (Gal. 2:20); "Not I, but the grace of God" (1 Cor. 15:10).

b. Christ's great title in Isaiah is "the Servant of Jehovah"; and He is there seen as accomplishing the purpose of God in earnest, loving work on behalf of man.

c. Having taken "the form of a servant" (Phil. 2:7), His first recorded words refer to His being about His Father's business (cf. Luke 2:49); and in the same spirit of selflessness John the Baptist later said of Him, "He must increase, but I must decrease" (John 3:30).

As we review this whole passage, we must ask ourselves: If these privileged disciples failed, where do we stand today? Who can tell the weakness and treachery of his own heart? If only we knew it, perhaps we are as blind, as selfish, and as unsympathetic as they were. If so, we need a searching revelation from God's Holy Spirit and His cleansing power, in order that we may walk with Christ in comprehending sympathy and self-sacrificing service. Our greatest encouragement is that He not only is our example, but is also the Source of all needed grace and strength.

43

FINAL OFFER TO THE NATION

Matthew 20:29—21:17

AFTER THE announcements already made to the disciples about Christ's imminent death, the time had come for His
last presentation of Himself to the Jewish nation. Gradually
our Lord drew near to Jerusalem where He was about to appear
publicly as God's Representative, an action very different from
His previous procedure when He so often counseled secrecy and
requested privacy. Now He seems even to court publicity among
the excitable crowds assembling for Passover.

I. The Last Miracle (20:29-34)

1. *The Appeal* (vs. 29-31)

   a. Approach to Jerusalem lay through Jericho (cf. Luke
   18:35 to 19:27), with multitudes following Jesus from
   there (v. 29); and on way He gave remarkable illustration of His power.

   b. Two blind men in great need sought favor from Him,
   addressing Him as "Son of David"; and thus they indicated their acknowledgment of His Messiahship (v. 30).

   c. People around rebuked them, but they were all the more
   insistent as they cried for mercy and continued to appeal
   to Christ as Messiah (v. 3); and it is noteworthy that He
   was recognized by blind men while those who could see
   physically but were spiritually blind were unable, because
   unwilling, to recognize Him (cf. John 9:39, 40; 12:35,
   36; 15:21-25).

2. *The Answer* (vs. 32-34)

   a. Immediately our Lord's compassion manifested itself in
   bestowal of blessing; for, in response to these men's call,
   He halted, called them to Him, and asked what they
   wanted (v. 32).

   b. Then, in answer to their prayer (v. 33), He put forth His
   power and gave them their sight; and their eyes, when

opened, must have realized strangeness of scene and press of crowds, but we are told "they followed him" (v. 34).

N.B. Probably differing accounts of healing of blind at Jericho is to be explained by Matthew's two men including Mark's one (cf. Mark 10:46-52), while Luke would seem to describe preceding, similar healing while entering city (cf. Luke 18:35-43).

c. It is interesting to wonder whether these men were among those who continued with Christ all through dark days that followed; and, if they were, it must have been great mystery to them that One who had done such marvels for them should not deliver Himself from His enemies.

d. But we know today explanation of it all: "He saved others; himself he [could] not ˉsave" (27:42), because it was only through surrender to God's will by way of cross that He could manifest His Divine love and saving grace — "to give his life a ransom for many" (v. 28).

3. *The Analogy*

a. This procession from Jericho may have reminded Christ, and perhaps others, of progress of Joshua from Jericho to conquest of promised land (cf. Josh. 8:13); for, although this Messianic progress from thence ended with its Leader being handed over to Gentiles, it was in higher sense another conquest over promised inheritance and victory over evil.

b. Let us note also that miracle of healing near Jericho beautifully illustrates how Christ deals with man's spiritual blindness; and in it we see, in response to human need, His instant readiness to put forth His Divine power in salvation.

Illus.: It is said that Moslem pilgrims, having arrived after years of effort at Mecca and gazed upon its holy places, knelt on white-hot bricks, heat from which, as they bent over, burned out all power of sight forever, lest it should be profaned by unhallowed scenes, for it was said: "See Mecca, and henceforth be blind!" How much better is effect of gospel! "See Christ," says Christian," "and henceforth find ever-increasing vision!" To one, vision is end; to other, it is beginning. Pilgrim sees Mecca, and straightway it is night; sinner sees Christ, and lo! it is daybreak.

II. The Last Opportunity (21:1-11)

1. *The King's Claim* (vs. 1-5)

a. This journey from Jericho to Jerusalem was one of great turning points in Christ's life on earth; it signified His acceptance of Messianic hopes of people, as He allowed Himself for first time to be heralded publicly as God's Anointed One (cf. v. 9).

b. His friends doubtless regarded it as royal or coronation procession, though Christ Himself must have realized it was mission of redemption; for He knew what they did not, namely, that crown could come only through cross.

c. Earlier in His ministry people had sought to make Him king (cf. John 6:15), but movement originating with them had been of earth, earthy; now, however, all initiative comes from Himself, and He approaches capital city not to be made King, for He was that already, but to be recognized as such, welcomed to Mount Zion, and honored and obeyed in Temple which was His House.

d. At Bethphage two disciples are instructed to bring colt, together with its mother (vs. 1-3), on which, according to magnificent prophecy of O.T., He was to make His entrance (cf. Zech. 9:9); for this prediction had to be fulfilled (vs. 4, 5) even though, serving as definite claim to Messiahship and cause for accusing Him, it would bring Him to cross.

N.B. Mention of two animals by both Zechariah and Matthew is better understood when A.S.V. rendering of former is used: "— riding upon an ass, *even* upon a colt the foal of an ass." The *Speaker's Commentary* suggests Matthew mentioned presence of mother because she actually accompanied colt of necessity, and that he thereby gave more complete narrative than other evangelists, though one in no way opposed to theirs.

2. *The King's Coming* (vs. 6-11)

a. Every point in story betokens majesty never before dreamed of — Divinely great and yet gentle, perfectly holy and yet approachable, absolutely kingly and yet very human.

b. Devoted disciples not only obeyed (v. 6), but contributed their outer garments, "and they set him thereon" (v. 7);

while enthusiasm of crowd would not even allow feet of beast to touch ground (v. 8).

c. Rumor of procession reaches Jerusalem and great multitudes stream out to meet it (v. 9); no wonder whole city is moved (v. 10) and both sections of crowd burst out in glad greeting: "Hosanna to the son of David: Blessed is he that cometh in the name of the Lord" (v. 9; cf. Ps. 118:26).

Illus.: In English school, some years ago, boys were to parade in salute of Royal Standard on king's birthday; but one boy refused and, when asked his reason, said proudly: "You forget, sir, I am a Spaniard; I own no king but Alfonso!" Of such hearts, risking disgrace for a name's sake, kingdoms, earthly or heavenly, are made.

III. The Last Claim (21:12-17)

1. *Its Assertion* (vs. 12, 13)

   a. Time had evidently come for definite, public claim about which there could be no mistake; and so, on reaching Jerusalem, our Lord entered Temple and authoritatively drove from it those who were misusing it (v. 12), basing what He did on Scripture (cf. Isa. 56:7, Jer. 7:11).

   b. This action of purification should be compared with that on His first official visit to Jerusalem, His offer of Himself to nation at opening of His ministry; but during interval conditions had gone from bad to worse, and "house of prayer" had become not only "an house of merchandise" (John 2:16), but "a den of thieves" (v. 13).

   c. Submission of these buyers and sellers, who by physical force might easily have overpowered one man alone, proves strength of moral influence with which Christ performed this act of cleansing; for even such profane men as these were evidently awed enough to yield without so much as a murmur.

2. *Its Acknowledgement* (vs. 14-17)

   a. As first result of our Lord's visit to Temple, blind and lame came there to Him; and, as so often before during His days on earth, "he healed them" (v. 14).

   b. In addition, even children were still calling out their hosannas in Temple (v. 15); and what Matthew calls "the wonderful things that he did," both in rebuke and in blessing, together with these echoing praises, sorely displeased authorities.

c. Their question (v. 16) doubtless implied Christ should silence children and thereby refuse this testimony to His Messianic character (cf. Luke 19:39, 40); but His response to their challenge referred them to well-known O.T. passage (Ps. 8:2) in tacit claim to its fulfillment.

d. This also was beautiful testimony to way in which God in heaven accepts praise even of infants; and, further, that He is glorified by those whom men regard as insignificant, typified by smallest and most helpless of beings, even "babes and sucklings."

e. It is no wonder that, after this willful blindness on part of chief priests and scribes, we are told "he left them, and went out of the city into Bethany" (v. 17); and there, no doubt, He "lodged" with his friends Lazarus, Mary, and Martha, for quiet night's rest and refreshment (cf. John 11:5, 12:1).

Conclusion

Let us think of what all this means to us today:

1. Christ comes to us as He came then to Jerusalem with a manifold revelation of Himself: as Light (20:34), as Seer (21:2), as Owner (v. 3), as King (v. 5), as God's Representative (v. 9), as Prophet (v. 11), as Reformed (vs. 12, 13), as Healer (v. 14), as Teacher (v. 16), as Friend (v. 17).

2. But most of all He comes to us as Lord; although in the Gospels and in Revelation He is shown to be potentially King, in the present dispensation, as taught in the Acts and the Epistles, He is preeminently the Lord and Head of His Church.

3. Christ claims our allegiance by the highest of all rights, and expects to be recognized, received, and honored; if, therefore, we can say with Thomas, "My Lord and my God," it will mean absolute surrender, trust, and obedience.

44

PARABLES OF JUDGMENT

Matthew 21:18—22:14

A s THE crisis of our Lord's ministry approached, the lessons taught by Him in parables were becoming increasingly solemn and, in particular, the subject of judgment was made prominent.

I. The Parabolic Act (21:18-22)

1. *The Symbol for the Nation* (vs. 18, 19)

   a. Christ's hunger, as He and His disciples returned next morning to Jerusalem, was at once literal, illustrating His real humanity, and also symbolic, expressive of His great desire to see fruit in men's lives (v. 18).

   b. Leaves on fig tree had attracted His attention because time for figs (July) was not yet (it was then April); and nature of eastern fig is such that as soon as leaves appear fruit should be there also.

   c. It was natural, then, for our Lord to look for leaves' proper accompaniment, figs; but He was disappointed (v. 19), for leaves hid real condition, barrenness.

   d. Since reality was so different from appearance, He bestowed on tree His malediction, pronouncing solemn judgment, which was immediately effected; for "the fig tree withered away."

   e. This symbolic action was teaching by act of great truth later taught in words (cf. vs. 28ff.); judgment of tree was not on barrenness as such, but on premature leaves without corresponding fruit.

   f. Thus Christ was condemning tree's deceptive appearance of fruitfulness as symbolic of hypocrisy of Jewish nation at that time; so that warning of fig tree is against unreality of national life, e.g., confession without conduct, outward show and no inward sincerity.

2. *The Lesson for the Twelve* (vs. 20-22)

   a. It was solemn warning also for Christ's disciples as individuals; they were doubtless surprised not only at speed of what had happened, but also at revelation of their Master's power (v. 20).

   b. Apparently they did not grasp full truth our Lord intended; but He immediately lifted incident into higher and more personal sphere, making it occasion for two great lessons on power of faith (v. 21), and prayer of faith (v. 22).

> *There is a place where Heaven's resistless power*
> *Responsive moves to thine insistent plea;*
> *There is a place — a silent, trusting hour —*
> *Where God Himself descends and fights for thee.*
> *Where is that blessed place? Dost thou ask where?*
> *O soul, it is the secret place of prayer!*
>
>   ADELAIDE A. POLLARD

II. The Challenged Authority (vs. 23-27)

1. *The Question* (v. 23)

   a. It was natural, in view of all that had happened (see vs. 1-16), that Christ's authority should be challenged at this very juncture.

   b. When He arrived once more at Temple, time was ripe for issue to be joined and for Him to be manifested as One with supreme right to be heard and followed.

2. *The Counter Question* (vs. 24, 25a)

   a. Manner in which our Lord met their challenge demonstrates unreality of foes' attitude; for He replied by asking them concerning His forerunner, John the Baptist, as to whether his baptism had been from heaven or of men, agreeing that if they could answer this question He would answer theirs about His own authority.

   b. Leaders at once saw what this question implied and dilemma on which it impaled them (vs. 25b, 26):

      (1) Being hypocrites, they would not say John's baptism had come from heaven because they knew this would involve them in inconsistency as religious leaders

and in condemnation for not having received his
message;

(2) Being cowards, they would not say John's baptism
had been of men for they were afraid of consequences
from people, by whom John had been received as
prophet.

3. *The Outcome* (v. 27)

a. With this blend of unreality and fear, leaders were compelled to admit they did not know origin of John's baptism;
and at once, with supreme dignity and calm, our Lord
definitely refused reply to their question about His
authority.

b. Thus unbelief is unmasked when confronted with Jesus
Christ; while, in professing inability to characterize John
the Baptist's ministry, Jewish leaders showed their complete unfitness to be religious teachers.

c. Too plainly to be evaded, John had uncovered two classes
among Jews of his day:

(1) Irreligious who were reproached but repented;

(2) Religious who were esteemed but did not repent; and
these, in addition, professed authority while resisting
light already offered and showing indifference to
spiritual claims.

d. By His question concerning John, Christ accomplished
three things:

(1) He compelled these men to show how much they
differed from the people as to John's work;

(2) He convicted them of guilt in rejecting Baptist's
expressed testimony to Jesus as Messiah; and —

(3) He caused them to pronounce their own sentence
upon themselves as wholly incompetent for their
office; so that it was evident that wickedness in
religious leadership could scarcely go further.

III. The Parabolic Teaching (21:28 to 22:14)

In discourse following exchange of words with chief priests and
elders, Christ goes on to unfold their full guilt, its forms, and
its punishment:

A. The First Parable — The Two Sons (21:28-32)

By His counterquestion (v. 25) our Lord had compelled His enemies to reveal their unbelief and ignorance, but now, in this first parable, He does more — He compels them to realize and even to declare their own guilt. His story of two sons shows situation exactly:

1. *The Father's Requirement* (v. 28)

   a. It was justified — addressed to his "son."

   b. It was definite — no mistaking its nature — "go work."

   c. It was urgent — there was to be no delay — "today."

   d. It was direct — in one specific place — "in my vineyard."

2. *The Sons' Response* (vs. 29, 30)

   a. *Immediate refusal* (vs. 29)

   (1) First son flatly declined, insolently telling his father "I will not"; yet "afterward he repented and went."

   N.B. "Atfterward" is word used often in Scripture, e.g., of riches (Gen. 15:14); of reception (Ps. 73:24); of rest (Prov. 24:27); of responsibility (John 13:36); of righteousness or rejection (Heb. 12:11, 17); of resurrection (1 Cor. 15:23, 46); and here it is used of repentance.

   (2) This picture is that of daringly ungodly ones who say No to Almighty God, and sometimes to earthly parents as well; but there is a place of repentance for them, with pardon and new life.

   N.B. "He repented and went" — this is not usual N.T. word for repentance, or "afterthought," act of thinking differently after consideration; it means, rather, "after-care" and seems to involve reaction of feelings, which, on human plane, involves regret or even remorse (cf. v. 32, 27:3, 2 Cor. 7:8). In Heb. 7:21 it is used in negative on Divine plane and implies absence of any change in attitude. Two together suggest different aspects of repentance, intended to issue in attitude expressed in Anglican Catechism by phrase, "repentance, whereby we forsake sin."

b. *Prompt Consent* (v. 30)

(1) Second son replies at once that he will go, showing not only compliance, but respect — "I go, sir," as much as to say, "My brother is a shameless fellow, but you have only to say one word to me, dear father."

(2) He represents easygoing, self-complacent people, who take their own virtue for granted; they make promises quickly, expressing warm feelings and good intentions.

(3) But, after all, his was hypocritical spirit, for "he went not"; and thus his guilt far surpasses that of insolent brother who afterwards repented and obeyed.

3. *The Searching Application* (vs. 31, 32)

a. By direct question, to which they had to give obvious answer, and by even more direct statements, Christ clearly showed Pharisees definite application of this parable.

b. Outcasts (v. 31) represented by first son had originally said No to God; but they had repented since coming of John the Baptist.

c. By contrast with them, Sanhedrin, as seen in second son and by their own doctrine and hypocrisy, had appeared to be pious and obedient; yet all the while they had been contemptuous toward others and were even now repudiating God's overtures in Jesus Christ.

d. This type of man is most hopeless of all, with his knowledge exceeding his action and his false profession of religion; while what God requires is not word, but work, not voice, but life.

B. The Second Parable — The Householder and the Vineyard (21:33-46)

This parable reviews briefly entire Jewish history in relation to God, points to utter unfaithfulness of leaders, and compels them to declare their own punishment.

1. *The Repudiated Servants* (vs. 33-36)

   a. Vineyard of householder (v. 33) represents Kingdom of God (cf. v. 43), privileges of which were, at this stage, exclusively Jewish; cf. Isa. 5:7, where earlier parable of vineyard is said to apply to "the house of Israel" and "the men of Judah."

   b. Hedge represents its distinguishing limits, winepress its distinctive function, and tower its Divine protection; cf. Isa. 5:2 for all of these in earlier parable.

   c. Laborers are official leaders, and servants are prophets, sent by owner who, representing God the Father, is looking for "the fruits" (v. 34) of vineyard; but all His servants received was beating, or killing, or stoning vs. 35, 36; cf. 23:37).

2. *The Rejected Son* (vs. 37-39)

   a. Owner's son in parable is, of course, Messiah; and sending of Him represents God's crowning effort to win His people and set up Kingdom at this time (v. 37).

   b. Attempt of laborers to gain inheritance for themselves by killing one whom they recognize as heir to it represents overweening ambition and ultimate wickedness of these Jewish leaders (vs. 38, 39).

   c. This parable not only predicts future punishment of Messiah's enemies, but it also definitely specifies nature of their sin in murder of Son of God, Messiah Himself.

   d. Quite apart from Christ's own application of parable, which has yet to be considered (cf. vs. 42-44), we can see how true story is to our own time; God, having done for Jews all, and more than all, that could have been expected (cf. Isa. 5:4), His grace and goodness are now being exercised to bring us Gentiles to repentance (cf. Rom. 2:4).

3. *The Deserved Penalty* (vs. 40-44)

   a. In reply to our Lord's direct question (v. 40), His hearers expressed their very frank opinion as to what lord of vineyard would do (v. 41); and then Christ brought to their remembrance very psalm of triumph from which children and their elders had so recently taken their Hosannas (v. 42; cf. Ps. 118:22, 23).

b. Action of lord of vineyard thus symbolized God's judgment on Jewish nation that would culminate with destruction of Jerusalem in A.D. 70; and it was also striking prophecy of conduct of Sanhedrin against Messiah.

c. Because they had rejected Cornerstone of national edifice there would be positive punishment for them, and Greek word translated "rejected" is in reality much stronger, viz., utterly repudiated as unfit after trial; so that it is difficult to imagine such effrontery.

d. Same passage was afterwards used by Peter and definitely applied to Christ (cf. Acts 4:11, 1 Pet. 2:4, 6, 7), as does Paul (cf. Eph. 2:20); and Peter goes on to say what Paul writes in two of his Epistles, that Christ was also to be a "stone of stumbling" (1 Pet. 2:8; Rom. 9:32, 33; 1 Cor. 1:23).

e. Now Christ declares rejection of Him constitutes both removal of "the Kingdom of God" from Jews and its transfer to Gentiles (v. 43; see Rom. 10).

   N.B. Meaning of term "Kingdom of God" is one of most difficult of N.T. problems because it has so many aspects. Plummer speaks of it as "the rule of God whether in the human heart or in society," and adds, "It exists now, but it has its realization in eternity." He goes on to observe that Christ Himself never gave any definition of it, so that perhaps it would be wise for us to follow His example. It should be noted that Kingdom comes before us in Gospels, Acts, and Revelation, while it is Church that is seen in between, in Epistles; and this suggests main idea of Kingdom is still future and has no reference to any organization, ecclesiastical or national, in present age.

f. It has, indeed, been questioned as to what "nation" is referred to in verse 43; but it does not seem possible to press word literally, as is evident from Peter's words to Hebrew Christians: "Ye are . . . an holy nation" (1 Pet. 2:9); certainly history does not record anything like literal fulfillment of our Lord's words.

g. Continuing metaphor from O.T. quoted in verse 42, Christ then declared (v. 44) that this Stone would fall on those who had first fallen on it; that is, those who would reject Him would be rejected by Him.

h. This expression seems to have been chosen with reference to stone mentioned in Daniel's prophecy (cf. Dan. 2:34, 35); it is very graphic way of foretelling punishment that would fall on Jews for their opposition to Christ — they would be not only "broken," but ground "to powder" (cf. Gen. 13:16).

4. *The Delayed Perception* (vs. 45, 46)

   a. These Jewish leaders at last recognized that our Lord was referring to them; and, in their rage and exasperation, they attempted to lay hands on Him at once (vs. 45, 46a).

   b. But, though they had already decided to kill Him, dread of people prevented them from carrying out their resolve immediately; for, as in case of His forerunner, "the multitude . . . took him for a prophet" (vs. 46b; cf. v. 26).

   c. Thus it was proven that this parable constituted justifiable indictment of nation represented by these men; high privilege had been sacrificed to self-seeking, and they were even then contemplating murder of their Messiah and King.

   d. Sinful heart of man could scarcely go further, and sin always involves judgment; this is one of most solemn facts emphasized in Scripture.

   e. It is also an eternal and inexorable law of Kingdom of God and, indeed of whole universe: "Be sure your sin will find you out" (Num. 32:23).

C. The Third Parable — The Marriage Feast (22:1-14)

This parable, telling of God's gracious offer to man, marks the end of our Lord's conflict in the Temple with the Jewish leaders, and it indicates not only the mercy of God, but also their responsibility in rejecting it. The parable is peculiar to this Gospel and quite distinct from the one recorded in Luke 14:16-24 which was spoken in Perea some three months before this one in Jerusalem. While there are resemblances, there are also important differences of detail, and the general tenor is not at all similar. In Luke the goodness and grace of the Lord are uppermost; while here

His severity and judgment are emphasized; and thus the lessons taught are not the same. In comparison with the two preceding parables, which referred to the history of the Jewish nation up to the slaying of the Son of God (vs. 38, 39), the one now to be considered was prophetic of the continuing sin of the people in the light of that transcendent offer of Divine grace that would be made as the result of Christ's death.

1. *The King's Invitation* (vs. 1-6)

   a. Those who had heard Jesus in Temple were now addressed (v. 1); and this parable illustrates method adopted by Him to lead people to think out its meaning for themselves.

   b. Kingdom of Heaven is here compared to king who made marriage feast for his son (v. 2), thereby indicating Divine purpose for world; indeed, Jews were accustomed to thinking of future kingdom under figure of feast, doubtless suggested by Paschal meal (cf. Exod. 12:8, 24:11, Isa. 25:6).

   c. This feast is also symbol of blessedness and fellowship in life of faith here and now, which will find its culmination hereafter (cf. Rev. 19:7-8); and figure of marriage state is another illustration of union and communion in things spiritual (cf. Eph. 5:25).

   d. King sent his messengers to call those who were invited; and this first call (v. 3) illustrates O.T. history as prophet after prophet was sent to Jewish nation by God, only to be disregarded and even opposed.

   e. When Jews refused to listen, second and stronger appeal was made (v. 4); and this may be taken as expressive of commissioning of Apostles (cf. Acts 1:8).

   f. But of this appeal guests made light, each being concerned with material things, such as farm and merchandise (v. 5); and here is shown solemn truth that it is possible to refuse God's invitation by insulting indifference, such as Jewish nation later showed in rejection of Apostle Paul's teaching (cf. Acts 28:25-27).

   g. Only interest any of these men would show was in doing harm to king's messengers and even in killing them (v. 6); and if it appears strange that invited guests would ill-treat and slay those sent to benefit and serve them, it is because this senseless conduct is intended to point to awful folly of those who then acted, and of those who are now acting, in same way with regard to God's messengers.

h. We think of infinite majesty of One who stoops to invite, of His loving eagerness, patience, and condescension in repeating invitation; and, above all, we marvel at provision made and great occasion for feast of love, for it is surely amazing in eyes of angels above that anyone on earth could refuse such grace and favor.

N.B. Thought of feast suggests fact that, while practically every faculty of human body is used in Scripture to illustrate and symbolize spiritual attitudes and blessings (e.g., eye, cf. Isa. 45:22; hand, cf. Isa. 27:5; ear, cf. Isa. 55:3; foot, cf. Gen. 17:1, and many others), perhaps most interesting and impressive of all is mouth (cf. Ps. 34:8). Thought of eating is frequently found in Scripture and is full of meaning:

(1) Food is necessary. Just as body requires food for life and health, so man is to live not by bread only, but by Word of God (cf. Luke 4:4).

(2) Food should be regular. As body must have its food at proper intervals, so soul, if it is to be healthy, strong, and vigorous, should have its regular and constant supplies of spiritual nourishment.

(3) Food is pleasant. When people are in bodily health their food always gives them satisfaction; and it is mark of true spiritual health that grace of God has revealed in His Word His joy to be bestowed on our life (cf. Ps. 119:103, Heb. 6:5, 1 Pet. 2:3).

2. *The King's Judgment* (v. 7)

a. Then king in justifiable anger sent his armies (no longer his servants); and solemn outcome of both indifference and animosity was destruction of "murderers" and burning of "their city."

b. It is most impressive to realize that within forty years of rejection and crucifixion of Christ this prophecy was literally fulfilled in destruction of Jerusalem by Titus in A.D. 70.

3. *The King's Decision* (vs. 8-10)

a. Notwithstanding refusal of those originally invited, king declared wedding feast was still to be held (v. 8); and so servants were commanded to go to places where people naturally gather and invite as many as possible of those who had hitherto been uninvited (v. 9).

b. This was done, with result that wedding of King's son was finally "furnished with guests" (v. 10); and this, of course, is significantly symbolic of what actually followed when Christianity was accepted by Gentiles (cf. Acts 11:18, 13:45-49, 28:28).

c. It is at this point, indeed, that this parable goes beyond that of Luke 14:16-24, quite apart from other differences; for commission here is to go immediately beyond doomed city, into highroads of world, and all, both bad and good, are invited.

4. *The King's Warning* (vs. 11-14)

a. With filling of wedding chamber, feast was consummated; and picture of host coming in to see guests (v. 11) is searching symbol of that spiritual inspection and inquiry that God is bound to make of every man.

b. Guest without wedding garment was quite evidently considered blameworthy in that he might and should have procured one, whether through host's provision or in some other way; and it is said that guests of eastern kings were indeed presented by hosts with long, white festal robes.

c. At any rate, custom would seem to be assumed in this parable (v. 12a); and it certainly agrees with truth of Divine grace and of God's gift of "robe of righteousness" (Isa. 61:10; cf. Rev. 7:14, 19:8).

d. As people gathered at this particular feast could scarcely have afforded such garments themselves, it is more than probable they were provided; and for this reason man in question, being obviously guilty of disrespect and ingratitude, clearly recognized he was without excuse for his unreadiness (v. 12b).

e. It was on this account he was punished; he was bound hand and foot to keep him from returning to feast, and then cast outside, beyond its light, warmth, and joy (v. 13).

f. Our Lord's comment on parable (v. 14) states that, while there are many invited to become Christians, comparatively few really accept Divine invitation (cf. 20:16); and He distinguishes between those within sound of gospel and those who, having accepted it, are proved by wearing of "wedding garment" of Christ's righteousness to be God's choice.

g. Thus we have here two great aspects of truth, Divine and human, sometimes called predestination and free will; and these are always found in Christian experience.

h. We have already seen sin and shame of refusing by insulting indifference, but here we have refusal by insolent acceptance; for we may profess to accept, or imagine we have accepted, God's salvation without any real reception of Christ Himself, and no one can truly have received Him without definite change of heart and of conduct.

Conclusion

1. *The King Teaching*

   a. Lesson of fig tree is against inconsistency, unreality, profession without practice; it rebukes confession without conduct and outward show without inward sincercerity, affecting of saintliness without actuality of sainthood.

   b. Fruitlessness is also loss, because it means inability to help others; since fruit is intended for blessing and usefulness, fruitless Christian is not only not helpful, but positive hindrance.

2. *The King Challenged*

   a. Christ is our supreme authority; and those willing to acknowledge Him and obey His Word will find only firm basis for life.

   b. Sinful men unwilling to acknowledge His claim reveal themselves as wholly unworthy; but convicted sinner is quick to recognize Christ as Saviour to be accepted, and genuine seeker will go on to find Him as Truth to be followed and obeyed.

3. *The King Answering*

a. There are elements of evil in both types of response to God's call as indicated in this first parable of judgment: initial refusal with belated repentance; and impulsive consent with hypocrisy or inconsistency.

b. There is something better: instant response with permanent consecration and sincere determination to continue; therefore, let us realize God's claim, respond to His call, and render Him service all the days of our lives.

4. *The King Warning*

a. This second parable of judgment is awful unveiling of fallen heart of man, because it reveals terrible possibilities for evil even in those given leadership; and some set in charge of God's heritage today are keener for their privileges than for their responsibilities.

b. When God sends His servants to reprove them, they count such as their enemies; but, since the Lord Jesus Christ is God's last appeal to man, sooner or later these unworthy ones will be brought face to face with Him as Judge.

5. *The King Offering*

a. Divine purpose is seen in this third parable of judgment to be fellowship between God and man; and Divine preparation of redemption took infinite pains from all eternity.

b. Human response shows people making light of God's desire and disregarding His invitation; but this is followed by Divine persistence in offering His blessings to others, and by Divine provision of Christ's righteousness as the wedding garment, that they may be clothted forever in "fine linen clean and white . . . the righteousness of saints" (Rev. 19:8; cf. 1 Cor. 1:30).

> *The Master came to the fig tree,*
> *And saw the foliage there,*
> *The thick and shady branches*
> *To hungry eyes so fair;*

But He found that it was barren
  And bore no luscious fruit,
Then life was gone, and even
  'Twas withered from its root.

The Master came to the Temple,
  And saw the worship there,
The ritual and the customs
  To Jewish eyes so fair;
But to Him 'twas all corruption,
  His House a den of thieves,
And all its boasted glory
  Was fruitless — only leaves.

The Master comes to the churches,
  And sees our service here,
The busy, nightly meetings
  To worldly hearts so dear;
And still He probes the motive,
  And still His Spirit grieves
To find our modern methods
  So fruitless — mostly leaves.

Lord Jesus, quicken our vision
  That we may see our state;
Show us if we are guilty
  Of doing what Thou dost hate;
Help us to bring true worship
  And give Thy Word its place,
And henceforth live to witness
  To Thine unbounded grace!

H. K. BENTLEY

45

THE DEEPENING CONFLICT

Matthew 22:15—23:12

C HRIST'S PARABLES of judgment had fallen on deaf ears, for the Jewish leaders were absolutely determined to find some occasion for apprehending Him. In this passage, therefore, we see the various methods adopted to "ensnare him in his talk" (v. 15), all in the form of questions. Questions propounded for purposes of education or enlightenment are good and useful, but those asked for such a wrong purpose as this are dangerous. But at the same time it is important and impressive to note the remarkable intellectual power and swift perception with which Christ first met these specious attacks, then seized His opportunity to ask a telling question of His own, and finally pointed out the chief faults of His foes and warned His disciples against them.

I. Controversy (22:15-40)

Perhaps, indeed, we do not sufficiently consider our Lord's fine powers of mind. Many persons when faced with difficult questions have time in which to ponder their answers; but He invariably replied at once, without hesitation, and with telling effect. It will be useful to link together the three main problems which Christ had to face on this occasion:

1. *A Political Problem* (vs. 15-22)

   a. *The Snare Laid by Human Wickedness* (vs. 15-17)

      (1) Pharisees wanted politically-minded Messiah, which Jesus would not become; and yet now they endeavored to make Him appear one in order to hand Him over to Romans (v. 15).

      (2) How bitter their hostility was is shown by their willingness to unite with Herodians (v. 16) who, accepting Roman authority, were abject creatures of emperors; but so utterly blinded by prejudice were they that they were prepared to say and do anything

to harm and involve our Lord (cf. earlier instance, Mark 3:6).

(3) Those who were sent were spies (cf. Luke 20:20), as with words of hypocritical respect they acknowledged Him to be sincere teacher of God's way of truth and impartial in His judgments; and even though they intended this as flattery it was striking testimony to His orthodoxy, fearlessness, and justice.

(4) Then came dangerous question (v. 17), whether or not it was lawful to pay taxes levied by Rome, thus involving whole problem of Jews' attitude to this foreign power, since according to true Jewish principles Jehovah was their only King; and so inquiry was meant to imply possibility that, as true servants of theocracy, Jews ought to refuse tribute and, resisting Roman dominion, rise up in rebellion.

(5) Pharisees themselves hated Gentile domination, yet were compelled to endure it; but they did not hesitate to use critical situation to their own advantage in trying to ensnare Jesus Christ by raising seemingly natural and merely disputatious issue.

(6) They were doubtless waiting to take opposite view whatever He said: if He answered them Yes, He would lose His popularity with people; if He should say No, leaders would be able to report Him to Pontius Pilate as seditious.

b. *The Snare Escaped by Divine Wisdom* (vs. 18-22)

(1) With truly unique spiritual perception, Jesus was enabled to meet this attack, and showed what He thought of His opponents by calling them "hypocrites" (v. 18); so that their purpose was soon seen and shown to be treacherous and wicked.

(2) When He asked to see tribute money, and coin was brought to Him (v. 19), it was simple but significant thing to inquire as to its "image and superscription" (v. 20); and mere fact that coin was current was quiet but ample testimony to Roman power.

(3) Furthermore, as Jewish leaders carried and acknowledged such currency (v. 21a) they were com-

pelled to admit thereby that they were subjects of very Tiberius Caesar whose image appeared on it, since everyone has tacitly subjected himself to state obligations who uses that state's currency; and, as Christ pointed out that, since coin was already Caesar's, its use included taxation and all other obligations to state, His answer was both impressive and convincing (v. 21b).

N.B. Plummer in commenting on this passage says: "The coin (denarius) represented Roman organization, security of person and property, facilities of transit, and other beneficent elements of stable government. Was it just to accept all these advantages and then refuse to pay for their maintenance? To pay tribute to Caesar was not merely lawful — it was a moral obligation, as the change from 'give' in their question to 'pay' in Christ's answer indicates. The tribute to Rome was not a gift; it was the payment of a debt; and it was no impediment to the discharge of any obligation to God."

(4) It is probable, moreover, that our Lord's words about rendering "unto God the things that are God's" was addition deliberately intended to show all that there was duty higher than that to state; and, while this duty is not here defined, one may rightly infer that man is to give to God that which bears Divine image and inscription (cf. Gen. 1:26, Rev. 3:12) — himself, even though likeness has been blurred by sin.

(5) Thus does Christ establish rights, and regulate duties, while distinguishing authority, of spiritual and temporal elements in life; and, further, He sets forth fundamental principles for guidance of all in both state and Church.

(6) If this rule of rendering rightful obedience were always adhered to, there would be no difficulty, still less conflict, between two powers that are Divine in origin; for one represents temporal, and other, eternal, welfare of man.

(7) It is no wonder, then, that when Pharisees and Herodians had heard Christ's reply to their question

they "marvelled, and left him, and went their way" (v. 22).

2. *A Doctrinal Problem* (vs. 23-33)

   a. *The Question of the Sadducees* (vs. 23-28)

      (1) It might have been expected that experience of Pharisees would suffice to keep other groups quiet, but hostility to Jesus was too intense for that; and so Sadducees came to Him with question of their own (v. 23).

      (2) They were the "rationalistic party" among Jews of that day, many of them being also wealthy and belonging to priestly families; they accepted only Pentateuch and denied doctrine of resurrection.

      (3) Realizing their opponents had been overcome, they hoped by making Christ appear nothing but one of themselves, a Sadducee, they would effectively destroy His influence with people.

      (4) They also wanted to show out of Law itself that doctrine of resurrection was absurd and therefore untenable; and question propounded was entirely in line with their methods of thinking.

      (5) They remind our Lord of well-known enactment of Mosaic code known as Levirate Law, based on family honor and preservation of property (cf. Deut. 25:5-10); and they invent improbable instance of no fewer than seven brothers who married in turn one woman, according to this requirement (vs. 24-27).

      (6) Then Sadducees put their hypothetical problem: "In the resurrection whose wife shall she be of the seven?" (v. 28); and, in spite of its absurd exaggeration, it was, for their purpose of ridicule at least, an acute question, and one that few would have been able to face.

   b. *The Answer of the Master* (vs. 29-33)

      (1) Yet at once Jesus declared Sadducees mistaken, and on two grounds: they were ignorant of Scripture, and they did not understand God's power (v. 29).

      (2) These two points He takes up in reverse order:
         (a) As to power of God (v. 30), there is no marriage

in resurrection, for all will have been transformed and made "as the angels in heaven";

(b) As to Word of God (vs. 31, 32), opponents are shown to have missed meaning of well-known passage from that very Pentateuch they themselves professed to believe, in which God revealed Himself to Moses as God of living and not of dead (cf. Exod. 3:6).

(3) Thus Christ was not content merely to reply to their immediate question, but showed that all along covenant people were in such close and permanent relationship to God that resurrection of their bodies followed as naturally as possible; yet His words indicate not only fact of future life, but also its obscurity in O.T. times.

(4) Since text did not say, "I *was* the God of Abraham, etc." as though relationship to patriarchs were something no longer in existence, but "I *am*—," implying that, since God continues to be their God, patriarchs must of necessity be continuing to live to Him; and Christ's interpretation of passage throws flood of light over Scripture, suggesting something of its wonderful hidden meaning.

(5) For thousands of years this precious jewel of truth had been obscured; but now, as Christ unveiled it, familiar words are seen to be glorious revelation of present condition of blessed dead.

(6) Our dear ones who used to be with us are now with Him and alive as never before; and the closer we draw to Him the nearer we shall be to them, since God is their God too and "all live unto him" (Luke 20:38).

(7) Thus, flippant question intended to ridicule very idea of life beyond grave is more than met by statements of our Lord; and we sense also that conditions of spiritual world cannot possibly be measured by those of this present life.

(8) As with Sadducees, so with many others, errors often flow from twin sources of ignorance of God's Word and incomprehension of His omnipotence; for if only we become better versed in Scripture and gain

a real experience of God's saving power in Christ, we shall not yield to unbelief, but rather await God's time and accept His way.

N.B. In verse 21 we find another instance of uniform view of O.T. in N.T. — i.e., that it is characterized both by authority and by inspiration.

(9) We are not surprised to read, therefore, that when multitudes heard Christ's twofold answer "they were astonished at his teaching" (v. 33); and they might well have been so, since it revealed superlative quality of intellect in our Lord for which His opponents had not hitherto given Him credit.

3. *A Moral Problem* (vs. 34-40)

a. *A Question About the Law* (vs. 34-36)

(1) After unbelief, worldliness, and rationalism had been defeated in debate, formalism came forward with its preoccupation with law; and it has been pointed out that these four are still chief enemies of Christianity, and usually in this order.

(2) Pharisees, probably gratified by way Jesus had silenced their inveterate foes, the Sadducees (v. 34), determined to try again in spite of their former defeat; but, instead of deputation (cf. v. 16), they evidently planned for individual question, with definite purpose of testing or tripping our Lord (v. 35), to be propounded by teacher of law (not lawyer in modern sense of pleader in court).

(3) Such men, or scribes, were in habit of making fine distinctions between one Mosaic requirement and another; so this man asked slyly, "Master, which is the great commandment in the law?" (v. 36).

(4) There was same lack of sincerity as before, and Pharisees probably took it for granted that Christ's answer would be something like "Thou shalt love God above all," thereby emphasizing importance of what we call monotheism; yet their idea of this subject was far removed from practical, everyday life.

(5) Not only so, but Christ had declared Himself to be Son of God; and Pharisees wanted above all else to get hold of something that might again show Him

guilty of blasphemy in making Himself equal with God (cf. John 10:33).

b. *An Answer About Love* (vs. 37-40)

(1) Our Lord's reply was soon given: "Thou shalt love the Lord thy God. . . . This is the first and great commandment" (vs. 37, 38); but when He went on to add a second which was "like unto it, Thou shalt love thy neighbor as thyself," Pharisees must have felt His addition of love to man had gone contrary to their plan, because His answer skillfully covered whole Decalogue, leaving no room for any real distinction between commandments.

(2) Later, when Sanhedrin placed Jesus before Pilate, they charged Him with making Himself Son of God, as well as King of Jews in political sense (cf. Luke 22:66 to 23:2); and former of these two considerations is seen in this inquiry about supreme commandment in Law.

(3) By "the great commandment," Pharisees meant greatest, and in Christ's quotation from Deut. 6:5 they recognized not only that God must necessarily come first as in Decalogue (cf. Exod. 20:1-11), but that everything turned on attitude of love.

(4) When He added second commandment as like unto first, He showed them He had penetrated their wicked design by acknowledging distinction between "great commandment" and remainder, and yet at same time was stating that second derived its authority from first.

(5) Then Christ applied truth by saying that on these two commandments everything in law and prophets depended (v. 40); and so from question of conduct He led this learned man to think of character, from precept to principle.

(6) Since man's love for his neighbor is greatest possible proof of his love for God, it was demonstrated by our Lord that if entire being with all its powers is full of love towards God and man, essential commandment will have been obeyed.

(7) St. Paul tells us "love is the fulfilling of the law"

(Rom. 13:10); and "these two commandments," perfectly expressing ideal attitude of man to God and to his fellows, are in reality inseparable.

II. Challenge (22:41-46)

1. *A Threefold Question* (vs. 41-45)

   a. It was then Christ's turn to interrogate; and solemn problem He poses for His enemies is universally vital one, because answers to it must always reveal human attitudes towards Him.*

   b. As at Caesarea Philippi disciples had been asked, "Who say ye that I am?" (16:15), so here our Lord desired to raise similar inquiry in minds of Pharisees as they were still "gathered together" (v. 41) to plot against Him; and this form of question, "What think ye of Christ? whose son is he?" (v. 42) would both confound these obstinate foes who had, at very least, to reply, from their knowledge of Scripture, "The son of David," and at same time instruct disciples further.

   c. Then Christ had another question for them: "How then doth David in the Spirit call him Lord —?" (v. 43, A.S.V.).

   N.B. Commenting on this verse, Plummer says finely: "Christ's argument is seriously misapprehended when it is supposed that He criticized the assertion that the Messiah is the Son of David as *untrue*. He criticized it as *inadequate*."

   d. Our Lord's reference to Ps. 110 (vs. 44, 45) was intended to prove that Messiah was not only Son of David, as Pharisees had agreed, but also Lord of David, i.e., both Son of man and Son of God; and subject it raises is one of perennial importance.

   e. Many modern writers have denied both Davidic authorship of this Psalm and its reference to Messiah as Priest-King upon Jehovah's throne (cf. Ps. 110:1, 2, 4, 5); and yet Christ quotes from it as veritable utterance of David

---

*Ed. Note: For the expansion of a series of seven addresses on the theme "What Think Ye of Christ?" often given by the writer, see his volume entitled *Christianity Is Christ*, Kent Publishing Inc., New Canaan, Conn.

speaking by Holy Spirit (cf. v. 43, A.S.V.), and as though Himself alone were its subject.

f. Then comes third and crucial question respecting this One: "If David then call him Lord, how is he his son?" (v. 45); and thus Christ turned tables on His interlocutors and clinched argument, for it was —

2. *An Unanswerable Question* (v. 46)

a. It is against natural procedure for human father to concede lordship over himself to his equally human son, so no wonder everyone present was rendered speechless, both on that day and "from that day forth"; and thus there was an abrupt end to questioning.

b. We may note in conclusion that it was left to one standing by, Simon Peter, to give true answer to this question when, in his Pentecost sermon (cf. Acts 2:29-36), he quoted from same Psalm; and later St. Paul was to write of "his Son Jesus Christ our Lord, which was made of the seed of David according to the flesh; and declared to be the Son of God with power, according to the Spirit of holiness, by the resurrection from the dead" (Rom. 1:3, 4).

> *"What think ye of Christ?" is the test*
> *To try both your state and your scheme;*
> *You cannot be right in the rest*
> *Unless you think rightly of Him.*
> *As Jesus appears in your view,*
> *As He is beloved or not,*
> *So God is disposed unto you*
> *And mercy or wrath is your lot.*
>
> *Some take Him a creature to be,*
> *A man or an angel at most;*
> *Surely these have not feelings like me,*
> *Nor know themselves wretched and lost!*
> *So guilty, so helpless am I*
> *I dare not confide in His blood*
> *Nor on His protection rely*
> *Unless I am sure He is God.*

Some call Him a Saviour in word
But mix their own works with His plan;
And hope He His aid will afford
When they have done all that they can.
If such doings prove rather too light
(A little, they own, they may fail),
They purpose to make up full weight
By casting His Name in the scale.

Some style Him "the Pearl of Great Price"
And say He's the fountain of joys;
Yet feed upon folly and vice,
And cleave to the world and its toys.
Like Judas, the Saviour they kiss
And, while they salute Him, betray;
Ah! what will profession like this
Avail in His terrible day?

If asked what of Jesus I think.
Though still my best thoughts are but poor,
I say, He's my meat and my drink,
My life, and my strength, and my store;
My Shepherd, my Husband, my Friend,
My Saviour from sin and from thrall;
My hope from beginning to end,
My portion, my Lord, and my all!

JOHN NEWTON

III. Conduct (23:1-12)

After the controversy stirred up by the Pharisees between themselves and Jesus Christ, and His answering challenge that so effectively silenced them, it was natural for Him to turn "to the multitude, and to His disciples" (v. 1) and, first, make some trenchant observations concerning His enemies and, second, draw from them a needed lesson in humility:

1. *False Pretensions* (vs. 1-7)

   a. In this section of passage Christ again denounced formallism as that which was in some respects more deadly than worldliness or rationalism; but Pharisees were admittedly in position of traditional authority and, so far as what they commanded was true to Scripture (v. 2), they were to be obeyed (v. 3a).

b. It was only their works that were not to be followed because, said Jesus, "they say and do not" (v. 3b); and not only so but they, by their insistence on traditions, placed intolerable burdens on consciences of men (v. 4).

c. This heavy weight did not belong to law itself, but was caused only by rigor of Pharisees' reverence of its letter and their neglect of its spirit; and exposure of their conduct is most impressive for, unless teacher or preacher practices what he preaches, there will be no power or blessing in or through his life.

d. This cannot mean perfect behavior, since he is but human, but it does mean earnest, sincere effort, with sorrow over every failure and inconsistency; for, especially when there is willful discrepancy between preaching and practice, former goes for nothing.

e. Another sin of Pharisees was their overweening desire to stand well with their fellow men (v. 5); they had applied literally some figurative expressions found among Divine directions in Exod. 13:9, 16, and repeated in Deut. 6:8.

f. Their very clothes were so made as to set them apart as pious leaders; and Christ implies their motive for all this, "to be seen of men" (v. 5), is essentially ungodly.

g. But strongest of all was their partiality for most important places, for public notice, and for honorable titles (vs. 6, 7); this was root of all their pride, for had they shown "love" (v. 6) for other people instead, they would have preferred them to themselves and avoided these serious pitfalls.

Now comes a warning application to our Lord's disciples of what He had just said about the Pharisees; and so emphasis is placed throughout the remainder of the passage on the pronouns "ye" and "yours":

2. *True Relations* (vs. 8-12)

a. Disciples were first to think of themselves as pupils in school of Christ their "Master" — in sense of Teacher (v. 8, Greek); and then, instead of seeking to be regarded as directors of spiritual things, they were to remember they were but followers of Christ their "Master" — in sense of "Leader" (v. 10, Greek).

N.B. This Greek word occurs only here, and means guide, one who goes in front.*

b. Also, they were to remember absolute authority of God as their Father in heaven (v. 9), and were not to usurp such authority over others.

c. Christ did not mean, of course, to prohibit titles in secular sphere because, as we know, this is impossible and impracticable; it is also opposed to instinctive standards of ordinary courtesy.

d. It is in relation to spiritual things that abject submission to any human authority signified by use of certain titles is forbidden; and, on positive side, our Lord's words were actually concerned most with man's fundamental relation to God.

N.B. H. G. Weston has pointed out three elements that make up a Christian: what he is, what he believes, and what he does; or, life, instruction, and practice. Thus we need, as in St. John's reverse order, "the way, the truth, and the life" (John 14:6), and these three only God can give, in Christ. Therefore, we are to call no man spiritual Father, or giver of life; no man infallible Teacher of truth; and no man spiritual Director for way.

e. Indeed, it has been well said that to interpret such commands slavishly according to letter of law is to fall into very Pharisaic evil against which our Lord here cautioned His disciples.

f. Spiritual ambition and pride (vs. 11, 12a) thus call for constant watchfulness; and it is only in power of genuine Christian life of faith that all such pretensions can be overcome (v. 12b) — faith in Christ as our Teacher and Guide, and faith in God as our heavenly Father; and it has been well expressed thus: "Out of the humility of fidelity springs the courage of freedom."

Conclusion

This entire section reveals our Lord in a new light:

---

*See following Study, No. 46, under I, 2, p. 333.

1. *Christ Debating*

   a. His foes' questions were prepared, studied, and arranged beforehand, and yet His answers were necessarily spontaneous; how remarkable, therefore, are His acuteness, intellectual force, and completeness of knowledge, and how striking His acquaintance with Scripture!

   b. Whether inquiry comes from criticism, or curiosity, or controversy, His reply is immediate, full, pointed, and amazing; not only so, but each questioner received far more than he expected, and thus evil is confounded and earnestness recommended.

2. *Christ Defending*

   a. In series of questions with which our Lord challenged His opponents, perhaps He wished to prepare His disciples for what was to come just two or three days later; foreseeing that at His trial He would be allowed no real opportunity of defense against accusation about His claim to be Son of God, He stated His position now and, as usual, based it on Scripture.

   b. Certainly, when He came before high priest, He referred to Son of man "sitting on the right hand of power" (26:64); and this looks very much like adoption of Jehovah's words in Ps. 110:1.

   c. Truth at length triumphs even though its defenders have much to undergo; in fact, it is often found that the more triumphant truth is, the more its supporters may be called upon to endure for its sake.

3. *Christ Disapproving and Directing*

   a. Sins of hypocrisy, boastfulness, and self-seeking on part of Pharisees called forth not only rebuke, but exposure from our Lord; and it is part of wisdom for men to study their hideousness and subtlety.

   b. Then, as Christ warned His disciples, there must be true humility based on godly fear and on submission to Himself as Master.

Our Lord is still ready to answer our questions, to prove Himself the unique Defender of truth, and to preserve us from what

David called "presumptuous sins" (Ps. 19:13). If, like the Queen of Sheba to Solomon, we come in sincerity, pouring out our hearts before Him, He will give us all our desires (1 Kings 10:13) and satisfy our every longing.

46

ROYAL AND LOYAL—A WORD STUDY

Matthew 23:8, 10

T HE CROWN and culmination of the Divine purpose and plan of redemption is "that God may be all in all " (1 Cor. 15: 28), and this will be reached in one way only — "that in all things he [Christ] might have the preeminence" (Col. 1:18). In view of this, our Lord's relation to us as supreme, and ours to Him as subject, become of immediate and intense practical importance. Consequently, the New Testament makes very prominent the thought of Christ as Master, Lord, King, and of ourselves as His servants, slaves, subjects. He is royal and we must be loyal. There are eight Greek words associated with His royalty, and eight more, expressive of our loyalty:

I. The Royalty of Christ

1. *As Possessor*
   a. This is the most common of all His titles, occurring hundreds of times, and usually translated "Lord" or "Master" (cf. Rom. 14:9, Eph. 6:9).
   b. It implies ownership and, therefore, perfect control.

2. *As Leader*
   a. This word occurs once only, in present passage, viz., Matthew 23:10; it means guide, leader, one who goes in front.
   b. It suggests capability, and calls for perfect acceptance of our Leader's wisdom.

3. *As Prince*
   a. This word appears in two forms: one of them four (Acts 3:15, 5:31, Heb. 2:10, 12:2), but other one (Rev. 1:5).

b. It implies primacy of position and power (cf. "prince" and "principal"); to Christ we must "give place."

4. *As Superintendent*

a. This term is found only in St. Luke's Gospel, but six times (5:5, 8:24, 8:45, 9:33, 9:49, 17:13).

b. It indicates overseership, one "standing over" us, exerting close inspection, attention, and authority; it calls for our own watchfulness, in instant obedience and complete sincerity.

5. *As Master*

a. This word is used by Simeon (Luke 2:29), by early Church (Acts 4:24), of attitude of apostates (2 Pet. 2:1, Jude 4), and by saints (Rev. 6:10).

b. It implies absolute possession and uncontrolled power — unrestricted domination in addition to simple ownership (cf. English words "despot" and "lord"); it calls for unquestioning submission (cf. 2 Tim. 2:21, Tit. 2:9).

6. *As King*

a. Note usages of this word in relation to Christ (John 1:49, 19:19, Acts 17:7, 1 Tim. 1:17).

b. It indicates reign, rule, glory (cf. Jas. 2:8, 1 Pet. 2:9), and our corresponding position and duties as subject.

7. *As Potentate*

a. This term is found only in 1 Tim 6:15, used of our glorified Lord.

b. It involves ability as well as authority, power as well as position; and it suggests to us both warning and comfort.

8. *As Teacher*

a. This word is frequently translated "Master" in Gospels (as in present passage, Matt. 23:8); and it implies schoolmaster, since Christ can teach only in so far as He is Master.

b. Note association and order of words "Teacher" and "Lord" in John 13:13, from disciples' standpoint, in order of their experience; in next verse, however, Christ changes order to correspond to His own standpoint, "Lord" and "Teacher" — i.e., Teacher because Lord.

II. The Loyalty of Christians

1. *As Bond Servants*

   a. This word with its cognates appears very frequently, notably as one of St. Paul's favorite designations of himself (Rom. 1:1, Gal. 1:10, Phil. 1:1, Tit. 1:1); he was "in slavery" to Jesus Christ, hence neither free nor independent.

   b. It implies living chattel, one who is our Lord's in everything; and it suggests devotedness and thoroughness of our service.

2. *As Ministering Servants*

   a. This term with its cognates denotes true "deacon" or "minister" (Matt. 20:26, 2 Cor. 6:4).

   b. Its derivation is uncertain but, if connected with Greek word "to pursue," it may suggest activity and celerity of our service, as in pursuit of tasks (cf. 1 Sam. 21:8)

3. *As Household Servants*

   a. This word is used of our Lord's followers in Luke 16:13 and 1 Pet. 2:18 (cf. Acts 10:7, Rom. 14:4).

   b. It suggests inwardness and intimacy of our service in "household" of God (cf. Gal. 6:10, Eph. 2:19).

4. *As Subordinate Servants*

   a. Literal meaning of this word is nautical — "under-rower" or crew-member, and may be translated "assistant" or "attendant" (Luke 1:2, John 18:36, Acts 13:5, 26:16, 1 Cor. 4:1).

   b. We are "under-lings" and, like rowers, we must work hard, since in boat not all can be "stroke," and in orchestra there must be "second fiddles"; so that this term suggests both subordination and strenuousness of our service.

5. *As Confidential Servants*

   a. This word is used only of Moses (Heb. 3:5; cf. Num. 12:7), and is connected with medical care (English word "therapy").

   b. It suggests tenderness and privilege of our service.

6. *As Public Servants*

   a. This word with its cognates indicates duty done in some public capacity (Acts 13:2, 2 Cor. 9:12, Phil. 2:17, 30).

   b. It suggests value and importance of our service, as it extends in influence and is not confined in sphere.

7. *As Temple Servants*

   a. This word with its cognates is used in connection with Tabernacle and Temple (Heb. 9:1, Luke 1:74).

   b. It suggests sacredness and dignity of our service (cf. Rom. 1:9).

8. *As Responsible Servants*

   a. This term with its cognates designates "steward," or head servant, to whom has been entrusted provision for whole household (Luke 12:42, 1 Cor. 4:1, 2, 1 Pet. 4:10).

   b. It suggests opportunity and faithfulness of our service.

Conclusion

1. *The Word "Lord"*

   a. This comes from an old Saxon term "loafward," or "bread-keeper" of the house, one who guarded the loaves; and Christ as Lord is indeed the secret of our "Bread of Life" for daily living.

   b. But He is this spiritual food to us only in proportion as He is our Lord; this is the condition of all His gifts to us, such as pardon, peace, purity, power, and progress.

2. *The Word "Master"*

   a. This comes from the Latin word for "the greater" and there must be whole-hearted acknowledgment and acceptance of this term in relation to Christ.

   b. Only twice in the N.T. do we find the word "pre-eminence" — in Col. 1:18 and 3 John 9 — but note the sad contrast in its use; and in the original of the latter passage the phrase describing Diotrephes, "who loveth to have the pre-eminence among them" points us back to our passage in chap. 23 descriptive of the scribes and Pharisees — they "love the most prominent places" (v. 6, Greek).

Instead, let our true attitude be one of submission, followed by admission, permission, commission, transmission! And all this is in order that we may "crown Him Lord of all."

47

DENUNCIATION AND DOOM

Matthew 23:13-39

THIS PASSAGE contains a most remarkable contrast to the usual utterances of our Lord. He turns again towards His enemies, the scribes and Pharisees, of whom, doubtless, there still were many among the crowd listening to Him; and He pronounces a solemn sentence on them and on their city. The epithets alone indicate the overwhelming force of His feeling: hypocrites, blind, fools, whited sepulchres, serpents, etc. It is well for us to remember, however, that "the Man of Sorrows" was also a Man of severity. Both denunciations and appeals are inherent in His character and therefore appear in His utterances; there is a balanced combination of appalling sternness and intense pity, according to circumstances and motives. At this time the enemies of Christ had reached the height of their opposition to Him, and it was essential to deal with them plainly and uncompromisingly, and in only a lesser degree of severity with the ordinary inhabitants of Jerusalem.

I. Woe for the Leaders (23:13-36)

Most authorities omit verse 14 of K.J.V. as less suitable to this situation and because, since it is found in Mark (12:40), and in Luke (20:47) expressed in warning people against scribes, who were demonstrating sad connection between covetousness and hypocrisy (cf. 6:16-21), it would seem in Matthew to be a marginal addition. If this omission is correct, there are seven "woes" here pronounced on Jewish leaders, a sevenfold, or perfect, revelation of Divine wrath. If verse 14 should be retained, however, there are eight "woes," which some writers contrast with eight Beatitudes with which Jesus Christ commenced His Sermon on the Mount (cf. 5:1-12). In any case, it is unutterably sad to realize that it was as He was closing His last public address that these dreadful words had to be directed against national leaders; for they, notwithstanding high responsibility of their office, were guilty of deplorable wickedness of life.

1. *The Relation of the Pharisees to the Kingdom* (vs. 13-22)
   First three woes show them to be blind guides and fools, light in them being darkness:

   a. First woe (v. 13) points out their utter antagonism to good in opposing Kingdom of Heaven:

   (1) This is represented as gathering-place with open doors: and these men were guilty of twofold sin, neither entering in themselves nor, so far as they were able, allowing others to enter.

   (2) How often, when people had been on point of believing in Christ, these religious leaders had drawn them away into unbelief!
   N.B. According to old version, woe in verse 14, as we have noted, is directed against avarice and hypocrisy, both having their roots in worldliness of mind.

   b. Second of seven woes (v. 15) deals with Pharisees' religious zeal and is against proselytizing in interests of fanaticism:

   (1) While they had taken away key of real knowledge they were zealots of false one, and so eager to gain adherents they put forth immense effort to make single follower.

   (2) Outcome was that proselyte became even worse than his teacher; while misleader is more to blame than misled, it is clear that Phariseeism can be intensified, making convert morally lower than leader.

   c. Third woe (vs. 16-22) deals especially with sin of casuistry, perversion of fundamental laws of religion and inversion of true proportions of facts:

   (1) Divine institution, like Temple or altar, that imposes solemn obligations, is regarded as unimportant, while human works, such as gold of Temple or gift on altar, are placed in its stead and more highly valued (vs. 16, 17).

   (2) Pharisees failed to see that Divine element, as original holy thing, was superior to human element that

becomes holy only through its relation to Divine; and this false reasoning was used to teach men how to swear vain oaths, thus ridding themselves of responsibility (vs. 18-22).

N.B. It has been well said that "casuistry cuts asunder the living relations of religion, kills its life, denies its spirit, and idolizes its body."

2. *The Relation of the Pharisees' Public and Private Lives* (vs. 23-28)

Next three woes mark double lives of these men, with emphasis on their own personal characters which exhibited hypocritical legalism:

a. Fourth woe (vs. 23, 24) shows that in their opposition to difficult demands of inward spiritual religion they had concentrated attention on outward and visible things:

   (1) They had been scrupulous in paying tithes of least products of their fields, and yet had revealed utter deficiency in what ought to have been given priority, "the weightier matters of the law" (v. 23); but these moral elements of law, those which Luke calls "judgment and the love of God" (11:42), had indeed no weight with them.

   (2) Yet true adherence to law always puts great matters first without neglect of lesser; legalism, however, inevitably fails to appreciate these true proportions.

   (3) For this reason Pharisees had become "blind guides" (v. 24) of their people, not only acting, but also influencing others to act, as hypocrites; for, like people who believe that to swallow so small a thing as gnat would defile them and consequently strain their wine to prevent this, these men were guilty of such enormous impurities that they might be said to be swallowing so huge a thing as a camel.

   N.B. This proverbial expression, though hyperbolic, has its point in fact that by Mosaic law camel was unclean, as well as "winged creeping things," or insects, that included gnats (cf. Lev. 11:4, 20, A.S.V.); and even such an imaginary action would involve violation.

b. Fifth woe (vs. 25, 26) continues to criticize Pharisees' pretensions to holiness by means of another metaphor:

(1) They were zealous in cleansing "the outside of the cup and of the platter" (v. 25) while neglecting inside; for outward appearance was everything to them and internal, moral side of life was nothing.

(2) In their blindness (v. 26) they are rebuked and urged to sanctify inner life by practice of righteousness and temperance (opposites of "extortion and excess" (v. 25); and at same time they are reminded that external cleanliness is not useless, though admittedly less important than purity of inner man.

c. Sixth woe (vs. 27, 28) emphasizes same element of utter duplicity:

(1) Christ speaks solemnly of spiritual death within, together with manifestation of attractive exterior, even as "whited sepulchres" (v. 27) hide decay.

(2) This antithesis is most striking, for in outward appearance Pharisees seemed "righteous unto men" (v. 28), although inwardly they were utterly unclean.

3. *The Relation of the Pharisees to God* (vs. 29-36)

a. *The Condemnation* (vs. 29-32)

(1) This was expressed most completely in seventh and last woe, which brings denunciation full circle; for it implies and re-emphasizes leaders' opposition to Christ and His Kingdom (cf. v. 13).

(2) They were ready to glorify the past in building sepulchres for honoring of dead prophets (v. 29); but profession of regard for dead was no substitute for consideration of present-day opportunity through living.

(3) They were also boasting of superiority to their fathers who killed prophets (v. 30); and yet they were showing by both actions and attitudes that they were lineal descendants of these same murderers (v. 31).

(4) They were continuing to acknowledge false principles that would inevitably express themselves in unholy action; and so with Divine irony our Lord called upon

them to fill up measure of ancient crime in same spirit that killed prophets of old and that they themselves condemned (v. 32).

(5) This seventh woe is most terrible of all because, in failing to recognize authority of Christ as their Messiah and in plotting His death, these wicked men were actually condemning themselves as true successors of those who had in olden times slain earlier messengers from God.

b. *The Judgment* (vs. 33-36)

(1) In view of past unbelief and opposition, judgment on these men was solemnly declared; and to do this Christ used strongest of terms (v. 33).

(2) Then in prophetic strain He declared He would send messengers whom Pharisees would ill-treat and even kill (v. 34); and His description fits exactly what happened to His Apostles in coming years.

(3) He adds that Divine purpose of this was that longstanding wickedness of nation from its earliest days would find its logical and terrible culmination (v. 35); and we know how literally all this was fulfilled in catastrophe of A.D. 70, during lifetime of most who were present (v. 36).

N.B. Scofield comments: "It is the way also of history: judgment falls upon one generation for the sins of centuries."

(4) Zachariah mentioned in verse 35 was probably one mentioned in 2 Chron. 24:20-22, last of O. T. books according to order of Hebrew canon; and it is suggested that this last of God's messengers to be put to death before captivity of Judah (2 Chron. 36: 15-21) was indeed son of Barachiah, and "Jehoida the priest" his grandfather.

N.B. Bishop Moule interprets Greek adjective twice translated "righteous" as "being attentive to God's revealed will," surely prominent characteristic of prophet, and striking confirmation of presumed revelation to Abel regarding sacrificial approach to God (cf. Gen. 4:4).

Now, after denouncing His enemies in these strongly worded

"woes," our Lord looks beyond the leaders to lament their evil influence on their city:

II. Warning for the People (23:37-39)

1. *Their Denial* (v. 37)

   a. This verse has been well called a "parting wail of rejected love" as pent-up emotion in heart of Christ breaks out in lamentation for city that had denied Him; His language, though sternly expressive of judgment, was also beautifully indicative of feeling.

   b. He would have drawn Jerusalem, notwithstanding its hatred of truth and murder of prophets, close to His heart, even as hen gathers her chicks under her wings for protection.

2. *Their Desolation* (v. 38)

   a. This is sad story of what might have been, but now it was too late; "your house [He could no longer call it "my Fahter's house," John 2:16] is left unto you desolate" (Greek, "abandoned to its own resources").

   b. City of Jerusalem had had its magnificent opportunity and had deliberately refused it.

3. *Their Discipline* (v. 39)

   a. People are told they would have no further chance until compelled to acknowledge Christ as their Messiah, and all, instead of few, would use words of Psalmist (Ps. 118:26; cf. Matt. 21:9).

   b. Thus, with surpassing love amidst judgment, He reveals possibilities they had lost, and warns of solemn future to which they were by their sin committed.

   N.B. Three "untils" of Israel's blessing are, according to Scofield: (1) Israel must say, "Blessed is he" (v. 39); (2) Gentile world power must run its course (Luke 21:24); (3) Elect number of Gentiles must be brought in (Rom. 11:25-27). With these, in inverse order, Dr. George Guille associated Dan. 9:15-17: (1) Restoration of people (v. 15; Rom. 11:25); (2) Restoration of city (v. 16; Luke 21:24); and (3) Restoration of sanctuary (v. 17; Matt. 23:39). Phrase "fulness of the Gentiles" (Rom. 11:25) would seem to emphasize opportunity for making up full complement of Christ's Church, while phrase "times of the Gentiles" (Luke 21:24) indicates period it would take for this completion.

With this discourse, the public ministry of Christ draws to a close on a twofold note: a passion for righteousness and a passion of love. Righteousness flames out in hatred of falsity, as seen in the Jewish leaders whose sins were inexpressibly foul in His sight; and from these scathing words of His can be sensed something of what is meant by "the wrath of the Lamb" (Rev. 6:16). Yet these were Divine tears melting His holy denunciation into a wailing lament over Jerusalem, the city that had shared in the sins of her leaders.

Conclusion

As we contemplate this last recorded public discourse (cf. Luke 21:37, 38), filled with denunciation and doom, two strong elements in our Lord's character are outstanding:

1. *The Sternness of Divine Judgment*

    a. Let no one think God is indifferent to human unrighteousness; on the contrary, severity of perfect love is most righteous fact in universe.

    b. Faithfulness with which God's Son describes sin shows also His undaunted courage in face of evils of His time.

    c. How searching is this description, and how complete a delineation of human character; very sinlessness of our Lord enabled Him to see more deeply into heart of things than can sinful man himself.

    d. No aspect of sin of that period in Jewish history seems to have been left untouched upon; both personal characters and official teachings of men in question were thoroughly dealt with and exposed with completeness and accuracy.

2. *The Sadness of Divine Love*

    a. After torrent has spent its force, our Lord speaks of His past willingness to deal gently with Jerusalem; and even His utter despair with it is expressed in tender yearning.

    b. This is same Saviour with whom we have to do today; at present time, it is His mission, by His Spirit and through His messengers, to "proclaim the acceptable year of the Lord."

c. But, if this is neglected, opposed, despised, there is nothing left but, later on, "the day of vengeance of our God" (Isa. 61:2; cf. Luke 4:16-23).

This was the lesson driven home by our Lord as He closed His public ministry, and this must be the burden of many a message today, so that a great company may pray with the hymn writer —

> *When He shall come with trumpet sound,*
> *O may I then in Him be found,*
> *Dressed in His righteousness alone,*
> *Faultless to stand before the Throne!*

EDWARD MOTE

48

FINAL PREPARATION OF THE DISCIPLES (1)

Matthew 24:1-51

AFTER CHRIST had solemnly declared the rejection of the nation that had rejected Him, He turned away from the Temple and was rejoined by His disciples who, doubtless as the group walked farther on, drew His attention to the striking view of its buildings from rising ground. When they had left the city behind and had reached the Mount of Olives the disciples asked their Master three questions in reply to His prediction of destruction and desolation: When should these things be? What should be the sign of His coming? What should be the sign of the end of the age? (v. 3). It has been suggested that verses 4-6 give the answer to the first question; verses 7-28, the answer to the second; and verses 29 to 25:46, the answer to the third. It has also been thought impossible to distinguish between the events of A.D. 70 and those connected with Christ's second advent. But Scofield believes that since "these things" (vs. 2, 3) undoubtedly refer to the destruction of Jerusalem, which did take place under Titus in that fateful year, Luke's Gospel is the only one that answers the disciples' first question (cf. Luke 21:20-24). According to this view, Matthew and Mark answer the second and third questions only, by recording our Lord's predictions regarding the course of this age (vs. 4-14, Mark 13:5-13), the tribulation (vs. 15-26, Mark 13:14-23) leading up to His coming in glory, and the end of the age. But, whether either of these views is correct, or neither, both this chapter of Matthew and the next are so worded as to preclude a literal application to the Christian Church in this dispensation. Instead, they seem to have explicit reference to Jewish believers in the period following it. We must, of course, always distinguish between the primary interpretation of prophecy and its secondary, spiritual application; but it is the former that is the fundamental meaning of this passage. However, the actual words of Christ as they appear call for our closest attention and also, though primarily addressed to representatives of the Jewish nation, our spiritual and individual application.

I. Destruction (vs. 1, 2)

1. *The Definite Statement*

    a. Evidently disciples were still so impressed by buildings of Temple that they could not take seriously its ultimate destruction (v. 1); Christ then uttered more explicit and positive prediction on subject than before (v. 2; see also v. 15).

    b. His supernatural vision enabled Him to see what could not have occurred to any human being, namely, that overthrow of Temple worship was certain, and that entire Jewish nation would find its future determined by its present relation to Himself.

2. *The Implied Danger*

    a. Implicit in these verses is possibility of over-emphasizing holy things and places; this is what we might call ritualism.

    b. But Jews had sense of sanctity of Temple that is scarcely conceivable today; and even Jesus Christ had called it "my Father's house" (John 2:16).

    c. Yet it was doomed to desecration; and so it is evident there is no building, institution, or spiritual organization, however sacred and useful, that will not utterly perish if pride, selfishness, and other forms of sin are allowed to enter in.

II. Explanation (vs. 3-14)*

To approach an answer to His disciples' questions (v. 3), our Lord commences His "Olivet Discourse" by emphasizing the practical issue of all this discussion of the future:

1. *Personal Precautions* (vs. 4-6)

   a. They were not to be led astray by many who would attempt to deceive them about His coming (v. 4); there would even be those masquerading as Christ Himself (v. 5).

   b. They were not to be afraid with respect to terrible upheavals that were to come, caused not only by "wars," but by "rumors of wars," or times of uneasy peace; for all these were necessary even though end was not indicated by them (v. 6).

2. *External Convulsions* (vs. 7, 8)

   a. There would be political revolutions, dangerous famines, nation-wide pestilences, and great earthquakes; that is to say, crises covering social, physical, medical, geographical developments of human life (v. 7).

   b. So far from all these things belonging to "the end," actually they would be merely "the beginning of sorrows" (v. 8).

3. *Internal Relations* (vs. 9-14)

   a. Then disciples are told of personal experiences during these troublous times; opposition to them as Christ's followers will extend to intense animosity and even to martyrdom (v. 9).

   b. There will be traitorous acts (v. 10), very opposite of Christ's call to His people to love one another (cf. John 15:17).

   c. Further, there will be pretenders to Divine claims who will lead people astray (v. 11); and, inasmuch as sin of all sorts will be multiplied, love of majority will grow cold (v. 12).

   d. On other hand, there will be faithfulness in midst of apostasy, and one who patiently endures to very end will

---

*See also the author's, *The Apostle John*, Kregel Publications, 1984, p. 364.

find complete deliverance (v. 13; cf. Luke 24:19); and good news of Divine Kingdom will be universally proclaimed as witness to all nations, and then end will come (v. 14).

e. This passage does not refer to coming of Christ *for* His people, which is never described as "the end," for there are several events to follow it; reference is rather to subsequent period connected with Israel, and it has still to be fulfilled when our Lord reveals Himself once more to that nation.

f. This seems to show we are not to expect conquest of world for Christ before end of this age; while we do our utmost to evangelize, by means of "gospel of the grace of God" (Acts 20:24), actual winning of world is left for next age and for same people He chose of old.

g. When, therefore, Jews shall have proclaimed "gospel of the kingdom" (v. 14) as their testimony to all, then our Lord will appear *with* His redeemed ones to usher in His glorious reign; and thus, though our immediate anticipation is Christ coming *for* us, this chapter does not seem to be concerned with that (cf. 1 Thess. 4:13-18).

h. But after later coming, bringing us with Him in His Divine glory and supreme authority, "then" (and not till then) "shall the end come" (v. 14; cf. 2 Thess. 5:1-4).

III. Prediction (vs. 15-44)

1. *Tribulation* (vs. 15-28)

   a. *Physical Protection* (vs. 15-22)

      (1) It would seem as though primary interpretation of these directions is connected with destruction of Jerusalem; but it is sometimes possible to see double meaning, primary and secondary, same principles being applicable to different occasions.

      (2) Word "therefore" (v. 15) indicates transition, looking back probably to verses 7-9; phrase "abomination of desolation" has been given several interpretations, including Roman eagles as military ensigns and under them imperial busts that were worshipped and placed in Temple, and therefore abhorrent to Jews.

      (3) If so, these would signify holy city was surrounded

and on point of capture, with phrase in parentheses, "whoso readeth, let him understand," constituting call to observe near approach of these signs in beginning of what Josephus called "The Jewish War"; this parenthetical phrase is found also in Mark's account (13:14), and is almost certainly interpolated exhortation by Evangelists.

(4) In these instructions (vs. 16-20) one is impressed by their practicality for emergency such as this, e.g., reference to Sabbath, on which Jew might go distance of only about one mile (cf. Acts 1:12), ordinance based on Exod. 16:29; this custom with regard to Sabbath travel, involving closing of city gates, and Jewish fanaticism, would make journeying on that day very difficult for escaping Christians.

(5) This tribulation is literally true to history of Jerusalem's destruction in A.D. 70 (v. 21), for by sheer awfulness of terror disciples were to measure swiftness of their flight; but here surely, that double meaning emerges, with foreshadowing of "Great Tribulation" of future ushered in by "abomination that maketh desolate" (Dan. 12:11; cf. 9:27).

(6) If so, "the elect" (v. 22) are not primarily Christians of first century, but God's elect nation in future; for O.T. prophecies tell us predicament of Jews just before Christ's coming will be most serious, hemmed in within Jerusalem and surrounded by foes whom Messiah will drive back at His appearing.

(7) But even we today, in very different circumstances, may yet take to our own hearts assurance that, whatever may be our troubles, there will be protecting mercy and Divine presence and power (cf. Isa. 43:2).

b. *Spiritual Perception* (vs. 23-28)

(1) This section seems to look forward to whole period of restrained judgment; and here is another instance where perspective of prophecy is important, as mountain peaks viewed from afar seem to be close together, but when seen at closer range are found to be widely separated by valleys.

(2) So with our Lord's references to future: destruction

of Jerusalem was to be regarded as manifestation of Himself, a "coming" in judgment; but it was only, as it were, one mountain peak in chain of comings.

(3) Thus it might seem from passage like this that everything follows quite consecutively, even immediately; and yet, in reality, there is often, and almost certainly here, definite period of time between, and even in one verse long ages may be included (e.g., 1 Cor. 15:23).

(4) Warning is given (vs. 23-25) lest disciples then (vs. 23, 25) and elect nation in future (v. 24) should be led astray by those professing to be Messiahs and prophets; although there is paradoxical inference in original that it is impossible for true believers thus to be deceived.

(5) This contrast between unreal and real, false and true, is often found in Scripture (e.g., 1 John 4:1-3, 2 John 9-11); for power to work miracles, even spiritual ones, is not necessarily proof of genuine Divine authority (cf. 7:22, Deut. 13:1-5, 2 Thess. 2:8-12).

(6) Christ was not to be identified with any particular location or faction, whether here or there, then or now (v. 26); on contrary, His coming would be like lightning, universal in its visibility (v. 27), thought here being not that of suddenness, but of omnipresence.

(7) Then comes solemn statement expressive of universal law of nature, having its counterpart in moral world; "eagles" here (v. 28) are carrion vultures, and grim figure gives profound expression of certainty of judgment.

(8) As carcass attracts eaters of carrion, so moral corruption demands punishment; thus, from time of Jerusalem's destruction onwards, all judgments would prove inevitable and at length would extend to entire world, morally corrupt and spiritually dead.

N.B. Canon Charles T. P. Grierson, noting how our Lord was accustomed to use mysterious and general language when dealing with His return, interprets verse 28 as meaning "when circumstances are ripe, the event happens"; and he adds that this statement by its enigmatic form covers all His future comings.

2. *Consummation* (vs. 29-44)

a. *Signs of Christ's Coming* (vs. 29-31)

(1) As mentioned above, it has been suggested that from verse 29 to end of chap. 25 Christ gives answer to third question of verse 3, "What shall be the sign of . . . the end of the age (Greek)?" if so, in verses 29-31 we have coming of Son of man in judgment, and not coming of our Lord for His people.

(2) These verses emphasize three points of time by words "immediately" (v. 29), "then" and "then" (v. 30); and it appears impossible to limit words to fall of Jerusalem when "tribulation" began only as its first and partial fulfillment (cf. v. 21).
N.B. James Morison, in stating there is no slightest necessity for such an assumption, speaks of it as "a "a microscopic way of peering toward telescopic objects."

(3) On contrary, it seems best to interpret whole passage of period after Church has been taken up; for, since context seems to point to what follows "Great Tribulation," this section in its primary interpretation has nothing to do with present dispensation, however much we may apply it spiritually and in secondary way.

(4) Moreover, coming of our Lord for His people appears to be unconnected with any "times and seasons" and is not at all dependent upon earthly events as far as we can know; on other hand, Great Tribulation and His coming in judgment seem very much to depend on "times and seasons" (cf. 1 Thess. 5:1 with closing verses of previous chapter).

(5) These verses, therefore, almost certainly deal with latter days when Jews have returned to their land, rebuilt Temple, re-established sacrifices, and made covenant with Antichrist; he will, of course, later break this agreement and desecrate altar of God (cf. Dan. 9:24-27).

(6) Then Christ will "immediately" appear; and thus

there can hardly be room for millennium before His coming — this period must follow it.

(7) Reference to sun and other heavenly bodies (v. 29) is from Isaiah 13:9, 10 and 34:4, and is perhaps to be understood as describing end of all things earthly rather than mere figurative expression; or perhaps it means these heavenly bodies shall hide their lights at manifestation of Divine Lord, thereby recognizing His superiority.

(8) At any rate, transformation of universe prepares way for "sign" of Christ's immediate coming (v. 30), some indication in form of "power and great glory" that solemnizes "all the tribes of the earth"; and then will follow complete gathering together of Israel from all parts of world (v. 31).

b. *Imminence of Christ's Coming* (vs. 32-44)

   (1) *Its Certainty* (vs. 32-36)

      (a) This section of chapter contains one of our Lord's shorter parables — hardly more than a metaphor; from fig tree disciples were to learn that "all these things" would mean His near approach (vs. 32, 33).

      (b) With solemn affirmation they were told generation in which they were then living would not pass away till all these things — not would "be fulfilled," but "commenced to take place" (v. 34, Greek); for word is not ordinary N.T., word for "fulfilled," and surely it cannot bear that translation in this context.

      (c) Strange to say, however, nearly all commentators overlook its plain, literal sense, i.e., "shall have become," or "shall have arisen," or "shall have begun to be" — referring not to end of something but to its beginning; in fact, out of 630 instances in N.T. this word means "fulfilled" only three times.

      (d) Thus phrase simply indicates generation of Jews then living would see commencement of "these things" mentioned in verses 3, 6; and this is exactly what took place, for they had their primary fulfillment not forty years after, i.e., in A.D. 70, though their complete realization would be in His second coming, still future even today; when thus understood verse is perfectly clear. *N.B.* In parallel passage, Luke 21:20-33, we find both verbs: in verse 24, "fulfilled," ordinary N.T. word; in verse 32, "become," "arisen," "begun to be" (as in Matt.). Cf. John 13:2, "supper having begun," or "during supper" (A.S.V.) — not "being ended" as in K.J.V., for cf. verses 4, 12, 26, in which supper is shown to be still in progress.

(e) This outcome was so certain that, even though material heaven and earth should pass away, Christ's words would still stand (v. 35); and yet of actual day and hour of fulfillment God the Father alone knew, for not even Christ in His human condescension and earthly limitation had this exact knowledge (v. 36).

(f) This is clearly associated with those limitations of Deity that were not only inevitable during earthly life of our Lord, but inherent in very idea of Incarnation; for Gospels seem unanimous that our Lord suspended use of His Godhead during most of His earthly life and that His utterances partook of this accepted position.

(g) There is something beautiful in thought that He lived His life on earth as man, not using His own Divine power but receiving knowledge and power every moment from His Father (cf. John 5:19, 20); and there is no difficulty whatever in such limitation since it was included in His Father's will for God the Son during His earthly life.

(h) Limitation of knowledge does not involve error; and what He as man did know He knew perfectly, and everything He said, moment by moment, was given Him of His Father to speak (cf. John 12:49, 50).

(i) Thus, while time of Christ's coming was to be unknown, fact of it was absolutely assured; and this adds to importance of considering entire discourse in its proper perspective and of bearing in mind double fulfillment of its predictions.

(2) *Its Unexpectedness* (vs. 37-44)

    (a) In this section coming of Christ is illustrated, not by parable but by history; in days of Noah there was seeming prosperity and people lived as though only physical well-being and social relationships were worthy of attention (vs. 37, 38).

    (b) They did not believe disaster was coming until after Noah had entered ark before their very eyes; and soon flood "came, and took them all away" (v. 39; cf. Gen. 6:21-23).

    (c) Christ says it will be similar when He comes again for, of two men working in field or two women grinding at mill, one may be taken and other left (vs. 40, 41); and this constitutes urgent call to watchfulness, because of similar ignorance of time when our Lord will come (v. 42).

    N.B. Since it is almost certain this entire chapter refers to Christ's coming in judgment, question arises as to who are "taken" and who are "left." Some writers follow view that it is judgment that, like flood in verse 39, takes away, that ones left are for blessing. Others incline to view that those taken are righteous, as Noah and his family were taken into ark, away from danger, and left ones are ungodly. Question of disciples in Luke 17:37, which follows this statement and which Christ answers with His cryptic saying about dead body and eagles would substantiate this latter interpretation.

    (d) Furthermore, just as householder does not know hour of thief's coming, but must constantly provide for safety of his possessions, so it is essential for all to be ready, since Christ will come when He is unexpected (vs. 43, 44); and similitude of thief is found elsewhere and is very striking in regard to those not ready for Master (cf. 1 Thess. 5:2, 4; 2 Pet. 3:10; Rev. 3:3; 16:15).

N.B. Cf. verses 42 and 44; disciples are to watch because of their lack of knowledge; and they are to be ready in order to guard against over-confidence.

IV. Application (vs. 45-51)

This closing passage, in form of another illustration, seems to suggest our Lord's judgment will begin with those who hold office as servants among His people:

1. *The Reward of Faithfulness* (vs. 45-47)

   a. Watchfulness will naturally be accompanied by faithfulness and wisdom; and these will lead to responsibility (v. 45).

   b. "That servant" (v. 46) is spoken of as "blessed" because his lord when he comes will find him engaged in his ordinary work; and result of this diligence will be reward in form of promotion, from "ruler over his household" (v. 45) to "ruler over all his goods" (v. 47).

2. *The Retribution of Unfaithfulness* (vs. 48-51)

   a. "That evil servant," presuming on his lord being delayed, is depicted as indulging in cruelty and excess (vs. 48, 49); but master of house returns quite unexpectedly, surprising evil servant (v. 50).

   b. He receives deserved result of his misdeeds; he is sent away where there are other deceivers and where there is remorse and unutterable grief (v. 51).

Conclusion

As we look back over this remarkable chapter, the following considerations stand out:

1. *The Inevitability of Judgment*

   a. This solemn truth is especially important today; and, as in Moses' time, God is still saying by various means, "Be sure your sin will find you out" (Num. 32:23).

   b. Everything we know about sin and, still more, about character of God shows disobedience cannot be thing of indifference or indulgence, but of necessity must be dealt with judicially and with utmost solemnity.

2. *The Perspective of Prophecy*

   a. This vital truth dominates so much of prophetic teaching that, while it is impossible to give detailed interpretation of all of Christ's words on subject of future, there is no doubt that important principles are declared and great certainties emphasized.

   b. We must, therefore, occupy ourselves with God's Word as it stands and endeavor not only to interpret future events by it, but also to apply it definitely to our own present needs.

3. *The Necessity of Watchfulness*

   a. This fundamental requirement of Christian life will place us always on alert, lest our Lord come for His own and find us sleeping.

   b. If Jewish disciples, representing elect nation, were thus solemnly warned to watch for coming that would be associated with definite signs, much more should Christians be watching for coming that evidently will be completely unexpected.

   c. At least part of world will be buried in sleep so that, when such people first open their eyes, all old condition of affairs will be gone forever; but it is significant that, when speaking of believers, Apostle Paul says they are not in darkness, that dawning of that day should overtake them as thief (cf. 1 Thess. 5:4ff.).

4. *The Commendation of Faithfulness*

   a. Contrast between good servants and wicked servants in relation to their master's coming is particularly impressive in its message for those Christian people who have special duties in Church; and seven commands in this connection are given in N.T.:

      (1) Awake (Rom. 13:11-13) — alertness;
      (2) Watch (v. 42, 25:13) — carefulness;
      (3) Wait (1 Thess. 1:10) — patience;
      (4) Expect (Phil 3:20, Heb. 9:28) — eagerness;
      (5) Pray (6:10, Rev. 22:20) — desire;

(6) Hasten (2 Pet. 3:11, 12) — earnestness; and —

(7) Love (2 Tim. 4:8) — devotion.

b. These are at once test and call to us today; and means to carry them out are found in St. Paul's words to Roman Christians (Rom. 13:14): "Put ye on the Lord Jesus Christ, and make not provision for the flesh."

Lord Jesus, come, and quickly come, we pray;
Dirges and tears hold universal sway;
We look for judgment, and behold, a cry!
Oppression rules and, o'er a groaning land,
The Church and world walk blindfold, hand in hand,
While Thy true children for deliverance sigh.
Cut short the blood-bedewed Gethsemane,
Hasten our Easter, though through Calvary,
And on a sinless earth let us see Thee!

49

FINAL PREPARATION OF THE DISCIPLES (2)

Matthew 25:1-46

P RIMARILY, this chapter continuing Christ's Olivet discourse is entirely Jewish, and the scenes depicted represent those that will be enacted on the earth at the close of the Jewish age, or Daniel's seventieth week, the "end" mentioned more than once in chapter 24, with which this chapter is linked by its first word "Then." This word definitely marks the exact time indicated by the first of three parables and means "at that time," immediately following 24:45-51. However, the solemn secondary application of the chapter about watchfulness concerns all Christian people today — "written for our learning" (Rom. 15:4) — and should therefore be carefully pondered.

Each of the three parables in this chapter has its own message, and yet all are concerned with the one idea of faithfulness. Besides giving three pronouncements of reward and retribution, and illustrating three principles of life, they present three striking pictures of Christ:

I. Christ as Bridegroom (vs. 1-13)

This first test of faithfulness is concerned with inner life as it will be when Christ returns at close of Great Tribulation (cf. 24:29, 30, 2 Thess. 1:7-10). It is Eastern picture and time is night:

1. *The Bridegroom*

a. Christ has many aspects in Gospels, where He is seen, e.g., as Saviour, Teacher, Lord; and many are the recorded responses to His claims.

b. Here, thought is that of fellowship, expressive of love between Christ and His followers, which is highest potentiality in Christian life; for Christianity is devotion to Person, not principle, and that devotion is at its best, fullest, and deepest in friendship born of love, as typified by marriage.

2. *The Virgins*

a. These attendants at Eastern wedding symbolize professing Jewish disciples during Christ's absence and just before His return (cf. Rev. 14:1-5); and they are represented as being in two groups, for "five of them were wise, and five were foolish" (v. 2).

b. But they had three things in common: "they took their lamps, and went forth to meet the bridegroom" (v. 1); they had oil in their lamps (vs. 3, 4; cf. v. 8, Greek); and, "while the bridegroom tarried, they all slumbered and slept" (v. 5).

3. *The Lamps*

a. These are typical of God's Word (cf. Ps. 119:105, Prov. 6:23; and see Rev. 1:20, 2:5, Greek, "lampstands" being churches witnessing to that Word); and all ten virgins were well-disposed towards light-bearing.

b. There was no idea of indifference among five foolish ones but, in fact, worthy intention; it is rare to find any believer, Jewish or Gentile, with entire lack of interest in Bible and in second coming.

4. *The Oil*

a. Five wise virgins had oil both in and with their lamps, while foolish ones thought "in" was sufficient and "took no oil with them" (v. 3); and, since oil in N.T. is usually typical of Holy Spirit, it will help us to understand full meaning of this parable if we consider all ten virgins as genuine disciples possessing Him as source of grace in inward life.

b. But we may think also of five wise ones as "spiritual" and five foolish as "carnal" (cf. Rom. 7:7 to 8:13); for trouble with latter is not that they have no grace, but that they have so little grace that their "lamps are going out" (v. 8, Greek), and thus difference is one of degree rather than of kind, between enough and not enough.

c. Certainly absolute necessity of Holy Spirit to Christian life is shown elsewhere (cf. Rom. 8:9); but N.T. also makes distinction between having Him, which is true of all believers, and being "filled with the Spirit" (Acts 2:4, 4:31, Eph. 5:18; cf. John 20:22, Eph. 1:13), and this is every believer's duty as well as his privilege (see Scofield on Acts 2:4).

d. Just as reserve of physical strength is advisable in case of illness or sudden test, so spiritual reserve of vitality and character through Holy Spirit, typified by "oil in their vessels" (v. 4) makes ready for every emergency; conversion is to be followed by consecration, human potentiality to be fulfilled by Divine power.

5. *The Waiting*

a. Because bridegroom tarried, "they all slumbered and slept" (v. 5); but they were not blamed for this, for it is not possible always to be watching in sense of sight and of conscious thought.

b. Blame was for lack of preparedness before sleep was taken; St. John calls this readiness "abiding in him," so that there may be confidence instead of shame at His coming (cf. 1 John 2:28).

6. *The Call*

a. Coming of bridegroom was both certain and expected, but time was unknown; and if this will be true of advent of Christ in judgment, much more ought our present-day witness to make reference repeatedly to His coming for His own; and we know it will be personal, not merely by means of some influence (cf. Acts 1:11).

b. Life is full of crises, and emergencies test and reveal us; and either of Christ's comings will be greatest crisis ever to those concerned (vs. 6, 7).

c. There was apparently tremendous difference between those called "wise" and those called "foolish," for "oil" was not transferable (vs. 8, 9); and gifts of Spirit are imparted direct to individual soul by God Himself (cf. 1 Cor. 12:1-11, Gal. 5:22-25).

d. Rewards and punishments followed (v. 10), wise ones going into feast with bridegroom, foolish being shut out from "marriage supper of the Lamb" (Rev. 19:9); so that in that day there will be two consequences only — entrance or exclusion.

e. It is awfulness of exclusion that explains severity of bridegroom's disclaimer of recognition (vs. 11, 12) and intensity of our Lord's appeal for watchfulness (v. 13); and although we of true Church are called "the bride, the Lamb's wife" (Rev. 21:9) and not represented by wedding attendants (cf. John 3:29), we also must be watching and prepared to meet Him when He comes for us, and this is only possible when our "oil" is our own, not borrowed (cf. 2 Pet. 1:1-11).

f. But if we look into our hearts we shall despair; if we look around at men we shall be baffled; and if we look towards our enemies we shall be alarmed.

g. If we look to Christ, however, we shall see ourselves as He sees us, and we shall see the precious blood and the merit of the atoning sacrifice; so that, occupied with Him, we shall be guarded, guided, and blessed in all things, as we watch and wait in full expectation of His coming.

II. Christ as Master (vs. 14-30)

First parable has to do with watching, this second one with working; first, with fellowship, second with stewardship; first with character, second with conduct:

1. *Responsibility* (vs. 14, 15)

a. This parable concerns servants to whom master has committed his goods; we must, therefore, avoid any interpretation that refers to all men, for it applies only to those who have been entrusted with specific responsibilities.

b. This is test of faithfulness in servants, and thought is still of Christ's coming in judgment; each is given "talents," referring to large sums of money (one talent being worth at least one thousand dollars), proportionate "to his several ability" to use and invest (v. 15; cf. v. 27).

N.B. (1) Our use of word "talented" is inaccurate, for talents bestowed are shown here to be effect, not cause, of abilities.

(2) To compare this parable with that of Pounds (Luke 19:11-27), note differences: of place — Jericho and Jerusalem; of time — before triumphal entry, and during last week; of audience — crowd, and disciples; of purpose — to show equal gifts leading to unequal results, and unequal gifts according to ability. Former seems best understood of gift of Divine grace, which is same to everyone who receives it.*

c. In this parable recounted by Matthew, different numbers of talents necessarily imply natural differences of temperament and opportunity; and so they may be interpreted also as spiritual endowments, such as Christian graces, knowledge of God's Word, appropriation of Spirit's power, i.e., everything that equips for the Lord's work.

d. Master's one requirement was that talents were to be used for his profit, and hence servants' one business was to make utmost use of his sacred trust, with thought of his return ruling day and night; and amount of work would be as nothing if only they could meet him without shame.

2. *Result* (vs. 16-18)

a. Faithful servants immediately set to work, and did good service; the one with five talents gained five more (v. 16), and the other, with two talents, gained two more (v. 17).

b. But third servant, with but one talent, was disobedient and neglectful, and buried his lord's money in ground for alleged safekeeping (v. 18);

N.B. Note modern proverbial way of speaking of "hiding one's talent in a napkin" is both incorrect and improb-

---

*For treatment of this parable, see the author's volume, *Outline Studies in Luke*, Kregel Publications, 1984, pp. 299ff.

able, for no napkin is likely to have held so many large coins; it was "pound," much smaller amount of money (about fifteen dollars), that was "kept laid up in a napkin" (Luke 19:20).

3. *Reckoning* (vs. 19-28)

   a. When ample time for required activity had passed, master returned and made personal, thorough inquiry; no one was overlooked, and evidently there was no hurry or partiality (v. 19).

   b. After reports from faithful servants (vs. 20, 22), there comes, first, word of commendation, then announcement of promotion, and then invitation to companionship with master (vs. 21, 23); and it is most significant that man who had two talents and made them four received exactly the same words of commendation as man who had five talents and made them ten, because each was proportionately faithful.

      N.B. In case of pounds, however, man who made his pound into ten received both praise and reward, while one who made his pound into five only had proportionate reward but without praise, because he was not as faithful as he might have been (cf. Luke 19:17, 19).

   c. Here, increased grace is its own reward; and believers will be given more work to do as they acquire greater capacity.

   d. Then came servant who had received only one talent and gave several excuses for simple fact of not having used what he had (vs. 24, 25); and his words seem on surface to plead extreme caution, but they also cast suspicion on his master's character as heartless and even unprincipled.

   e. Instead, it is his own character that is shown up, as slothful, disobedient, and inconsistent; but basis of evil was wrong opinion of his master, for servant's fear was clearly in error in view of wholehearted trust reposed in them all (cf. vs. 14, 15).

   f. Then his master denounced him as both "wicked and slothful" because he had professed to misinterpret master's characteristics of shrewdness and thrift instead of striving to satisfy them by wise investment (vs. 26, 27); and then he was deprived of his trust, which was given to fellow servant who had most (v. 28).

4. *Reward and Retribution* (vs. 29, 30)

a. Whatever primary application is given this parable, there is moral obligation here for every one of us — "thou oughtest" (v. 27); for sin is not merely in abuse, but in non-use of what is given us.

b. Great law of spiritual capital (v. 29) is found four other times in Gospels (cf. 13:12, Luke 8:18, 19:26, John 15:2); in short, if we do not use we lose.
Illus.: There are many instances of this in human experience, such as atrophy in unused limbs; and in nature — e.g., moles and mine ponies who live underground and fish who swim in caverns are blind.

c. On other hand, there always comes special momentum after reaching certain point in development or progress, whether in recovery after sickness, or in use of money or knowledge; so also in regard to things spiritual — use of Bible, of prayer, of Christian fellowship, exertion of giving, of obedience, of faith, will increase, after certain stage of growth, in truly marvellous way, enabling us through God's grace to multiply our labors for Christ.

d. Our service ought indeed to be profitable to our Master and means of glorifying Him; for this, however, we are not called upon for success, but only for faithfulness, which is one great lesson of this parable.

e. "Outer darkness" refers primarily, of course, to period of tribulation into which unfaithful ones are to return with grief and regret; and it is quite probable that all these parables in this Jewish Gospel have yet to find their full interpretation quite apart from Church of God.

f. But let us bear in mind solemnity of these words for all God's servants during either period of Christ's absence; for not only sin, but even neglect may result in awful loss.
N.B. Joseph Parker once said: "The ground which received the one talent will also receive the five; you can easily find a spade to dig a grave for your talents and abilities, your money and your time, but understand that in burying your talent you are burying yourself; in burying ought that God has given you, you are burying part of your very life."

III. Christ as Judge (vs. 31-46)

Our chapter is still concerned with faithfulness, although this third parable extends to Gentile nations and is concerned with judgment of such as are in existence when our Lord comes in glory with His people to set up His Kingdom. It is not a general judgment; that is not found in Scripture. Judgment of sins is connected with the cross (cf. John 3:24); judgment of believers in regard to their works since conversion will have taken place when our Lord comes for His people (cf. 1 Cor. 3:11-15); and judgment of wicked dead will not occur until after the millennium (cf. Rev. 20:11-15). But, again, it is important to distinguish between future, full realization and present, partial application.

1. *The Scene* (vs. 31, 32a)

   a. This has been called most astonishing pageant described in antiquity: Christ's glorious coming as King (cf. vs. 34, 40), attended by angels, and taking His place on His throne (v. 31) as nations assemble before Him (v. 32a); and claim of "Son of man" (v. 31) to be Judge of mankind, prerogative of God only, is most striking (cf. 7:22, 23).

   b. Apparently it is same judgment as found in Joel 3:1-8; however, it is not national judgment in general, but of individuals included in Gentile nations referred to (cf. 28:19), and on specific charge, to take place at opening of millennium.
   N.B. Whether these nations are to be distinguished from or regarded as identical with nations of Rev. 20:8 is matter of opinion; but it would seem that those mentioned in Rev. 21:25 have already been judged and are walking in light of city of God.

2. *The Separation* (vs. 32b-36, 40-43, 45)

   a. This is first announced (vs. 32b, 33), and then justified (vs. 34-36, 40-43, 45); and there are three classes mentioned here: "sheep," "goats" (vs. 32, 33), and "brethren" (v. 40).

   b. "Brethren" are Jewish remnant who will have turned to the Lord during Great Tribulation, and who will have gone everywhere evangelizing (cf. 24:14); those Gentiles ("sheep") who accept their message will show it by their kindly attitude to messengers, and those ("goats") who reject it will oppose and reject them also.

c. There is no idea here of great realities of grace and of sin in general, but only of philanthropic reception and lack of it; and result is plainly seen in great severance of people and their being placed on right or left hand of King.

d. It is solemnly important to realize that our Lord's dealings at that time will be based upon treatment meted out to Israel; and those who have been kind and true will inherit Kingdom prepared for them (v. 34).

e. Since Church of Christ will have been previously caught up to meet Him in air (cf. Phil. 3:20, 21; 1 Thess. 4:17; Tit. 2:13, 14), it is clear those set on right hand of King, described as blessed and invited to inherit kingdom, cannot possibly be either Bride of Christ or His "brethren" mentioned in indictment.

N.B. (1) R. V. Bingham wrote in this connection: "The sentence of judgment is based not on benevolent acts done during the Church age, but on the disposition made by the nations of the gospel witness during the tribulation at the hands of Christ's brethren."

(2) During this time, it would seem Israel's national salvation will take place (cf. Rom. 11:25-27), because Jews will have been able for first time to look on Him whom they have pierced (cf. Zech. 12:10, Rev. 1:7).

3. *The Surprise* (vs. 37-39, 44)

a. Righteous were astonished to hear their actions had been remembered and applied to Christ Himself (vs. 37-39); but what they had done to others had indeed, in His mind, been done to Him (cf. v. 40).

> *Still, wherever pity shares*
> *Its bread with sorrow, want, and sin,*
> *And love the beggar's feast prepares,*
> *The uninvited Guest comes in.*
>
> *Unheard, because our ears are dull,*
> *Unseen, because our eyes are dim,*
> *He walks the earth, the Wonderful,*
> *And all good deeds are done to Him.*
>
> J. G. WHITTIER

b. In opposite direction, it would seem there was surprise as to sin of merely doing nothing (v. 44); for Christ tells those on left that because they had not done good to others they had not done good to Him (v. 45).

c. Sin of omission here is emphasized as in two earlier parables: foolish virgins, slothful servant, those whom Christ actually called "ye cursed" (v. 41) — all teach danger of doing nothing; and first will come blame, then utter loss, especially if by such neglect gospel itself is rejected.

4. *The Sentence* (v. 46)

a. Both sides are thus definitely declared, and sent to eternal life or eternal loss; future life will be marked by fundamental, continuing differences between people, with evil impossible to transform into good.
Illus.: (1) The mark indelible in yonder fossil was imprinted thousands of years ago, when the stone was in a semi-liquid state, by the claw of a passing bird; but it has petrified since then, and it cannot be altered now.
(2) "Do not write there," said a boy who saw a man scratching with his diamond ring on a window pane. "Why not?" asked the other. "Because you cannot rub it out," said the boy. No, you cannot rub out the past in the future.

b. Destiny is distinct, just, irrevocable; and verdict separates honor from dishonor, fellowship from banishment, blessing from cursing, Kingdom of Heaven from everlasting fire, God the Father from devil and his angels.

c. If it be asked how we can reconcile verses 41, 46 with earlier phrase, "Come, ye blessed of my Father" (v. 34), we must remember that correct conception of fatherhood involves not only parental love, but righteous government and true discipline; all the more, then, must Divine Fatherhood invariably mean not something soft, sentimental, or partial, but essential righteousness, justice, and truth, which are eternal (cf. 1 Pet. 1:17).

d. It may well be noted in this connection that only adjectives, aside from word "heavenly," our Lord ever connected with His term for God, "Father," were "holy" and "righteous" (John 17:11, 25); so that when man errs of his own deliberate choice God the Father cannot be indifferent, but must deal justly with one who is sinning against available light and grace.

e. This leads us to distinction made by our Lord between two judicial sentences here: to those on His right hand, words are "Come, ye blessed of my Father" (v. 34); to those on left, they are simply "Depart from me, ye cursed" (v. 41), omission in latter phrase indicating curse was solely of themselves.

f. There is further departure from strict parallelism in contrast between "the kingdom prepared for you" (v. 34) and "everlasting fire, prepared for the devil and his angels" (v. 41); and this is borne out in all of N.T. by ascribing to God work of grace for believer and associating doom for evil doers not with God, but with Satan and with willful sinners themselves (cf. Rom. 9:22, 23; Eph. 1:5-14; 2:1-3).

g. There is one parallel in original to be noted, however: adjectives in verse 46, translated "everlasting" and "eternal" are identical, qualifying both "punishment" and "life"; and if this word includes idea of character as well as that of duration (cf. John 3:15-17; 17:2, 3; Eph. 3:21), its use to describe separation from God as well as fellowship with Him is very solemn indeed.

Conclusion

This chapter, in setting forth by parable some of the principles of judgment, points to three of life's lost opportunities:

1. *The Lost Opportunity of Rejoicing* (vs. 1-13)

   a. It is possible to be so "foolish" — not necessarily wicked — as to forfeit our own joy in Christ and His in us by forgetting true spirituality cannot be borrowed from fellow Christians, nor even from our own feelings or past experience.

   b. It is possible to commit what has been called "the crime of the impromptu" when tested by crisis or emergency, through having courted danger of neglect and postponed decision until midnight of life overtakes us.

   c. Rather, we should seek, directly and daily, Holy Spirit's power, and be ready to receive it in simple trust to be used in faithful service; thus and only thus shall we enter into full joy of "marriage supper of the Lamb."

2. *The Lost Opportunity of Reward* (vs. 14-30)

   a. It is important to remember that each believer, without exception, has some ability, however small; and we may observe force of "every man" in Mark's parallel passage (Mark 13:34), and "every one of us" in Paul's phrase (Eph. 4:7).

   b. It is vital for "one-talent men" to avoid danger of thinking they can do nothing; for when one has not as great ability as he would like he is tempted to give up entirely, lose himself in crowd, and leave his work undone.

   c. Rather, our encouragement should be that most of world's work is done by average, ordinary men — "common people, because there are so many of them," to borrow well-known phrase; and, though responsibility may lie heavily on some of us, equally impressive will be reward of hearing our Lord's words, "Well done, good and faithful servant" — faithful because good, and both because "full of faith."

3. *The Lost Opportunity of Realization* (vs. 31-46)

   a. It is interesting to note how many things God has "prepared" for His people, e.g.: "the kingdom" (v. 34); "the marriage feast" (22:4, A.S.V.); and "for them that love him . . . the deep things of God" (1 Cor. 2:9, 10), and "good works . . . that we should walk in them" (Eph. 2:10, A.S.V.).

   b. Wherever soul looks it finds God's wisdom and love exercised on its behalf; in past, atoning sacrifice has been prepared (cf. Heb. 10:5, Rev. 13:8), and in future "a city" (Heb. 11:16).

   c. If only His people are faithful they will realize and rejoice in His great goodness laid up for them that fear Him and wrought for them that trust in Him (cf. Ps. 31:19); let us therefore respond by exclaiming, "O how great is thy goodness!" — in all experiences of life since our Lord is with us in loving ministry every hour — and hear Him say to us —

> *My child, be faithful!*
> *Is the work small? This I require of thee,*
> *Do it with all thy heart as unto Me.*
>
> *My child, be faithful!*
> *Great is thy task? My grace will suffice thee,*
> *In well-doing weary not, co-labor with Me.*

Thus, as we look back over the whole of this great Olivet discourse, we see, on the one hand, the dangers to which God's people will be subjected, and yet, on the other hand, the assurance that is theirs of protection, peace, and eventual triumph. To those who watch and wait, the personal appearing of the Lord will be a remarkable and welcome contrast to this present age. As in winter we look longingly for spring, and hail every sign of its approach, so we are bidden to live now in eager expectation of our glorious future. While we avoid the folly of those who fix dates, we are also to be wise enough to keep our eyes set on the Master and trace each possible indication of His approach. Then, faithful in spirit, in service and in sympathy, we shall know what it is to be among those whom our Lord twice described as "blessed" (24:46, 25:34).

50

"OIL IN THEIR VESSELS"—A WORD STUDY

Matthew 25:4

T HE USE of oil, the oil of the olive, of course, was very common indeed in the East in Bible times, as it still is; hence the frequency of its figurative use and spiritual application in Scripture. It was used not only for lighting (as here) and for other domestic needs, but also for applying to the person, or anointing. This is inherent in the meaning of the words "Christ" and "Christians," of "the Anointed One" and His "anointed ones"; and it refers especially to the Holy Spirit's presence, preparation, and power (cf. Isa. 61:1, Acts 4:27, 10:38, 2 Cor. 1:21, 1 John 2:20, 27). The use of oil is associated in Scripture specifically with six types of persons and with the Tabernacle worship:

I. The Leper (Lev. 14:15-29)

1. *For Consecration.* After cleansing by blood came oil of consecration on right ear, hand, and foot, token that atonement had been made and every power belonged to God.

2. *For Authorization.* Remaining oil was poured on head (v. 29), and then leper went back restored by authority of priest and empowered to resume fellowship.

   N.B. Consider this in light of leprosy of sin. Are we healed, consecrated, and authorized by the Holy Spirit of God?

II. The Sick (Jas. 5:13-15)

1. *For Restoration.* Curative powers of olive oil are well known and widely used even today (cf. Luke 10:34).

2. *For Holiness.* There is spiritual as well as etymological connection between salvation (for soul) and health (for body); and the Holy Spirit is "healing" Spirit.

   N.B. Are we "whole," which also means "healed"? Why should we remain spiritual invalids?

III. The Prophet (Isa. 61:1, 1 John 2:20-27)

1. *For Illumination.* This is in order to understand will of God.
2. *For Revelation.* This is so as to declare will of God to others.
   N.B. We all may be "prophets" in N.T. sense of "teacher" (cf. 1 Cor. 14:1, 3), and our testimony must ever be in power of Spirit.

IV. The Priest (Exod. 40:12-15, Lev. 8:30, Rev. 1:6)

1. *For Sacrifice.* This was in order to approach God; but now, since Calvary, we as "an holy priesthood" (1 Pet. 2:5) may offer our bodies (Rom. 12:1, 1 John 3:16), our praise (Heb. 13:15), and our substance (Phil. 4:18, Heb. 13:16).
2. *For Intercession.* This was in order that man might be represented before God; and we all, as "a royal priesthood" (1 Pet. 3:9), may have similar privilege on behalf of others (Eph. 6:18, Col. 4:12, 1 Tim. 2:1-4).
   N.B. Our priesthood as believers can never be properly exercised except in power of Holy Ghost (Jude 20).

V. The Tabernacle (Exod. 30:25, 26)

1. *For the Abode of God.* As of old Moses was told to use oil for perpetual light in tabernacle (Exod. 27:20, 21), so we as "temple of God" (1 Cor. 3:16, 17) are to have Spirit of God dwelling always in us (Eph. 2:21, 22).
2. *For the Worship of God.* Within our souls there is to be true recognition of and reverence for Him (Gen. 28:18, Exod. 40:9-11, John 4:23, 24).
   N.B. There can be no such attitude without the Holy Spirit of God (John 4:23, 24).

VI. The King (2 Sam. 5:3)

1. *For Victory.* Anointing with oil was associated with deliverance and leadership (1 Sam. 10:1, Isa. 10:27).
2. *For Government.* But it was principally used to denote one who was set apart for rulership (1 Sam. 16:13, 2 Sam. 23:1).
   N.B. If we would "reign in life" (Rom. 5:17) here and now, let us seek anointing of Spirit's power as "kings . . . unto God" (Rev. 1:6).

VII. The Guest (Luke 7:46)

1. *For Provision.* Oil was important feature of Eastern meal (Ps. 23:5, 104:14, 15).
2. *For Gladness.* It was always associated with joyous communion (Ps. 45:7, Heb. 1:9).
   N.B. Our life of fellowship as guests of God (Rev. 3:20-22) is possible only in the Holy Ghost.

Conclusion

1. Let us see, therefore, the need of the Holy Spirit in every part of our lives (Acts 2:1-4):
   a. As an illuminant — light, fire;
   b. As a lubricant — tongues unloosed; and —
   c. As a motive power — wind energizing.
2. Let us seek, therefore, power of Holy Spirit on every day of our lives (Ps. 92: 10):
   a. "Fresh oil" sought in daily prayer;
   b. "Fresh oil" received in daily trust; and —
   c. "Fresh oil" utilized in daily service.

51

THE SERVICE OF GOD*

Matthew 25:21

THE MOTTO of the Prince of Wales is a short but very expressive one — *"Ich dien."* — "I serve." At first sight it may seem a strange motto for a prince but, when it is remembered that in our Christian era no royal personage is more truly royal than when he is giving himself to the service of his people, it follows that a true prince is a servant and that, conversely, the true servant can be a very prince among men. Indeed, the highest positions on earth are here demeaned by being occupied for the good of others; on the contrary, they are dignified by such public service, and may be glorified by being consecrated to the service of God as well.

A greater than any earthly royalty, even "the prince of life" (Acts 3:15), had a name and a character similar in import. In the Old Testament He is called the Servant of Jehovah, and in the New He is said to have taken the form of a servant, and to have come not to be ministered unto, but to minister; and if we are to follow in His steps, the motto of each may well be "I serve." It will not, therefore, be amiss if we use our text in order to emphasize some of the characteristics of true Christian service, although the interpretation of the parable in which these words appear does not lie within the scope of our present intent. They form the commendation of the lord in the story to the servant who had rightly used what had been entrusted to him: "Well done, good and faithful servant: thou hast been faithful over a few things, I will make thee ruler over many things: enter thou into the joy of thy lord." From this meditation may we both perceive and know what things we ought to do, and also have grace and power faithfully to fulfill the same.

---

*Ed. Note: This was a sermon apparently preached first in 1885, when the preacher's age was twenty-four.

I. The Relationship — "Well done, thou . . . servant"

As his master gives him name of servant, so our Lord names us; therefore let us consider —

1. *The Ground of the Relationship*

Just as name of servant can be given only when certain conditions are fulfilled, no man cannot be servant of God except on acceptance of His stipulations. While in certain sense "all are thy servants" (Ps. 119:91), there is peculiarly Christian sense in which believers "being made free from sin . . . become servants to God" (Rom. 6:22). There are two qualifications:

a. *Salvation from Sin*

(1) This is primary and all-important (cf. Luke 1:72); it is vital and absolutely necessary to true service (cf. Rom. 6:16).

(2) No service can be for God unless we have renounced all other service, notably that of sin (cf. John 8:34, 1 Thess. 1:9); and we must definitely experience conversion and forgiveness (cf. Heb. 9:14).

(3) Further, we are unable to do anything for God until, first, we receive things Christ has done for us and, second, we have power of Holy Spirit in our souls.

(4) Let us beware of even attempting to work for God while we are living for Satan and sin; no service will be accepted until there first has been surrender and enlistment.

(5) Power is needed for God's work and that He alone can give; true service is heart service, and for that, heart must be changed.

(6) Enslaved in bondage of sin, we must have redemption before we can serve God; dead in trespasses and sins, we must have new life before we can do God's will.

(7) Since all things are of God, all energies and weapons we need from conversion to consummation come from above, being work of His own grace and power.

Resulting from this salvation as necessary consequence comes next qualification for this relationship:

b. *Separation to God*

(1) Redeemed by precious blood of Christ, we are no longer our own, but His; and therefore there must be entire separation from everything contrary to His will.

(2) We cannot serve God unless we are unmistakably under His sole guidance and care, free from all other claims; just as when Pharaoh wanted Israelites to stay in Egypt and sacrifice there God's message to him was, "Let my people go, that they may serve me" (Exod. 7:16).

(3) Egypt was no place for God's people, and so now: life must be wholly, all, only, and always for Christ our Lord.

(4) We often fulfill first qualification but fail lamentably in this one; content with mere deliverance from sin, we are satisfied to "take it easy," troubling little, if any, about God's full purpose concerning us.

(5) Surely it is obvious that in such high and holy service there must be no compromise with unbelief or wrongdoing, but entire separation from all sins that beset us; there must be no looking back to Sodom, no hankering after Egypt, but instead a looking straight off to Jesus and going with Him, definitely, persistently, and triumphantly.

We are the Lord's; then let us gladly tender
Our souls to Him in deeds, not simply words;
Let heart and tongue and life combine to render
No doubtful witness that we are the Lord's.

These, then, are the two great grounds of relationship with God, without which we cannot be His true servants nor do any real good to His cause. Now let us note —

2. *The Character of the Relationship*

What about service itself? Surely true service of God consists of —

a. *Love to the Master*

(1) Here is unique feature of Christian work — it is service of love; it is not drudgery nor servitude under hard taskmaster.

(2) Hebrew slave at certain time was entitled to free himself, but if he did not wish to do so he would come and say, "I love my master, . . . I will not go out free" (Exod. 21:6); he then dedicated himself to his master for life.

(3) So it is with Christian — love of Christ to him constrains him to love and serve Christ, who has redeemed him from fate worse than human bondage; and so "by love" (Gal. 5:13) he serves and will not "go out free."

(4) But we are not only servants, but sons, adopted into God's own family, and because we are sons we serve, for there is no contradiction between spirit of sonship and spirit of obedience.

(5) We have but to think of our Lord Himself, who was "a Son, yet learned he obedience" (Heb. 5:8), and who declared to His disciples, "I am among you as he that serveth" (Luke 22:27); indeed, He laid down His life because of His Father's commandment, and how reverently He always approached Him.

(6) So our sonship and service will not clash; on the contrary, our oneness with Christ will give us His Spirit, so that His "service is perfect freedom."

(7) It is a great mistake to imagine God's service is compulsory on His part or galling in effect; no, compulsion is from us, we cannot help serving Him if we truly know and love Him.

(8) Through His great love towards us we find His yoke easy and His burden light, and in highest degree ennobling; so much so that we cry from fulness of heart, "I delight to do thy will, O my God" (Ps. 40:8).

b. *Loyalty to the Master*

(1) This is natural result of love; for true love is always manifested in loyal devotion towards its object.

(2) Genuine servant, like those of old, will measure his service by words of our Lord's mother: "Whatsoever he saith unto you, do it" (John 2:5); not one thing, but anything, everything — "whatsoever my lord the king shall appoint" (2 Sam. 15:15).

(3) Doubtless this is high standard, but nothing less will do, for God has bidden it and will enable for it; only let there be readiness on our part, and His power to be loyal will be ours.

II. The Requirement — "good and faithful"

Here emphasis is on servant, rather than on service, and these two words descriptive of his character are in sharp contrast with those used of unfaithful servant (v. 26): "good" — "wicked"; "faithful" — "slothful." There must be —

1. *Goodness*

a. This has to do with inward character and obviously comes first, for only good servant will be faithful; but, while we may distinguish between these two characteristics, it is almost impossible to separate them.

b. Every good servant of God lives according to God's standards, and one of these is to walk by faith; only by so doing can he acceptably do work of faith (cf. Isa. 29:13).

2. *Faithfulness*

a. This has to do with outward conduct; for good servant works only on lines of his master's will, getting to know it so that he may obey it.

b. He believes it is not enough to be engaged on a good work — he must do it according to his master's desires; for if he follows his own counsel, he is not really serving but directing.

c. We may ask God's blessing on our work, but first we ought to ask His will for it; and it is better to be occupied with small tasks in path of His choosing than to be doing great work in accordance with our own ideas.
   Illus.: We recognize this principle in daily life. We ask for glass of water — that is our wish; but our servant thinks he will do something better — he will gather a basketful of fine fruit and bring it. Will he be good servant of ours, doing us true service? No, he will be asked again for water for our thirst; and so must we keep in path of God's will.

d. The nearer we approach to fulfillment of God's will the simpler we shall find our duty to be, and the more freedom we shall find in which to do it; only let us surrender ourselves wholly to Christ and exercise our highest wisdom in learning His way in simple obedience.

e. Again, let us not wait for great occasions, but make every occasion great.

N.B. George Macdonald said: "Obedient love learnt by the meanest abigail [servant girl] will make of her an angel of ministration, such an one as he who came to Peter in prison, at whose touch the fetters fell from the limbs of an apostle."

Illus.: It is recorded of a certain great philosopher that his little daughter met his friend who, knowing her father was very learned, assumed he was teaching her something very deep and unique; so he asked her what she was learning from her famous father. Her answer was simple: "Obedience, sir!" What, indeed, are we in God's hand but children whose most important lesson is the same — obedience!

f. Further, even though we may not be called upon to do, but instead to endure, that, too, is obedience, and part of our faithfulness to God; and, as in war we are grateful for active fighting men but cannot win without those who stand steadily behind them, often under harrowing fire, to do more inconspicuous tasks, so those Christians whose lives have been darkened, whose hopes disappointed, may well be among bravest of brave in battle for God.

> *Who best*
> *Bear His mild yoke, they serve Him best. His state*
> *Is kingly: thousands at His bidding speed*
> *And post o'er land and ocean without rest;*
> *They also serve who only stand and wait.*
>
> JOHN MILTON

This leads us to the culminating phrases of our text, namely —

III. The Recompense — "ruler over many things . . . the joy of thy Lord."

Now we contemplate final scene in service of God, with task done, struggle past, victory won, and servant not only acknowl-

edged, but honored. Here, again, we have two results —
exaltation and entrance; and, as before, their connection is
very close, for one speaks of present promotion and other of
future felicity:

1. *The Privileges of Service*
    a. These are neither few nor small, for even now true servant
    of God may be much cheered and blessed by results of
    faithfulness; even now it is true that "if any man serve
    me, him will my Father honor" (John 12:26), and that
    "the king's favour is toward a wise servant" (Prov.
    14:35).
    b. Even now His "servants shall sing for joy of heart"
    (Isa. 65:14), and by taking His yoke upon us we find rest
    to our souls (cf. 11:29); above all, "it is enough for the
    disciple that he be as his master, and the servant as his
    lord" (10:25).
    c. Since these are but a few of present privileges of Christ's
    servants, let no one think there is no immediate joy in
    Christ's service; and besides all this there is honor of
    added responsibility here and now — for "many things,"
    after "few things" have been faithfully attended to.

2. *The Prospects of Service*
    a. Chief among these is to be in very presence of our Lord
    (cf. John 12:26); here is great difference between earthly
    service and heavenly — Master and servants together,
    indeed, servants no longer, but friends (cf. John 15:15).
    b. Not only with Christ, but like Christ (cf. 1 John 3:2),
    for in all their future service "they shall see his face"
    (Rev. 22:3, 4); they will work and gaze, gaze and work,
    and shall be changed into His likeness, with His Name, i.e.,
    His claim of ownership, in their foreheads.
    c. Yet again, another prospect is rejoicing with Him, ac-
    cording to concluding words of our text; into all joy
    filling His heart when He sees everyone redeemed and
    safe for whom He died, we shall enter (cf. Isa. 53:11).
    d. More yet — there will be perfect service of our Lord
    (cf. Rev. 7:15) for, though in one sense "they rest from
    their labors" (Rev. 14:13), in another "they rest not"
    (Rev. 4:8); "from their labors" — yes, from toil un-

congenial or disproportioned to capacity, from distrac-traction, discouragement, disappointment.

e. But rest from vigorous, co-operative service to full extent of individual powers — never; for in this fellowship of labor, severed from all that is wearisome or unwelcome, will be found deepest and most perfect repose.

f. And, yet once more — eternal rule with Christ will crown their efforts, for His servants "shall reign for ever and ever" (Rev. 22:5; cf. 2 Tim. 2:12, Rev. 5:10, 20:6).

These, then, are some of the privileges and prospects of service for Christ.

Conclusion

In considering the final outcome of all these grand and glorious truths, and in order to turn them into living realities, let us ask an age-old question: "Who then is willing to consecrate his service this day unto the Lord?" (1 Chron. 29:5):

1. *There are Some Serving Sin and Satan.*

   They will get their "wages . . . death" (Rom. 6:23); but there is a nobler Master and a greater service whose "gift . . . is eternal life through Jesus Christ our Lord."

2. *There Are Some Halting Between Two Opinions.*

   But this cannot continue indefinitely; there must be decision, for they "cannot serve God and mammon" (cf. 6:24).

3. *There Are Some Serving Christ in a Limited Way.*

   But He wants all their powers, for they came from Him and belong to Him; and so these must be "ready to do whatsoever" their Lord and King "shall appoint" (2 Sam. 15:15).

4. *There Are Some Serving Christ with All Their Might.*

   They are as conscious as any human being can be that they are His alone, and yet when they keep yielding more and more to Him they will find how much more there is that He can use; and so each will be "a workman that needeth not to be ashamed" (2 Tim. 2:15).

Yes, the sublime potentialities of a life fully dedicated to God cannot be measured; but let each of us make the words of his lips, the desire of his heart, and the endeavor of his whole existence to be —

In full and glad surrender I give myself to Thee,
O Son of God who lovest me, I will be Thine alone,
Thine utterly, Thine only, Thine evermore to be;
And all I am and all I have forevermore Thine own.

52

THE CROWNING WORK BEGUN

Matthew 26:1-46

"The Old, Old Story" of the cross, as Matthew tells it, begins here. Familiar though it be, there is a perennial freshness in everything connected with that "wondrous cross"; and each of the accounts found in the closing chapters of the Gospels has its own special characteristics traceable by careful study. Let us look at this section of Matthew's version as illustrating various aspects of the Person of our Lord Jesus Christ on the eve of His crucifixion and of the cross itself as He drew nearer and nearer to it.

It is customary to speak of our Lord as Prophet, Priest, and King; and His work as King and Prophet has already been illustrated throughout this Gospel. In particular, His prophetic office, that of representing God to man, was historically closed in the discourse just considered. The teaching of the three-years' ministry with all its wonderful revelation of Divine truth was at an end, and now the third aspect of the Master's life and work is to be seen. It has to do with the coming sacrifice of Himself, and is twofold in the very nature of it. Instead of the Prophet, we see foreshadowed the Priest, the one who represents man to God. This was begun as He hung between heaven and earth, although He did not exercise His permanent priestly function until His ascension (cf. Heb. 8:4), after which it became "unchangeable," or "untransmissible" (Heb. 7:24, Greek). Further, instead of the Teacher, we begin to sense more immediately the Victim and in this record of His passion we see our Lord almost wholly in this capacity of suffering Saviour. The prominence given to His sufferings by all the Evangelists is particularly noteworthy.

This can most easily be seen by a comparison of the full content of the record for the last week of Christ on earth, compared with what actually are selected, even fragmentary, accounts of His ministry during the three eventful years that preceded it.

I. The Cross in the Foreknowledge of Christ (vs. 1-5)

1. *The Prediction* (vs 1. 2)

   a. As we have already seen, in more than one passage of this Gospel and of others Christ's death was no afterthought either with the Father or with Himself; and nothing is more striking than our Lord's calm, quiet consciousness of what was about to take place.

   b. As Peter on day of Pentecost told Jews, Christ had been delivered up "by the determinate counsel and foreknowledge of God" (Acts 2:23); and, without any interference with freedom of His enemies or any reduction of their guilt, fact and circumstances of His death were fully known to God and as fully arranged.

   c. We have very striking illustration of this in fact that our Lord was crucified at Passover, contrary to intention or desire of Jews; so that now, having completed His teaching (v. 1), He announced again His approaching betrayal and suffering in connection with this feast, two days thence (v. 2).

2. *The Plot* (vs. 3-5)

   a. Ever since conflicts with Jesus in Temple leaders had been planning to do away with Him, their hostility intensified by defeat in debate; at this time, therefore, they gathered in high priest's palace for purpose of consulting how they might take Him and kill Him (vs. 3, 4).

   b. They had hitherto found it impossible to arrest Him in any properly authorized, legal way, so they were compelled to resort to "subtilty" (v. 4) and plan to take Him by craft, hoping to have Him put to death on charge of sedition against Roman power.

   c. Feast refers to entire festival, covering one week, for which occasion Jerusalem was crowded; and since Jesus was still popular with people it was thought dangerous to deal with Him during that period, lest they rise in opposition and give Pontius Pilate, Roman governor at

time, excuse for avoiding treatment Jewish leaders contemplated for Christ (v. 5).

d. But "Christ our passover . . . sacrificed for us" (1 Cor.
5:7) had to be slain at feast; and, though He had several
times in past escaped from His enemies (e.g., John 10:
39), He quite evidently determined now to be taken
at very time when they especially desired not to take Him
(cf. vs. 18, 46, 53-56).

e. Thus leaders, though unwilling to do so then, were
compelled to apprehend Him, thereby fulfilling prophecies
concerning Him as true Passover (cf. vs. 26-28; also
John 1:29, 36; Exod. 12:11); and story goes on to
tell how marvellously God's designs were accomplished
and those of Jews set at nought.

II. The Cross in the Action of Mary (vs. 6-16)

How, then, did it come to pass, humanly speaking, that our Lord
was taken and crucified at very time when rulers were opposed
to it? It seems to have been due to revelation by Him in
incident now before us, which, placed here by both Matthew and
Mark out of its chronological position (cf. John 12:1 — "six
days before the passover"), shows reason why plans of council
failed to this extent, and why Christ was apprehended at beginning of feast and not after it closed.

1. *The Hospitality of Simon* (v. 6)

a. At Bethany, two miles east of Jerusalem, where Christ
was lodging at this time (cf. 21:17, 18, Mark 11:11,
12, 19), lived man known as "Simon the leper."

b. Nothing else is known of him, though we may conjecture
he had been healed by Christ of his leprosy; and it is
probable this occasion, "as he sat at meat," was feast given
in gratitude.

2. *The Devotion of Mary* (v. 7)

a. "There came a woman" and, though not named here,
she certainly was Mary of Bethany, sister of Lazarus and
Martha, for clearly story is to be identified with that in
John's Gospel, where her name is given (John 12:3)
and her identity noted on another occasion (John 11:2);
but it is to be equally clearly distinguished from incident
in Luke 7:36-50.

b. Anointing with oil was associated all through O.T. with consecration of persons and things (cf. i.e., Gen. 28:18, Lev. 8:12, 30; 1 Sam. 10:1);* and Moses was commanded also to make and use "an oil of holy ointment" (Exod. 30:22-33) containing precious spices for anointing.

c. Among Jews, anointing of head was distinction conferred upon guest of honor (cf. Luke 7:46 with Ps. 23:5), and anointing of body last token of respect to dead (cf. v. 12, Mark 16:1, Luke 23:56); so that Christ graciously accepted Mary's gift of "an alabaster cruse of exceeding precious ointment" (A.S.V.).

d. Mark speaks of her breaking this beautiful flask, doubtless to pour out ointment lavishly upon His head (Mark 14:3); and John says she anointed His feet and wiped them with her hair (John 12:3).

3. *The Indignation of the Disciples* (vs. 8, 9)

a. In mere money value Mary's offering was notable for, comparing 20:2 and Mark 14:5, it seems to have been equal to laborer's wage for perhaps an entire year, or even more; and very probably it represented Mary's savings of many years.

b. Disciples murmured at "this waste" (v. 8), with John revealing Judas Iscariot was their spokesman (John 12:4, 5); and he was evidently instigator of their indignation, though there was no real desire on his part to give money to poor (v. 9; cf. John 12:6).

4. *The Vindication by the Lord* (vs. 10-13)

a. When Christ noticed this furtive, ungracious murmuring, He immediately urged disciples not to trouble Mary by slighting her splendid deed (v. 10); there is no waste in love and, as someone has helpfully remarked, while disciples were thinking only of expediency of gift, Christ had its moral significance in view.

b. Then He told them they could always help poor, but that, because of His own imminent departure through death, it was only on such an occasion as this that good could be done to Him (v. 11); and, His Divine insight having penetrated into real meaning of what Mary had

---

*See Study No. 50, p. 369.

done, He then revealed her act was symbolic, similar to Jewish custom of anointing body for burial (v. 12; cf. Mark 14:8, John 12:7), and she had actually performed sacred service by anointing His body as though it were already a corpse.

N.B. Scofield says: "Mary of Bethany, who alone of our Lord's disciples had comprehended His thrice-repeated announcement of His coming death and resurrection, invested the anointing with the deeper meaning of the preparation of His body for burying. Mary of Bethany was not among the women who went to the sepulchre with intent to embalm the body of Jesus."

c. Further than this, Christ declared, there would be permanent distinction for this devoted and discerning woman since, wherever "this gospel," good tidings of salvation through His death, would be proclaimed, this story would also be "told for a memorial to her" (v. 13), and we know today remarkable way in which these words have been fulfilled, e.g., inclusion of incident in three of four Gospels and special mention by John in connection with previous incident (John 11:2; cf. Luke 10:39, 42).

d. It is plain, then, from this story that His death was becoming more and more prominent in Christ's thought, coloring everything connected with these closing days; and it is also clear that Mary's action, full of glowing love and sympathy, showed Him that, in some measure at least, she realized burden that weighed upon His heart.

e. It is noteworthy, also, that Christ is here indebted to another, though in so many other instances others were indebted to Him; and this shows devotion of human heart is very dear to Him, so that we may believe, with due reverence, that our Lord hungers for man's love.

f. Certainly, when our motive is loving gratitude towards Him, sacrificial giving is our most priceless privilege; and because Mary had "done what she could" (Mark 14:8), viz., everything possible, her act was recognized, approved, and accepted by her beloved Master.

N.B. It should be noted that in Luke 7:36-50 we have another and quite different anointing for, although the two incidents have similarities, there are also distinct

differences. There is not the slightest evidence, inciden-
tally, that "woman in the city, which was a sinner,"
mentioned by Luke, was Mary Magdalene; while it is
also certain that modern efforts to identify Mary of
Bethany with Mary of Magdala have no basis at all.

5. *The Determination of Judas* (vs. 14-16)

   a. *The Occasion Seized* (vs. 14, 15)

   (1) These verses immediately follow interpolated story
   of Mary (cf. also Mark 14:10, 11); and thus it
   would seem it was indeed her faith and devotion
   that were used to bring about Divinely planned
   result — death of Passover Lamb at Passover time.

   (2) Having shown her realization of Christ's imminent
   suffering and formed her preparation for His burial,
   her lavish "waste" had aroused Judas to anger (cf.
   John 12:4, 5); and strong approval by his Master
   of Mary's act stirred yet further indignation in his
   self-seeking mind (cf. John 12:6) and thus hastened crisis.

   (3) Having begun seriously to yield to thought of
   betrayal, he formed his fateful decision; and, since
   it was necessary to make arrangement with Jewish
   authorities, he hurried off to bargain with those who
   were even then assembled in high priests' palace for
   consultation (v. 14; cf. vs. 3-5).

   (4) This infamous bargain was soon struck, for leaders
   were only too glad of so fine an opportunity of cap-
   turing their enemy (cf. Mark 14:11); and Luke adds
   what seems to be last consideration of effect upon
   multitude (cf. Luke 22:6).

   (5) Yet "thirty pieces of silver" (about $15.00) do not
   seem to be very much to pay or to receive (v. 15), although it is striking that this was amount of com-
   pensation for slave (cf. Exod. 21:32); and, prophetically, it was also amount at which Divine Shepherd
   was valued by his followers (cf. Zech. 11:12).

   b. *The Opportunity Sought* (v. 16)

   (1) From moment covenant was executed Judas watched
   for chance to betray his Master; but it would be

well-nigh incredible, had we not this record, that so terrible a crime could even have entered his mind.

(2) Three years of fellowship counted for nothing; and baseness of this disciple's action stands out as most treacherous act of friend against friend that history records.

(3) Of sins that crucified Christ, that of Judas is generally regarded as unprecedented in enormity, unique in character, and exclusively his; and various theories have been advanced to account for him and to analyze his sin.

(4) Sober reflection may decide, however, that uniqueness of it lies rather in outward opportunity than in inward spirit, in form more than in fact; and so we may well go deeper and ask in relation to Judas, "What shall a man give in exchange for his soul?" (16:26).

(5) We shall find our answer, perhaps, in N.T. phrase about Judas and his "reward of iniquity" (Acts 1:8) and may well heed Paul's warning to Timothy about those who "will be rich" (1 Tim. 6:9, 10); for Judas committed common sin of avarice, or "the love of money";

   (a) He respected Christ — but he respected money more;

   (b) He was under obligation to Christ — but he felt bound to continue amassing as much money for himself as possible for, according to John, as manager of common purse for apostolic band, "he was a thief" (John 12:6);

   (c) He may not have wished to injure Christ (cf. 27:3, 4) — but he wished even less to miss his profit on transaction with Jewish leaders.

   N.B. According to John Ruskin: "We do great injury to Judas in thinking him wicked above all common wickedness. He was only a common money-lover and, like all money-lovers the world over, did not understand Christ, could not make out the worth of Him, or the meaning of Him. This is the money-lover's idea the world over; he doesn't hate Christ but can't understand Him, doesn't care for Him, sees no good in such benevolent business, makes his own little job out of it, come what will."

(6) It is necessary, however, to be quite clear here for, since money represents product of toil and medium of exchange for necessities of life, making or getting of it is worthy aim if done honestly and dispassionately; but only knaves and misers are money-lovers, for love is strong, personal term as distinct from mere liking or preference for material things.

(7) Avarice, or love of money, therefore, is centering of devotion on unworthy object and sacrificing of right things for wrong; e.g., laborer who does defective work for extra profit, merchant who adulterates food or medicine, employer who exploits workers, corporations that indulge in "cut-throat" competition.

(8) But further, since Judas undoubtedly shared undue aspirations to secular leadership and "delusions of grandeur" indulged in so mistakenly by Twelve, his main motive is usually thought to be combination of ambition and greed; and by this he was easily led into hypocrisy and then, through disappointment, into intense hostility towards all for which Jesus Christ stood.

(9) Judas was, of course, perfectly free in entering company of apostles, and all along was under no constraint to betray his Master nor, on other hand, to refrain from so doing; but problem of relationship between human freedom and Divine responsibility is certainly acute in case of Judas, although not essentially different from that which arises in lives of all of us.

Now we come face to face with the solemn closing scenes between our Lord and His disciples:

III. The Cross in the Passover and the Last Supper (vs. 17-30)

1. *Preparing the Passover* (vs. 17-19)

   a. Feast called Passover (cf. Exod. 12) had in Jewish usage become very elaborate; and on fourteenth of month

Nisan, first day of unleavened bread (v. 17), Jews put all leaven out of their houses (cf. Exod. 12:8).

b. Typifying sin (cf. 13:33; 1 Cor. 5:6-8), its absence indicated repentance, just as Passover itself symbolized faith in God's deliverance from bondage through Christ as Passover Lamb (cf. Lev. 23:5, 6 Mark 14:12, Luke 22:7-13); thus these two elements are seen to be inseparably essential to Christian life.

c. Then, when Christ's disciples wanted to know where they were to eat Passover together, two of them (cf. Mark 14:13), Peter and John (cf. Luke 22:8), were directed to house of one in city who must have been in some way a follower of Jesus, for term "The Master saith —" is used (v. 18); also, here, "large upper room" (Luke 22:12) was already partly prepared (cf. Mark 14:15).

d. Readiness with which this man was willing to allow use of his house indicates real devotion to our Lord; it was evidently sufficient for Master to express His desire and servant obeyed.

N.B. There is reason from history to assume that this same upper room was also scene of Pentecost (cf. Acts 1:13, 2:1), and it is likely to have been in house of John Mark's mother (cf. Acts 12:12); so that this unnamed man may well have been Mark himself or his father (cf. fuller detail in Mark 14:12-16 and also in Luke 22:7-13). It is striking that our Lord's directions to disciples should have been at once so exact and yet seemingly so careful to avoid householder's name, and this suggests there was need for caution at this juncture, or at least for seclusion from crowds. He would probably provide lamb (cf. Exod. 12:3-6), which Peter and John would present in Temple and slay in presence of Priest. Then would follow all other necessary preparations, though no details are given.

2. *Observing the Passover* (vs. 20-25)

a. When all requirements had been fulfilled our Lord and His disciples celebrated this Jewish feast in usual manner of that day; although original order had been to partake standing, with staff in hand (cf. Exod. 12:11), this had been modified in course of time (v. 20).

b. Passover meal would occupy long while, for rites observed were numerous and consisted of several stages, connected by sips of wine; but at some moment during celebration came Christ's startling announcement that one of those seated at table with Him would actually betray Him (v. 21).

c. This led to great sorrow on part of each disciple, and question asked, one by one, "Is it I?" (v. 22), seems to indicate not only surprise and instinctive denial, but also measure of self-distrust and distrust of each other (cf. Luke 22:23); and reply of Christ did not definitely identify Judas as betrayer, but referred as yet only to one who would dip his hand with him in dish, thereby indicating traitor in general terms without naming him (v. 23).

d. Perhaps this was last appeal in effort to lead Judas to repentance; and reference to O.T. is characteristic of this Jewish Gospel (v. 24; cf. Ps. 41:9), although it is John who quotes specific Scripture (cf. John 13:18).

e. At same time there was solemn warning of woe against betrayer, with deeply impressive statement that it would have been good for that man if he had never been born. *N.B.* It has been claimed it is possible that Christ meant it had been good for Himself if Judas had not been born. Plummer allows this rendering to be grammatically possible, as though to say it would have been happy thing for Jesus if there had been no Judas, and then adds: "But the context is wholly against this interpretation. Our Lord is pointing out the miserable condition of the traitor, not His own sufferings. The common rendering gives the right meaning." Indeed, if one looks at entire verse, whether in English or in Greek, one sees how difficult it would be to distinguish between two uses of phrase "that man," making one refer to Judas and other to our Lord; for two clauses in which they appear seem to be strict parallels. As another commentator has stated, "There is a tragic emphasis in repetition of 'that man'."

f. It is astonishing to find that at length even Judas could dare to follow example of his companions and ask same question, "Is it I?" (v. 25), although, of course, he knew what had taken place between himself and chief priests (vs. 14, 15); and thus he maintains his hypocrisy to end, and only now does our Lord make significant reply by usual formula of affirmation, "Thou hast said" (cf. 26:64).

3. *Superseding the Passover* (vs. 26-30)

a. *The Transition*

(1) On that solemn night of Paschal supper, old dispensation of Judaism actually came to an end; and Jesus Christ as true Paschal Lamb, typified for so long by Passover, took its place in anticipation (cf. John 1:29, 1 Cor. 5:7, 1 Pet. 1:18-20).

(2) Now there was to be new Feast, embodying essence of Christianity even as Passover had embodied essence of Judaism; and they have one great characteristic in common — they typify deliverance, or salvation (cf. 1:21, Exod. 2:27), the one from temporal bondage, the other from spiritual.

N.B. There is, however, no evidence to support theory that the Lord's Supper was to take place of Jewish sacrifices; on contrary, it cannot be too strongly emphasized it was Christ Himself, not Supper, that was to be anti type of Passover Lamb. Cf. clear teaching of Epistle to Hebrews that all old sacrifices found their fulfillment in Him (chaps. 9 and 10).

(3) In this ordinance instituted by Christ, therefore, we see transition from law to gospel, and there is very much about it we might profitably contemplate; but it is possible here only to dwell upon some of its outstanding features in light of this particular chapter.*

b. *The Institution*

(1) It is not certain, but quite probable, that Judas withdrew before actual partaking of the Lord's Supper (cf. Luke 22:21, John 13:30); and its institution was solemn but also very simple in character.

(2) Our Lord took Passover bread and broke it, and cup of Passover wine, and gave them to His disciples with new meaning, viz., as outward and visible ex-

---

*For a more general discussion of the Lord's Supper, see the following Study, No. 53, p. 400.

pressions of His coming work of sacrifice for them
and of their fellowship with Him; bread was to be
symbol of His body given (v. 26; cf. Luke 22:19),
and cup symbol of His "blood of the new testament
[or covenant] which is poured out for many" (vs.
27, 28; cf. A.S.V.; also Luke 22:20).

N.B. Greek word translated "poured out" has Divine, not human usage, and usually indicates God's
bountiful munificence (cf. Acts 2:17, 18, 33; 10:45);
see also Hebrew of Lev. 8:15, where blood was
"poured out" on sin offering only, others being
merely sprinkled; and note Isa. 53:12 and Mal.
3:10. But, *contra,* see Rev. 16, where vials of God's
wrath are also "poured out."

(3) Passover having fulfilled its purpose, true Paschal
Lamb was about to be slain; and new Feast was to
express same truth, only spiritually instead of tem-
porally.

(4) It is impressive to note, as has often been stressed,
that Christianity is unique among religious systems in
commemorating death of its Founder by means of
feast; for, while world rejoices with feasting over
births of great men and dates of great discoveries,
victories, or other accomplishments, it usually thinks
of death with sorrow and regret and never with joy
and satisfaction.

(5) Also, Christianity actually concentrates such thought
and devotion on One whom world regarded as male-
factor or, at very least, failure; and no other religion
has ever done this.

(6) It is clear this Feast, which was to be observed in
remembrance of our Lord, was intended to be permanent (cf. 1 Cor. 11:26); and today it is celebrated
as reverently and faithfully as ever, because it is
more than remembrance, it is also expression of
covenant, solemn agreement ratified by blood.

N.B. Our Lord used word "remembrance" (cf. Luke
22:19), not "memorial"; i.e., meaning is subjective
as distinct from objective, emphasizing act of mind
recalling, rather than exterior object that reminds.
These two words in Greek are always carefully dis-

tinguished (cf. use of latter in this very chapter, v. 13).

(7) Covenants in olden times were entered into by eating and drinking in company; and the Lord's Supper is at once expression of our union and communion with Him, opportunity of fellowship with each other, and wonderful prophecy of future.

(8) Thus there followed Christ's anticipation of this glorious future when He and His disciples would have renewal of fellowship (v. 29); and His words seem to suggest at once symbolism of joy and solemnity of thought that He would be unable to have such fellowship with them again until He met them in His Father's Kingdom.

(9) After singing hymn, probably one of psalms of praise, they left upper room (cf. John 14:31b), never to meet again in exactly the same way (cf. Luke 24:36-45); and Matthew adds "they went out into the mount of Olives" (v. 30).

N.B. It is suggestive that, though there is no record of our Lord actually praying with His disciples, only of praying alone in their presence or nearby (cf. vs. 36ff., Luke 11:1), He did offer praise with them. Explanation doubtless is He had no sins to confess, and confession is so prominent a part of human prayer, as in model He gave His disciples (cf. 6:12), but is not necessarily involved in praise. This uniqueness in prayer is, of course, striking testimony to our Lord's unique Person and to His Deity, while His oneness with men in praise to the Father reminds us of His essential humanity.

IV. The Cross in the Garden of Gethmane (vs. 31-46)

1. *On the Way to Gethsemane* (vs. 31-35)

   a. *Prediction and Promise* (vs. 31, 32)

   (1) Our Lord now had some solemn words, both of warning and of comfort, for His disciples; and it is sad beyond measure that even then Peter and rest had no conception as to what would so soon happen.

   (2) As they were going out of city, Christ foretold

what His sufferings would mean to disciples; they would cause Him, their own Master, to be offense, or snare, to them (v. 31).

(3) Then He quoted prediction from prophecy of old (Zech. 13:7), but notwithstanding announced fulfillment of this He gave them wonderful promise; after His resurrection, which they seem to have totally ignored ever since incident recorded in 16:21 (cf. also 17:23), He would go before them into Galilee (v. 32).

(4) His word must be fulfilled, His character vindicated, and His work accepted; and yet risen Christ was to be living, present reality in Galilee, His earthly home, scene of much of His ministry of teaching and healing.

(5) Here He would gather His followers together once more (cf. 28:7, 16, 1 Cor. 15:6); and perhaps there is allusion here to closing words of prediction (cf. Zech. 13:9).

b. *Protest and Plainness* (vs. 33-35)

(1) Then Peter, once more with characteristic impulsiveness, asserts categorically that, though all others should be upset by what would happen, he himself would "never be offended" (v. 33); whereupon Christ told him with great frankness that, so far from this being true, he would do worse, deny his Master not once, not twice, but three times, on that same night (v. 34).

(2) This prediction was met by protestation that, even though death itself should be involved, denial of Christ would not occur, and this statement was made by rest of disciples also (v. 35); and yet within very short time, before dawn of next day, Peter was to deny he ever was associated with Christ or even knew Him (cf. vs. 69-75).

(3) We can but marvel at how little any of these men knew weakness of their own hearts or strength of powers of evil that would so soon be arrayed against them; but at same time we must confess our own ignorance in comparable situations.

2. *In the Garden of Gethsemane* (vs. 36-46)

   a. *Christ Agonizing* (vs. 36-39)

     (1) Story of Gethsemane has no parallel in record of our Lord's life and calls for deepest reverence in presence of profound mystery into which it is hardly possible to enter; notwithstanding this, we must try to apprehend, if only dimly, that which in its completeness is beyond our comprehension (vs. 36, 37).

     (2) When our Lord told Peter, James, and John, "My soul is exceeding sorrowful, even unto death" (v. 38), we may be sure He referred to something far beyond mere physical pain; and many writers have thought our Lord in Gethsemane did indeed shrink, in His perfect, sinless human nature, from deep significance of awful cross before Him.

     (3) Yet, in view of way in which He had hitherto steadfastly set His face in that direction (cf. Luke 9:51; see also Isa. 50:7), it is surely perplexing to imagine His shrinking at last moment; would it not, therefore, be more natural to consider Gethsemane as scene of terrible conflict with Satan, seeking to overwhelm Christ and actually to prevent Divinely planned death on cross?

     (4) There are also differences of opinion as to what our Lord meant by "this cup" (vs. 39, 42), some thinking it was cup of His Father's will as expressed in death for man's redemption; but others think it was cup of premature death in Garden, with our Lord fearing He would be overcome and not able to reach cross.

     (5) Record does seem to hint His overpowering agony was due to this fear of not accomplishing man's redemption (cf. v. 41, Luke 22:43, 44); and for this reason His prayer for cup to pass from Him was surely earnest request to be delivered from death in Garden and to be strengthened physically in order to reach cross set before Him.

     (6) Certainly if Scriptures were to be fulfilled, Christ had to die, but it would be on cross (cf. Ps. 22),

not in Garden; and later, looking back at His passion, we read of our Lord offering "prayers and supplications with strong crying and tears unto him that was able to save him from death," and being heard, as original has it, "by reason of his reverent submission" (Heb. 5:7, Greek).

(7) He had determined to go forward towards cross, but from outset, in wilderness (4:1-11), then in person of Peter (16:22, 23), and now surely in Gethsemane, Satan tried desperately to turn Him aside and prevent His accomplishment of redemptive purpose of God; hence it would seem Christ felt need to lift up His heart in agonizing prayer to His Father to be saved from this premature death, and He was heard (cf. v. 45).

b. *Christ Alone* (vs. 40-46)

(1) Being perfect man as well as very God, our Lord in His agony expressed intense desire for human sympathy (vs. 38, 40, 41; cf. Mark 14:37); but comradeship of these three most intimate disciples that Christ had so naturally craved failed Him at this crisis (vs. 43, 45).

(2) In supreme loneliness of situation He maintained His close fellowship with His Father (vs. 36, 39, 42, 44); and it was only when agony was over and victory won that He called three disciples, arousing them from sleep because of what was about to happen (v. 46).

(3) It is indeed sad to realize that, after all their protestations of faithfulness and loyalty, not one of these men could spare even "one hour" (v. 40) for vigil with his Master; yet, if tempted to deplore their conduct, let us remember this was before Pentecost and we who live after coming of Holy Spirit are often guilty of far more serious failures.

> *Have Thou Thy way with me, O God,*
> *Although I beg my own;*
> *Heed not the body's noisy cry,*
> *But the soul's undertone.*

> *Have Thou Thy way with me, O God,*
> *Nor let me dread the proof*
> *Thine unguessed way may put me to*
> ~~*For Thy Divine behoof.*~~
>
> *Have Thou Thy way with me, O God,*
> *And O, my soul, take care*
> *To have thy daily attitude*
> *In keeping with thy prayer!*
>
> C. F. BATES

Conclusion

This solemn passage may be usefully summed up by considering its revelation of certain basic human attitudes towards our Lord Jesus Christ which, in turn, reveal some of His most gracious attributes:

1. *Conspiracy*

   a. Declaration of council, as its enmity to Jesus mounted, remarkably epitomizes common policy of sin; for, while determined to carry out its dastardly purposes, it is crafty enough to have some regard for appearances, for timing, and for its own advantage.

   b. But obedience of our Lord, as He approached moment of death, is complete, for as Israelite He must keep Passover feast in Jerusalem although it would result in His own capture; and, in fact, it was His very submission to Mosaic law that brought Him to His death.

   c. In full anticipation of His heavenly destiny, however, He not only is prepared for death but faces it clearly and resolutely, even though He is surrounded by most intense hostility.

2. *Consecration*

   a. We see in Mary of Bethany who, by both attitude and action, showed eagerness to put Christ first and to give Him everything she possessed, true spirit of Christian life; for, having received from Him salvation and blessing, we shall gladly yield ourselves to Him without reserve, to live with all our might for His service.

b. Wholehearted devotion is best way of showing true gratitude (cf. 2 Sam. 23:15-17); for love in Biblical sense is not mere feeling but genuine fact — not emotion only, but devotion — not aspiration, but action — not sentiment, but sacrifice.

c. We see this in God's love to us, invariably proved by giving (cf. John 3:16, Gal. 2:20, Eph. 5:25) and expressed also by such Pauline phrases as "riches," "abun-"dance," "fulness," "shed abroad" ("poured out," Greek of Rom. 5:5); and our love to Him must be in accordance —

That all our powers with all their might
In His sole glory may unite.

3. *Criticism*

a. This is seen in disciples, particularly Judas, whose remarks were altogether unworthy of occasion and did not even express his real sentiments; for under veil of philanthropy and frugality there was deep selfishness and deceit.

b. That which is sometimes called altruism, claiming to be opposed to individualism, is often in reality antagonistic to genuine devotion; it may appreciate good works done for men, but has no regard for honor due to God.

c. Here Christ's disapproval of disciples' spirit, together with His commendation of Mary's action, sanctioned important principle that our relation to Himself stands first; this is because only true basis of love to man is love to God (cf. 1 John 4:21).

4. *Covetousness*

a. It is Judas, of course, who eximplifies this; and perhaps most solemn thought of all is that man could be in close contact for nearly three years with Jesus Christ and yet make gain of Him, betraying Him at last for sake of mere money.

b. It shows how easy it is to ignore goodness and to resist even strong influence of beautiful life; and it reminds us who belong to Christ of importance of striving to keep Divine love flowing through us by maintaining delicate balance between getting and sharing, i.e., by proportionate giving (cf. 10:8).

c. In this connection, our Lord's words at table pronounced on Judas should be realized at their full force because, while there was special sense in which they were true only of traitor, they may also be said of every sinner in general; and, notwithstanding this fearfully solemn statement, we cannot but feel Christ's infinite pity was still at work, at last moment, not willing that even such a man as Judas should perish.

5. *Communion*

a. Since supreme purpose of God in Christ was to bring man into fellowship with Himself, the Lord's Supper may be said to typify and express whole gospel of His grace; and hymn writer has said, "No Gospel like this Feast," because it includes in its beautiful symbolism every truth connected with our Saviour:

(1) *Christ for Us — Commemoration.* Bread broken and wine poured tell of our Lord's sacrifice on our behalf (cf. 1 Cor. 10:16).

(2) *Christ in Us — Realization.* Bread eaten and wine taken speak of our participation in Christ and of Him as life of our souls (cf. Gal. 2:20).

(3) *Christ with Us — Manifestation.* We are all one in Him and this feast gives opportunity of demonstrating this oneness of life and love and His presence in our midst (cf. 1 Cor. 10:17).

(4) *Christ through us — Proclamation.* By this observance we bear witness to Him, confessing Him before others and telling what we think of His death (cf. 1 Cor. 11:26).

(5) *Christ Coming for Us — Anticipation.* We keep this feast "until that day" (v. 29) and "till he come" (1 Cor. 11:26), thereby linking cross and crown.

b. Thus the Lord's Supper includes retrospect, aspect, and prospect; past, present, and future all are there, with food for faith, love, and hope.

N.B. Canon A. E. Barnes-Lawrence speaks of five "looks" in observance of Holy Communion: (1) look back, to cross; (2) look up, to throne; (3) look in, to presence of Christ; (4) look around, to fellow Christians; and (5) look on, to second coming.

    c. Simple yet searching requirement for partaking is that we should remember our Master; and, as we cannot remember person whom we do not know, it is manifestly impossible for anyone to remember Christ in this holy Feast or to eat and drink it worthily who does not know Him personally as Saviour and Lord.

6. *Contradiction*

    a. Attitude of disciples after they and their Master had left city may be frankly characterized as contradictory and unworthy; but, unfortunately, it is also very human.

    b. Perhaps relief of each at not being betrayer had made them all boastful of not being offended or unfaithful; and doubtless many elements, both mental and physical, contributed to their falling asleep and failing their Master in His hour of need.

    c. How different are utterances of our Lord, showing His clear consciousness of what was about to take place and His remarkable calm and balance with which everything was anticipated and accepted; and all this shows clearly Divine secret of earthly life of Jesus Christ, whose fellowship with His Father was so real that none of these things moved Him except "godly fear" of not fulfilling Almighty's perfect will.

    d. His concern was for disciples, and even during His agony He cautioned them to "watch and pray" lest testing overcome not only flesh but spirit (v. 41); and when it was over He urged them to take their rest.

    e. It is significant that in N.T. there is never any object attached to verb "watch" — neither enemies, friends, Satan, nor selves; and this grammatic freedom from definite object may be intended to teach us to be concerned only with "looking unto Jesus" (Heb. 12:2), and with watching for His return (cf. 24:42, 25:13).

As we recall these attitudes to Christ and His related attributes, we note that there are indeed two "suppers" in this passage. One, John tells us, "they made him" (John 12:2). Have we a feast to make Him? If we have but a little He will as gladly accept and use that as though we had marvellous powers, rich possessions, and unlimited opportunities. But before we can make Him a supper we must accept the one He has made for us, the supper typifying salvation (cf. Luke 14:16-24) and symbolized in turn by the Lord's Supper. To this He invites us, saying, "Come, for all things are now ready!" (Luke 14:17) Indeed, "blessed are they which are called unto the marriage supper of the Lamb!" (Rev. 19:9).

53

THE LORD'S SUPPER*

Matthew 26:26-29
1 Corinthians 10:16-21
1 Corinthians 11:20-34

I T IS indeed deplorable that the Lord's Supper, an ordinance intended to emphasize Christian love, trust, and fellowship, should have become the occasion of some of the most acute differences of opinion among the followers of Christ. In a larger area of Christian doctrine it has been said that we have allowed three material elements to cause our most serious spiritual divisions — bread, wine, and water, the third of these referring, of course, to baptism with the well-known differences of interpretation as to its mode and even as to its very significance. This must not prevent us, however, from seeking to know clearly and exactly what the New Testament teaches about the meaning and purpose of the Holy Communion; in fact, it makes such a return to sources all the more essential. These are but few in number, for there are only five passages which deal with the meaning of the ordinance, and three of these are parallel records of the original institution. Mark's account (cf. Mark 14:22-26) is very like Matthew's, the differences probably being due to the individual purposes of the writers. Although Luke's account (cf. Luke 22:14-20) resembles in format those in the other two Synoptic Gospels, it is more like the remaining two passages (in 1 Cor. 10 and 11), due doubtless to Luke's close association with St. Paul, their author, whose writings, of course, were chronologically the earliest of all. We may note that the passages

---

*For a much fuller treatment of this subject see the author's volume entitled *A Sacrament of Our Redemption,* chapters 2-5, now out of print.

in Acts that mention the Lord's Supper simply refer to its observance, e.g., Acts 2:42, where it is listed as part of a fourfold means
of maintaining adherence to the apostolic Church (cf. also Acts
20:7, 11).

I. The Institution (26:20-29)

1. *The Occasion* (vs. 20-25)

    a. It is important to keep this clearly in mind because it
sheds light on purpose of new ordinance; it was occasion
of Jewish Passover supper.

    b. Time was eve of Christ's death and ushering in of new
dispensation; thus the Lord's Supper has intimate connection with both.

2. *The Delineation* (vs. 26-29)

    a. Every word and act should be carefully studied: "bread"
used for food was fitting symbol of spiritual things; and
verb "blessed," having no object in original, refers to
blessing or praising God as Giver of bread (v. 26),
just as thanksgiving is associated with "cup" (v. 27), full
phrase being, as Westcott says, "to bless God for the
thing."

    b. Words "This is my body" should be read in connection
with Luke's fuller version — "which is given for you"
(Luke 22:19), and are thus seen to refer specifically to
Christ's sacrifice on our behalf; so also "cup" is similarly
mentioned in connection with His "blood . . . which is
shed for many for the remission of sins" (v. 27).

    c. Thus separation of "bread" from "cup" applies one to
"body . . . given" and other to "blood . . . shed," act and
fact, respectively, of His sacrificial death; and verb is in
both connections "is," not "becomes," i.e., elements were
not about to be changed but were simply metaphorical representation (cf. 1 Cor. 10:17, Rev. 19:8; see also "I am,"
in John 8:12, 9:5, 14:6, 15:1).

    d. Our Lord is not referring to actual literal identity, whether
physical or spiritual; He is speaking to His disciples'
faith and spiritual perception, with view to what was still
in future, next day specifically, even though to us it is
in long-ago past.

    e. Word "testament" (v. 28) means covenant and refers

back to O.T. prophecy of redemption (cf. Jer. 31:31-34; see also Heb. 8:8 to 9:18); word always describes God's solemn pledge and promise on man's behalf, to be accepted through faith.

f. Here, as in all records, phrase "the fruit of the vine" (v. 29) is employed; and, in fact, word "wine" is not found in connection with the Lord's Supper, though it seems natural to suppose beverage used was common wine of country that appeared on Passover table.

g. It is uncertain, however, whether this was fermented or unfermented, but certainly Jews in their Passover feast today do not limit themselves to latter; it would follow, therefore, that matter of wine at Holy Communion is one for individual liberty and sense of what is appropriate.

II. The Exposition (1 Cor. 10:16-21, 11:20-34)

In these two passages St. Paul corrects errors and gives warnings concerning conduct of the Lord's Supper in Church at Corinth:

1. *Correction* (1 Cor. 10:16-21, 11:20 22)

He stresses need for considering certain aspects:

a. *Communion* (10:16, 17)

(1) "The cup of blessing" means cup over which thanksgiving is offered to God (cf. Matt. 26:26); and "communion" suggests fellowship.

(2) This feast is meant to imply our fellowship in sacrificial death of Christ (v. 16); and it also includes our union in His body (cf. 1 Cor. 12:27) as "one loaf" (Greek), and our consequent unity with other Christians (v. 17).

b. *Separation* (10:18-21)

(1) But it also means separation, of most definite sort: from "idols" (vs. 18, 19), which are nothing except for what they represent; and from "devils" or "demons" (vs. 20, 21), which are hideous reality behind representation.

(2) It goes without saying that if we have true fellowship with Christ and His people we must be separate from all that is wrong; and this includes not only

actual evil, but "all appearance of evil" (1 Thess. 5:22; cf. 2 John 9-11), not only wrongdoing, but also false doctrine.

c. *Veneration* (11:20-22)

(1) Christians at Corinth were evidently accustomed to community life based on religion and associated with meals in common; and they naturally continued good elements in these customs after their conversion.

(2) Abuses crept in, however, and their observance of the Lord's Supper was actually marked by irreverence (v. 20, Greek, "it is not possible to eat —"); by selfishness and excess (v. 21); and by desecration of holy things and disregard of poorer Christians (v. 22a); and for these disgraceful actions Paul certainly could not commend them (v. 22b).

(3) There was thus urgent reason for writing to point out abuses by reminding Corinthian Church of original institution by Christ; for best way to correct error is to re-state truth.

2. *Revelation* (1 Cor. 11:23-26)

a. The Lord's Supper was evidently important enough to warrant special revelation about it from Christ directly to Paul (vs. 23-25); and reference to betrayal (v. 23) is further emphasis on its solemnity, as though Apostle would say it was possible to betray his Lord in other ways than that chosen by Judas.

b. Then Paul adds two important truths as to meaning of this holy feast (v. 26):

(1) It is opportunity of proclaiming death of Christ to others — "shew" means "declare"; and —

(2) It is to be observed until the Lord comes again — "till he come."

3. *Exhortation* (1 Cor. 11:27-34)

a. First, Apostle Paul sought to guard his readers against unworthy behavior; they must not use the Lord's Supper for wrong ends or they would be actually guilty of profaning His death (v. 27).

b. Then he tried to lead them toward careful action; but

they must first test themselves as to whether they really understood meaning of ordinance (v. 28).

c. Next, Paul warned these people against Divine chastisement; for if they did not realize spiritual nature of the Lord's Supper they would bring trouble on themselves: moral judgment (v. 29); physical sickness and even death (v. 30); and risk of condemnation with worldly folk (vs. 31, 32).

d. Summing up, the Apostle urges them positively towards establishing orderly type of service (vs. 33, 34); and his words remind us afresh of simplicity of original institution of the Lord's Supper — in private house, at close of meal, and quite apart from any association with Temple or priesthood.

III. The Application

Foregoing study leads us to apply its principles to present-day conditions by raising some contemporary questions:

1. *Is the Lord's Supper a "Service," an "Act of Worship," a "Celebration," an "Administration"?*

   a. Strictly speaking, it was not originally a service as instituted; and, in view of many references to prayer and praise in N.T., and gatherings of people of God apart from Holy Communion, it does not seem Scriptural or true to describe it as "the one service instituted by our Lord."

   b. Again, term "highest act of worship," or "greatest act of worship," is ambiguous and, indeed, inaccurate; worship is worship wherever it is offered and, as it is attitude to God consisting of several elements or acts, such as praise, prayer, thanksgiving, adoration, each of which is essential, it is obviously impossible to describe any one act of worship as "highest" or "greatest."

   c. Further, only acts ordained by our Lord at this time were "take," "eat," "drink," "do," although He Himself set an example of "blessing" or "giving thanks"; but these acts imply, rather, receiving, appropriating, feasting, which are not in themselves acts of worship though, of course, they are indeed occasion and opportunity for precious times of worship.

d. Also, according to N.T., our Lord is brought before us in Holy Communion as crucified, i.e., His body is regarded as dead, and His blood as shed and therefore separated from His body; obviously, then, it is Christ crucified who is offered to our faith in the Lord's Supper, while our *worship* of Him is not as crucified, but as alive for evermore, ascended in fullness and glory of His Godhead (cf. Luke 24:52a), and not partially, in dead body and shed blood of His manhood.

e. Then, if words "celebration" and "administration" are carefully considered, they suggest two different but complementary aspects of the Lord's Supper; thus, celebration seems to look towards God, as we "honor" Him, praising Him for what Calvary means, while administration looks towards man, as sacred symbols of our Lord's atonement are, literally, "served to" us.

2. *Is the Lord's Supper "Our Richest Means of Grace?"*

a. Such a phrase does not seem true to N.T. concept of grace, for amid hundreds of references to it there is no single one that connects it with the Lord's Supper; however, we believe grace is amply received in due and faithful use of this feast.

   N.B. Bishop Drury of Ripon put it thus: "There is nothing in Scripture . . . to lead us to suppose that in Holy Communion we receive a special kind of grace, which can be received then and then alone. But there is every reason to believe, humbly yet trustfully, that times of Holy Communion are times of special opportunity, when we may with clearer faith, and fuller hope, and warmer love, embrace God, as He offers Himself in holy symbol to be embraced by us, and when we may receive 'without measure' the blessed benefits of Christ's body and blood."

b. The Lord's Supper is not only feast to be enjoyed by Christian soul, for he can "feed on Him" in his "heart by faith" altogether apart from ordinance, as Cranmer long ago taught concerning John 6; and Paul's words in 1 Cor. 5:7 are particularly applicable here — literally: "Christ our passover was sacrificed for us; therefore let us keep a continual feast."

c. That which believers do spiritually and in symbol at

stated intervals, in special places, they may do spiritually, apart from symbols, "at all times and in all places"; they can indeed "feed on" Christ in their hearts "by faith with thanksgiving."

3. *Is the Lord's Supper a Sacrifice, or a Sacrament?*

a. It is not, according to all we know from N.T., in itself a sacrifice; but it does symbolize and pledge our Lord's sacrifice "of himself once offered" on Calvary, and it gives opportunity for His people's own spiritual sacrifices, notably, "this our sacrifice of prayer and thanksgiving" — His expiation, our sanctification.

b. It is, however, a sacrament, which may be said to include outward sign, inward grace, and due use of elements; there is no magic, no altar, but a meal on a table.
N.B. Bishop Beveridge wrote: "There is a vast difference between a sacrament and a sacrifice, for in a sacrament God offereth something to man, but in a sacrifice man offereth something to God. What is offered in a sacrifice is wholly or in part destroyed, but what is offered in a sacrament still remaineth. And there being so great a difference betwixt the one and the other, if it be a sacrament it is not a sacrifice, and if it be a sacrifice it is not a sacrament, it being impossible that it should be both a sacrament and a sacrifice too."

c. We believe with all our hearts in presence of our Lord at time of Holy Communion, but not that His presence is *in* sacramental elements; those who hold this latter view fail to realize one of primary principles of spiritual religion, and lose sight of fundamental element of that worship which is "in spirit and in truth" (John 4:24) as opposed to worship connected with localized presence of Deity (cf. 2:11, 8:2, etc.).

4. *Is the Lord's Supper To Be Observed at Any Particular Time of the Day, Month, or Year?*

a. Our Lord's example is best understood and carried out in spirit, not in letter; for Christianity is religion of principles, not of rules.

b. So long as we observe the Lord's Supper in true spirit in which our Lord intended it, it seems perfectly immaterial whether we receive it in morning or in evening, before or after meals, kneeling or sitting; for slavish adherence to any letter of law is always unwise and un-scriptural.

N.B. As to use of leavened or unleavened bread, it is noteworthy that latter was not known in Church till eleventh and twelfth centuries, and is now almost solely associated with churches that use wafer rather than actual bread, or Jewish matzos.

c. There is danger that constant use of this "means of grace" may obscure its real meaning and detract from spiritual blessing, so that some are inclined to feel less frequent administrations with more thorough preparation are spiritually more profitable; conversely, longer intervals may tend to suggest too much of a spectacle with over-crowding, etc.; but this is one matter on which, naturally, everyone should be "fully persuaded in his own mind" (Rom. 14:5).

d. Spiritual preparation is absolutely essential for due reception of the Lord's Supper, and if our enlightened reason and conscience find weekly administrations not conducive to this, one should not attend so frequently. On other hand, if they are most spiritually helpful, no one should criticize, for in both cases great requirement is Christian liberty (cf. 1 Cor. 14:26b).

e. It would seem to very many earnest believers that Easter Sunday is one of most appropriate times for this holy feast; not only does it always fall on first day of week when, as we know, disciples gathered together "to break bread" (Acts 20:7), but it is altogether fitting that on this particular Lord's Day we commemorate Him who once was dead, but is now alive for evermore.

f. While it is true we remember our Lord's death in His Supper, we must never forget Good Friday and Easter Day are inseparable; for that death would be spiritually invalid and inefficacious without His resurrection, since one held permanently in grave could not be Divine.

Conclusion

As Jewish children were expected to inquire and to be told about the meaning of the Passover (cf. Exod. 12:26, 27), so it is vital for us to know and transmit the true meaning of the Lord's Supper, especially because of the many and unfortunate differences that appear among Christian people on this subject. The simplest and safest way is to keep as close as possible to Scripture; and the words "Do this in remembrance of me," engraved on so many Communion tables, practically sum up all that the Holy Feast means:

1. *The Person*

   a. The Lord's Supper calls attention to a Person — "me," One who claims remembrance, having now set aside national observance of Passover; and Christianity rests on Christ Himself as Divine Lord, true man, Holy One, crucified, risen, ascended, and coming Saviour.

   b. The Lord's Supper does indeed direct our thoughts to Him; and in all these capacities and attributes He calls on us to remember Him.

2. *The Remembrance*

   a. To keep Him "in remembrance" means first to know Him, and then to think of Him, to trust Him, to obey Him, to imitate Him, to value Him, to confess Him, and to expect Him.

   b. Thus we recall Him as historic Personage, accept Him as Saviour, appreciate Him as Friend, proclaim Him to others by lip and life, and anticipate His return.

3. *The Ordinance*

   a. The Lord's Supper enables us to do this by giving us something tangible to help our hearts and minds — "This do"; broken bread representing His body sacrificed is also symbol of food for soul, bringing eternal life, just as was lamb at Passover, while wine symbolizing His blood poured out for our salvation tells of forgiveness.

   b. But breaking and pouring is not enough; there must be appropriation, Christ's death being accepted personally by faith on part of each participant.

   c. Eating and drinking together with others expresses unity, love, and fellowship, including spiritual relationship not only to God, but to our fellow Christians; while wine is further symbol of "the joy of the Lord," telling of what Christ is to His own.

Thus the Lord's Supper, as has been said, expresses "the totality of salvation" and is at once simple, searching, and satisfying. It speaks of Jesus Christ in His threefold aspect, Prophet, Priest, and King — in the past, in the present, and in the future. It proclaims to us at once union, communion and, finally, reunion, all of which have a blessed application to Him and to one another in Him. It is only for the friends of Christ and illustrates His atonement for us, His life in us, His presence among us, and His promise to come again for us. In all these blessed aspects it appeals to intellect, heart, conscience, and soul; and well may we render unto God the Father "most hearty thanks for the innumerable benefits procured unto us by the same."

54

THE CROWNING WORK CONTINUED

Matthew 26:47-75

THE CLOSING portion of this chapter and the whole of the next reveal more of those basic human attitudes towards our Lord Jesus Christ by which, in turn, some of His greatest attributes, human and Divine, are revealed to us in all their beauty and righteousness, pathos and glory.

I. The Betrayal (vs. 47-56)

1. *The Dissembler* (vs. 47-50)

   a. With strength derived from communion with His Father, our Lord was enabled to meet His foes; and while He was still speaking to arouse His disciples (cf. v. 46), traitor appeared, together with large armed crowd (v. 47).

   b. Surely there was never provocation like this; actually to be betrayed, and that to death, by intimate, trusted friend and, above all, with words "Hail, Master!" and with hypocritical kiss, would be incredible if we had not these records (vs. 48, 49).

   c. Yet our Lord's loving heart was still open towards Judas; and in gentleness He received that crowning insult and black treachery with perfect patience and exquisite calm.

   d. Even now He has no thought for Himself, but all consideration for Judas, making in pure pity one last appeal; calling him not "Traitor," but "Friend" (v. 50), Christ would remind him of old times and former associations.

   e. With mild inquiry, "Wherefore art thou come?" He would arouse Judas to sense of enormity of what he was doing; and so suffering love forgets itself in final effort to rescue its betrayer.

2. *The Defender* (vs. 51-54)

   a. John tells us it was actually Simon Peter who "drew his sword" (v. 51; cf. John 18:10, 11) in typically impulsive defense of his Master; and for this blundering zeal he was immediately rebuked (v. 52).
   N.B. Contradiction between these verses and Luke 22:36-38 has been suggested, but is only apparent, not real; here our Lord is rebuking Peter for mistakenly using sword in defense at that particular time, while in latter passage He spoke in symbolic language expressive of need for disciples to take care of themselves after He had left them. He reminded them that while He had been with them they had needed nothing (cf. Luke 22:35); but soon entirely new set of circumstances would arise, and then all due caution would be necessary.

   b. Then Christ declared that, so far from His enemies triumphing over Him, He could, if expedient, obtain hosts of angels to take His part (v. 53); but such a request of His Father would interfere with fulfillment of Scripture (v. 54).

3. *The Deserters* (vs. 55, 56)

   a. Our Lord then turned and rebuked crowd for coming out against Him armed as against robber, for He had been apparently at their mercy during His daily visits to Temple and they had not laid hold on Him (v. 55); doubtless this implied not only that they were now being incited against Him by their evil leaders (cf. Luke 22:53b), but also that not until now was appointed hour for which He had come (cf. John 12:27, 18:37).

   b. Christ then repeated His declaration that everything was happening in fulfillment of Scriptures (v. 56a); and at this moment, when His disciples saw Him not merely taken, but actually agreeing to His capture, they all "forsook him and fled" (v. 56b).

c. It was easy to boast presumptuously when no danger threatened (cf. v. 35); it was hard to stand their ground when surrounded by bitter hostility; and this was where Christ's followers failed miserably then, and where they too often fail today.

II. The Trial (vs. 57-68)

This was threefold — Jewish, Roman, Herodian; and the Jewish trial had three stages: a preparatory examination before Annas, the real high priest deposed by the Romans (cf. Luke 3:2, John 18:13); then an examination during the night before Caiaphas, his son-in-law and Roman official appointee (cf. John 18:19-24), who, though hostile to Jesus, had earlier prophesied His death and its meaning (cf. John 11:49-52, 18:14); and, finally, the formal examination, in the morning, before both Caiaphas and the council, described in this passage:

1. *Jesus Defamed* (vs. 57-66)

a. Immediately upon His capture, our Lord was taken to house of high priest (v. 57; cf. John 18:13, 24); for Jewish leaders, having already decided case among themselves, wanted only pretense of legal hearing.

b. Meanwhile, Peter arrested his flight and returned to city also; and even though he "followed him afar off into the high priest's palace" (v. 58), it was better than not following Him at all.

c. It was at first futile effort to obtain credible false witnesses against Jesus (vs. 59, 60a); but at last two men came who twisted and misconstrued Christ's words about raising up Temple (vs. 60b, 61; cf. John 2:18-22).

d. When high priest appealed to Jesus to defend Himself (v. 62) he obtained no answer (v. 63a), because our Lord, declining to recognize good faith of judge or competency of tribunal, could not but maintain silence in face of such patently false testimony.

N.B. This is first of Christ's three recorded silences before His judges: (1) Before high priest He was silent in face of prejudice; (2) before Pilate He was silent in face of worldliness (27:14; cf. John 19:9); (3) before Herod He was silent in face of curiosity (Luke 23:8, 9). Truly, "as a sheep before her shearers is dumb, so he openeth not his mouth" (Isa. 53:7).

e. Yet, when high priest put Him upon His oath as to whether He were Messiah and Son of God (v. 63b), Christ replied with customary form of definite affirmation, "Thou hast said"; and then He made remarkable claim to participation in Divine glory and power (v. 64).

f. This statement was deemed sufficient proof so that charge of blasphemy was made by high priest (v. 65); and verdict of death was immediately pronounced (v. 66).

g. It is both striking and tragic that this Man, acknowledged to be world's greatest Teacher and to be flawless in character and in conduct, should be rejected and condemned to die not on any such testimony as that given by false witnesses, but for His own assertion in reply to an appeal on His oath that He was Son of God, Deity's veritable Representative on earth.

h. As accused prisoner He would say nothing, but as Judge and King He had much to say; and this claim to Divine position and authority constituted not only prime reason for His death, but also essential feature of His redemptive purpose.

N.B. Gospels can never be understood without continual recognition of fact that it is Christ's Deity that makes Him Saviour of mankind. Only One both God and man could save us, and it was this great claim, and not primarily His claim to Messiahship, that made Jews hate Him and put Him to death (cf. Luke 22:70, 71, John 19:7). This Son of God and Son of man is still foundation-stone of Holy Spirit's work, convincing of sin for very same reason, i.e., that men refuse to believe in Jesus Christ as Divine Saviour (cf. John 16:8-10).

2. *Jesus Derided* (vs. 67, 68)

a. Verdict was immediately followed by inflictions of atrocious indignities on part of servants and others (v. 67; cf. Mark 14:65) in contemptible opposition to Christ; just as Roman governor and his soldiers were to jest at His kingly office (cf. 27:27-31, 37, 42), so these Jews now derided His prophetic office (v. 68).

b. This outburst of savagery in absence of any wrong done is testimony to low morals of men who, like animals, are ready to trample on fallen; for rude natures have rude ways of showing their rudeness.

c. These same men had been afraid as they arrested Him because they knew His power; but now they thought He was helpless because physically bound, and so took revenge for their fears.

d. Whatever our feelings of consternation let us ponder solemn yet blessed truth that all these sufferings and indignities were borne by our Lord not only on our behalf, but because of all our individual types of human depravity; and in return we must abhor any heartlessness that under guise of superior sensitiveness would hide its face from tortures that led to Calvary.

e. In all these sufferings of our Divine Saviour we have revelation of unutterable love, so that, beyond all else, our hearts should open themselves to reality of cross; there is absolutely nothing so glorious, so beautiful, or so precious.

III. The Denial (vs. 69-75)

At this point Matthew inserts the story of Peter's denial, as another of the sad accompaniments to the main account of our Lord's last hours on earth:

1. *The Circumstances*

This fearful lapse was at once climax of Peter's sins and shortcomings and, as we read later, occasion of new start; and actual circumstances appear to be associated with three stages of denial rather than with three distinct persons or groups:

a. First stage of denial took place at gate of palace and was marked by mere evasion (vs. 69, 70):

(1) All this time Peter was sitting outside in entrance amid doubtful, if not evil, surroundings; and he was cold and exhausted, perhaps shivering and sleepy.

(2) Woman's sharp eyes recognized him and blurted out, "Thou also wast with Jesus of Galilee" (v. 69); and result of his feelings of weakness and fear in

these surroundings was that he "denied before them all" (v. 70), cravenly pleading lack of comprehension.

(3) We may ask why Peter was here among his Master's enemies when John had gone in unmolested, evidently unafraid of being "known unto the high priest" (John 18:15); for we know we owe much to our surroundings and find duty difficult where no one agrees with us.

b. Second stage of denial occurred beside fire in court (cf. John 18:18, 25), and was strongly expressed by oath (vs. 71, 72); for in little while another maid saw him and charged him with being with Jesus, and this time Peter denied even knowing Him.

c. Third stage of denial was also in court of palace and resulted in intense anger (vs. 73, 74a), for same charge was made for third time; and Peter was denying yet again, with cursing and swearing, when cock crowing (v. 74b) according to his Master's prophecy (cf. v. 34) brought him to his senses, "and he went out and wept bitterly" (v. 75).

2. *The Causes*

a. Peter's acting thus is usually attributed to cowardice, and yet few men were so naturally courageous; others think he was too self-confident.

b. Predisposing causes of his fall probably were natural self-sufficiency due to consciousness of inner force coupled with consequent rashness; imperfect knowledge, since Christ's teaching about cross had been entirely ignored by Twelve; and spiritual negligence, sleeping in Gethsemane and following his Master afar off.

c. These conditions make Peter's denial intelligible, for, as has been said, "no one suddenly becomes base," and moral steps downward may exist in secret long previous to actual fall; but it is more likely main cause in this case lay deeper.

d. In face of his Master's apparent helplessness after all His manifestations of superhuman power, there may well have come thought he had been mistaken in thinking Jesus of Nazareth was Messiah; and in support of this statement we recall our Lord's words in upper room,

"Simon, Simon, . . . I have prayed for thee that thy faith fail not completely" (Luke 22:31, 32, Greek).

e. Not "thy courage," but "thy *faith*" — "faith in Me, thy Master, thy Messiah"; and when "the Lord turned, and looked upon Peter" (Luke 22:61), it all came back again.

f. Jesus was same still, and that look which must have been one of sorrow, yet one of love and mercy too, broke faithless disciple's heart and brought him back to loyalty that never again faltered; for our Lord, knowing immense value of this man, did not misunderstand his nature; there always would be fierce struggle around him because he was so well worth capture by enemy.

g. All disciples were self-confident (cf. v. 35) ; and yet they denied their Master by deed if not by word, through not following Him at this time at all, with exception of John, who tells us he "went in with Jesus into the palace of the high priest" because he "was known unto the high priest" (John 18:15), which may or may not have made his action easier.

h. But in upper room Christ had first used plural in warning Simon Peter — "Satan asked to have *you* (all) that he might sift *you* as wheat; but I made supplication for *thee,* that *thy* faith fail not" (Luke 22:31, 32, A.S.V.) ; and thus was Peter sifted so that, as our Lord told him further, when he was "converted" (lit., "turned back again"), he might establish his errant fellow disciples in their faith.

3. *The Contrast*

Peter's restoration was real, proved by immediate withdrawal and bitter sorrow; and contrast with case of Judas is striking, especially as similar terms for departure are used in original (cf. 27:3-5).

a. Judas lost his faith, cast away whatever love he may have had, and became traitor; Peter's lack of faith at crisis caused him to try to save himself but without harming Christ, which made him selfish, weak, even wicked, but not apostate.

b. Judas thought of consequence of his sin, and so became remorseful; Peter thought of sin itself, and so was led to repentance.

c. Satan tripped Peter; but he trapped Judas, causing him to "go to his own place" (Acts 1:25).

As we have seen, Peter's supreme lack seems to have been his loss of belief in his Master as Messiah and Son of God (cf. Luke 22:32); true faith in Christ would have enabled him to anticipate and comprehend the cross, which would have given him all needed strength and boldness.

Conclusion

In all of this tragic story we notice:

1. *Man's Guilt*

   a. The sin of distrust in Peter:
   A good man suddenly carried away by doubts gave one more pang to the heart of Christ, grieving more over His disciples' faults than over the willful sins of any others.

   b. The brutality of the high priest's servants:
   A coarse joy over the downfall of greatness was caused by the latent savagery of unregenerate human nature.

   c. The malice of Judas and the rulers:
   This was religious perjury, and a mockery of religion is the worst sin of which man is capable.

It is sad when the will fails to do good for lack of faith, as did Peter's; it is even sadder when ignorance is pleased to destroy good, as in the case of the servants; but it is saddest of all to see the good, and deliberately to reject it, as did the betrayer and the nation's leaders. But we know that all sin, of whatever kind or degree, hurts our Lord Jesus Christ, as He was grievously hurt at this time by Peter and all the rest.

2. *God's Grace*

   a. To Judas there was the last appeal of friendship, and to the malicious rulers there was a warning of judgment and its implied consequences to them.

   b. To the brutal servants there was shown patience, and later there was prayer for forgiveness towards all who had any part in that day's dreadful doings.

   c. To the weak Peter there was the look of recall, and later the message of reassurance (cf. Mark 16:7), the encounter of loving reunion (cf. Luke 24:34, 1 Cor. 15:5), and the final commission to service (cf. John 21:15-22, Acts 1:15, 2:14).

The message for all is found in Isa. 1:18: "Come, let us reason together, saith the Lord . . . ." It is easy to point the finger of scorn if we ourselves are not ready to run any risk for Christ. Like the disciples, we think ourselves strong when in reality we are morally and spiritually weak; in fact, our greatest danger is at our strongest, not at our weakest, point. But God's provision is perfect, and so we never need yield to temptation or fall into sin. The one thing needful is trust in our Master, for faith will give foresight and insight; and the one great secret of the retention of faith is abiding in Christ, keeping close to Him, not following afar off. Then faith will develop into experience, enabling us to remain "strong in the Lord and in the power of his might" (Eph. 6:10).

55

THE CROWNING WORK ACCOMPLISHED

Matthew 27:1-66

WE HAVE come now to the very heart not only of Matthew's Gospel, but of the New Testament itself, the death of our Lord Jesus Christ. It is important to dwell on it because, although it is so familiar, it has a great and constant value and a universal meaning that are enhanced by any amount of study. The way in which the details are emphasized and elaborated shows that Christ's death occupied a very prominent, indeed, a pre-eminent place in His purpose; for He came not so much to live, as do others, but to die. Among other considerations, as before noted, the notable brevity of the Gospel accounts of His three years' ministry contrasted with the remarkable detail in the events of His last week on earth shows the degree of importance to be placed on His death.

The cross was at once natural, unnatural, and supernatural: natural, because our Lord died as a human being; unnatural, because He was innocent and not guilty; and supernatural, because it was so important a part of the purpose of God, in providing pardon for the past, power for the present, and peace for the future. This threefold purpose is expressed very simply in one of the verses of a well-known children's hymn:

> *He died that we might be forgiven,*
> *He died to make us good,*
> *That we might go at last to heaven,*
> *Saved by His precious blood.*

MRS. C. F. ALEXANDER

Let us keep these solemn yet precious thoughts in mind as we study this all-important chapter:

I. Condemnation (vs. 1-10)

To casual onlooker that early morning, and to superficial readers of these verses today, there was but one condemnation carried out in high priest's court; yet it is possible to note no fewer than three verdicts pronounced:

1. *Christ Condemned* (vs. 1, 2)

   a. This was unthinkable result of our Lord's arraignment before representatives of His own people (v. 1); but their hostility to Him was being brought rapidly to a head.

   b. As we are later told, it was "for envy" (v. 18) they delivered him up to "Pilate the governor" (v. 2), i.e., feeling of strong resentment of advantages shown by another; for high priests and elders prized their positions of power and privilege as heads of governmental and ecclesiastical systems, and respected traditions of centuries were threatened by influence of Jesus on their people.

2. *Judas Condemned* (vs. 3-5)

   a. When Judas saw by this procession to Pilate that Christ was condemned to death, he was filled with fearful remorse; and, since this was caused by consideration of consequences of his deed, it would seem he had never fully anticipated such an outcome.

   b. Perhaps he had thought, as on former occasions, Jesus Christ would deliver Himself by some superhuman method from His enemies' power so that he, Judas, might as well profit from betraying his Master into it; and he also was probably filled with anguish as he recognized fulfillment of Christ's prediction concerning him, seeing in this a proof of fulfillment of other sayings that he had not chosen to consider seriously.

c. His remorse (v. 3) was not repentance, since latter is always due to consciousness of sins and their guilt quite apart from their results; and this mere change of attitude is in clear contrast with genuine penitence and sorrow of Peter.

d. It was too late for Judas to turn back or to change his course; and his fearful agony must have been intensified by callous indifference of chief priests and elders to whom he went to return his ill-gotten gain (v. 4).

e. As Bengel put it, those who are our companions in evil usually desert us after committal of that evil; and Judas thereupon went away from Temple precincts and committed suicide, his despair beyond any mitigation (v. 5). *N.B.* Question has often been raised in regard to reconciling of accounts of Judas' death (cf. Acts 1:18-20), but it is probable we are to understand he fell headlong after hanging himself from some tree branch or other height. Matthew deals with traitor's suicide and uses general term, while Luke's account in Acts is precise report "known unto all the dwellers of Jerusalem," and dealing with Divine visitation following that act of self-destruction. Thus, two accounts may be considered complementary, and not at all in contradiction of each other.

f. And so Judas gained nothing by his sin but, rather, lost everything, and this is always true of evil; at first, sin seems profitable, but though it asks for "water" and is given "milk," even "butter in a lordly dish" (Judg. 5:25), outcome is finally seen to be death, for, as has been well said, "the nails and the hammer are not far behind."

g. One thing is certain in regard to the devil — he always pays his servants their wages, and "the wages of sin is death" (Rom. 6:23); and so Judas by his suicide stands self-condemned.

3. *The Rulers Condemned* (vs. 6-10)

a. Chief priests took action at once though they had been unsympathetic to Judas; for their insistence upon mere ceremonialism impelled them to use money only to buy burying-ground for strangers, viz., Gentiles (vs. 6-8).

b. Their suggestion that it was not lawful to use money for any other purpose was terrible condemnation of their own hypocrisy in paying out this same "price of blood" (v. 6); and thus these Jewish leaders also stand self-condemned.

c. Reference to fulfillment of prophecy (vs. 9, 10) raises one of greatest difficulties in N.T. criticism, more particularly as Matthew quotes in these verses passage found fully neither in Jeremiah, which is cited in most versions, nor in Zechariah, which comes closer in wording (cf. Zech. 11:12, 13; Jer. 32:6-15).

d. Case in point is purchase of potter's field, though in Zechariah no mention is made of field, only of potter, while in Jeremiah there is full account of buying of field, but for another purpose, and with no mention of its belonging to potter; again, money mentioned in Jeremiah is seventeen shekels, while in Zechariah it is indeed "thirty pieces of silver."

e. It is possible here only to cite briefly several solutions suggested by various writers:

(1) Name of Jeremiah is said to be error of copyist, for some ancient versions give merely "the prophet"; this seems most likely since it would have been easy for some commentator to write in margin and for some later copyist to insert such a marginal note in text.

(2) Ryle and Bullinger express view that Matthew writes of that which was "spoken" by Jeremiah, not of anything found in his book, and this is illustrated by Paul's use of saying of Christ not found in Gospels (cf. Acts 20:35); but this suggestion may be classified as purely subjective criticism of evangelical type that may well be as unconvincing as are many of purely subjective and etymological emendations of higher criticism.

(3) Several authorities claim that since books in each division of O.T. canon were called by name of first author, and "former prophets" began at Joshua, in ancient order "latter prophets" began at Jeremiah; thus, entire section in which Zechariah was included would bear name of Jeremiah; against this, however, is fact that in present Hebrew canon first book of "latter prophets" is not Jeremiah, but Isaiah.

(4) It is not at all likely, of course, that Matthew was so ignorant of his Bible as to write Jeremiah when he should have written Zechariah; it may be suggested, therefore, that both quotations are embodied in Matthew but that only one author is mentioned, and that the more important.

N.B. Broadus, after enumerating several of above points with others, wisely adds: "If not quite content with any of these explanations, we had better leave the question as it stands, remembering how slight an unknown circumstance might solve it in a moment, and how many a once celebrated difficulty has been cleared up in the gradual progress of Biblical knowledge. . . . The two cases [in Matthew and Zechariah] are similar internally as well as in striking external points, and the Evangelist declares them to have a prophetic relation."

II. Interrogation (vs. 11-25)

According to Luke's account of trial of Christ, that part of it before Pilate was divided into two sessions, between which Luke places our Lord's appearance before Herod (cf. Luke 23:1, 25); and in both these sessions questions were asked, as at any hearing:

1. *Of the Defendant* (vs. 11-14)

   a. When He stood before this Roman governor He was immediately asked, "Art thou the King of the Jews?" (v. 11); and the circumstances leading up to this question are also seen elsewhere (cf. John 18:29-32).

   b. At once Christ answered affirming this fact, though to accusations of chief priests and elders in court He made no reply (v. 12), and this silence caused Pilate to ask Him second question, i.e., whether He had indeed heard number of things witnessed against Him (v. 13); and then we are told this prolonged silence was matter of great amazement to Pilate (cf. John 19:10).

c. But this second recorded silence of Christ before His accusers need not surprise us, His followers; for it was doubtless compounded of holy indignation, invincible love, and helpless grief which He had voluntarily permitted to take place of irresistible power (cf. 26:63, Luke 23:8, 9).

Then questions were asked —

2. *Of the Accusers* (vs. 15-25)

   a. *The Choice Offered* (vs. 15-20)

      (1) Pilate now stands revealed as advocate of expediency; for, though evidently convinced of Christ's innocence and told by conscience what his duty in case was (cf. Luke 23:13-22), he nevertheless proposed choice between Barabbas and Christ, asking his first question of leaders (vs. 15-17).

      (2) Barabbas, this notorious prisoner (cf. Mark 15:7, Luke 23:19, John 18:40), contrasted with Jesus Christ, shows extent to which both Pilate and Jews were prepared to go; and Matthew adds here that governor "knew that for envy they had delivered him" (v. 18) — envy based on hatred and fear, attitude towards innocence and righteousness that should never have been given official support.

      N.B. John McNeil once said: "Let me recommend to you Barabbas' theory of the Atonement! It is a good theory to preach on, to pray on, to live on, and to die on: he knew he was guilty as well as condemned; he knew Jesus Christ had done no sin; yet he knew Jesus Christ would be for him a true substitute; he knew he himself had done nothing to merit such interposition; and, finally, he knew Christ's death would be perfectly efficacious for him with the one who provided Him as substitute. Do you know any other theory that will stand these tests?"

      (3) At this moment, as Jews received Pilate's alternatives, strong warning came to him from his wife

(v. 19), fact mentioned by Matthew only, along with references to earlier visions of others bearing testimony to Christ (cf. 1:20; 2:12, 13, 19, 22); and she, in calling Jesus "that righteous man" (A.S.V.), strongly implies that Pilate by hurting Him might subject himself to some punishment.

(4) We do not know nature of dream which caused this woman so much trouble, but that it was sufficient to lead her to send this message shows deep impression made upon one who evidently knew something of Christ's mission and ministry; and it is tempting to think of her as one of those God-fearing, heathen persons who, without actually accepting Jewish religion, were earnestly seeking in their darkness after "the unknown God" (Acts 17:23).

(5) This reference to Christ is rightly called, like Plato's description of perfectly righteous man, "one of the most memorable, unconscious prophecies of heathenism"; and it is remarkable that this heathen woman should be only human being with courage enough to plead our Lord's cause, when even His own disciples had forsaken Him.

(6) This warning was second at this fateful time, first being from Judas to priests about "innocent blood" (cf. v. 4), and both proved entirely fruitless; indeed, members of council used delay caused by message to Pilate from his wife to stir up people in support of their determination to encompass Christ's death (v. 20).

b. *The Choice Made* (vs. 21-24)

(1) Leaders might once have been content with Roman governor's confirmation of their condemnation for blasphemy and then that Jesus should have been left to Jewish method of execution by stoning (cf. Lev. 24:16, John 10:33, 19:7); but they went further and, when Pilate interrogated them a second time (v. 21), and a third (v. 22), they demanded his active co-operation in executing their prisoner as an insurrectionist like Barabbas (cf. Mark 15:7), thus compelling Him to be crucified according to Roman custom.

(2) Perhaps this extreme to which they went was intended to blot out all thought of Christ from minds of people, involving Him, as they would think, in most utter disgrace; but Pilate asked them his fourth and final question, urging them to give positive reasons for crucifixion of their Prisoner (v. 23a).

(3) When they persisted in their demand (v. 23b), Pilate adopted Jewish custom of washing hands before them (cf. Deut. 21:1-9), to make it fully understood that he freed himself from this bloodguiltiness (v. 24); perhaps it was also endeavor to dissuade them from their terrible course but, as someone has said, Pilate "washed his hands before the multitude, but could not wash his heart."

(4) In washing his hands of fate of One he knew to be innocent, he himself certainly could not be "innocent of the blood of this just person," but rather was condemning himself with every word he uttered; and by delivering Jesus over to Jewish council Pilate was sacrificing his position as representative of Roman law and, in his weakness, becoming tool in hands of strong religious fanaticism (cf. Acts 3:13, 14).

(5) Thus, he affords still further proof of Christ's innocence, showing only fear of people was real cause of his action; for, while longing to do justice, he dared not do it at such a risk.

(6) It is unutterably sad to realize that, though Pilate strove his utmost up to certain point to free Jesus, beyond that he would not go, for fear of man; and one who hates evil enough to shun it at great cost, but not enough to face any loss on earth, is still its slave.

(7) No one is ever obliged to do wrong, although price of refusal may be very high; man who trusts in God will pay that price to remain true and just, drawing on Divine grace for necessary strength.

c. *The Choice Confirmed* (v. 25)

(1) Matthew is only Evangelist who records this act on part of people; but history of Jews ever since

has been continuing fulfillment of this their awful imprecation on themselves.

(2) These words were in nature of prayer, that their God might actually transfer, as it were, blood of their Prisoner from Pilate's hands to their own, and even to those of generations unborn; it was prayer offered in blind hatred of right and cross ignorance of extent of their sin.

(3) It was prayer answered from that day on (cf. 23:34, 35; Acts 5:28), notably in A.D. 70, and down through ages; "the Jew" has always stood for separation, persecution, punishment, as well as for God's eternal laws of retribution.

(4) But it is also prayer that may be transformed as Christians pray for Jewish people that, in Peter's later words, there may be to them "sanctification of the Spirit, unto obedience and sprinkling of the blood of Jesus Christ" (1 Pet. 1:2; cf. Heb. 9:14; 1 John 1:7) — of that same blood of which they spoke so callously and rashly to Pilate.

N.B. Collect for Good Friday in Book of Common Prayer refers appropriately to Jewish people because of part they took in crucifixion: "Have mercy upon all Jews, . . . and take from them all ignorance, hardness of heart, and contempt of Thy Word; and so fetch them home, blessed Lord, to Thy flock, that they may be saved among the remnant of the true Israelites, and be made one fold under one Shepherd, Jesus Christ our Lord." Such prayer for our Lord's brethren after flesh, in spirit of His own prayer in first of Last Words from cross (cf. Luke 23:34), returns great good for great evil and petitions for them three great boons — pardon, salvation, and fellowship with all God's people of every race and nation, punished, persecuted and separated no longer.

III. Humiliation (vs. 26-30)

1. *Scourging* (v. 26)

   a. Meanwhile, we see in Christ marvel of One who was "The mighty God" (Isa. 9:6) tried for His human life as common criminal; but, further, Christ "at Pilate's bar" brings crisis of Pilate's life, for he has to decide what to "do then with Jesus which is called Christ" (v. 22).

b. There is to be no escape for Prisoner, and yet that decision also fixes judge's own destiny; and Pontius Pilate still lives, awaiting day when he will be called before bar of Christ and meet as his Judge that Prisoner of long ago, as also all others who refuse Him as Saviour and Lord.

c. So now, having actually released Barabbas, insurrectionist, robber, and murderer, Pilate delivers Christ to be scourged by Roman method, much more severe than Jewish which was limited by Mosaic law (cf. Deut. 25:1-3); and yet scourging as punishment of One whom he knew to be innocent was, according to Luke (cf. Luke 23:16, 22), vain ˊattempt to satisfy accusers (cf. also John 19:1-13) and, it may be, to move them to something like compassion.

2. *Mocking* (vs. 27-30)

a. As our Lord leaves hand of Pilate, at end of His three-fold trial, it is impossible to avoid thinking of Pilate and Herod and Caiaphas in terms of their attitude of hostility to Christ and its varied but related causes:

  (1) Caiaphas, in common with other Jewish leaders, was moved by "envy" of Christ leading to intense hatred of Him;

  (2) Herod was consumed with frustrated curiosity about Christ leading to spiteful treatment of Him; and —

  (3) Pilate was activated by political ambition overcoming his natural admiration of Christ, and leading to cowardly surrender of Him so as to be known as "Caesar's friend" (John 19:12).

  N.B. It has been remarked more than once that no parent calls child by names such as these, nor after betrayer, Judas; instead, names of John, James, Peter, Mary, and others of most obscure Galileans who loved our Lord are chosen names of Christendom, for what men and women are to Christ, that they are unconsciously honored for by others.

b. Pilate's sentence was immediately carried out, though persons taking part in these awful events could not have imagined connection of their deeds with that which has become most far-reaching act in history of mankind; and these "soldiers of the governor" (v. 27), calling their "whole band" to join them, were but thoughtless creatures of circumstance, yet eternally guilty (cf. Rom. 1:20ff.).

c. When Christ was handed over to them, instead of leading Him away immediately, they took Him only as far as "common hall," or barracks of Praetorian guards (cf. A.S.V.) on duty at residence of governor; and, following example of crowd in hostility, they commenced to make sport of their Prisoner, continuing godless mockery begun earlier by Herod (cf. Luke 23:11).

d. Every detail is full of sacred meaning, part of all that Cross signified; so that even this mockery with robe and crown (vs. 28, 29) is remarkable in its symbolism.

e. Christ was indeed a King, though His Kingship was "not of this world" (John 18:36) and was ultimately to be won through suffering instead of being recognized as His right; while reed, first in His hand indicative of royal scepter and then in soldiers' hands as weapon (vs. 29, 30), was reminder of weakness of man (cf. 11:7) that became power of God (cf. Phil. 2:5-11).

IV. Crucifixion (vs. 31-61)

Now that we have reached the very center of the gospel, we shall, if we are truly Christ's, ponder again this moving story with brokenness of heart and melting of emotion. Only the Holy Spirit, who is the Author of the story, can enable us to enter into its spiritual meaning and teach us, on the one hand, its love and power and, on the other, the blackness of the sin that brought about all these sorrows.

1. *To the Cross* (vs. 31-34)

a. Executions took place outside city of Jerusalem (cf. Heb. 13:13), and our Lord was conducted thither not by Roman officials, but by ordinary soldiers (v. 31); and since, according to custom, criminals were obliged to carry their own crosses to place of execution, Christ evidently bore His for part of way (cf. John 19:17).

b. But en route to Golgotha they found man named Simon from Cyrene in African Libya, where many Jews were living (cf. Acts 2:10), and for remainder of way he was compelled to bear cross (v. 32); perhaps he was present for Passover and may already have been disciple, but some think, rather, that this experience was means of leading him to become one (cf. Mark 15:21, Acts 13:1, Rom. 16:13).

c. It is generally thought draught offered to Christ on arrival at Golgotha (vs. 33, 34) was intended to deaden intense pain of crucifixion, which was especially cruel method of death used by Romans for slaves and non-citizens, for death usually came slowly and torture was severe and lingering; but it was evidently for just this reason that our Lord refused to drink.

2. *On the Cross* (vs. 35-44)

a. *Suffering* (vs. 35-38)

(1) Victim was usually fastened to cross as it lay on ground, and then cross was raised and placed in hole prepared for it; but brevity with which Matthew describes our Lord's sufferings is very noticeable (v. 35a).

(2) Nothing is actually said about agonies of cross, although crucifixion was indeed most extreme form of torture devised at that time; apparently everything physical is transcended by thought of what cross is intended to mean, and yet we must never lose sight of this mind-picture of suffering Love incarnate, for our Substitute is none other than the great Creator Himself.

(3) Union of Divine and human natures in our blessed Lord is so close and so sacred that it is possible to attribute to one that which logically belongs only to other (cf. Acts 20:28, 1 Cor. 2:8); while, therefore, it is not strictly correct or fitting to say God died on cross, although John did write, "He laid down his life for us" (1 John 3:16) with nearest Greek antecedent "God" (v. 10), it is perfectly true to state categorically that He who died on Calvary was not only "Son of God" (1 John 3:8), but indeed God the Son.

N.B. Richard Hooker used notable phrase, "the infinite worth of the Son of God," meaning it was Divine nature in Christ that gave efficacy to His human death as our Redeemer.

(4) Between verses 34 and 35, it is well to read and ponder 2 Cor. 5:21 — "made . . . sin for us" — and Gal. 3:13 — "made a curse for us"; for deepest reason of all for our Lord's crucifixion was that "He was wounded for our transgressions; he was bruised for our iniquities" (Isa. 53:5).

N.B. As P. T. Forsyth accurately said, our keenest interest in Christ "made flesh" lies in His also having been "made sin."

(5) Another notable feature of Matthew's account is his inclusion of fulfillment of O.T. prophecies (cf. vs. 35, 46), although casting of lots for Christ's clothing (vs. 35, 36) is given in fuller detail by John (John 19:23, 24); and "his accusation" (v. 37) should be compared with words recorded in other Gospels (cf. Mark 15:26, Luke 23:38, John 19:19).

(6) Crosses in use at that time were of three kinds: one was like letter X, another almost like capital T, and third of shape most familiar to us, and in view of Matthew's statement that accusation was "set up over his head," last-named seems most likely; and it is probable Pilate's use of term "King of Jews" was for purpose of mocking Jewish leaders.

N.B. Critics have contended that variations in wording of superscription given by Matthew, Luke, and John prove inaccuracy of Gospels. But Arthur Gook points out that use of three languages, with well-known space differences in translations, may well be explanation. He believes Matthew, with his taxgatherer's knowledge of Latin, chronicled Roman-initiated inscription thus; Luke, who not only wrote in excellent Greek, but was traditionally Greek by birth, would describe inscription as it appeared in that language and mention it first (cf. Luke 23:38); and John, Galilean, better acquainted with

Aramaic dialect of Hebrew, seems to think in Hebrew though he writes in Greek, and probably reports inscription as in language of common people, mentioning it first (cf. John 19:19, 20). Gook sums up by saying: "We conclude, therefore, . . . that the Gospel records are entirely unimpeachable on this point; . . . taken together they give us the tablet as it left the hand of Pilate's secretary."

(7) Crucifixion was usual punishment in those days for robbery, but it is possible these "two thieves" (v. 38) were no common criminals; in fact, they may well have been fellow conspirators with Barabbas (cf. Mark 15:7, 27, 28), with that center cross intended for him.

N.B. Consider eternal centrality of that Figure hanging there "lifted up" (cf. John 3:14, 8:28, 29), surrounded not only by guilty thieves and rough soldiers as Barabbas would have been, but also by priests, rulers, and common people, friends and foes, angels and devils. "He was numbered with the transgressors" (Isa. 53:12) but, lifted up, He was commencing to draw all men to Himself, in one relationship or another (cf. John 12:32, 33).

b. *Reviling* (vs. 39-44)

(1) Passersby then took their part in indignities and taunted our Lord, misusing His words, as had false witnesses at trial (vs. 39, 40; cf. 26:61); they little dreamt that within three days He would indeed rebuild Temple that they had destroyed, "the temple of his body" (John 2:21).

(2) But meanwhile it was just because He was "the Son of God" (v. 40) that He would not and could not descend from cross; and, as crowd was thus blaspheming, members of council also mocked, using title similar to Pilate's for Him, "King of Israel" (vs. 41, 42) and implying they had obtained so complete a victory they were safe in promising belief in Him.

(3) Yet even their mockery includes wonderful twofold

testimony to Him — that "He saved others" (v. 42) and that "He trusted in God" (v. 43); nothing could be truer than these ironic comments, as also statement that "He said, I am the Son of God."

(4) Even two thieves at first "cast upon him the same reproach" (v. 44, A.S.V.); we know, however, that afterwards one of them was led to repentance and trust in Christ (cf. Luke 23:39-43).

(5) Reference to O.T. in this section (cf. v. 35) draws our attention to one of wonders of God's Word, namely, that it has given us not only historic account of Christ's crucifixion, but also prophetic description (see Ps. 22, Isa. 53); and it is intensely interesting to compare these three passages.

(6) In Isa. 53, inspiration singles out silence of Jehovah's Servant for special notice (Isa. 53:7); and here in Gospel history it is also His silence that impresses us and we realize the solemn reasons for it.

(7) But Ps. 22 reveals something of intensity of provocation He endured, giving us, about one thousand years before event, cross from within, from standpoint of our Saviour Himself; and we sense how that taunting crowd looked to Him, and how He felt under their "mocking scorn."

(8) In this Gospel record we have greatest horror of of history, assault of human malice on Deity by group after group: but in combined prophecy we learn Christ's sensitivity to it all and His tenderness of spirit with its infinite, because Divine, capacity for suffering; and yet, nevertheless, "he opened not his mouth" (Isa. 53:7).

(9) Son of God though He was, He suffered in silence because He had committed Himself and His cause to His Father, and therefore would make no attempt to defend Himself (cf. 1 Pet. 2:23, 4:19); yes, He was there as Sin-bearer and, as such, "bore our sins" (1 Pet. 2:24) and "carried our sorrows" (Isa. 53:4).

> *Himself He could not save,*
> *For justice must be done;*
> *Our sins' full weight must fall*
> *Upon the sinless One;*
> *For nothing less can God accept*
> *In payment of that fearful debt.*

3. *From the Cross* (vs. 45-50)

a. "The sixth hour" (v. 45) was twelve o'clock noon, when sun was highest and daylight at its brightest; and "darkness over all the land" cannot have been caused by ordinary eclipse, even one to which events were Divinely timed, because Passover was always celebrated at time of full moon when eclipse of sun is impossible with moon at opposite side of earth.

b. This darkness is therefore to be understood as supernatural phenomenon associated with death of Jesus Christ in uniquely close and yet mysterious manner; thus His crucifixion was accompanied by extraordinary occurrence in physical world.

c. After three hours of darkness and agony, our Lord's cry "with a loud voice" (v. 46)* proved it was not uttered because of physical exhaustion; and words He used from Ps. 22:1 are full of sacred mystery, indicating heavy weight of sin's burden He was bearing (cf. 2 Cor. 5:21), so that for that awful period of time God the Father could not even look upon Him (cf. Heb. 1:13).

d. In approaching this great mystery we must remember our Lord's perfect manhood as well as His Godhead; and surely, since, if we may thus phrase it, He was not availing Himself of latter, but living moment by moment as man, by faith in God the Father, we can well understand His anguish, indeed, His very human surprise at depth of loneliness of being "made sin" and "made a curse" (cf. 2 Cor. 5:21, Gal. 3:13).

e. On cross He was our Sin-bearer and, as such, was without conscious Divine fellowship, and so this was first and only time He used term "My God" instead of His usual "My Father"; and yet we must bear in mind He

---

*For more detailed treatment of this verse, see Study No. 57, p. 445.

as man had not lost His faith, for He does speak of God as "my" God.

f. As His cry is cited in original tongue of Ps. 22 we are able to appreciate mockery of "some of them that stood there" (v. 47), which rests upon similarity of sounds in Hebrew, followed by their translation into Greek; and yet there was very real difference between names "Eli" and "Elias," especially with former repeated, showing mistake was really willful and spiteful (cf. also v. 49).

g. Draught of vinegar, or sour wine (v. 48), was doubtless given in response to cry, "I thirst" (cf. John 19:28, 29); and, "when he had cried again with a loud voice" (v. 50) — His final word from cross (cf. Luke 23:46) — this handing over of His spirit to His heavenly "Father," shows His death was no ordinary one, result of weakness and pain, but instead an act of His own will after He could say of His mission, "It is finished" (John 19:30).

h. Thus Christ's human experience of sin and of death was in intimate connection with indescribable anguish of His perfect nature; and all this shows once more there are depths connected with Calvary that have never yet been fathomed by wisest of men, where our Lord "suffered for sins, the just for the unjust, that he might bring us to God, being put to death in the flesh" (1 Pet. 3:18).

4. *Around the Cross* (vs. 51-66)

a. *Convulsion* (v. 51)

(1) The moment Jesus Christ died there was extraordinary occurrence in religious world — rending of veil of Jewish Temple from top to bottom; this signified, of course, old covenant was no longer in existence, and way into very presence of God had been made possible through death of His own great Sacrifice (v. 51a; cf. Heb. 10:19, 20).

(2) Then followed another phenomenon in physical world — immediate quaking of earth and breaking of rocks; and while no contemporary secular record of these remarkable events is known to exist, its absence does not in any way set aside their historical probability in view of ample proofs of other N.T.

events, otherwise unrecorded, including Christ's resurrection itself (cf. 28:2).

b. *Resurrection* (vs. 52, 53)

(1) Breaking of rocks naturally meant opening of tombs as well, although we are told it was not until three days after, following Christ's own resurrection, that those who had been dead arose from their graves and appeared to many in Jerusalem (vs. 52,53); and here, again, we know only what we are told in these verses.

(2) It is true many modern scholars are in favor of omitting these verses as legendary, but textual evidence of N.T. manuscripts and versions is exactly the same for this passage as for remainder of Matthew's Gospel; and in view of its precision and restraint, record seems quite credible — tombs being cracked open by earthquake at time of our Lord's death and yet only "after his resurrection," with its own earthquake (cf. 28:2), not before, did these "saints" come forth.

(3) Tombs being near Jerusalem, with fact of recognition implied in narrative, suggests "saints" were some of those who during their recent earthly life had been led to faith in Jesus as Messiah; certainly this meaning of word "saint," i.e., one made holy through faith in Christ, is only one recognized by N.T.

(4) It is striking to note how much Evangelist leaves unsaid, and how great is contrast between this simple veracity and certain grotesque legends that have grown up around our Lord's life story; and we may regard passage as full of spiritual meaning and as striking testimony to supernatural character and far-reaching power of His death.

(5) Scripture has indeed been given to familiarize us with Divine life in relation to our own interests; and value of any assurance contained in it of raising of dead, especially holy dead, is very great and real, as another manifestation of Christ's instant power over grave and of His graciousness in typical triumph here recorded (cf. Eph. 4:8).

(6) Thus, not only was Christ victorious over death, but

others shared His victory; resurrection of saints accompanied His and will follow it in future, being both guarantee and model.

c. *Attraction* (vs. 54-61)

(1) Gathering of persons about cross was striking prophecy of way in which all kinds of people would be attracted to it and influenced by it along various lines in all ages; some have merely watched (cf. v. 36), some have actively scorned (cf. vs. 39-49), and yet others have been impressed, as in these verses.

(2) Already atoning death of Christ was having its effect upon mankind, first on realm of dead, and now on Gentile world as represented by Roman centurion and those with him (v. 54); for they evidently could not help crying out, in fear and conviction, "Truly this was the Son of God."

(3) Not least of all there were "many women ... who had followed Jesus from Galilee, ministering unto him" (v. 55, A.S.V.), as representing those who had loved Him; and, while they saw Him die, His crucifixion must have been profound mystery to them all — including Mary Magdalene* and mothers of two pairs of His disciples (vs. 56, 61).

(4) At this point, at last, we see practical ministry of love towards our Lord and, after evil had done its worst, proof of real discipleship coming from unexpected quarters; for Joseph of Arimathea, rich man and secret disciple (cf. Mark 15:43, Luke 23:50, 51, John 19:38), begged Christ's body at eventide and with tender hands prepared it for burial, laying it in his own new tomb (vs. 57-60).

(5) It is indeed remarkable this work was limited to Joseph and, according to John, to Nicodemus (cf. John 19:39); for apparently not one of eleven apostles came out of hiding to help in burial.

(6) These two men had been secret disciples and it was they who came out into the open, reminding us of flower that blooms at night and shrub that blossoms in winter; for, when night of sin is darkest and winter

*See separate Study, No. 58, p. 454.

of neglect coldest, we sometimes see men step forth to honor Christ just as His enemies are exulting and even His friends considering His cause hopeless.

(7) From this action of Joseph we learn also that glory of God is seen in fulfilling to letter Word He inspired; for, hundreds of years before, Isaiah had prophesied Messiah's appointment to criminal's grave but His actual occupation of rich man's tomb (cf. Isa. 53:9).

(8) None but God, it would seem, understood or remembered this saying, but when time came His instruments were ready; and thus these ancient words came true although what they prophesied had seemed so improbable and even contradictory.

(9) Then, too, we may learn from Joseph and Nicodemus to beware judging people, since those whom we despise for cowardice may some day put us to shame at time of sore trial; let us, therefore, walk in love, and lowliness, and large-heartedness, judging nothing hastily and being thankful our Lord still has disciples in unexpected places.

d. *Precaution* (vs. 62-66)

(1) Not only love, but hate also was active at time of Christ's death, for opposition of His enemies did not cease with His life; they revealed what they both understood and feared in proposal they made and action they took, for they well remembered He had said repeatedly He would rise again (vs. 62, 63; cf. John 2:19, Matt. 12:40, 16:21, 26:61).

(2) On this account they asked Pilate that sepulchre should be made secure against opening until after third day (v. 64); and this effort on part of His foes to guard dead body of Jesus is most significant.

(3) Some think Pilate was being ironic when he said, "Make it as sure as ye can" (v. 65), but others interpret his words to mean he merely granted petition, placing soldiers at Jews' disposal while leaving to them actual deployment of men as guardians of tomb, and agreeing that Roman force might be utilized as long as necessary.

(4) If latter is true interpretation, Pilate once again revealed his weakness in yielding to Jewish demands;

for it was mere question of their religion with which he, as civil ruler, should have had nothing to do, unless he also was apprehensive.

(5) Then cord would be stretched across large stone that Joseph had rolled to door of sepulchre (cf. v. 60), and its ends sealed to rock with wax on which would be stamped official seal of Roman governor; and thus, even though Jesus of Nazareth was dead, their precautions testify to leaders' fear of Him, for men who were most hostile were conscious that, somehow or other, He could still be force to be reckoned with.

(6) It is most impressive that members of Sanhedrin were impelled to go on morning of one of their most sacred days to sepulchre of Christ for this purpose of sealing its stone; quite evidently their anxiety was too great to be allayed, and so they were ready to desecrate this special Sabbath by seeking to secure grave of One whom they had accused for doing beneficent works on ordinary Sabbath days (cf. 12:1-14, Luke 13:14, John 5:9-18).

(7) Folly and unbelief could hardly go further, and it is remarkable in its quiet significance that by waxen seal and borrowed guard it was thought to make sure Jesus Christ was indeed dead; but, as we know from sequel, all these efforts were in vain, for it is always thus with opponents of our Lord.

(8) Whatever may be done in hope of silencing Him, or or of dismissing Him as unworthy of notice, He invariably reasserts Himself and demands answer from man's conscience to Pilate's own question: "What shall I do then with Jesus?" (v. 22); this is essential spirit of Christianity, for He who once died is now "alive for evermore" (Rev. 1:18), compelling everyone to decide either for or against Him.

Thus, even in death Christ is seen to be victorious — over pain and shame, over mockery and loneliness; and the depth of human sin is wonderfully contrasted with the height of Divine love. We may know, as never before, that the Lord Jesus by that death became the power of God unto salvation to everyone who believes in Him. Thus love, forgiveness, grace, and power are all represented in the cross, which as the very heart of Christianity will be the theme of the redeemed throughout eternity.

Conclusion

Our study of Matthew's account of our Lord's passion has surely impressed us with the uniqueness of it; through the fullness of detail as compared with the remainder of the Gospel, and through Christ's own utterances in Gethsemane and on Calvary, added to His earlier references to His death, we have seen that it is central and therefore vital in Christianity. There is only one satisfactory explanation: Christ shed His precious blood as atonement for human sin, a purchase price for man's redemption. There now follow three considerations associated with this transcendent truth:

1. *The Need of Redemption*

    a. Man has broken God's law and his conscience condemns him; he knows sin will separate him from God unless it is removed.

    b. Man's wrongdoing has many aspects, but these three may be said to stand out, showing why atonement was necessary:

    (1) Sin is a burden of debt which needs to be removed by forgiveness;

    (2) Sin is a bondage of degradation which needs to be broken by grace; and —

    (3) Sin is a barrier of defilement which needs to be taken out of the way by love.

2. *The Means of Redemption*

    a. Sacrifice being necessary, God who required it also provided it; and Christ's sacrifice on the cross was perfect, precious, and permanent.

    b. The cross is a revelation of Divine love, moral strength, and restoring grace; because it meets the deepest of human needs it was central in the purpose of God and became the source of His pardon and peace.

3. *The Power of Redemption*

    a. Christ's death first removes the burden and reinstates us in our true position with God;

b. Then it breaks the bondage and renews our true condition of soul; and —

c. Then it displaces the barrier and restores us to full fellowship with God.

This, therefore, is the heart of Christianity. Sin is the great problem of human life, and Christ's atonement the glorious solution. Christ crucified, being central in the New Testament and in the preaching of the gospel, is central also in true Christian experience; and this appeal to experience constitutes the final and supreme proof of the eternal value of the cross. No wonder that the great Apostle exclaimed: "God forbid that I should glory, save in the cross of our Lord Jesus Christ" (Gal. 6:14).

Christ does not save men by His life,
  Though that was holy, sinless, pure,
Nor even by His tender love,
  Though that forever shall endure;
He does not save them by His words,
  Though they shall never pass away,
Nor by His vast creative power
  That holds the elements in sway;
He does not save them by His works,
  Though He was ever doing good.
The awful need was greater still,
  It took His death, His cross, His blood.

Men preach today a crossless Christ,
  A strengthless Saviour, vague and dim;
They will not see their sinful state,
  They will not own their need of Him.
They will accept the man-made God,
  Since for themselves this right they claim,
But not the God sent forth as man
  To suffer agony and shame;
They will not know the Lamb of God,
  Despised, rejected, crucified.
That were to humble into dust
  Their boasted intellect, their pride.

> Yet no man cometh unto God
>   Save by the Son alone, He saith;
> The deathless life for which we long
>   Can only — ever — come through death.
> Not Bethlehem or Nazareth
>   Stern Justice' lifted hand could stay;
> To Calvary the soul must go
>   And follow Jesus all the way!

ANNIE JOHNSON FLINT
(Used by permission.)

56

REJECTION OF THE KING

Matthew 27:22

THREE GREAT facts, like the three strands of a rope, run through the Gospel story: Revelation, Rejection, Reception. The personal revelation of Christ is met on the one hand by rejection on the part of the majority of men, even after many and varied public presentations of Himself; on the other hand, it is met by reception on the part of certain other persons who form a minority of His contemporaries. The rejection culminates in the crucifixion, and the reception is crowned by the resurrection.

Throughout the Gospel narrative there is repeated mention or implication of the sin that was the foundation of the rejection of Christ; but now, as we look at the story of His crucifixion, we can see most clearly the sins that were the immediate cause of this rejection. We have, therefore, a twofold subject for careful study, the sin and the sins, the source and the streams, the root and the fruits, the fundamental cause and the instrumental occasions. Taking the latter element first, let us look at the streams before tracing them back to the source:

I. The Sins That Rejected Christ

There are five different but associated classes or persons concerned with the crucifixion and they represent five different views:

1. *The Multitude*

   a. This word describes generally inhabitants of Palestine of our Lord's day, but especially those who lived in Galilee;

and they were impulsive, easily influenced, and deeply impressed by miracles.

b. These people wished to make Christ king, and followed Him in crowds, hanging on His words and crying "Hosanna" on Palm Sunday; and yet they were as easily influenced by their rulers to cry out, "Crucify him!" on Good Friday.

c. Their sin was fickleness based on superficiality, and this is one of ways by which Christ is still rejected; for such men are easily stirred, full of emotions and impulses, but essentially unstable, because they have no depth of conviction or force of character with which to choose the right and adhere to it at all costs.

2. *The Jews*

a. These are clearly distinct from multitude and represent inhabitants specifically of Jerusalem and Judaea; this was party of patriotic hopes, nationalistic ideas of Messiah and His sovereignty, and included sect called Pharisees.

b. In religion they represented narrow, prejudiced, bigoted Judaism, so that, when Jesus came preaching gospel that opposed their views and traditions, they resented it and forthwith persecuted Him; they even charged Him with blasphemy, willfully misinterpreting and misstating His words, and when climax came they made accusations in which there was grain of truth with ton of error (cf. Luke 23:1):

(1) They said He had been "saying that he himself is Christ a king"; true, but not their kind of king.

(2) They said He had been "forbidding to give tribute to Caesar"; very opposite of truth.

(3) They said He had been "perverting the nation"; absolutely false.

c. Their sin was slander based on prejudice, and so is Christ rejected today; since He opposes men's errors by truth, men's iniquity by righteousness, men's impurity by holiness, they object to Him, misunderstand and misinterpret Him because of their deeply rooted prejudices, and so, afraid of consequences of light, they walk on in darkness.

3. *The Chief Priests*

   a. These were of Sadducees' party and were chief movers in rejection of Christ, representing power, privilege, and position, possession of which led to intolerance and arrogance; they had behind them traditions of centuries and were exponents of official religion, so could not brook any opposition.

   b. Then came Jesus of Nazareth teaching in simplicity and power that which undermined their position, cutting at root of their ecclesiastical rank and personal influence, and bidding fair to supersede them altogether; and so to them Jesus was dangerous revolutionist to be crushed, and yet, under guise of vindicating their loyalty to God and their nation, they were really gratifying their own ambitions.

   c. Their sin was envy based on hatred, for we read "for envy they had delivered him" (v. 18), and same principle is at work today whenever Jesus Christ strikes at root of unworthy ambitions, entrenched traditions, erroneous ways of living; He is resented and opposed by men who will not yield to His claims because of false conservatism encrusted with personal claims and vested interests.

4. *Judas the Disciple*

   a. Here we see primary instrument in actual delivery of Jesus to death — man who followed Him not for what He was, but for what He presumably could give; and when these personal advantages proved unsubstantial and even non-existent, then Judas turned from Jesus to others who seemed more promising.

   b. Key to his character appears to be in words, "What will ye give me —?" (26:15), for he was rank materialist who could not appreciate Christ's spirituality; self-seeking was his standard, so that he was prepared to sacrifice Jesus to love of gain.

   c. His sin was avarice based on selfishness, and unfortunately this is one all too prevalent today because, though money-making is legitimate and even necessary, money-loving is not (cf. 1 Tim. 6:10); moreover, there is scarcely another sin more frequently denounced in N.T. than covetousness (e.g., Acts 5:1 11; Col. 3:5), and when it is brought face to face with Christ there can be nothing but absolute defeat on one side or the other.

5. *Pilate the Governor*

    a. Last in order of instruments that compassed our Lord's downfall, this Roman viceroy did not believe in accusations or accusers; indeed, he was so deeply impressed by his interviews with Jesus, so confirmed in his impressions by message from his wife, and so unwilling to condemn his Prisoner that he actually tried, up to a point, to liberate Him.

    b. Yet Pilate yielded step by step until he, "willing to content the people, . . . delivered Jesus . . . to be crucified" (Mark 15:15); and ever since then he has borne stigma of creedal phrase "crucified under Pontius Pilate"; having lived by expediency and not by principle, fear of disgrace prevailed (cf. John 19:12, 13), and yet, ironically, everlasting dishonor was natural result.

    c. His sin was weakness based on cowardice, and still, today, many people are afraid to do right lest love of position, fear of man, social opinion, or worldly prospects may become involved; they are for ever "letting I dare not wait upon I would," in Shakespeare's phrase, so that when Christ stands before them they hesitate, they shrink, they yield, they are lost, not so much by weakness of wickedness as by wickedness of weakness.

These are the sins that led to the rejection of Christ — fickleness, slander, envy, avarice, and weakness. These sins are still very much with us in various forms, doing their deadly work of rejecting Christ from our life today. But what is at the root of them?

II. The Sin That Rejected Christ

Is there any one foundation, root, wellspring of such hostile attitudes towards our blessed Lord? Yes, the one source of them is the sin of unbelief; the sin that led to the Fall in Eden is the root of every sinful thought, word, and deed today. This is because unbelief implies self-assertion, with absolute refusal to depend on God and consequent belief in self rather than in Him — not only echoing the serpent's sceptical question, "Hath God said?" (Gen. 3:1), but adding, in effect, "Even if He has, I will not believe!"

1. *Unbelief Produces Instability*

   This is because it prevents man's intellectual nature from forming deep, strong convictions and keeps it shallow, superficial, virtually useless.

2. *Unbelief Produces Prejudice*

   This is because it prevents man's moral nature from seeing truth whole and, therefore, from gaining poise in experience and balance in judgment.

3. *Unbelief Produces Hatred*

   This is because, in preventing man's social nature from having faith that works through love — love that seeks not her own, but welfare of others — it opens door to pessimism, envy, jealousy, and all uncharitableness.

4. *Unbelief Produces Selfishness*

   This is because it prevents man's spiritual nature from finding room for Divine grace — "the expulsive power of a new affection" — with all its possibilities for aiding apprehension of spiritual realities.

5. *Unbelief Produces Cowardice*

   This is because it prevents man's physical nature from enjoying safeguard of moral ideals and righteous living, thereby allowing everything in him to be sacrificed to himself, his desires, and often to tyranny of wicked associates, so that he is actually afraid of doing right.

Conclusion

It follows that, contrariwise, at the root of all true Christian life lies belief, faith, trust. This attitude is the very absence of self-assertion and the expression of dependence on God. As such, it is the basis of every grace of character possible to man:

1. Trust produces *steadfastness,* the opposite of fickleness and instability, because its roots are in God.

2. Trust produces *truthfulness,* the opposite of prejudice and slander, because it follows the light of truth at all costs.

3. Trust produces *love,* the opposite of hatred and envy, even to the point of conflict with one's own interests.

4. Trust produces *unselfishness,* the opposite of selfishness and

avarice, because it sees the true proportion of things and considers the interests of all.

5. Trust produces *courage,* the opposite of cowardice and weakness, because it dares to do right and to stand alone, even against the whole world, relying on Divine strength and acting in accordance with the will of God.

Yes, trust in God, belief in His Word, faith in His Son Jesus Christ — these set free the expulsive power of love, the expansive power of humility, the uplifting power of sincerity, and the transforming power of contentment, so that we can say with St. John, "We have known and believed the love that God hath to us" (1 John 4:16) — that love of God which St. Paul describes as "shed abroad in our hearts by the Holy Ghost" (Rom. 5:5).

57

THE LONELINESS OF CHRIST*

Matthew 27:46

T HE NEW TESTAMENT contains many momentous questions, asked by different persons on various occasions, but the question in our text transcends all others both in sublimity and in poignancy. Its wording, appropriated by Jesus Christ from Ps. 22, one of the greatest Messianic Psalms, as prophetic of Himself, introduces us into a field of inquiry instructive and illuminating, and yet having depths that we cannot fully penetrate. But we can gather something of the significance of this question in relation to the whole account of our Lord's mission on earth, and, of course, the circumstances in which it was spoken are very familiar.

To meditate on any of the words of Him who "spake as never man spake" is of the utmost importance, but especially is it incumbent upon us to linger over His last and dying utterances. Few and brief though they were, there is not one of the memorable Seven Last Words from the cross that does not contain truths of the deepest import to us; so that, in spite of their familiarity, they repay constant reiteration.

---

*Notes of sermon preached first in 1885, when the author was twenty-four years old.

Let us, then, endeavor to find out something of the meaning of this the only question asked from the cross, and also to ponder something of its message for us today:

I. The Meaning

"My God, my God, why hast thou forsaken me?" The emphasis seems clearly to be on the word "why," so we may well seek, first, the reason for this utterance and, second, the reason why God the Father had forsaken His Son. Christ had challenged the Jewish rulers to find any fault in Him, and Pilate had declared Him innocent; yet now He is evidently forsaken by God and, conscious of His blamelessness, He appeals to His Father as to the explanation.

1. *This Cry Was Not the Result of Corporeal Pain Endured.*

   a. It is true Christ had been hanging for hours under oriental midday sun, with both fever and thirst having their effect, and wounds on head and in hands and feet causing terrible agony; but relation of these sufferings to His question was remote.

   b. Indeed, history provides numerous instances in which even men living and dying without moral support of eminent purity of character have yet been unmoved by bodily suffering more protracted, if not more intense, than our Lord's; and not only are there instances of pagan fortitude in agony, but countless instances also of Christian courage, such as that of martyrs in times of unbridled pagan and papal Rome.

   c. Shall we, can we, say Son of God, who foresaw all these sufferings and "set his face like a flint" towards them, shrank where His followers and others did not? No, surely not, and therefore physical pain gives us no satisfactory solution to His mental anguish in this last hour.

2. *This Cry Has To Do Solely with the Relationship Within the Godhead.*

   a. In manner beyond human comprehension, God the Father was then withholding from His Son consciousness of His supporting presence; and Jesus Christ therefore realizes, in full, exile's relation to One with whom He had been equal in heavenly home.

b. It was not that union between Divine and human nature was in least degree weakened, but there was no sensible apprehension of God's presence and fellowship; and necessity for this eclipse of His Father's face, this paternal desertion, He cannot, humanly speaking, understand.

c. During Christ's life on earth He had never once complained of absence from God; again and again, rather, He had announced His union with His Father:

   (1) After the temptation God sent Him angels to minister to His wants (cf. 4:11); and twice, on His baptism (cf. 3:16, 17), and at His transfiguration (cf. 17:2), He was openly acknowledged from heaven.

   (2) At grave of Lazarus His prayer was heard (cf. John 11:41-44), and soon after, when His soul was troubled, voice came from heaven promising further glory through Him (cf. John 12:27, 28); and in Gethsemane He did not plead in vain, for angelic aid again was sent to support Him (cf. Luke 22:43).

d. But now, surrounded by enemies, deserted by friends, and unsupported by angels, Christ, realizing His Father had actually forsaken Him, directs, amid tumult around His cross, this agonized question towards heaven; and utterance is all the more remarkable because, only day or so before, He had deliberately told His disciples He was not alone for, said He, "the Father is with me" (John 16:32).

e. It is striking to realize that, in demonstration of moral fidelity, such a man as Daniel went down into den of lions and God was with him, and in executing Divine will three Jewish youths passed harmless through fire, for Son of God walked with them (cf. Dan. 6 and 3, respectively); yet Jesus Christ, conscious through life of doing those things that pleased His Father (cf. John 8:29), was only Servant of His, dying for God's vindication and glory, who could not secure consciousness of Divine favor and presence.

Therefore we find that reason of our Lord's cry certainly was not anguish caused by bodily pain but, rather, distress caused by realization of having been abandoned by Him with whom, all His life long, He had been in closest fellowship; but now we ask, if cry was caused by God's forsaking Him, what was reason of this forsaking? Here we tread on holy ground and must be careful not to overstep bounds of truth revealed to us, as we suggest that —

3. *This Abandonment Was the Crowning Manifestation of God's Wrath Against Sin.*

    a. In being there as man's representative, Christ's mission was to show on Calvary enormity of sin as well as to provide plan of salvation; for on human souls chains of guilt were strongly riveted and through sin there was changeless antagonism of nature between God and man.

    b. Character of God demanded either every offender should suffer penalty of law or else atonement be made that should satisfy law's demands; and at crucifixion it was necessary God should (so to speak) exhaust methods by which He might impress mankind with terrible nature of sin, and in so doing "He . . . spared not his own Son" (Rom. 8:32).

    c. It was because Christ there stood in place of sinful man that God had to forsake Him, and yet, since He did not hate Bearer of guilt but burden itself, His condemnation really fell on that; in other words, since on cross Saviour and sin were so closely connected, that wrath which God directed against sin fell on Sin-bearer, even though His Person as such must still have been acceptable to His Father.

    d. Fact of God's so loving world as to send His Son teaches His tender compassion for mankind, and fact that Christ's death was necessary proves God's inflexible justice; and now fact that He hid His face shows how revolting sin is in His holy sight.

    e. Cross of Christ is loftiest observatory from which men can look at sin for, there and then, on Jesus was rolled this whole world's iniquity in thought, word, deed, and tendency; and yet no artist can paint nor author compose faithful picture of results of sin, for its relations to God's government, to man's unhappiness and doom are best seen at Calvary and most clearly heard in this cry of anguish.

    f. There, with spotless Lamb of God in awful solitude because Representative of sin, we can begin to grasp sin's ravages on human character, on domestic life, on civil government, and on international relations.

N.B. Sin has been aptly described as "perverting every faculty of the human mind, pearling every teardrop, generating every sigh of sorrow, unsheathing every sword, lighting every canon, digging every grave, and surging as a never-ebbing tide against the throne of God."

g. It is only when we take this broad and radical view of sin, and find an omnipotent God at labor to unfold its enormity, that this mournful inquiry of our Lord becomes transformed from theological enigma into very central doctrine and truth of gospel; for this desertion of Christ was God's final, culminating illustration of sin's terrible character, and from this experience Jesus could not free Himself and at same time make complete atonement.

h. He had offered to bridge gulf between heaven and earth and now, literally hanging between them, He could not save Himself from this desolation, even though during His life on earth He could calm storm or not, multiply loaves as He willed, call dead to life or leave them to sleep on until resurrection; this dilemma was final drop emptied into that cup which Jesus drank to its dregs and then, drawing all mankind to His heart, cried, "It is finished!" and bowed His head in death.

II. The Message

This cry of our Lord has in it lessons for our lives today to which we shall do well to take heed. We see in it —

1. *God's Eternal Estimate of Sin*

a. These are days in which sin in many forms is only too apparent, and yet is lightly passed over as of small moment; and since men have so superficial an idea of what sin really is, there is greater need of emphasizing its true character in sight of God.

b. To do this we must take our stand at cross of Christ, for there it is best seen as that which caused humiliation, suffering, and cruel death of Son of God; and when men gain some conception of depths to which He descended they realize something of nature of sin and, contrariwise, those with superficial views of sin can have no appreciation of His work of redemption.

    c. Clearly, this cry of Christ during His last agony reveals
what sin is, causing infinitely holy God to forsake His
Son; it is same sin that seduced angels from their allegiance, that brought Divine condemnation upon Adam and
Eve in Eden.

    Illus.: Nine-headed monster of Greek fable whose heads
sprang again to life as fast as blade of Hercules severed
them is but emblem of power of sin.

    d. Revolutions may be checked, conflagrations may be ex-
tinguished, great rivers may be diverted from their
channels; but sin dies very reluctantly even in regenerated
soul, when Holy Spirit co-operates with consenting human
will for believer's entire sanctification.

    e. Sin is architect and builder that has made this world one
vast penitentiary of perdition; and to set men free from
its galling fetters, to purify them from its abominable
pollutions, Christ experienced awful solitude implied in
our text.

    f. To enable us to live above its conquests, to strengthen our
moral natures against its ravages, Christ died with midnight within and around Him; let us gaze, then on cross
of Christ, listen to this cry of desolation from lips of
perfect Holiness, dwell upon abandonment of Him by His
Father, and gain some conception of character, extent, and
power of sin.

2. *God's Eternal Valuation of a Human Soul*

    a. Twice in His public ministry, Jesus Christ sought to
impress men with soul's surpassing worth:

      (1) On one occasion, He indicated, as it were, pair of
scales:

        (a) On one balance He placed "whole world"
(16:26) — all happiness ever purchased by
fortune, all satisfaction ever acquired by ease,
all position ever obtained by fame.

        (b) On other balance He placed immortal soul of
man, with its magnificent endowments — mind
creating thought and drawing inferences, memory
holding chain of recollections, imagination paint-
ing unrivaled pictures, conscience striking alarm
against danger, will-power determining eternal
destiny, affection uniting with God and with
fellow man — all these.

      (c) As world scale shot up like rocket and soul scale fell like millstone, Divine Teacher presented to men problem with which mathematicians have vainly wrestled: "What shall it profit a man, if he shall gain the whole world, and lose his own soul? Or what shall a man give in exchange for his soul?" (Mark 8:36, 37).

   (2) Now, again, expiring in blood and gloom, our Lord's thought must have reviewed worth of human soul:

      (a) Did His vision sweep over its vast reasoning powers, its marvelous ability to call up past impressions and paint future with hope, its far-reaching power of free agency, its affections rising again and again above all calamities, its ambitions satisfied with nothing terrestrial, and its immortality burning like an unquenchable flame?

      (b) This we may say — as from cross Christ looks out on darkness around Him, He knows that to complete only possible plan of redemption and indicate God's estimate of even pauper's soul, God must smite Him as man's Substitute; and by this darkness at noonday, by this awful solitude of spirit, by these wounded hands and feet, He holds up human soul as masterpiece of God's workmanship and sole object in entire universe precious enough to cost for its ransom death of God the Son.

b. Yes, at Casarea-Philippi we sense value of man, but in cross of Christ we see it with our own eyes of faith; although, to lesser degree, we sense it also from human experience with government, science, invention, art, philosophy, it is only when we take our stand with Him on Calvary that we grasp true conception of man's worth, for there we see sacrifice of God for man's salvation.

c. But worth of human soul should be related not only to our own personal salvation, but also to our dealings with others; and, whatever man's origin and place, his stages of development and of power, one thing at least is certain, that he is a being whose rescue from moral evil is held on high to be worth agony and bloody sweat, cross and passion of Christ.

d. His sacrifice is eternal witness to truth that man at his very worst is worth being ministered to from heaven itself and at cost that defies expression in terms of earthly sacrifice; and, if we are tempted to think meanly of man, if, face to face with dark facts of his frailty and even of his vice, all fine things said of him by poet and prophet, historian and preacher seem to be but hollow mockeries, we must remember there is judgment above our own.

e. However little we can see to admire, there must be something of infinite value, since God has redeemed each one, potentially, by infinite sacrifice; by this the humblest is glorified, whatever his race, creed, or character, because he is one of those whom God loved and for whom Christ died, as He testified in His expiring cry to inherent grandeur of immortal spirit of man as well as to disastrous effect of sin upon it.

Conclusion

1. *Believers Will Never Be Forsaken.*

a. This is why Christ lived, suffered, and died — that God might never have to forsake us — and here is our stay and hope — Jesus forsaken for us; pall of darkness falling on His soul has hung canopy of hope over our future.

b. Gloom that gathered around His cross has lit up our sky with great and precious promises; and desolation that fell on His sad heart has kindled beacons of rejoicing throughout our lives.

c. Because of His mournful cry we have His promise, "I will never leave thee nor forsake thee" (Heb. 13:5), and He endured this agony that our sins might be canceled, our hearts sanctified, and our future secured; He was bereft of God and left solitary that we might never lose our sight of God's face nor strength and joy of His presence.

d. Let us, then, bow our hearts in hushed and grateful reverence, so that, trusting in Him, we never shall be solitary; for He has said, "Lo, I am with you alway" (28:10) in order that we may boldly say, "I will fear no evil" (Ps. 23:4) and look forward to day when we shall "ever be with the Lord" (1 Thess. 4:17).

But this cry from Calvary shows us also the full measure of the responsibility of those who are unsaved:

2. *Unbelievers Will Be Forsaken Hereafter.*

 a. Christ paid penalty of violated law, but not debt of human duty; and man who voluntarily rejects personal concern with Christ's atonement commits unpardonable sin, only overshadowing iniquity that has no forgiveness, so that he becomes moral suicide.

 b. For ignoring Christ's death God will forsake that man forever and, standing where no light breaks on eternal darkness, his wail will echo, "My God, my God, why hast thou forsaken me?"; and to that dread question his conscience will respond in solemn words of Apostle Paul: "If any man love not the Lord Jesus, let him be anathema" — accursed (1 Cor. 16:22).

 c. Forsaken of God beyond grave means deserted by all agencies for human salvation; and eternity will be spent in fruitless study of contrast between what is and what might have been, deathless present and ruined past.

Oh, yield to him now as Saviour and Lord, in heart and in life, and you will never have to cry from the depths of eternal misery, "My God, my God, *I know* why Thou hast forsaken *me!*"

> *"Why hast Thou forsaken?"*
> *List to that sad, sad moan!*
> *Oh, His heart was broken,*
> *Suffering there alone;*
> *Broken then that mortals*
> *Ne'er need cry in vain*
> *For God's love and comfort*
> *In the hour of pain.*

> MAUD FRAZER

58

MARY MAGDALENE

Matthew 27:55, 56, 61; John 20:14-18

CAREFUL study of these verses, together with other related New Testament passages, will enable us to note, in the familiar phrase of Philip Doddridge, "the rise and progress of religion in the soul" of one of Christ's followers, Mary Magdalene. There were four stages in this woman's spiritual experience and her relation to her Master:

I. Salvation

1. *Mental Healing*

   a. Mary of Magdala had been among group of women "healed of evil spirits and infirmities" (Luke 8:2); and in her case malady had been of exceptional severity, for Christ had cast out of her no fewer than "seven devils."

   b. Whether number is to be taken literally, as is quite likely, or as expression of total possession, seven being representative of completeness, result is much the same; it was case of terrible affliction.

   c. Demon-possession is still known today, especially on mission field, where symptoms in certain cases of distress can be explained only in this way; and in N.T. it is clearly distinguished from ordinary illness and insanity (cf. 4:24).

   N.B. As already noted (see Study No. 52, under II, 4, f), there is not the slightest evidence from any Gospel record that the woman mentioned in Luke 7:36-50 was Mary Magdalene.

2. *Spiritual Regeneration*

   Demon-possession expresses spiritual condition of many unsaved persons:

   a. It is fit symbol of sinful nature, for at least three things followed it; evil power, shameful bondage, and intense misery; and these are still results of sin in our own day.

b. Its healing is beautiful symbol of salvation, for Mary's blessing, like ours, was due to three things: the Saviour's loving pity, His infinite mercy, and His Divine power.

c. Its result is appropriate symbol of those who have been saved, for there came to Mary, as to us, three things: absolute freedom, perfect peace, and complete satisfaction.

Christ is always the Master of Satan, but only those who accept His victory by faith and reckon it theirs know what His grace can do.

II. Service

Outcome of this healing, this salvation of mind and soul, was soon evident; for it proved itself by its fruit in Mary Magdalene's life:

1. *Fellowship*

She was "with him" (Luke 8:1, 2), and this new friendship must have been very precious; we have only to compare it with her old life of decidedly different associations (cf. also Luke 8:38, 18:43).

2. *Consecration*

Her life and "substance" (Luke 8:3) henceforth belonged to Him who had done so much for her; in company with other women in group, she gave what she had, which must have been of real help to Christ (cf. Rom. 21:1).

III. Sorrow

But time came when Mary's devotion to her Master was tested to uttermost, for, having "followed Jesus from Galilee, ministering unto him" (vs. 55, 56), she saw Him die and watched by His tomb (v. 61).

1. *Gratitude Shown* (Mark 61:1, Luke 23:55 to 24:1)

a. Even now, she wished to do all she could for her Benefactor; and so, in company with other women, she "bought sweet spices, that they might come and anoint him" (Mark 16:1).

b. Then, very early on Easter morning, these faithful friends "came unto the sepulchre, bringing the spices which they had prepared" (Luke 24:1).

2. *Grief Experienced* (John 20:1, 2)

    a. Christ's death must have been to Mary, as to others, profound mystery; and as she recalled past she realized great loss, for blessings of that friendship with Him were, as she thought, forever at an end.

    b. Then, too, empty tomb seemed to mean loss even of dead body of her Lord; and thus she could do nothing, after all, to show her love for Him.

3. *Grief Expressed* (John 20:11-13)

    a. Her weeping, as Greek word suggests, was intense and audible; and even sight of angels in tomb did not check it.

    b. In answering their question, her devotion to Christ is simply but beautifully indicated by words she used of Him — "my Lord" (v. 13).

IV. Solace (John 20:14-18)

Mary Magdalene little knew how near time was for her sorrow to be forever dispelled (v. 14). She remembered much but, like all the rest, she had forgotten Christ's words about rising again; and so His question was particularly to the point — "Why weepest thou?" (v. 15a)

1. *The Revelation* (vs. 15b, 16)

    a. Her reply showed not only mistaken identity," "supposing Him to be the gardener," but impulsive devotion as, in her intensity of feeling, she forgot her woman's weakness and thought she could unaided take body away (v. 15b).

    b. But her name, spoken in dear, familiar voice, broke spell and dispersed gloom instantly; and her heart was wondrously relieved as she realized who it was who spoke and that He was indeed alive.

2. *The Restraint* (v. 17a)

    a. In her new-found joy, Mary Magdalene evidently wanted to cling to her Master, so that many writers have interpreted text by emphasizing her desire to resume former fellowship; and they suggest our Lord, in checking this impulse, would remind her that not until His promised coming again in the Spirit after His bodily ascension would fellowship be possible.

b. At same time, we must not overlook difficulty of this view in face of Matt. 28:9, and there is much to be said for more natural interpretation: as He had only just risen, His words to Mary meant He had not then gone up to His Father to present Himself as One who had accomplished salvation, in manner of high priest of old, who entered Holy Place with blood of sacrifice to show it had been duly offered (cf. Lev. 16:14, 15; and Heb. 9:12 with 9:24).

c. With this type in mind to be fulfilled, He would say, "Touch me not, for I have not yet ascended," although a little time afterwards He was to allow other faithful women not only to touch Him, but to hold Him by the feet (cf. Matt. 28:9); thus, explanation seems to be that He had meanwhile, on very morning of resurrection, appeared before His Father.

d. Further, it would seem impossible to interpret these words of His final ascension of forty days later; for He used present tense of verb, "I ascend," and if He had not intended to do so at once it seems difficult to understand why He had any need to send message to His disciples.

e. Moreover, since later on in day our Lord urged His disciples' to touch Him (cf. Luke 24:39), it would seem something had occurred to remove prohibition to Mary; and if this was due to His having ascended and come back again to appear before them everything is quite simple and clear.

f. There seems to be no reason why Christ's priestly act of entering Holy Place should have been deferred for forty days; we can, however, easily understand why it was necessary for Him to come back at times during that period in order gradually to train His disciples to do without His visible presence and to lean instead upon His spiritual presence.

N.B. It is, perhaps, neither necessary nor possible to decide dogmatically between these two views, so both should be kept clearly before us. We can at least consider how —

> *Love, with infant haste, would fain*
> *Touch Him and adore;*
> *But a deeper, holier gain*
> *Mercy keeps in store:*
> *"Touch Me not; awhile believe Me;*
> *Touch Me not till heaven receive Me;*
> *Then draw near, and never leave Me,*
> *Then I go no more."*

JOHN KEBLE

3. *The Requirement* (vs. 17b, 18)

   a. Mary was to go and announce Christ's ascension to His "brethren" (v. 17b) ; and, thus commissioned and signally honored as first messenger of His resurrection, she joyfully obeyed (v. 18).

   b. We can easily imagine this faithful woman's feelings as she must have hastened to do her Master's bidding, for her sorrow was past; and once again she was engaged in service for Christ that not only recalled former days, but was beginning of far higher service that would not cease.

Conclusion

What was the keynote of the spiritual life of Mary Magdalene? We may trace it in the word she used when she became conscious of the Lord's return from the grave — "Rabboni!" (John 20:16). The sincere employment of this title acknowledges the true relationship between Jesus Christ and His followers:

1. *Rabboni Means Teacher*

   John interprets Hebrew word thus, and we are reminded of shorter word "Rabbi"; Christ is our greatest Teacher, and teaching, education, is need of all His disciples, or "learners."

2. *Rabboni Also Means Master*

   We speak of "schoolmasters," those with authority over ones they teach; and Christ can be our Teacher only in proportion as He becomes Lord and Master of our lives (cf. Rom. 14:9).

3. *Rabboni Presupposes Saviour*

   Christ is our Teacher and Master only if He is, first of all, our Saviour from sin, as He was to Mary Magdalene, for our minds, like hers, need His gracious influence, His purifying and strengthening power.

4. *Rabboni Means, Strictly, "My Master"*

This suggests very personal acceptance and acknowledgment of Christ, as also when Mary said, "My Lord" (v. 13); and if we can truthfully say "My —" we have commenced to be true followers of the Lord Jesus, ready to "go . . . and say" to others what He has done for us and can do for them. Armed with a threefold message —

a. To a world under condemnation, we proclaim the atonement of Christ; and —

b. To a world in bondage to fear, we proclaim the resurrection of Christ; and —

c. To a world at enmity with God, we proclaim the ascension, intercession, and return of Christ.

This is the full and glorious gospel!

59

THE KING'S TRIUMPH

Matthew 28:1-20

T HE RESURRECTION of the Lord Jesus Christ is the basis of Christianity; it covers every spiritual truth relating to our past, our present, and our future. All four Evangelists record it, agreeing that it took place on the first day of the week, as befitting a new life, a new era; and it is at once intensely interesting and vitally important to compare the various appearances of the risen Christ. Matthew does not give much of the detailed history associated with the resurrection, but the record found in his Gospel clearly indicates Christ's Kingship and majesty.

I. The Culmination (vs. 1-7)

1. *The Reassuring Message* (vs. 1-7)

a. Since Jews reckoned their days from evening to evening, statement of time probably means night after Sabbath day was included as part of it (v. 1); and just before

daybreak on our Sunday some women who had been
faithful followers of our Lord came to His tomb, intending
to anoint His body with spices (cf. Mark 16:1, Luke
24:1).

b. Mary Magdalene was one who had been healed by our
Lord (cf. Luke 8:2); and "the other Mary" was mother
of James and Joses (cf. 27:56, 61).

c. They and other women (cf. Mark 16:1, Luke 24:10)
found tomb empty, with "angel of the Lord" (vs. 2, 3)
in charge; and when they saw what had evidently happened they were naturally afraid, as were "keepers" or
members of Roman guard set to watch tomb (v. 4; cf.
27:66).

d. Angel then reassured women, telling them not to fear,
because their Master was risen, according to His own
word (vs. 5, 6a); just as at our Lord's birth (cf. Luke
1:30, 2:10), so here first word from heaven was "Fear
not."

e. Then women were invited to see for themselves that
Jesus was not there (v. 6b); and finally came angel's
command to go quickly and tell His disciples what had
happened and that He would meet them in Galilee (v. 7).
N.B. As an ancient writer once said: "Through woman
death was first introduced to the world; to women the
first announcement was made of the resurrection."

2. *The Risen Master* (vs. 8-10)

a. Blending of fear and joy in these faithful women (v. 8)
was perfectly natural, and as they went, their Master
met them with usual greeting (v. 9a); original is literally "Rejoice!" and it is noteworthy that His first word
on resurrection morning spoke of joy, while that evening
He gave His disciples greeting of "peace" (John 20:19).

b. His followers were clearly intended to possess what St.
Paul afterwards called "joy and peace in believing" (Rom.
15:13) — believing on Saviour who, because living, is
present, powerful, perpetual.

c. No wonder these women "held him by the feet" (v. 9b)
in their rejoicing and adoration; and it is evident they
were allowed to cling to Him, probably because, since His
refusal to allow Mary Magdalene to touch Him (cf.

(John 20:17), He had presented Himself to God in heaven.*

d. Then Christ continued to reassure them by repeating angel's admonition against fear and also his direction for disciples; and our Lord's choice of Galilee for meeting with them would both prove their faith by their taking sixty-mile journey and provide link of past with present by visit to scene of former labors and fellowship.

e. Thus, key word in Matthew's account would seem to be "Fear not," first spoken by angel and then by Christ Himself; and His resurrection is shown not only to remove fear, but also to introduce His people to courage and hope, peace and joy that come from fellowship with Him as risen Lord.

Illus.: There was once a "Cape of Storms" at southern tip of Africa, so named because of many shipwrecks off its coast. But after that intrepid navigator Vasco da Gama succeeded in rounding it safely its name was changed to "Cape of Good Hope," by which it is still known. Up to time of Calvary, likewise, death was "cape of storms," but Christ has contained it by His resurrection and "has begotten us again to a living hope" (1 Pet. 1:3; cf. v. 21).

II. The Contrast (vs. 11-14)

This incident, which is found only in Matthew's Gospel, is in striking contrast to his emphasis on the Kingly glory of Christ:

1. *The Conspiracy* (vs. 11-14)

a. News of empty tomb soon reached city by means of members of watch; and immediate action on part of Christ's enemies was felt to be necessary (vs. 11, 12a).

b. Chief priests and elders taking counsel together decided to bribe these soldiers to spread abroad impression that His body had been stolen during their sleep (v. 13); and Sanhedrin hastened to express its readiness to intercede with Pilate (v. 14), probably knowing well his weakness and corruption.

---

*For a fuller discussion of this question, see Study No. 58, under IV, 2, p. 456.

    c. They would use Roman soldiers just as they had employed Judas; and then by means of similar bribe they would keep governor quiet and thereby free soldiers from punishment and themselves from ridicule (cf. Acts 12:19, 16:27).

    d. But story was so manifestly impossible that it is incredible that it should have satisfied even man like Pontius Pilate; if soldiers had been asleep, itself matter of very serious moment, how could they have been aware that body had been stolen, and that by disciples?

2. *The Condemnation* (v. 15)

    a. But bribe was accepted and plan carried out; and lying statement went abroad, becoming common report among Jews, although it may be questioned whether it was really believed by any who gave it serious consideration.

    b. Reference to "this day" is to time Gospel was written, probably twenty years or more after event; but lie carries its own condemnation down centuries, for its improbabilities amount to impossibilities and show only how intense was animosity of contemporary Judaism against Christ, and how concerned leaders were by His evident influence over their people.

    c. That religious men should have resorted to this extremity reveals deplorable deterioration of their lives; and contrast between truth of Christ's resurrection and untruth of this account of it calls for special emphasis.

    d. There is nothing in history more striking than earthly action that put Jesus Christ to death contrasted with heavenly power that raised Him from dead; and antithesis between these two paragraphs of Matthew's Gospel (28:1-10 and 11-15) is antithesis between reality and unreality, indeed between righteousness and unrighteousness.

    e. While Christianity fears nothing and is ready to be tested by every available standard of truth, purity, and righteousness, here enemies of Christ are compelled to resort to most unworthy methods, including falsehood, bribery, and corruption; and thus it remains true that best proof of our Lord's resurrection is genuine follower of His who shows forth in life and witness "the power of his resurrection" (Phil. 3:10).

III. The Commission (vs. 16-20)

It may be noted that the Ascension, mentioned by Mark and Luke in their concluding paragraphs, is omitted here, doubtless because it does not come within the scope of this Gospel, which is to set forth the Kingdom of Heaven and the Kingship of the Messiah. Instead, the Gospel of Matthew closes with the record of our Lord's commission to His disciples. The need for such a commission may be illustrated by the condition of the world at that time: the Jews had failed in the realm of religion; the Greeks had failed in the realm of philosophy; and the Romans had failed in the realm of law and rule. Now the moral and spiritual guidance of the world was to be entrusted to other hands, those of Christ's Apostles, as they witnessed to that "light for revelation to the Gentiles" (Luke 2:32, A.S.V.) of which old Simeon had spoken.

A. The Scene (vs. 16, 17)

1. *The Reunited Disciples*

   a. When our Lord and Eleven met again in Galilee, it was "into a mountain" (v. 16) that they went; although precise one is not known, its location was probably near Sea of Galilee (cf. 5:1, 17:1), and would remind them they were once more apart from world and in communion with God.

   b. Some of them at once recognized their Master and worshipped Him, but others hesitated in doubt until they, too, must have been convinced of His identity and of reality of His resurrection life (v. 17) by His presence and His authoritative words.

2. *The Risen Lord*

   a. Our Lord's body after His resurrection may best be described in St. Paul's words, as "a spiritual body" (1 Cor. 15:44), although to us, with our present limited knowledge, term "spiritual" seems to contradict idea of "body"; and it is evident there was identity between body buried and body raised.

   b. But at same time there was equally clear dissimilarity; it was same though different, and different though same.

   c. It would appear, therefore, that our Lord's resurrection body is best, and indeed only, illustration we have of what resurrection bodies of His saints will be (cf. 1 Cor. 15:20-23, 35-49, 2 Cor. 5:1-10).

B. The Service (vs. 18-20)

These verses give Matthew's account of Great Commission, words from our Lord's lips called by Duke of Wellington "the Marching Orders of the Church," for they constitute Divine warrant for all types of Christian service and witness. Four times in original, word "all" is used and, when these are put together, they give explicit directions to Christ's followers:

1. *The Secret of Service* — *"all authority"* (v. 18, A.S.V.)

   a. This comes first as basis of missionary work; and such universal authority was claimed by Christ to have been given Him by His Father.

   b. It would naturally be greatly needed as work began and developed; and so it was hereby assured at very outset of our Lord's final commands to His apostles.

2. *The Scope of Service* — "all the nations" (v. 19, A.S.V.)

   Following command to "go . . . and teach ("make disciples," Greek), baptizing —," scope is shown to be universal too; Christ's followers were to proceed everywhere and, as Mark expresses it, "preach the gospel to the whole creation" (Mark 16:15):

   a. *Apostles Were To Lead People To Become Disciples, or Learners.*

      (1) English phrase, "make disciples of all the nations," is ambiguous, for literal rendering of Greek is, rather, "make all nations disciples" and not "make disciples out of all nations"; thus, commission embraces whole nations rather than indicating individuals from among them (cf. Acts 14:21, which means that apostles "made many people disciples").

      (2) But at once comes question whether phrase here defines other passages, teaching that scope of work was to be national rather than individual conversion; or is it to be understood, in light of these other passages, as meaning presentation of gospel to people of all nations without exception?

(3) Certainly words "to take out of them" (Acts 15: 14) indicate individual evangelization and discipleship; and neither immediate followers of Christ nor any since then made all those to whom they preached so much as even professed disciples.

(4) However, if Matthew gives aim and scope of Great Commission, and passages like Acts 14:21 and 15:14 actual results, everything is clear; and that this is true view exegetes of first rank bear witness:

N.B. F. B. Meyer interprets passage as "all nations without exception" and compares wording of 24: 14, 25:32, and 26:13; and Plummer similarly refers passage to "the whole human race"; while both writers contrast it with now canceled limitation of 10:5.

b. *Apostles Were Then To Form These Disciples Into Christian Community*

(1) This was to be by means of ordinance of baptism in Divine Name, and therefore baptism was intended as badge of their relationship to Christ, proof that they were real disciples; and since disciple is always learner, and all disciples were to be baptized, all those baptized were regarded as learners in school of Christ.

N.B. This is especially true of mission field where, from moment convert is baptized, there comes separation from old associations, often with persecution and even with death.

(2) It should be noted that verb "baptize" in N.T. is always in passive or middle (quasi-passive) voice, never in active, for people never baptize themselves, but allow themselves to be baptized, and thus, fundamental thought of baptism is something done to us, not something we do or witness we bear; it is, first and foremost, symbol of act of God towards us, not of ours towards God.

(3) Its exact meaning, however, is not spelled out in N.T., probably because rite was already familiar, since Jews used water in similar way (cf. Heb. 9:10, Greek), and John the Baptist baptized (also

with no explanation given, cf. 3:6ff.) ; but there was one idea common to all three, that of washing or purification.

(4) There is one Greek preposition always used and, though variously rendered in English (cf. 3:11, 28: 19, Acts 2:38, Rom. 6:3), it always means "with a view to"; and thus we get idea that baptism is symbolic washing with view, respectively, to Jewish community, to John's call to repentance, or, as here, to Divine Name.

(5) From this we see purpose of Christian baptism is with view to union with God and forgiveness by Him (cf. Acts 2:38, 39), so it is primarily act by which He sets us apart for blessings included in gospel; and, further, it is witness to and pledge of His mercy and grace in Christ, so that when we respond to this Divine act by repentance and faith His blessings become ours.

(6) It is sometimes questioned why in Acts there is no reference, as here, to baptism in Name of Trinity, but only in Name of our Lord Jesus (Acts 2:38, 8:16) :

(a) It is generally understood that baptism in His Name is, to all intents and purposes, equivalent to baptism in Name of Trinity; and it would seem Matthew's words are not to be regarded as express terms of baptismal formula so much as statement revealing spiritual meaning of rite.

N.B. When thus understood, Bishop Chase of Ely suggests, "the question ceases to be one of rival formulas, and becomes one of Christian theology"; and he adduces way in which writer of *Didache* first gives explicit direction for baptism in words of Matthew, but later uses phrase, "baptized into the Name of the Lord." As illustration, the Bishop adds, St. Paul is not inconsistent in ending one Epistle to Corinth with words "The grace of our Lord Jesus Christ be with you" (1 Cor. 16:23), while in another he expands benediction into well-known long form (cf. 2 Cor. 13:14).

(b) Further, since significance of these baptisms was always conversion to faith in Christ, it was not necessary to repeat full form each time; besides, baptism "into Christ" carries with it relation to God of which Trinity is full expression, arising out of Christ's claim to Deity.

(c) Perhaps, also, we may regard complete realization of Great Commission as to be expected in future, when God's Kingdom will be manifested at close of present dispensation of Christ's Church.

(7) While we adhere closely to N.T. teaching on baptism with water, we must never forget supreme necessity of being "baptized with the Holy Spirit" (Acts 1:5; cf. Matt. 3:11); for word when associated with Him seems to refer only to initial work of God uniting us to Christ and to one another in Him (cf. 1 Cor. 12:13).

(8) Following analogy of water baptism, so clearly symbol of Holy Spirit's "descending and remaining" (John 1:33), this baptism is never repeated; rather, that which Christians must face and realize is great necessity for continuing fullness of Holy Spirit, not His baptism, in their daily life and service — as it has been well expressed, "one baptism, but many fillings."

3. *The Substance of Service — "teaching . . . all things"* (v. 20a)

a. Having made disciples, or learners, and having initiated them by rite of baptism, it was most natural and necessary that Apostles were to instruct them in everything previously given by Christ for guidance of His followers; so ministry of teaching is seen to be most important.

b. This command, though first addressed to Eleven, was not limited to them, for later on Paul associates various gifts of ministry, including that of teaching, with our Lord's Divine gift to entire Church on His ascension (cf. Eph. 4:7-16); yet there is equal certainty N.T. emphasizes Divinely commissioned, specially trained ministry (cf. 1 Cor. 12:28).

c. Development of this was, of course, gradual, as required, for at first Apostles only were all that were needed; and then in sequence came the Seven (cf. Acts 6), evangelists (Acts 21:8, 2 Tim. 4:5), elders and deacons (1 Tim. 3), as spiritual organism necessitated variety of function within its organization.

4. *The Strength of Service* — *"I am with you all the days"* (v. 20b, Greek)

a. This Divine commission from exalted Christ fitly closes with assurance of continuance of His own presence with His disciples in their work for Him; this would cheer, inspire, and strengthen them wherever they went and for however long a time.

b. This beautiful thought corresponds with statement (cf. Mark 16:20) that as they went forth the Lord worked with them and confirmed His Word through their lips by His own Divine power; and it assures us, in our turn, of continual power we shall experience in perpetual presence of our Master Himself, for He, in the Person of the Holy Spirit, has never left His Church, and we know He never will.

c. Thus there is complete equipment for Christian work and no excuse for not doing it; and however varied may be its forms, its full universality is clearly seen.

N.B. The presence of the Lord is prominent all through Scripture, e.g., — for salvation (Ps. 9:3); for victory (Isa. 19:1); for rest (Exod. 33:14); for separation (Exod. 33:16); for protection (Gen. 28:15); for deliverance (Jer. 1:19); for joy (Ps. 16:11); for courage (Acts 4:13); and, as here, for power.

> *When we walk amid the shadows*
> *And the skies are overcast,*
> *When we linger, half bewildered,*
> *'Twixt the future and the past,*

> *We shall always find the Saviour*
>   *At the parting of the ways;*
> *We shall hear His gentle whisper:*
>   *"I am with you all the days!"*

> *Yesterday, today, forever,*
>   *He's the same Lord Jesus still,*
> *Guiding, keeping those who love Him,*
>   *Shaping all things to His will.*

> *I would always trust my Saviour,*
>   *Let Him choose my times and ways,*
> *For the promise never fails me:*
>   *"I am with you all the days!"*

Thus it is clear that this "Great Commission" given by Christ at the close of His life on earth (cf. Mark 16:19) is in thorough harmony with His resurrection power and forms the "marching orders" whereby it may be manifested by His Church.

Conclusion

All through the Acts and the Epistles the resurrection is invariably attributed not to Christ Himself, but to God the Father. It was as though God would let His ancient people know, by the resurrection from the dead, what He thought both of His Son and of their own treatment of Him. It was this, doubtless, that led to the sending of an angel to open the grave (cf. v. 2), God thereby bearing witness to the righteousness of His Son. St. Paul desired to know the power of Christ's resurrection (cf. Phil. 3:10), and teaches us that the same power that God used in raising Christ is intended for His followers (cf. Eph. 1:19-23). What, then, is to be found in the resurrection for us?

1. *Vindication of Christ's Claims*

   The resurrection ratified these, testifying both to His Word and to His character.

2. *Verification of Christ's Atonement*

   The resurrection declared God's acceptance of His sacrifice, declaring His death was truly sufficient for redemption from sin.

3. *Vigor for Christ's Life in His People*

   The resurrection reveals that we may live to God as those

who are dead to sin and alive in Christ, through the power of His Spirit in our daily life.

4. *Vitality for Christ's Service*

The resurrection assures us of a present Friend and Master, for Christianity is not merely the remembrance of a dying Saviour, but companionship with a living Lord.

5. *Victory over Death*

The resurrection anticipates our future glory, because Christ's being raised guarantees our resurrection as well. Thus we are enabled to see that Christ is much more than a historical character with whom men came into contact centuries ago. He is One with whom we can still enjoy a personal relationship today. It is this truth of the Person of Christ that gives the resurrection its supreme importance and inestimable value.

> *Spring calls to the earth,*
>   *"Awake from thy dreaming;*
> *The winter is over;*
>   *Thy death was but seeming.*
> *In place of the shadows,*
>   *The cold, and the gloom,*
> *Bring brightness and warmth*
>   *And the flowers in bloom;*
> *Stir the sap in the trees,*
>   *Loose the streams from their prison;*
> *Oh, the joy of the world*
>   *That her Saviour has risen!"*
>
> *Christ calls to thy heart,*
>   *Its lonely watch keeping:*
> *"Thy hopes are not dead;*
>   *They have only been sleeping;*
> *After darkness comes light,*
>   *And smiles after sadness;*
> *After blight cometh bloom;*
>   *After grief cometh gladness;*
> *Out of death cometh life;*
>   *I have loosed it from prison.*
> *Share the joy of the world,*
>   *For thy Saviour has risen!"*
>   ANNIE JOHNSON FLINT
>   (Used by permission.)

60

THE MEANING OF EASTER

Matthew 28:5, 6

IT IS A curious thing that the English word "Easter" comes from the name of a Saxon goddess of spring, Eostre, and yet stands in the Christian Church for the day that is often called "Queen of Festivals." Indeed, in many churches today, the world over, Easter Day is regarded as the peak, the goal, of Christian corporate effort, and plans are made so as to lead up to it as a crowning-point. This is good, if there does not come afterwards a sense of recession and a desire for rest that may lead to reaction. To guard against any such peril it should be noted that the real life and power of the disciples came after Easter and because of it. The remarkable influence exercised by Christ's followers was due to the resurrection, suggesting that Easter should be regarded not as a goal, but rather as a starting point. "Once Easter, always Easter" — even on Good Friday — for "Christ being raised from the dead dieth no more" (Rom. 6:9).

The observance of Easter Day by Christians can be traced back at least to the middle of the second century, within about fifty years of the time of the Apostles; and it has always been regarded as a very important festival because the great event that it celebrates, the resurrection of Jesus Christ, is felt to be vital to Christianity. In fact, the Christian Church has had the conviction that Easter Day represents so essential a part of its doctrine that if it were lost it would mean destruction and disaster. It is important, therefore, to inquire into the reasons for this strong, persistent, and constant emphasis; for, as Easter is a permanent fact, so it has perpetual force. To the disciple of Christ today, in short, life should be a continual Easter, full of rich spiritual significance:

I. The Resurrection Means Victory Over Sin

1. *The Problem of Sin*

a. There is nothing in life more pressing than problem of

      sin and no fact more real than consciousness of guilt (cf. 1 Cor. 15:17); and, as consequence, deepest longing of human soul is for assurance of forgiveness.

    b. Question from *Macbeth,* "Canst thou not minister to a mind diseased?" is still being asked everywhere; and it can be answered only by death and resurrection of Christ.

  2. *The Power of God*

    a. Intellect, culture, morality, philosophy are all valuable and essential, but they are powerless to deal with sin; for only adequate force is "the old, old story" which, when received, becomes power of God unto salvation.

    b. Forgiveness has been aptly called "Christ's most striking innovation in morality"; and it becomes possible only through what happened on Easter day, since He lives forever, as Conqueror not only of death, but also of sin.

II. The Resurrection Means the Presence of Christ

  1. *Christ as Our Life*

    a. Because He is living He is directly interested in human life; and especially at times of sorrow and suffering, when burden of life presses as never before, there is no more clamant need than that of His constant presence.

    b. Further, Christ as our source of life is necessary consequence of resurrection and of our acceptance of it; He is described as "our life" (Col. 3:4), and it is further said that He lives in us and we in Him (cf. Gal. 2:20, 6:25).

  2. *Christ as Our Lord*

    a. This at once and inevitably involves His control over our lives, for Giver of life is Giver of law by means of which we obey His rule and live His life; and believer is described by St. Paul as "under law to Christ" (1 Cor. 9:21).

    b. This means every part of our life is subject to His authority and He is thus both Source and Standard of it; for He first bestows life, then prescribes its nature, and finally provides grace whereby we can realize His purpose for us, which is to be "in Christ Jesus" and to "walk not after the flesh, but after the Spirit" (Rom. 8:1).

    c. Thus Christ not only sets forth ideal, He provides dynamic whereby ideal can be realized; in fact, His gospel is full of ideals but, as has been well said, if it is only gospel of ideals, it is like Venus de Milo, very beautiful but without arms — i.e., incapable of reaching down to help men in their struggle with sin.

d. Christ's death and resurrection were for purpose of providing Divine grace whereby we may realize ideals set before us as His law; and, since without this grace they would remain unattained and unattainable, believer is now able to say with Paul, "I live; yet not I, but Christ liveth in me. . . . I can do all things in Christ who is strengthening me" (Gal. 2:29, Phil. 4:13, Greek).

III. The Resurrection Means That Christ Reigns as King

1. *It Reminds Us Not of His Death Only*

   a. Notwithstanding times of confusion, tyranny, and even brutality of war, it is still possible, in light of resurrection, to believe in Christ's Kingship; for, in spite of everything, we know He not only died, but also lives (cf. Rev. 1:18).

   b. Thus, crucifix is not full and complete symbol of Christianity as some would have us believe, because it may easily suggest presently emaciated, defeated, dead Christ — Jesus of Nazareth as disciples saw Him on that first sad Good Friday.

   N.B. Bishop Westcott wrote: "The crucifix . . . obscures our faith. Our thoughts rest not upon a dead, but a living Christ. The closed eye and the bowed head are not the true marks of Him who reigns from the cross, who teaches us to see through every sign of weakness the fulfillment of His own words — 'I, if I be lifted up from the earth, will draw all men unto me.' "

2. *It Reminds Us, Above All, of His Life*

   a. When Easter is invariably associated with Good Friday we have full and satisfying revelation of One who, although once dead, is now alive for evermore; and it is this that Greek Church endeavors to express in its striking picture of Christ on cross as living and arrayed in His priestly robes.

   b. This combination of death and life is very essence of Christian gospel, justifying old paradox: "He reigns from the tree"; and so today, not merely in spite of everything, but even because of everything, "He must reign, till he hath put all enemies under his feet" (1 Cor. 15:25).

N.B. As Charles Simeon put it: "He must reign; He will reign; He shall reign."

IV. The Resurrection Means That Christ Is Coming Back

1. *The Second Advent Is Believed by the Church*

   a. For ages past, and still, in present day, on Easter Sunday and week by week on the Lord's Day Christian Church has confessed that "from thence He shall come."

   b. Even modern scholarship has come to realize this doctrine as "fundamental and pervasive."

2. *The Second Advent Is Set Forth in Scripture*

   a. It is among most prominent aspects of N.T. teaching, being found in one way or another over three hundred times.

   b. St. Paul crowns his message with revelation and assurance of Christ's coming again, presenting it as supreme incentive to hope and to holiness, and as main inspiration of life here and hereafter.

Conclusion

We may thus sum up the Easter message:

1. *Christ Redeeming*

   a. This means perpetual victory over sin and is prominent in teaching of St. Paul; death had no more dominion over his Lord, and his followers were expected and urged to share this experience (cf. Rom. 6:9-14).

   b. Since he and other Apostles were so conscious of this victory, they proclaimed His triumph and ours wherever they went; and Church today should base on resurrection every appeal for acceptance of Christ.

   c. There are few things in N.T. more impressive than ringing note of victory that marks apostolic testimony; "Jesus and the resurrection" (Acts 17:18) was constant, exultant, satisfying theme of all preaching.

2. *Christ Risen*

   a. Since our Lord's entrance into human life was but prelude to His atoning death and glorious resurrection, Easter means also constant witness to Him as risen Saviour; and those who accepted apostolic message were to "walk in newness of life" (Rom. 6:4) because Christ was risen as both their pattern and their power.

b. Nothing can compare with life of believer when framed on living Christ and energized by Him; so we can readily understand why, from earliest days, dominant note in Christian message was this living Lord.

3. *Christ Reigning*

a. Earnest service for our King is another mark of Easter life of Christians; for it is significant that St. Paul's great chapter on Resurrection closes not with message about bereavement or with encouragement to halting and timid, but with clarion call to "the work of the Lord" (1 Cor. 15:58).

b. This has been well called "a strange conjunction," for immediately following elaborate argument for Resurrection comes this strong appeal to practical effort; and yet it is not really strange, because Easter message is only adequate reason, as it also is only sufficient power, for enlistment under banner of our King (cf. 1 Cor. 15:25).

4. *Christ Returning*

a. Easter abides, too, as guarantee of future in Him at His coming; this is only assurance that will meet our need, for He "shall so come in like manner" (Acts 1:11) in His risen form.

b. St. Paul comforts his readers by linking fact of Christ's victory over death with certainty of our resurrection at His coming (cf. 1 Thess. 4:14-18); and St. Peter attributes our "living hope" to Christ's resurrection from dead (cf. 1 Pet. 1:3, 4, A.S.V.).

Easter, then, must be both perpetual and prominent in the Christian's experience. Christ does not return to earth to re-enact His life and passion; He lives forever on the throne. In proportion as we enter upon these realities and live them out in trust, joy, and obedience, they will prove, as they have already proved in millions of lives, the foundation of peace, the secret of power, the spring of comfort, the source of influence, and the guarantee of progress. With His own, in short, it is always Easter!

Summary

Thus ends our study of the Gospel of the King. He has revealed to us the laws of the Kingdom and then has manifested that Kingdom in His earthly life. This was crowned by His submission to death, though resurrection immediately followed because it was not possible for the heavenly King to be held by death. From first to last the royal note is struck, and the One who was "born King of the Jews" (2:2) is finally seen to have potential dominion over "all nations" (28:18, 19).

With this in mind, we may summarize Matthew's account very briefly and simply as follows:

1. The Preparation of the King (1:1 to 4:11);
2. The Proclamation of the Kingdom (4:12 to 14:36);
3. The Preparation of the King's Ambassadors (14:37 to 25:46);
4. The Passion of the Kingly Saviour (26:1 to 27:66); and —
5. The Power of the Risen Lord and King (28:1-20).

Be it ours who read of this heavenly King first to accept and follow Him as our Saviour and our Lord, and then to proclaim far and wide the grace and glory of His gospel, exerting every talent and energy of our souls to "crown Him Lord of all"!